Makers of the Western Tradition

PORTRAITS FROM HISTORY
VOLUME 2
Fourth Edition

J. Kelley Sowards, editor
Wichita State University

Makers of the Western Tradition

PORTRAITS FROM HISTORY
VOLUME 2
Fourth Edition

St. Martin's Press New York

To my parents, in love and gratitude

Library of Congress Catalog Card Number: 86-60650

Manufactured in the United States of America.
10987
fedc

For information, write:
St. Martin's Press, Inc.
175 Fifth Avenue
New York, NY 10010

Cover design: Darby Downey

ISBN: 0-312-50616-3

ACKNOWLEDGMENTS

LOUIS XIV: From *Saint-Simon of Versailles*, selected and translated from the *Memoirs of M. le Duc de Saint-Simon* by Lucy Norton. Copyright © 1958 by Hamish Hamilton Ltd. Reprinted by permission. From *Louis XIV and 20 Million Frenchmen* by Pierre Goubert, translated by Anne Carter. Copyright © 1970 by Anne Carter. Reprinted by permission of Pantheon Books, a Division of Random House, Inc.

PETER THE GREAT: From "Panegyric to the Sovereign Emperor Peter the Great" by Mikhail Vasilevich Lomonosov, translated by Ronald Hingley, from *Russian Intellectual History*, edited by Marc Raeff. Reprinted by permission of Humanities Press International, Inc., Atlantic Highlands, NJ, and The Harvester Press Ltd. From *On the Corruption of Morals in Russia* by Prince M. M. Shcherbatov. Edited and translated by A. Lentin. Copyright © 1969 by Cambridge University Press and reprinted with their permission. From *A History of Russia*, 2nd edition, by Nicholas V. Riasonovsky. Copyright © 1963, 1969 by Oxford University Press, Inc. Reprinted by permission of Oxford University Press, Inc.

JEAN-JACQUES ROUSSEAU: From *The Social Contract* by Jean-Jacques Rousseau, translated and with an introduction by Maurice Cranston. Reprinted by permission of AD Peters & Co. Ltd. From *The Origins of Totalitarian Democracy* by J. L. Talmon. Reprinted by permission of Westview Press and Martin Secker & Warburg, Ltd. From *Jean-Jacques Rousseau: The Prophetic Voice (1758–1778)*, by Lester G. Crocker. Copyright © 1973 by Lester G. Crocker. Reprinted with the permission of Macmillan Publishing Co., Inc.

NAPOLEON: From *Madame de Stael on Politics, Literature, and National Character*, translated and edited by Morroe Berger. Copyright © 1964 by Morroe Berger and reprinted by permission of his estate. From *Napoleon: From 18 Brumaire to Tilsit, 1799–1807* by Georges Lefebvre. Translated by Henry F. Stockhold. Copyright © 1969 by Columbia University Press and reprinted with their permission.

CHARLES DARWIN: Extracted from *Darwin and The Beagle* by Alan Moorehead, published by Crescent Books, New York. © Alan Moorehead 1969. Reprinted with permission of The Rainbird Publishing Group Ltd, London. "Evolution As Fact and Theory" is reprinted from *Hen's Teeth and Horse's Toes, Further Re-*

Acknowledgments and copyrights continue at the back of the book on pages 324–325, which constitute an extension of the copyright page.

Preface

Are men and women able to force change upon history by their skill and wits, their nerve and daring? Are they capable of altering its course by their actions? Or are they hopelessly caught up in the grinding process of great, impersonal forces over which they have no real control?

Historians, like theologians, philosophers, and scientists, have long been fascinated by this question. People in every age have recognized great forces at work in their affairs, whether they perceived those forces as supernatural and divine, climatological, ecological, sociological, or economic. Yet obviously at least a few individuals—Alexander, Charlemagne—were able to seize the opportunity of their time and compel the great forces of history to change course. Still others—Moses, St. Francis, Galileo—were able, solely by the power of their thought or their vision, to shape the history of their period and of all later time more profoundly even than the conquerors or military heroes.

The purpose of this book is to examine the careers and the impact of several figures who significantly influenced the history of Western civilization, or who embodied much that is significant about the periods in which they lived, and at the same time to introduce the student to the chief varieties of historical interpretation. Few personalities or events stand without comment in the historical record; contemporary accounts and documents, the so-called original sources, no less than later studies, are written by people with a distinct point of view and interpretation of what they see. Problems of interpretation are inseparable from the effort to achieve historical understanding.

The readings in this book have been chosen for their inherent interest and their particular way of treating their subject. Typically, three selections are devoted to each figure. The first selection is usually an autobiographical or contemporary biographical account; in a few instances, differing assessments by contemporaries are included. Next, a more or less orthodox interpretation is presented; it is often a selection from the "standard work" on the figure in question. The final selection offers a more recent view, which may reinforce the standard interpretation, revise it in the light of new evidence, or dissent from it completely. In some cases, two very different recent views are set side by side.

A book of this size cannot hope to include full-length biographies of all the individuals studied. Instead, each chapter focuses on an important interpretive issue. In some chapters, the figure's relative historical importance is at issue; in others, the significance of a major point mooted in the sources; in still others, the general meaning of the figure's career, as debated in a spread of interpretive positions. In every chapter, it is hoped, the problem examined is interesting and basic to an understanding of the figure's place in history.

The fourth edition (like the second and third) is based in considerable part on responses to a questionnaire by colleagues across the country who used the third edition in their classes. Their comments about which chapters or selections appealed to students and which did not, their suggestions about which figures ought to be deleted and which added or substituted, and their general observations were extremely helpful in the revision.

As with the third edition, substantial changes have been made in the fourth. In order to conform to the practice of an increasing number of Western Civilization courses, I have decided to move the break between the two volumes to the early eighteenth century—thus making Louis XIV the overlap figure between the volumes. Even though the first volume will thus have an additional three chapters, for a total of fourteen, the instructor in a typical fifteen-week semester should be able to make use of all the figures if he or she wishes to do so.

The later starting point for the second volume allows me to include more twentieth-century figures—an often expressed wish of users. One of these, Joseph Stalin, is actually a substitute for Charles de Gaulle. Eleanor Roosevelt and Pablo Picasso are entirely new and move the coverage of the second volume into the decade of the 1970s. Counting Louis XIV, there are fourteen chapters in the second volume, as in the first.

In addition to adding Eleanor Roosevelt and Picasso, I have made a number of substitutions. In the first volume, we have brought back St. Augustine from an earlier edition; in the second, we have brought back Cecil Rhodes and prepared a new chapter on Stalin.

Furthermore, all the selections in the readings were carefully reviewed, and a number of them were replaced with either more current or more relevant selections. This was done in the chapters on Alexander the Great, St. Augustine, Charles Darwin, and Albert Einstein.

Finally, all the chapter reading lists were reviewed and updated.

J.K.S.

Contents

Contents

Makers of the Western Tradition

PORTRAITS FROM HISTORY
VOLUME 2
Fourth Edition

The Granger Collection

Louis XIV: "The Sun King"

1638	born
1643	succeeded to throne under a regency
1660	beginning of Louis' personal government
1667–1668	War of Devolution
1689–1697	War of the Grand Alliance
1701–1714	War of the Spanish Succession
1715	died

In 1661, on the death of the regent Cardinal Mazarin, the personal reign of Louis XIV of France began. Though he was just twenty-three years old, Louis had already been nominally the king for almost twenty years. And he was to rule for more than another half century, through one of the longest, most brilliant, most eventful, and most controversial reigns in the history of modern Europe.

It had been the aim of Cardinal Richelieu, the great first minister of Louis' father, "to make the king supreme in France and France supreme in Europe." And to an extent Cardinal Richelieu, as well as his successor, Cardinal Mazarin, had been successful. France was the richest and most populous nation in Europe. Her army had surpassed that of Spain as Europe's most formidable military machine. And the two wily cardinals had gained for France a diplomatic ascendancy to match her military might. It remained for Louis XIV to complete their work. In the process he became the archetype of divine-right monarchical absolutism, justifying later historians' labeling of the age that he dominated as the "Age of Absolutism." Louis took the sun as his emblem, as he himself wrote, for its nobility, its uniqueness, and "the light that it imparts to the other heavenly bodies," and as "a most vivid and a most beautiful image for a great monarch." [1]

From the beginning of his personal rule, Louis XIV intended to make the other states of Europe—"the other heavenly bodies"—swing in the

[1] Louis XIV, . . . *Mémoires for the Instruction of the Dauphin,* Paul Sonnino, trans. (New York: Free Press, 1970), pp. 103–4.

orbit of his sun. In 1667 he began the so-called War of Devolution to claim the disputed provinces of the Spanish Netherlands for his Spanish wife. He fought a series of wars with Spain and the Empire, the Dutch, and the English, culminating in the great European conflict, the War of the Spanish Succession (1701–1714), to set his grandson on the throne of Spain and create a Bourbon "empire" to dominate the continent. In the course of these wars, he gained the hostility of most of Europe and was finally brought to terms in 1715 at the Peace of Utrecht. Even though Louis was reported on his deathbed to have said, "I have loved war too much," he had, nevertheless, come closer to making France supreme in Europe than had any ruler before Napoleon.

Louis XIV disliked Paris. From early in his reign, he made increasing use of the royal estate of Versailles, some ten miles out of the city, as his principal residence and the locus of the court. Versailles grew in size and magnificence to become the most visible symbol of and the most enduring monument to Louis' absolutism. An English visitor, Lord Montague, sniffily called it "something the foolishest in the world," and thought Louis himself "the vainest creature alive." [2] But Versailles was far from foolish and, though vain indeed, Louis XIV was a consummate realist. Versailles was not simply a symbol of his absolutism; it was a working part of it. The function of Versailles was to help make the king supreme in France.

Royal supremacy was, in Louis' reign as before, most clearly threatened by the power and independence of the great nobility. On the very eve of Louis' personal rule, he, his mother, Mazarin, and the court had been faced with an uprising, called the Fronde, led by the great Princes of the Blood. Though it failed, Louis never forgot the Fronde. It became his deliberate policy to keep the great nobility at Versailles, separated from their provincial estates and the roots of their political power, and to redirect their interests and their energies. It may be argued that the elaborate court behavior that developed at Versailles with its perpetual spectacles and entertainments, its endless adulteries and affairs, its incredible tedium and banality—and its perpetual attendance upon the king—was really a device to neutralize the power of the great nobility while the king governed with the aid of a succession of ministers, appointed by him, answerable to him alone, and capable of being dismissed by him without question. It has been suggested by more than one scholar that Louis XIV was the archetype not only of the absolute monarch but of the "royal bureaucrat." The court life at Versailles was surely the most glittering side-show ever staged. But it was a show that fascinated the very people who played their parts in it; and it has fascinated—and distracted—observers ever since.

[2] Quoted in John C. Rule, "Louis XIV, Roi-Bureaucrate," in *Louis XIV and the Craft of Kingship,* ed. John C. Rule (Columbus: Ohio State University Press, 1969), p. 42.

The Memoirs

LOUIS, DUC DE SAINT-SIMON

The sources for the reign of Louis XIV are an embarrassment of riches—an enormous volume of public documents and official records, reports, and inventories and such a mass of royal correspondence that it still has not been completely edited. Many of the figures of the court wrote letters as prodigiously as the king, and almost as many wrote memoirs as well. Of these the most important are the memoirs of Louis de Rouvroy, Duc de Saint-Simon.

Saint-Simon was born at Versailles in 1675 and lived there for the next thirty years. Through much of that time—and throughout the rest of his long life—he kept his memoirs with a compulsive passion. In one edition, they run to forty-three volumes, and a complete text has yet to be published. Saint-Simon's memoirs are important not only for their completeness but also for the perspective they give on the age of Louis XIV. Saint-Simon fancied himself a chronicler in the tradition of Froissart or Joinville and saw his literary labor as preparing him in the knowledge of "great affairs" "for some high office." But preferment never came. Saint-Simon was never more than a minor figure of the court, moving on the fringes of the affairs that his memoirs so carefully record.

Saint-Simon blamed the king for his neglect—as he quite properly should have, for nothing happened at Versailles without the wish of the king, and the king simply disliked Saint-Simon. Saint-Simon also accused the king of demeaning the old aristocracy to which Saint-Simon so self-consciously belonged. This complaint is the nagging, insistent theme that runs like a leitmotif through the memoirs. Saint-Simon believed that Louis deliberately preferred "the vile bourgeoisie" to the aristocracy for high office and great affairs. Although the claim is somewhat exaggerated, it is indeed true that Louis preferred the lesser nobility for his bureaucrats because they had no separate power base beyond the king's preferment.

But while Saint-Simon hated his king, he was also fascinated by him, for, like it or not, Louis was the center of the world in which Saint-Simon lived. He set the fashion in dress, language, manners, and morals. Even his afflictions inspired instant emulation: after the king underwent a painful operation, no fewer than thirty courtiers presented themselves to the court surgeon and demanded that the same operation be performed on them.

Saint-Simon hated Versailles nearly as much as he hated the king, and he described it with the same malicious familiarity—its size, its vulgarity, its inconvenience and faulty planning. But he also described the stifling, debasing, desperate style of life that it dictated for the court nobility so grandly imprisoned there.

One modern scholar has called Saint-Simon "at once unreliable and indispensable." [3] *We can correct his unreliability, however, by consulting other sources, and he remains indispensable for the picture he gives us of the "other side" of royal absolutism.*

We turn now to Saint-Simon at Versailles *for Saint-Simon's appraisal of Louis XIV.*

HE WAS A prince in whom no one would deny good and even great qualities, but he had many others that were petty or downright bad, and of these it was impossible to determine which were natural and which acquired. Nothing is harder to find than a well-informed writer, none rarer than those who knew him personally, yet are sufficiently unbiased to speak of him without hatred or flattery, and to set down the bare truth for good or ill.

This is not the place to tell of his early childhood. He was king almost from birth, but was deliberately repressed by a mother who loved to govern, and still more so by a wicked and self-interested minister, who risked the State a thousand times for his own aggrandisement. . . .

. . . After Mazarin's death, he had enough intelligence to realize his deliverance, but not enough vigour to release himself. Indeed, that event was one of the finest moments of his life, for it taught him an unshakable principle namely, to banish all prime ministers and ecclesiastics from his councils. Another ideal, adopted at that time, he could never sustain because in the practice it constantly eluded him. This was to govern alone. It was the quality upon which he most prided himself and for which he received most praise and flattery. In fact, it was what he was least able to do. . . .

. . . The King's intelligence was below the average, but was very capable of improvement. He loved glory; he desired peace and good government. He was born prudent, temperate, secretive, master of his emotions and his tongue—can it be believed?—he was born good and just. God endowed him with all the makings of a good and perhaps even of a fairly great king. All the evil in him came from without. His early training was so dissolute that no one dared to go near his apartments, and he would sometimes speak bitterly of those days and tell how they found him one night fallen into the fountain at the Palais Royal. He became very

[3] Peter Gay, in the introductory note to Louis, Duc de Saint-Simon, *Versailles, the Court, and Louis XIV*, ed. and trans. Lucy Norton (New York: Harper & Row, 1966), p. vii.

dependent on others, for they had scarcely taught him to read and write and he remained so ignorant that he learned nothing of historical events nor the facts about fortunes, careers, rank, or laws. This lack caused him sometimes, even in public to make many gross blunders.

You might imagine that as king he would have loved the old nobility and would not have cared to see it brought down to the level of other classes. Nothing was further from the truth. His aversion to noble sentiments and his partiality for his Ministers, who, to elevate themselves, hated and disparaged all who were what they themselves were not, nor ever could be, caused him to feel a similar antipathy for noble birth. He feared it as much as he feared intelligence, and if he found these two qualities united in one person, that man was finished.

His ministers, generals, mistresses, and courtiers learned soon after he became their master that glory, to him, was a foible rather than an ambition. They therefore flattered him to the top of his bent, and in so doing, spoiled him. Praise, or better, adulation, pleased him so much that the most fulsome was welcome and the most servile even more delectable. . . .

Flattery fed the desire for military glory that sometimes tore him from his loves, which was how Louvois [4] so easily involved him in major wars and persuaded him that he was a better leader and strategist than any of his generals, a theory which those officers fostered in order to please him. All their praise he took with admirable complacency, and truly believed that he was what they said. Hence his liking for reviews, which he carried to such lengths that he was known abroad as the "Review King," and his preference for sieges, where he could make cheap displays of courage, be forcibly restrained, and show his ability to endure fatigue and lack of sleep. Indeed, so robust was his constitution that he never appeared to suffer from hunger, thirst, heat, cold, rain, or any other kind of weather. He greatly enjoyed the sensation of being admired, as he rode along the lines, for his fine presence and princely bearing, his horsemanship, and other attainments. It was chiefly with talk of campaigns and soldiers that he entertained his mistresses and sometimes his courtiers. He talked well and much to the point; no man of fashion could tell a tale or set a scene better than he, yet his most casual speeches were never lacking in natural and conscious majesty.

He had a natural bent towards details and delighted in busying himself with such petty matters as the uniforms, equipment, drill, and discipline of his troops. He concerned himself no less with his buildings, the conduct of his household, and his living expenses, for he always imagined that he had something to teach the experts, and they received instruction from him as though they were novices in arts which they already knew by heart. To the King, such waste of time appeared to deserve his

[4] Michel Le Tellier, Marquis de Louvois (1641–1691), Louis' great minister of war.—ED.

constant attention, which enchanted his ministers, for with a little tact and experience they learned to sway him, making their own desires seem his, and managing great affairs of State in their own way and, all too often, in their own interests, whilst they congratulated themselves and watched him drowning amidst trivialities. . . .

From such alien and pernicious sources he acquired a pride so colossal that, truly, had not God implanted in his heart the fear of the devil, even in his worst excesses, he would literally have allowed himself to be worshipped. What is more, he would have found worshippers; witness the extravagant monuments that have been set up to him, for example the statue in the Place des Victoires, with its pagan dedication, a ceremony at which I myself was present, and in which he took such huge delight. From this false pride stemmed all that ruined him. We have already seen some of its ill-effects; others are yet to come. . . .

The Court was yet another device to sustain the King's policy of despotism. Many things combined to remove it from Paris and keep it permanently in the country. The disorders of the minority [5] had been staged mainly in that city and for that reason the King had taken a great aversion to it and had become convinced that it was dangerous to live there. . . .

The awkward situation of his mistresses and the dangers involved in conducting such scandalous affairs in a busy capital, crowded with people of every kind of mentality, played no small part in deciding him to leave, for he was embarrassed by the crowds whenever he went in or out or appeared upon the streets. Other reasons for departure were his love of hunting and the open air, so much more easily indulged in the country than in Paris, which is far from forests and ill-supplied with pleasant walks, and his delight in building, a later and ever-increasing passion, which could not be enjoyed in the town, where he was continually in the public eye. Finally, he conceived the idea that he would be all the more venerated by the multitude if he lived retired and were no longer seen every day. . . .

The liaison with Mme de La Vallière,[6] which was at first kept secret, occasioned many excursions to Versailles, then a little pasteboard house erected by Louis XIII when he, and still more his courtiers, grew tired of sleeping in a low tavern and old windmill, after long, exhausting hunts in the forest of Saint-Léger and still further afield. . . .

Gradually, those quiet country excursions of Louis XIV gave rise to a vast building project, designed to house a large Court more comfortably than in crowded lodgings at Saint-Germain, and he removed his residence there altogether, shortly before the death of the Queen.[7] Immense numbers of suites were made, and one paid one's court by asking for one,

[5] A reference to the Fronde.—Ed.

[6] One of Louis' early mistresses.—Ed.

[7] The Spanish princess Maria Theresa died in 1683.—Ed.

whereas, at Saint-Germain, almost everyone had the inconvenience of lodging in the town, and those few who did sleep at the château were amazingly cramped.

The frequent entertainments, the private drives to Versailles, and the royal journeys, provided the King with a means of distinguishing or mortifying his courtiers by naming those who were or were not to accompany him, and thus keeping everyone eager and anxious to please him. He fully realized that the substantial gifts which he had to offer were too few to have any continuous effect, and he substituted imaginary favours that appealed to men's jealous natures, small distinctions which he was able, with extraordinary ingenuity, to grant or withhold every day and almost every hour. The hopes that courtiers built upon such flimsy favours and the importance which they attached to them were really unbelievable, and no one was ever more artful than the King in devising fresh occasions for them. . . .

. . . He took it as an offence if distinguished people did not make the Court their home, or if others came but seldom. And to come never, or scarcely ever, meant certain disgrace. When a favour was asked for such a one, the King would answer haughtily, "I do not know him at all," or, "That is a man whom I never see," and in such cases his word was irrevocable. . . .

There never lived a man more naturally polite, nor of such exquisite discrimination with so fine a sense of degree, for he made distinctions for age, merit and rank, and showed them in his answers when these went further than the usual *"Je verrai,"* [8] and in his general bearing. . . . He was sometimes gay, but never undignified, and never, at any time, did he do anything improper or indiscreet. His smallest gesture, his walk, bearing, and expression were all perfectly becoming, modest, noble, and stately, yet at the same time he always seemed perfectly natural. Added to which he had the immense advantage of a good figure, which made him graceful and relaxed.

On state occasions such as audiences with ambassadors and other ceremonies, he looked so imposing that one had to become used to the sight of him if one were not to be exposed to the humiliation of breaking down or coming to a full stop. At such times, his answers were always short and to the point and he rarely omitted some civility, or a compliment if the speech deserved one. The awe inspired by his appearance was such that wherever he might be, his presence imposed silence and a degree of fear. . . .

In everything he loved magnificently lavish abundance. He made it a principle from motives of policy and encouraged the Court to imitate him; indeed, one way to win favour was to spend extravagantly on the table, clothes, carriages, building, and gambling. For magnificence in such things he would speak to people. The truth is that he used this means

[8] "We shall see."—ED.

deliberately and successfully to impoverish everyone, for he made luxury meritorious in all men, and in some a necessity, so that gradually the entire Court became dependent upon his favours for their very subsistence. What is more, he fed his own pride by surrounding himself with an entourage so universally magnificent that confusion reigned and all natural distinctions were obliterated.

Once it had begun this rottenness grew into that cancer which gnaws at the lives of all Frenchmen. It started, indeed, at the Court but soon spread to Paris, the provinces, and the army where generals are now assessed according to the tables that they keep and the splendour of their establishments. It so eats into private fortunes that those in a position to steal are often forced to do so in order to keep up their spending. This cancer, kept alive by confusion of ranks, pride, even by good manners, and encouraged by the folly of the great, is having incalculable results that will lead to nothing less than ruin and general disaster.

No other King has ever approached him for the number and quality of his stables and hunting establishments. Who could count his buildings? Who not deplore their ostentation, whimsicality and bad taste? . . . At Versailles he set up one building after another according to no scheme of planning. Beauty and ugliness, spaciousness and meanness were roughly tacked together. The royal apartments at Versailles are beyond everything inconvenient, with back-views over the privies and other dark and evil-smelling places. Truly, the magnificence of the gardens is amazing, but to make the smallest use of them is disagreeable, and they are in equally bad taste. . . .

But one might be for ever pointing out the monstrous defects of that huge and immensely costly palace, and of its outhouses that cost even more, its orangery, kitchen gardens, kennels, larger and smaller stables, all vast, all prodigiously expensive. Indeed, a whole city has sprung up where before was only a poor tavern, a windmill and a little pasteboard château, which Louis XIII built so as to avoid lying on straw.

The Versailles of Louis XIV, that masterpiece wherein countless sums of money were thrown away merely in alterations to ponds and thickets, was so ruinously costly, so monstrously ill-planned, that it was never finished. Amid so many state rooms, opening one out of another, it has no theatre, no banqueting-hall, no ballroom, and both behind and before much still remains undone. The avenues and plantations, all laid out artificially, cannot mature and the coverts must continually be restocked with game. As for the drains, many miles of them still have to be made, and even the walls, whose vast contours enclose a small province of the gloomiest, most wretched countryside, have never been completely finished. . . . No matter what was done, the great fountains dried up (as they still do at times) in spite of the oceans of reservoirs that cost so many millions to engineer in that sandy or boggy soil.

A Rationalist View of Absolutism

VOLTAIRE

Voltaire (1694–1778) was the preeminent figure of what modern scholars call the Enlightenment, or the Age of Reason. He was also one of the greatest and most influential of early modern historians. Among Voltaire's most important books was The Age of Louis XIV *(1751), which he conceived as one of the earliest instances of what we would nowadays call "cultural history." His intention in writing this book was to illuminate the great achievements of Louis' "age"—as the title announces—rather than the king himself. Indeed* The Age of Louis XIV *is usually published as part of his later* Essay on the Morals and the Spirit of Nations *(1756). But Louis the king was as impossible for Voltaire to ignore as he had been for Saint-Simon, and as he has been for historians of his age ever since.*

Voltaire knew and cultivated many of the survivors of Louis' court, some of them important figures. He collected their letters and memoirs and those of other contemporaries—in short, he had much of the equipment of modern historical research. Although Voltaire also had strong and independent views on the past, as on most other subjects, his portrait of Louis XIV is surprisingly balanced. He does not evade Louis' faults, nor does he exploit them. Indeed, Voltaire seems rather to have admired the king, both as a person and as a ruler. We must remember, however, that, though a rationalist, Voltaire was not a revolutionary. He thought highly of what has come to be called Enlightened Despotism. At the time he completed The Age of Louis XIV, *for example, Voltaire was in Berlin as the guest, tutor, and "friend in residence" of Frederick the Great of Prussia.*

We must remember, too, that Voltaire was a French patriot who shared Louis XIV's love for the glory of France. We do not even find him denouncing Louis' militarism, so often the target of more recent criticism. Voltaire was especially mindful of the unprecedented domination of French culture in Europe during the age of Louis XIV and of the extent to which Louis himself exemplified that culture. Voltaire admired Louis' sound domestic economy and the diligence with which he worked at his craft of kingship, and he had considerable sympathy for his trials as a person. The picture that Voltaire gives us of Louis XIV is altogether a very different one from that created by Saint-Simon.

LOUIS XIV invested his court, as he did all his reign, with such brilliancy and magnificence, that the slightest details of his private life appear to interest posterity, just as they were the objects of curiosity to every court in Europe and indeed to all his contemporaries. The splendour of his rule was reflected in his most trivial actions. People are more eager, especially in France, to know the smallest incidents of his court, than the revolutions of some other countries. Such is the effect of a great reputation. Men would rather know what happened in the private council and court of Augustus than details of the conquests of Attila or of Tamerlane.

Consequently there are few historians who have failed to give an account of Louis XIV's early affection for the Baroness de Beauvais, for Mlle. d'Argencourt, for Cardinal Mazarin's niece, later married to the Count of Soissons, father of Prince Eugene; and especially for her sister, Marie Mancini, who afterwards married the High Constable Colonne.

He had not yet taken over the reins of government when such diversions occupied the idleness in which he was encouraged by Cardinal Mazarin, then ruling as absolute master. . . . The fact that his tutors had allowed him too much to neglect his studies in early youth, a shyness which arose from a fear of placing himself in a false position, and the ignorance in which he was kept by Cardinal Mazarin, gave the whole court to believe that he would always be ruled like his father, Louis XIII. . . .

In 1660, the marriage of Louis XIV was attended by a display of magnificence and exquisite taste which was ever afterwards on the increase. . . .

The king's marriage was followed by one long series of fêtes, entertainments and gallantries. They were redoubled on the marriage of *Monsieur,* the king's eldest brother, to Henrietta of England, sister of Charles II, and they were not interrupted until the death of Cardinal Mazarin in 1661.

The court became the centre of pleasures, and a model for all other courts. The king prided himself on giving entertainments which should put those of Vaux in the shade.

Nature herself seemed to take a delight in producing at this moment in France men of the first rank in every art, and in bringing together at Versailles the most handsome and well-favoured men and women that ever graced a court. Above all his courtiers Louis rose supreme by the grace of his figure and the majestic nobility of his countenance. The sound of his voice, at once dignified and charming, won the hearts of those whom his presence had intimidated. His bearing was such as befitted himself and his rank alone, and would have been ridiculous in any other. . . .

The chief glory of these amusements, which brought taste, polite manners and talents to such perfection in France, was that they did not for a moment detach the monarch from his incessant labours. Without such toil he could but have held a court, he could not have reigned: and had the magnificent pleasures of the court outraged the miseries of the people, they would only have been detestable; but the same man who gave these entertainments had given the people bread during the famine of 1662. He had bought up corn, which he sold to the rich at a low price, and which he gave free to poor families at the gate of the Louvre; he had remitted three millions of taxes to the people; no part of the internal administration was neglected, and his government was respected abroad. The King of Spain was obliged to allow him precedence; the Pope was forced to give him satisfaction; Dunkirk was acquired by France by a treaty honourable to the purchaser and ignominious to the seller; in short, all measures adopted after he had taken up the reins of government were either honourable or useful; thereafter, it was fitting that he should give such fêtes . . . that all the nobles should be honoured but no one powerful, not even his brother or *Monsieur le Prince*. . . .

Not one of those who have been too ready to censure Louis XIV can deny that until the Battle of Blenheim [9] he was the only monarch at once powerful, magnificent, and great in every department. For while there have been heroes such as John Sobieski and certain Kings of Sweden who eclipsed him as warriors, no one has surpassed him as a monarch. It must ever be confessed that he not only bore his misfortunes, but overcame them. He had defects and made great errors, but had those who condemn him been in his place, would they have equalled his achievements? . . .

. . . It was the destiny of Louis XIV to see the whole of his family die before their time; his wife at forty-five and his only son at fifty; but a year later we witnessed the spectacle of his grandson the Dauphin, Duke of Burgundy, his wife, and their eldest son, the Duke of Brittany, being carried to the same tomb at Saint-Denys in the month of April 1712, while the youngest of their children, who afterwards ascended the throne, lay in his cradle at death's door. The Duke of Berri, brother of the Duke of Burgundy, followed them two years later, and his daughter was carried at the same time from her cradle to her coffin.

These years of desolation left such a deep impression on people's hearts that during the minority of Louis XV I have met many people who could not speak of the late king's bereavement without tears in their eyes. . . .

The remainder of his life was sad. The disorganisation of state finances, which he was unable to repair, estranged many hearts. The complete confidence he placed in the Jesuit, Le Tellier, a turbulent spirit, stirred them to rebellion. It is remarkable that the people who forgave him all his mistresses could not forgive this one confessor. In the minds of the majority of his subjects he lost during the last three years of his life all the prestige of the great and memorable things he had accomplished. . . .

[9] Marlborough's great victory (1704) for England and her allies in the War of the Spanish Succession.—ED.

On his return from Marli towards the middle of the month of August 1715, Louis XIV was attacked by the illness which ended his life. His legs swelled, and signs of gangrene began to show themselves. The Earl of Stair, the English ambassador, wagered, after the fashion of his country, that the king would not outlive the month of September. The Duke of Orleans, on the journey from Marli, had been left completely to himself, but now the whole court gathered round his person. During the last days of the king's illness, a quack physician gave him a cordial which revived him. He managed to eat, and the quack assured him that he would recover. On hearing this news the crowd of people that had gathered round the Duke of Orleans diminished immediately. "If the king eats another mouthful," said the Duke of Orleans, "we shall have no one left." But the illness was mortal. . . .

Though he has been accused of being narrow-minded, of being too harsh in his zeal against Jansenism,[10] too arrogant with foreigners in his triumphs, too weak in his dealings with certain women, and too severe in personal matters; of having lightly undertaken wars, of burning the Palatinate and of persecuting the reformers—nevertheless, his great qualities and noble deeds when placed in the balance eclipse all his faults. Time, which modifies men's opinions, has put the seal upon his reputation, and, in spite of all that has been written against him, his name is never uttered without respect, nor without recalling to the mind an age which will be forever memorable. If we consider this prince in his private life, we observe him indeed too full of his own greatness, but affable, allowing his mother no part in the government but performing all the duties of a son, and observing all outward appearance of propriety towards his wife; a good father, a good master, always dignified in public, laborious in his study, punctilious in business matters, just in thought, a good speaker, and agreeable though aloof. . . .

The mind of Louis XIV was rather precise and dignified than witty; and indeed one does not expect a king to say notable things, but to do them. . . .

Between him and his court there existed a continual intercourse in which was seen on the one side all the graciousness of a majesty which never debased itself, and on the other all the delicacy of an eager desire to serve and please which never approached servility. He was considerate and polite, especially to women, and his example enhanced those qualities in his courtiers; he never missed an opportunity of saying things to men which at once flattered their self-esteem, stimulated rivalry, and remained long in their memory. . . .

It follows from what we have related, that in everything this monarch

[10] A sect named after the Flemish theologian Cornelis Jansen that was, though Catholic, rather Calvinistic in many of its views. Jansenism was bitterly opposed by the Jesuits who finally persuaded Louis XIV to condemn it.—Ed.

loved grandeur and glory. A prince who, having accomplished as great things as he, could yet be of plain and simple habits, would be the first among kings, and Louis XIV the second.

If he repented on his death-bed of having lightly gone to war, it must be owned that he did not judge by events; for of all his wars the most legitimate and necessary, namely, the war of 1701, was the only one unsuccessful. . . .

His own glory was indissolubly connected with the welfare of France, and never did he look upon his kingdom as a noble regards his land, from which he extracts as much as he can that he may live in luxury. Every king who loves glory loves the public weal; he had no longer a Colbert[11] nor a Louvois, when about 1698 he commanded each comptroller to present a detailed description of his province for the instruction of the Duke of Burgundy. By this means it was possible to have an exact record of the whole kingdom and a correct census of the population. . . .

The foregoing is a general account of what Louis XIV did or attempted to do in order to make his country more flourishing. It seems to me that one can hardly view all his works and efforts without some sense of gratitude, nor without being stirred by the love for the public weal which inspired them. Let the reader picture to himself the condition to-day, and he will agree that Louis XIV did more good for his country than twenty of his predecessors together; and what he accomplished fell far short of what he might have done. The war which ended with the Peace of Ryswick[12] began the ruin of that flourishing trade established by his minister Colbert, and the war of the succession completed it. . . .

. . . Nevertheless, this country, in spite of the shocks and losses she has sustained, is still one of the most flourishing in the world, since all the good that Louis XIV did for her still bears fruit, and the mischief which it was difficult not to do in stormy times has been remedied. Posterity, which passes judgment on kings, and whose judgment they should continually have before them, will acknowledge, weighing the greatness and defects of that monarch, that though too highly praised during his lifetime, he will deserve to be so for ever, and that he was worthy of the statue raised to him at Montpellier, bearing a Latin inscription whose meaning is *To Louis the Great after his death.*

[11] Jean Baptiste Colbert, Louis' great minister of finance (d. 1683).—ED.
[12] The War of the League of Augsburg (1688–1697).—ED.

Louis XIV and the Larger World

PIERRE GOUBERT

The historiography of Louis XIV is almost as vast as the original sources and almost as intimidating. Few figures in European history have been more variously or more adamantly interpreted. As W. H. Lewis has said, "To one school, he is incomparably the ablest ruler in modern European History; to another, a mediocre blunderer, pompous, led by the nose by a succession of generals and civil servants; whilst to a third, he is no great king, but still the finest actor of royalty the world has ever seen."[13] *And such a list does not exhaust the catalog of Louis' interpreters.*

There is at least one contemporary revisionist school that has turned again to "the world of Louis XIV," not the limited world that Saint-Simon saw—the world of the court and the hated prison of Versailles—but the larger world of economic and social forces beyond the court. One of the best exponents of this school is the French historian Pierre Goubert, from whose Louis XIV and Twenty Million Frenchmen *the following selection is taken. Goubert is essentially an economic historian, occupied with such things as demographic trends, price and wage fluctuations, gross national products, and the like. In this book he is concerned with Louis XIV as an able bureaucratic manager rather than as strictly an autocrat; as a king whose foreign policy was often governed, not by his own absolutist theories, but by the realities of economics and whose domestic policies were limited by the dragging, inertial resistance to change of the inherited institutions of his own nation.*

AS EARLY AS 1661, as he declared in his *Mémoires,* Louis meant to have sole command in every sphere and claimed full responsibility, before the world and all posterity, for everything that should happen in his reign. In spite of constant hard work, he soon found he had to entrust the actual running of certain departments, such as finance or commerce, to a few colleagues, although he still reserved the right to take major decisions himself. There were, however, some aspects of his *métier de roi* to which he clung absolutely and persistently, although his persistence was not invariably absolute. Consequently, it is permissible to single out a kind of personal sphere which the king reserved to himself throughout his

[13] W. H. Lewis, *The Splendid Century, Life in the France of Louis XIV* (New York: Doubleday, 1957), p. 1.

reign, although this sphere might vary, while the rest still remained, as it were, under his eye.

As a young man, Louis had promised himself that his own time and posterity should ring with his exploits. If this had been no more than a simple wish, and not an inner certainty, it might be said to have been largely granted.

As a hot-headed young gallant, he flouted kings by his extravagant gestures and amazed them by the brilliance of his court, his entertainments, his tournaments and his mistresses. As a new Augustus he could claim, for a time, to have been his own Maecenas. Up to the year 1672, all Europe seems to have fallen under the spell of his various exploits and his youthful fame spread even as far as the "barbarians" of Asia. For seven or eight years after that, the armies of Le Tellier and Turenne [14] seemed almost invincible while Colbert's youthful navy and its great admirals won glory off the coast of Sicily. Then, when Europe had pulled itself together, Louis still showed amazing powers of resistance and adaptability. Even when he seemed to be ageing, slipping into pious isolation amid his courtiers, he retained the power to astonish with the spendours of his palace at Versailles, his opposition to the Pope and the will to make himself into a "new Constantine," and later by allying himself with Rome to "purify" the Catholic religion. When practically on his death bed, he could still impress the English ambassador who came to protest at the building of a new French port next door to the ruins of Dunkirk. . . .

For precisely three centuries, Louis XIV has continued to dominate, fascinate and haunt men's minds. "The universe and all time" have certainly remembered him, although not always in the way he would have wished. From this point of view, Louis' personal deeds have been a great success. Unfortunately, his memory has attracted a cloud of hatred and contempt as enduring as that which rises from the incense of his worshippers or the pious imitations of a later age.

In his personal desire to enlarge his kingdom, the king was successful. The lands in the north, Strasbourg, Franche-Comté and the "iron belt" [15] are clear evidence of success. In this way Paris was better protected from invasion. But all these gains had been made by 1681 and later events served only to confirm, rescue or reduce them. . . .

As absolute head of his diplomatic service and his armies, from beginning to end, he was well served while he relied on men who had been singled out by Mazarin or Richelieu but he often made a fool of himself by selecting unworthy successors. He was no great warrior. His father and his grandfather had revelled in the reek of the camp and the heady

[14] Le Vicomte Henri de Turenne (d. 1675), one of Louis' generals. A holdover from Louis' father's reign, Turenne was the French hero of the Thirty Years War and the war against Spain.—ED.

[15] A reference to the fortifications—the *frontière de fer*—of the Marquis de Vauban (1663–1707), Louis' master military and seige engineer.—ED.

excitement of battle. His preference was always for impressive manoeuvres, parades and good safe sieges rather than the smoke of battle, and as age grew on him he retreated to desk strategy. Patient, secretive and subtle in constructing alliances, weaving intrigues and undoing coalitions, he marred all these gifts by ill-timed displays of arrogance, brutality and unprovoked aggression. In the last analysis, this born aggressor showed his greatness less in triumph than in adversity but there was never any doubt about his effect on his contemporaries whose feelings towards him were invariably violent and uncompromising. He was admired, feared, hated and secretly envied. . . .

More often than not, and permanently in some cases, administrative details and the complete running of certain sectors of the administration were left to agents appointed by the king and responsible to him. Louis rarely resorted to the cowardly expedient of laying the blame for failure on his subordinates. Not until the end of his life, and notably in the case of the bishops, did he indulge in such pettiness. Everything that was done during his reign was done in his name and Louis' indirect responsibility in matters he had delegated was the same as his direct responsibility in his own personal spheres. Moreover, the two sectors could not help but be closely connected.

A policy of greatness and prestige demanded an efficient and effective administration as well as adequate resources, both military and financial. . . .

In order to disseminate the king's commands over great distances and combat the complex host of local authorities, a network of thirty intendants had been established over the country. These were the king's men, dispatched by the king's councils and assisted by correspondents, agents and *subdélégués* who by 1715 were numerous and well organized. By this time the system was well-established and more or less accepted (even in Brittany). It met with reasonable respect and sometimes obedience. Sometimes, not always, since we only have to read the intendants' correspondence to be disabused swiftly of any illusions fostered by old-fashioned textbooks or history notes. The difficulties of communications, the traditions of provincial independence, inalienable rights and privileges and the sheer force of inertia, all died hard. Lavisse used to say this was a period of absolutism tempered by disobedience. In the depths of the country and the remote provinces, the formula might almost be reversed. Nevertheless, there is no denying that a step forward had been made and that the germ of the splendid administrative systems of Louis XV and of Napoleon was already present in the progress made between 1661 and 1715. . . .

In one adjacent but vital field, ministers and jurists laboured valiantly to reach a unified code of French law, giving the king's laws priority over local custom and simplifying the enormous tangled mass of statute law. . . .

The navy, rescued from virtual oblivion by Colbert who gave it arsenals, shipwrights, gunners, talented designers, its finest captains and fresh personnel obtained by means of seaboard conscription, distinguished itself particularly from 1672 to 1690. . . .

The greatest of all the king's great servants were those who helped him to build up an army, which in size and striking force was for the most part equal to all the other armies of Europe put together. They were first Le Tellier and Turenne and later, Louvois and Vauban. Many others of less fame, such as Chamlay, Martinet, Fourilles and Clerville would also deserve a place in this unusually lengthy roll of honour if the historian's job were the awarding of laurels, especially military ones. The fighting strength was increased at least fourfold, discipline was improved, among generals as well as officers and men, and a civil administration superimposed, not without a struggle, on the quarrelsome, short-sighted and in many cases incompetent and dishonest military one. New ranks and new corps were introduced; among them the artillery and the engineers, as well as such new weapons as the flintlock and the fixed bayonet, and a new military architect, Vauban, all helped to make the army more efficient. Most important of all, the army at last possessed a real *Intendance* with its own arsenals, magazines, and regular staging posts. Uniforms became more or less general, providing employment for thousands of workers. The first barracks were an attempt to put an end to the notorious custom of billeting troops on civilian households. The Hôtel des Invalides [16] was built, on a grand scale. The instrument which these invaluable servants placed at their master's disposal was almost without parallel in their time, a genuine royal army, growing ever larger and more diversified, modern and disciplined. . . .

An ambition to astonish the world with magnificence and great armies is all very well so long as the world is prepared to be astonished.

At the beginning of his reign, when Louis surveyed the rest of Europe, he saw nothing but weakness and decline. Some of his observations, as regards Spain and Italy, were perfectly correct. In others, he was mistaken. He stupidly underestimated the United Provinces, as though a small, bourgeois and Calvinist population were an inevitable sign of weakness. Yet another observation was swiftly belied by the changes which occurred in two highly dissimilar entities; England and the Empire.

Louis XIV found himself baulked at every turn by the diplomacy and dogged courage, as well as by the seapower and the immense wealth of the United Provinces. It is no longer fashionable to believe that the "Golden Age" of the Dutch was over in 1661. For a long time after that, their Bank, their Stock Exchange, their India Company, their fleets and their florins remained as powerful as ever. The invasion of 1672 weakened them only temporarily and even in 1715 . . . their wealth, currency and

[16] Now a military museum and the site of Napoleon's tomb but originally intended as an old soldiers' home.—ED.

bankers remained powerful and respected and often decisive. Their policy was not yet tied directly to England's. It was simply that they no longer enjoyed undivided supremacy: another nation's economy had reached the same level and was about to overtake them.

Louis XIV always did his best to ignore economic factors but they would not be denied and they took their revenge. . . .

Louis found other forces of opposition within the borders of his kingdom . . . the ancient, traditional and heavily calculated weight of inertia possessed by that collection of "nations," *pays, seigneuries,* fiefs and parishes which together made up the kingdom of France. Each of these entities was accustomed to living independently, with its own customs, privileges and even language, snug in its own fields and within sound of its own bells. The king consecrated at Rheims was a priest-king to be revered and almost worshipped, but from afar. . . .

If, dazzled by the splendours of Versailles, we let ourselves forget the constant presence of these seething undercurrents, we will have understood nothing of the France of Louis XIV and of the impossible task which the king and his ministers had set themselves, or of the massive inertia which made it so difficult. . . .

For some years now, younger historians of a certain school have tended to ignore the bustle of individuals and events in favour of what they call revealing, measuring, defining and illustrating the great dominant rhythms which move world history as a whole. These rhythms emerge as largely economic. . . . From 1600 onwards, the quantities of silver reaching Spain from America grew less and less until by 1650 the imports were only a fifth of what they had been in 1600. A probable revival of the mines of central Europe was insufficient to make up the deficit. First gold, and then silver, grew scarce, giving rise to hoarding. Copper from Sweden or Japan (via Holland) tended to take their place but it was a poor substitute. The whole age of Louis XIV was an age that Marc Bloch has called "monetary famine." . . .

Historians and economists have long been aware that the seventeenth century as a whole and the period from 1650-90 in particular, or even 1650-1730, was marked by a noticeable drop in the cost of basic foodstuffs as well as of a great many other things—a drop quite separate from annual "accidents." Landed incomes, offices and possible moneylending, all seem to have been affected by the same general reduction. . . .

There remains a strong impression that the period of Louis' reign was one of economic difficulties, suffering both from sudden, violent crises and from phases of stagnation and of deep depression. It is not easy to govern under such conditions especially when, like the king and most of his councillors, one is unaware of them. But what they tried to do and sometimes, despite such obstacles, achieved, remains nonetheless worthy of interest and even admiration.

It is possible, therefore, that France under Louis XIV may have been unconsciously subject to powerful economic forces which are still much disputed and not fully understood. Social, demographic, mental and other factors, wholly or partly incomprehensible to the rulers, may have played their part also. . . .

About the great mass of French society and its slow, ponderous development we know almost nothing, only a few glimmers here and there. . . .

It is true that Louis XIV, like most men who grew up between 1640 and 1660, was incapable of rising beyond the limits of his education, let alone of taking in, at one glance, the whole of the planet on which he lived, to say nothing of infinite space. A king to the depths of his being, and a dedicated king, he had a concept of greatness which was that of his generation: military greatness, dynastic greatness, territorial greatness and political greatness which expressed itself in unity of faith, the illusion of obedience and magnificent surroundings. He left behind him an image of the monarchy, admirable in its way, but already cracking if not outworn at the time of his death.

Suggestions for Further Reading

THE BEST BIOGRAPHY of Louis XIV is John B. Wolf, *Louis XIV* (New York: Norton, 1968), a comprehensive, analytical, and persuasive book. Another work, by an eminent French historian, Pierre Gaxotte, *The Age of Louis XIV*, tr. Michael Shaw (New York: Macmillan, 1970), can also be recommended, but it is not as readable as Nancy Mitford, *The Sun King* (New York: Harper & Row, 1966), a handsome book on Louis and the daily life at Versailles—the court intrigues and decisions of government—a lively and witty, if somewhat superficial, book by a popular British novelist and biographer. Two brief biographies can also be recommended: the older Maurice Ashley, *Louis XIV and the Greatness of France*, "Teach Yourself History Library" (New York: Macmillan, 1948), and the more recent and sympathetic Vincent Buranelli, *Louis XIV*, "Rulers and Statesmen of the World" series (New York: Twayne, 1966).

Louis XIV, no matter how he is judged, is the central figure in seventeenth-century Europe. Some works on that century and the age of Louis XIV are therefore necessary to an understanding of the Sun King. David Ogg, *Europe in the Seventeenth Century*, 8th rev. ed. (London: Macmillan,

1961), and G. N. Clark, *The Seventeenth Century*, 2nd ed. (Oxford, England: Clarendon Press, 1961), have long been the standard works of, respectively, the narrative and institutional history of the period. A famous interpretive book, somewhat like Clark, is W. H. Lewis, *The Splendid Century, Life in the France of Louis XIV* (New York: Doubleday, 1957 [1953]), but it is more lively and entertaining. More comprehensive and much more far-ranging in subject is Maurice Ashley, *The Golden Century, Europe 1598–1715* (New York: Praeger, 1969). Of the same sort, but more popular, is Ragnhild Hatton, *Europe in the Age of Louis XIV* (New York: Harcourt, Brace and World, 1969). J. B. Wolf, *Toward a European Balance of Power, 1620–1715* (Chicago: Rand McNally, 1970), deals almost entirely with the central role of Louis XIV's France in the evolution of that important political-diplomatic concept. Students interested in the intellectual history of Louis' France should consult the small but well-done work by Edward John Kearns, *Ideas in Seventeenth-Century France: The Most Important Thinkers and the Climate of Ideas in which They Worked* (New York: St. Martin's Press, 1979).

Through the last generation or so, seventeenth-century studies, and the study of Louis XIV, have passed through a major crisis of revision. One of the early works reflecting this is J. B. Wolf, *The Emergence of the Great Powers, 1685–1715*, "Rise of Modern Europe" series (New York: Harper & Row, 1951), a brilliant synthesis of narrative, analysis, and modern research. Students should read more extensively in the important work, Pierre Goubert, *Louis XIV and Twenty Million Frenchmen*, tr. Anne Carter (New York: Pantheon, 1970), excerpted in this chapter. Students interested in this sort of work might be interested in the vast, two-volume compendium of French institutional history by the great French authority, Roland E. Mousnier, *The Institutions of France under the Absolute Monarchy 1598–1789*, vol. 1 *Society and the State*, tr. Brian Pearce (Chicago and London: University of Chicago Press, 1979), vol. 2 *The Organs of State and Society*, tr. Arthur Goldhammer (Chicago and London: University of Chicago Press, 1984). There are three sets of readings that represent much of the newer research and interpretation of Louis XIV: *Louis XIV and the Craft of Kingship*, ed. John C. Rule (Columbus: Ohio State University Press, 1969), *Louis XIV and Absolutism*, ed. Ragnhild Hatton (Columbus: Ohio State University Press, 1976), and *Louis XIV and Europe*, ed. Ragnhild Hatton (Columbus: Ohio State University Press, 1976). Finally, students may be interested in an important thesis book on the so-called general crisis of the seventeenth century: Theodore K. Rabb, *The Struggle for Stability in Early Modern Europe* (New York: Oxford University Press, 1975), in which Rabb argues that the crisis was a search for a principle of authority.

The Bettmann Archive

Peter the Great and the Westernization of Russia

1672	born
1682	joint succession with Ivan V under a regency
1696	beginning of Peter's sole rule
1697–1698	the Grand Embassy (Peter's tour of the West)
1698	destruction of the *streltsy* army revolt
1700–1721	the Great Northern War against Sweden
1706	start of the building of St. Petersburg
1725	died

Peter the Great was six feet eight inches tall and so strong that he could break a horseshoe with his bare hands. He was practically indifferent to comfort, and he had a manic energy and a capacity for the most savage and destructive rage. Despite an education so scant and faulty that he was virtually illiterate, he became a competent expert in more than a dozen technical crafts and a more than respectable amateur scientist. The enormous mass of laws, regulations, and edicts he framed have not even yet been completely edited. He was apt to invite anyone to eat or drink with him and was fond of stopping in the huts or shops of the humblest artisans to admire their skill or try his own and to chat with them. Yet Peter the Great sacrificed the lives of uncounted thousands of his peasants in the building of his new capital city of St. Petersburg—his "window on Europe"—in the desolate, disease-ridden marshes at the mouth of the Neva River on the Baltic. He could endure a slur to his own son made by a drunken companion, yet he rode rough-shod over the customs and sensibilities of his boyar court nobility, forcing them to set aside their old ways in favor of Western fashions in dress and education. He cut their beards himself and even demonstrated the new Western craft of dentistry on a few unfortunates among them. When a revolt of the *streltsy,* the imperial musketeers, forced him to return to Moscow from his first journey to the West, he disbanded the unit, personally saw to the torture and execution of more than a thousand of them, and displayed their corpses throughout the city as a lesson to other rebels. When, later in his reign, he suspected his weakling son Alexis of taking part in a conspiracy, Peter ordered his arrest and watched the boy be tortured to death.

Peter the Great is, in short, the most contradictory and intriguing figure in Russian history—as well as the most important. For no matter how it is interpreted, the reign of Peter the Great marks the most fundamental turning point in the history of his nation. And the central issue of this significant reign is Peter's policy of Westernization.

The offspring of the second marriage of Czar Alexis and third in the line of succession, Peter was raised by his mother away from the court in the so-called German suburb, where all the foreign residents of Moscow were compelled to live. Here Peter made friends among the Western merchants, artisans, technicians, and adventurers and developed his passion for Western ways. In 1697, after his succession to the throne, Peter made his celebrated first journey to the West, ostensibly to solicit support for a war against the Turks and also to sample for himself the wonders of Western technology. Peter traveled simply as a member of the party, disguised as Bombardier Peter Mikhailov. His true identity was discovered, however, and he was received at the courts of Brandenburg and Hanover, he met William of Orange and the Emperor Leopold, and he made friends with Augustus the Strong of Saxony, the king of Poland. On the whole, Peter's diplomatic initiative failed, but not so his technological mission. He visited iron foundries in Brandenburg. In Amsterdam he actually worked on the docks and in the shipyards as a ship's carpenter. In England he found the shipyards at Deptford and the Woolwich naval arsenal more interesting than London or the Parliament.

When the revolt of the *streltsy* forced him to cut short his visit to the West, Peter returned to Russia with the resolve to Westernize his nation. He not only imposed such seemingly trivial reforms as cleanshaven faces and Western clothing; he instituted the most fundamental changes in every aspect of Russian government and society. He reformed the judicial system and created a senate, whose members were appointed by him, to replace the old council of boyars. A series of ministries for public affairs was established; their directors were both Russians and foreigners. Peter recognized the chaotic system of local government, imposing upon it a structure of governorships responsible to him, and he drove the old conservative religious faction of the nobility out of the court. The power of the Patriarch over the Russian church was broken, and in its place an administrative system like the other ministries of the state was instituted. Peter forced Western-style education upon the boyars and created a new structure of nobility and a "Table of Ranks" based entirely on merit and service to the state. He reformed the system of taxation as well. He invited Western advisors and experts to Russia in unprecedented numbers and gave them unheard-of status and authority. At the same time, thousands of young Russians were sent to study and train in the West.

Peter the Great founded a merchant marine and opened up the vast resources of Russia to foreign trade. He created the Russian navy and completely reorganized the military establishment into Russia's first standing army. Never content to stand on the sidelines, Peter himself passed through all the ranks and grades in all the services of both the army and the navy. Even his foreign policy marked a fundamental turn to the West. The war against the Turks, early in his career, was undertaken in the hope of gaining access to the Mediterranean through the Black Sea. And the major conflict of his reign, the Great Northern War (1700–1721), was waged to challenge Swedish supremacy in the Baltic and open Russia to the West. In the course of the war, he faced the greatest military genius of his age in Charles XII of Sweden; and, though defeated by him at Narva in 1700, Peter came back to defeat Charles at Poltava nine years later. In the treaty that ended the war at Nystadt, it was Peter's Russia that gained the lion's share of territory, and Peter gained his long hoped-for access to the West.

By the end of his reign in 1725, Peter the Great had changed the Russian monarchy into a Western absolutism; he had displaced Sweden as the dominant power in the Baltic; and he had thrust Russia as a new and powerful force into the family of European nations from which it would never again be excluded.

Panegyric to the Sovereign Emperor Peter the Great

MIKHAIL LOMONOSOV

Peter the Great not only had his detractors and opponents; he also had his champions, some of whom he had raised to high position and others, both contemporaries and near contemporaries, who shared Peter's vision of the future of their nation. One such defender was Mikhail Vasil'evich Lomonosov (1711–1765), as fanatic a champion of Russian cultural modernization as the great Czar himself and the author of "Panegyric to the Sovereign Emperor Peter the Great," from which the following selection is taken. The occasion for the panegyric was the coronation of Peter's daughter Elizabeth in 1741, and its purpose was clearly to remind the new empress of her father's policies. But the panegyric is important not only as a sympathetic retrospective survey of Peter's reign, but also as one of the first important contributions to the myth of Peter the Great, the founder of modern Russia, a man larger than life and altogether heroic. A contemporary of Lomonosov, P. N. Krekshyn, hailed the Czar in these terms, "Our father Peter the Great! Thou broughtest us from nothingness into existence!" [1]*—a sentiment thoroughly compatible with Lomonosov's views.*

. . . AS I EMBARK on this undertaking, with what shall I begin my discourse? With His bodily endowments? With the greatness of His strength? But it is manifest in his mastery of burdensome labors, labors without number, and in the overcoming of terrible obstacles. Shall I begin with His heroic appearance and stature combined with majestic beauty? But apart from the many who vividly call to mind an image of Him engraved in their memory, there is the witness of those in various states and cities who, drawn by His fame, flocked out to admire a figure appropriate to His deeds and befitting a great Monarch. Should I commence with His buoyancy of spirit? But that is proved by the tireless vigilance without which it would have been impossible to carry out deeds so numerous and great. Wherefore I do immediately proceed to present these deeds, knowing that it is easier to make a beginning than to reach the end and that

[1] Quoted in M. S. Anderson, *Peter the Great* (London: The Historical Association, 1969), p. 3.

this Great Man cannot be better praised than by him who shall enumerate His labors in faithful detail, were it but possible to enumerate them.

And so, to the extent that strength and the brevity of limited time will permit, we shall mention only His most important deeds, then the mighty obstacles therein overcome, and finally the virtues which aided Him in such enterprises.

As a part of His grand designs the all-wise Monarch provided as a matter of absolute necessity for the dissemination of all kinds of knowledge in the homeland, and also for an increase in the numbers of persons skilled in the higher branches of learning, together with artists and craftsmen; though I have given His paternal solicitude in this matter the most prominent place, my whole speech would not be long enough to describe it in detail. For, having repeatedly made the rounds of European states like some swift-soaring eagle, He did induce (partly by command and partly by His own weighty example) a great multitude of His subjects to leave their country for a time and to convince themselves by experience how great an advantage a person and an entire state can derive from a journey of inquiry in foreign regions. Then were the wide gates of great Russia opened up; then over the frontiers and through the harbors, like the tides in the spacious ocean, there did flow in constant motion, in the one direction, the sons of Russia, journeying forth to acquire knowledge in the various sciences and arts, and, in the other direction, foreigners arriving with various skills, books, and instruments. Then to the study of Mathematics and Physics, previously thought of as forms of sorcery and witchcraft, but now arrayed in purple, crowned with laurels, and placed on the Monarch's throne, reverential respect was accorded in the sanctified Person of PETER. What benefit was brought to us by all the different sciences and arts, bathed in such a glow of grandeur, is proved by the superabundant richness of our most varied pleasures, of which our forefathers, before the days of Russia's Great Enlightener, were not only deprived but in many cases had not even any conception. How many essential things which previously came to Russia from distant lands with difficulty and at great cost are now produced inside the state, and not only provide for our needs but also with their surplus supply other lands. There was a time when the neighbors on our borders boasted that Russia, a great and powerful state, was unable properly to carry out military operations or trade without their assistance, since its mineral resources included neither precious metals for the stamping of coins nor even iron, so needful for the making of weapons with which to stand against an enemy. This reproach disappeared through the enlightenment brought by PETER; the bowels of the mountains have been opened up by his mighty and industrious hand. Metals pour out of them, and are not only freely distributed within the homeland but are also given back to foreign peoples as if in repayment of loans. The brave Russian army turns against the enemy weapons produced from Russian mines and Russian hands.

In the establishment of the sizable army needed for the defense of the homeland, the security of His subjects, and the unhindered carrying out of important enterprises within the country, how great was the solicitude of the Great Monarch, how impetuous His zeal, how assiduous His search of ways and means! . . . The impossible was made possible by extraordinary zeal, and above all by an unheard-of-example. In former times the Roman Senate, beholding the Emperor Trajan standing before the Consul to receive from him the dignity of Consul, exclaimed: "Through this thou art the greater, the more majestic!" What exclamations, what applause were due to PETER the Great for His unparalleled self-abasement? Our fathers beheld their crowned Sovereign not among the candidates for a Roman consulship but in the ranks of common soldiers, not demanding power over Rome, but obedient to the bidding of His subjects. O you beautiful regions, fortunate regions which beheld a spectacle so wondrous! Oh, how you marveled at the friendly contest of the regiments of a single Sovereign, both commander and subordinate, giving orders and obeying them! Oh, how you admired the siege, defense, and capture of new Russian fortresses, not for immediate mercenary gain but for the sake of future glory, not for putting down enemies but to encourage fellow countrymen. Looking back at those past years, we can now imagine the great love for the Sovereign and the ardent devotion with which the newly instituted army was fired, seeing Him in their company at the same table, eating the same food, seeing His face covered with dust and sweat, seeing that He was no different from them, except that in training and in diligence He was superior to all. By such an extraordinary example the most wise Sovereign, rising in rank alongside His subjects, proved that Monarchs can in no other way increase their majesty, glory, and eminence so well as by such gracious condescension. The Russian army was toughened by such encouragement, and during the twenty years' war with the Swedish Crown, and later in other campaigns, filled the ends of the universe with the thunder of its weapons and with the noise of its triumphs. It is true that the first battle of Narva was not successful; but the superiority of our foes and the retreat of the Russian army have, through envy and pride, been exaggerated to their glorification and our humiliation, out of all proportion to the actual event. For although most of the Russian army had seen only two years' service and faced a veteran army accustomed to battle, although disagreement arose between our commanders, and a malicious turncoat revealed to the enemy the entire position in our camp, and Charles XII [of Sweden] by a sudden attack did not give the Russians time to form ranks—yet even in their retreat they destroyed the enemy's willingness to fight on to final victory. Thus the only reason the Russian Life Guard, which had remained intact, together with another sizable part of the army, did not dare to attack the enemy thereafter was the absence of its main leaders, who had been summoned by Charles for peace talks and detained as prisoners.

For this reason the Guards and the rest of the army returned to Russia with their arms and war chest, drums beating and banners flying. That this failure occurred more through the unhappy circumstances described than through any lack of skill in the Russian troops and that PETER's new army could, even in its infancy, defeat the seasoned regiments of the enemies, was proved in the next year and subsequently by many glorious victories won over them. . . .

Having covered Himself and His army with glory throughout the world by such famous victories, the Great Monarch finally proved that he had been at pains to establish His army mainly in the interests of our safety! For He decreed that it should never be dispersed, even in times of untroubled peace (as had happened under previous Sovereigns, frequently to no little loss of the country's might and glory), and also that it should always be kept in proper readiness. . . .

Having cast a quick glance over PETER's land forces, which came to maturity in their infancy and combined their training with victories, let us extend our gaze across the waters, my Listeners; let us observe what the Lord has done there, His marvels on the deep, as made manifest by PETER to the astonishment of the world.

The far-flung Russian state, like a whole world, is surrounded by great seas on almost every side and sets them as its boundaries. On all of them we see Russian flags flying. Here the mouths of great rivers and new harbors scarcely provide space for the multitude of craft; elsewhere the waves groan beneath the weight of the Russian fleet, and the sounds of its gunfire echo in the chasms of the deep. Here gilded ships, blooming like spring, are mirrored on the quiet surface of the waters and take on double beauty; elsewhere the mariner, having reached a calm haven, unloads the riches of faraway countries to give us pleasure. Here new Columbuses hasten to unknown shores to add to the might and glory of Russia; there a second Tethys dares to sail between the battling mountains; she struggles with snow, with frost, with everlasting ice, desirous to unite East and West. How did the power and glory of Russian fleets come to be spread over so many seas in a short time? Whence came the materials, whence the skill? Whence the machines and implements needed in so difficult and varied an enterprise? Did not the ancient giants tear great oaks from dense forests and lofty mountains and throw them down for building on the shores? Did not Amphion with sweet music on the lyre move the various parts for the construction of those wondrous fortresses which fly over the waves? To such fancies would PETER's wondrous swiftness in building a fleet truly have been ascribed if an exploit so improbable and seemingly beyond human strength had been performed in far-off ancient times, and if it had not been fixed in the memory of many eyewitnesses and in unexceptionably reliable written records. . . . From that very time when the contriving of a boat (which, though small in dimensions, was great in influence and fame) aroused in

PETER's unsleeping spirit the salutary urge to found a fleet and to show forth the might of Russia on the deep, He applied the forces of His great mind to every part of this important enterprise. As He investigated these parts, He became convinced that in a matter so difficult there was no possibility of success unless He Himself acquired adequate knowledge of it. But where was that to be obtained? What should the Great Sovereign undertake? . . .

. . . But greater still was the amazement that He aroused, greater the spectacle that He presented to the eyes of the whole world when, becoming convinced of the untold benefits of navigation—first on the small bodies of water in the Moscow area, then on the great breadth of Lake Rostov and Lake Kubensk, and finally on the expanse of the White Sea—He absented himself for a time from His dominions and, concealing the Majesty of His Person among humble workmen in a foreign land, did not disdain to learn the shipwright's craft. Those who chanced to be His fellow-apprentices at first marveled at the amazing fact that a Russian had not only mastered simple carpentering work so quickly, had not only brought Himself to the point where He could make with His own hands every single part needed in the building and equipping of ships, but had also acquired such skills in marine architecture that Holland could no longer satisfy His deep understanding. Then how great was the amazement that was aroused in all when they learned that this was no simple Russian, but the Ruler of that great state Himself who had taken up heavy labors in hands born and anointed to bear the Scepter and the Orb. But was it merely out of sheer curiosity or, at the most, for purposes of instruction and command, that He did in Holland and Britain attain perfection in the theory and practice of equipping a fleet and in navigational science? Everywhere the Great Sovereign aroused His subjects to labor, not only by command and reward, but also by His own example! I call you to witness, O great Russian rivers; I address myself to you, O happy shores, sanctified by PETER's footsteps and watered by His sweat. How many times you resounded with high-spirited and eager cries as the heavy timbers, ready for launching of the ship, were being slowly moved by the workmen and then, at the touch of His hand, made a sudden spurt toward the swift current, inspiring the multitude, encouraged by His example, to finish off the huge hulks with incredible speed. To what a marvelous and rousing spectable were the assembled people treated as these great structures moved nearer to launching! When their indefatigable Founder and Builder, now moving topside, now below, now circling round, tested the soundness of each part, the power of the machinery, and the precision of all the preparations and by command, encouragement, ingenuity, and the quick skill of His tireless hands, rectified the defects which He had detected. In this unflagging zeal, this invincible persistence in labor, the legendary prowess of the ancients was shown in PETER's day to have been not fiction but the very truth! . . .

I say nothing of the assistance afforded in this matter by other wise institutions, but will mention the increase of external revenues. Divine Providence aided the good designs and efforts of PETER, through His hand opening new ports of the Varangian [Baltic] Sea at towns conquered by His valor and erected by His own labors. Great rivers were joined for the more convenient passage of Russian merchants, duty regulations were established, and commercial treaties with various peoples were concluded. What benefit proceeded from the growth of this abundance within and without has been clear from the very foundation of these institutions, for while continuing to fight a burdensome war for twenty years Russia was free from debts.

What, then, have all PETER's great deeds already been depicted in my feeble sketch? Oh, how much labor still remains for my thoughts, voice, and tongue! I ask you, my Listeners, out of your knowledge to consider how much assiduous effort was required for the foundation and establishment of a judiciary, and for the institution of the Governing Senate, the Most Holy Synod, the state colleges, the chancelleries, and the other governmental offices with their laws, regulations, and statutes; for the establishment of the table of ranks and the introduction of decorations as outward tokens of merit and favor; and finally, for foreign policy, missions, and alliances with foreign powers. You may contemplate all these things yourselves with minds enlightened by PETER. . . .

Nothing can serve me so well to demonstrate the kindness and gentleness of His heart as His incomparable graciousness toward His subjects. Superbly endowed as He was, elevated in His Majesty, and exalted by most glorious deeds, He did but the more increase and adorn these things by His incomparable graciousness. Often He moved amongst His subjects simply, countenancing neither the pomp that proclaims the monarch's presence nor servility. Often anyone afoot was free to meet Him, to follow Him, to walk along with Him, to start a conversation if so inclined. In former times many Sovereigns were carried on the shoulders and heads of their slaves; graciousness exalted Him above these very Sovereigns. At the very time of festivity and relaxation important business would be brought to Him; but the importance did not decrease gaiety, nor did simplicity lessen the importance. How He awaited, received, and greeted His loyal subjects! What gaiety there was at His table! He asked questions, listened, answered, discussed as with friends; and whatever time was saved at table by the small number of dishes was spent in gracious conversation. Amid so many cares of state He lived at ease as among friends. Into how many tiny huts of craftsmen did He bring His Majesty, and heartened with His presence His most lowly, but skilled and loyal, servants. How often He joined them in the exercise of their crafts and in various labors. For He attracted more by example than He compelled by force. And if there was anything which then seemed to be compulsion, it now stands revealed as a benefaction. . . .

On the Corruption of Morals in Russia

PRINCE M. M. SHCHERBATOV

Lomonosov had proclaimed that the "compulsion" that had brought about Peter's reforms is "now revealed as a benefaction." To many, however, it continued to seem compulsion. One person who held this view was the conservative aristocrat Prince Mikhail Mikhailovich Shcherbatov (1733–1790). Shcherbatov belonged to one of the oldest and proudest families of the Russian traditional nobility, and throughout his life he was preoccupied with the status and the condition of the class to which he belonged. He was also a scholar and historian, one of the first to write a systematic, documentary history of his nation. Shcherbatov was commissioned by the Empress Catherine II to edit the private and public papers of Peter the Great. Thus, there was no one of his generation in a better position to assess Peter's accomplishments.

Shcherbatov was an admirer of Peter and even, to an extent, of Peter's Westernizing reforms. But, at the same time, he was alarmed by the consequences of those reforms, which he saw as undermining the position of the old aristocracy and corrupting the moral base that he considered to be fundamental to the greatness of Russia. These views are nowhere better or more succinctly expressed than in Shcherbatov's tract On the Corruption of Morals in Russia, *a work of his old age and a kind of summation of his reflections on the direction of Russian history. In Shcherbatov we have a cautious, even gloomy conservative to set beside Lomonosov, the euphoric enthusiast for Peter's reforms.*

PETER THE GREAT, in imitating foreign nations, not only strove to introduce to his realm a knowledge of sciences, arts and crafts, a proper military system, trade, and the most suitable forms of legislation; he also tried to introduce the kind of sociability, social intercourse and magnificence, which he first learnt from Lefort, and which he later saw for himself. Amid essential legislative measures, the organization of troops and artillery, he paid no less attention to modifying the old customs which seemed crude to him. He ordered beards to be shaved off, he abolished the old Russian garments, and instead of long robes he compelled the men to wear German coats, and the women, instead of the "telogreya" to wear bodices, skirts, gowns and "samaras," and instead of skull-caps, to adorn their heads with fontanges and cornettes. He established various assemblies where the women, hitherto segregated from the company of men, were present with them at entertainments. . . .

The monarch himself kept to the old simplicity of morals in his dress, so that apart from plain coats and uniforms, he never wore anything costly; and it was only for the coronation of the Empress Catherine Alexeevna, his wife, that he had made a coat of blue gros-de-tours with silver-braid; they say he also had another coat, grey with gold braid, but I do not know for what great occasion this was made.

The rest was all so plain that even the poorest person would not wear it today, as can be seen from such of his clothes as have remained, and are kept in the Kunst-Kamera at the Imperial Academy of Sciences.

He disliked cuffs and did not wear them, as his portraits attest. He had no costly carriages, but usually travelled in a gig in towns, and in a chaise on a long journey.

He did not have a large number of retainers and attendants, but had orderlies, and did not even have a bodyguard, apart from a Colonel of the Guard.

However, for all his personal simplicity, he wanted his subjects to have a certain magnificence. I think that this great monarch, who did nothing without farsightedness, had it as his object to stimulate trade, industries and crafts through the magnificence and luxury of his subjects, being certain that in his lifetime excessive magnificence and voluptuousness would not enthrone themselves at the royal court. . . .

As far as his domestic life was concerned, although the monarch himself was content with the plainest food, he now introduced drinks previously unknown in Russia, which he drank in preference to other drinks; namely, instead of domestic brandy, brewed from ordinary wine—Dutch aniseed brandy which was called "state" brandy, and Hermitage and Hungarian wine, previously unknown in Russia.

His example was followed by the grandees and those who were close to the court; and indeed it was proper for them to provide these wines; for the monarch was fond of visiting his subjects, and what should a subject not do for the monarch? . . . .

Closely copying him, as they were bound to do by their very rank, other leading officials of the Empire also kept open table, such as Admiral-of-the-Fleet, Count Fyodor Matveevich Apraxin, Field-Marshal-in-Chief, Count Boris Petrovich Sheremetev, the Chancellor, Count Gavrilo Ivanovich Golovkin, and the boyar, Tikhon Nikitich Streshnev, who as first ruler of the Empire during Peter the Great's absence abroad, was given estates in order to provide for such meals.

As these eminent men were copied by their inferiors, so the custom of keeping an open table was now introduced in many homes. The meals were not of the traditional kind, that is, when only household products were used; now they tried to improve the flavor of the meat and fish with foreign seasonings. And of course, in a nation in which hospitality has always been a characteristic virtue, it was not hard for the custom of these open tables to become a habit; uniting as it did the special pleasure of society and the improved flavour of the food as compared with the traditional kind, it established itself as a pleasure in its own right. . . .

With this change in the way of life, first of the leading officials of state, and then, by imitation, of the other nobles, and as expenditure reached such a point that it began to exceed income, people began to attach themselves more and more to the monarch and to the grandees, as sources of riches and rewards.

I fear someone may say that this, at any rate, was a good thing, that people began to attach themselves more and more to the monarch. No, this attachment was no blessing, for it was not so much directed to the person of the monarch as to personal ends; this attachment became not the attachment of true subjects who love their sovereign and his honour and consider everything from the point of view of the national interest, but the attachment of slaves and hirelings, who sacrifice everything for their own profit and deceive their sovereign with obsequious zeal.

Coarseness of morals decreased, but the place left by it was filled by flattery and selfishness. Hence came sycophancy, contempt for truth, beguiling of the monarch, and the other evils which reign at court to this day and which have ensconced themselves in the houses of the grandees. . . .

But despite [his] love of truth and his aversion to flattery, the monarch could not eradicate this encroaching venom. Most of those around him did not dare to contradict him in anything, but rather flattered him, praising everything he did, and never resisting his whims, while some even indulged his passions. . . .

I said that it was voluptuousness and luxury that were able to produce such an effect in men's hearts; but there were also other causes, stemming from actual institutions, which eradicated resoluteness and good behaviour.

The abolition of rights of precedence (a custom admittedly harmful to the service and the state), and the failure to replace it by any granting of rights to the noble families, extinguished thoughts of noble pride in the nobility. For it was no longer birth that was respected, but ranks and promotions and length of service. And so everyone started to strive after ranks; but since not everyone is able to perform straightforward deeds of merit, so for lack of meritorious service men began to try and worm their way up, by flattering and humouring the monarch and the grandees in every way. Then there was the introduction of regular military service under Peter the Great, whereby masters were conscripted into the ranks on the same level as their serfs. The serfs, being the first to reach officer's rank through deeds suited to men of their kind, became commanders over their masters and used to beat them with rods. The noble families were split up in the service, so that a man might never see his own kinsman.

Could virtue, then, and resolution, remain in those who from their youth had gone in fear and trembling of their commanders' rods, who could only acquire respect by acts of servility, and being each without any support from his kinsmen, remained alone, without unity or defence, liable to be subjected to violent treatment?

It is admirable that Peter the Great wished to rid religion of superstition, for indeed, superstition does not signify respect for God and his Law, but rather an affront. For to ascribe to God acts unbecoming to him is blasphemy.

In Russia, the beard was regarded as being in the image of God, and it was considered a sin to shave it off, and through this, men fell into the heresy of the Anthropomorphites.[2] Miracles, needlessly performed, manifestations of ikons, rarely proven, were everywhere acclaimed, attracted superstitious idolatry, and provided incomes for dissolute priests.

Peter the Great strove to do away with all this. He issued decrees, ordering beards to be shaved off, and by the Spiritual Regulation, he placed a check on false miracles and manifestations and also on unseemly gatherings at shrines set up at crossways. Knowing that God's Law exists for the preservation of the human race, and not for its needless destruction, with the blessing of the Synod and the Ecumenical patriarchs, he made it permissible to eat meat on fast-days in cases of need, and especially in the Navy where, by abstaining even from fish, the men were somewhat prone to scurvy; ordering that those who voluntarily sacrificed their lives by such abstinence, should, when they duly fell ill, be thrown into the water. All this is very good, although the latter is somewhat severe.

But when did he do this? At a time when the nation was still unenlightened, and so, by taking superstition away from an unenlightened people, he removed its very faith in God's Law. This action of Peter the Great may be compared to that of an unskilled gardener who, from a weak tree, cuts off the water-shoots which absorb its sap. If it had strong roots, then this pruning would cause it to bring forth fine, fruitful branches; but since it is weak and ailing, the cutting-off of these shoots (which, through the leaves which received the external moisture, nourished the weak tree) means that it fails to produce new fruitful branches; its wounds fail to heal over with sap, and hollows are formed which threaten to destroy the

[2] Attributing manlike qualities to God.—ED.

tree. Thus, the cutting-off of superstitions did harm to the most basic articles of the faith; superstition decreased, but so did faith. The servile fear of Hell disappeared, but so did love of God and his Holy Law; and morals, which for lack of other enlightenment used to be improved by faith, having lost this support began to fall into dissolution. . . .

And so, through the labours and solicitude of this monarch, Russia acquired fame in Europe and influence in affairs. Her troops were organized in a proper fashion, and her fleets covered the White Sea and the Baltic; with these forces she overcame her old enemies and former conquerors, the Poles and the Swedes, and acquired important provinces and sea-ports. Sciences, arts and crafts began to flourish there, trade began to enrich her, and the Russians were transformed—from bearded men to clean-shaven men, from long-robed men to short-coated men; they became more sociable, and polite spectacles became known to them.

But at the same time, true attachment to the faith began to disappear, sacraments began to fall into disrepute, resoluteness diminished, yielding place to brazen, aspiring flattery; luxury and voluptuousness laid the foundation of their power, and hence avarice was also aroused, and, to the ruin of the laws and the detriment of the citizens, began to penetrate the law-courts.

Such was the condition with regard to morals, in which Russia was left at the death of this great monarch (despite all the barriers which Peter the Great in his own person and by his example had laid down to discourage vice).

Peter the Great: A Modern View

NICHOLAS V. RIASANOVSKY

Modern historians of Russia, in their efforts to gain an objective view of Peter, have tried to uncover the real man behind the myth of Peter the Great. They have tried to strike a balance between the work of Peter's champions and the work of his detractors in order to put Peter's reign in proper perspective.

Their efforts have been complicated by the myths and prejudices not only of the eighteenth century but of the twentieth century as well. It is precisely on the issue of Peter's Westernization that the greatest difficulty arises. Through the late nineteenth century until the very eve of the revolution of 1917, one of the dominant themes of Russian intellectual life was Pan-Slav nationalism, with its extravagant praise of things Russian and its almost paranoid suspicion of outside, non-Slavic influences. The effect of such a point of view can be seen in the following conclusion of Vasili Klyuchevsky, the greatest Russian historian of the generation just before the revolution. "He was not a blind admirer of the West, on the contrary, he mistrusted it, and was not deluded into thinking that he could establish cordial relations with the West, for he knew that the West mistrusted his country, and was hostile to it. . . . Thus for Peter association with Europe was only a means to an end, and not an end in itself." [3]

Russian hostility toward the West was only increased by the revolution and by the events of Russian history ever since. The kindest treatment Peter the Great has ever received at the hands of Soviet historians is a kind of faint praise for his advancing of Russia's modernization. But even that faint praise is no longer heard: Peter's Westernization is now simply denounced as "cosmopolitanism," [4] *and work on the editing of the documentary sources for Peter's reign has been halted indefinitely.*

Despite such difficulties, a consensus view of Peter the Great is finally beginning to appear among modern, non-Soviet Russian historians. That view is represented in the following selection from A History of Russia *by the American scholar Nicholas V. Riasanovsky, considered by many Russian historians to be the best general treatment of Russia's history.*

AFTER PETER took over the conduct of state affairs and began to reform Muscovy, he found few collaborators. His own family, the court circles, and the boyar duma [5] overwhelmingly opposed change. Because he discovered little support at the top of the state structure, and also because he never attached much importance to origin or rank, the sovereign proceeded to obtain assistants wherever possible. Before long an extremely mixed but on the whole able group emerged. . . .

Among foreigners, the tsar had the valuable aid of some of his old friends, such as Patrick Gordon and the Swiss Francis Lefort, who played a prominent role until his early death in 1699. Later such able newcomers from Germany as the diplomat Andrew Ostermann and the military expert Burkhard Münnich joined the sovereign's entourage. Some of his numerous foreign assistants, for example, the Scot James Bruce who helped with the artillery, mining, the navy and other matters, had been born in Russia and belonged to the second generation of foreign settlers in Muscovy.

Russian assistants to Peter ranged over the entire social gamut. . . .

[3] Vasili Klyuchevsky, *Peter the Great, Liliana* Archibald, (London: Macmillan, 1961), pp. 262–63.

[4] *Rewriting Russian History, Soviet Interpretations of Russia's Past,* ed. Cyril E. Black, 2nd ed. (New York: Random House, 1962), p. 254.

[5] The old council of nobility.—ED.

War against Turkey was the first major action of Peter I after he took the government of Russia into his own hands in 1694, following the death of his mother.[6] In fighting Turkey, the protector of the Crimean Tartars and the power controlling the Black Sea and its southern Russian shore, the new monarch followed in the steps of his predecessors. However, before long it became apparent that he managed his affairs differently. The war began in 1695, and the first Russian campaign against Azov failed: supplied by sea, the fortress remained impregnable to the Muscovite army. Then, in one winter, the tsar built a fleet in Voronezh on the Don River. He worked indefatigably himself, as well as ordering and urging others, and utilized to the best advantage the knowledge of all available foreign specialists along with his own previously acquired knowledge. By displaying his tremendous energy everywhere, Peter the Great brought thirty sea-going vessels and about a thousand transport barges to Azov in May 1696. Some of the Russian fleet, it might be noted, had been built as far away as Moscow and assembled in Voronezh. This time besieged by sea as well as by land, the Turks surrendered Azov in July.

With a view toward a further struggle against Turkey and a continuing augmentation and modernization of the Russian armed forces, the tsar next sent fifty young men to study, above all shipbuilding and navigation, in Holland, Italy, and England. Peter dispatched groups of Russians to study abroad several more times in his reign. After the students returned, the sovereign often examined them personally. In addition to experts, the tsar needed allies to prosecute war against Turkey. The desire to form a mighty coalition against the Ottoman Empire, and an intense interest in the West, prompted Peter to organize a large embassy to visit a number of European countries and—a most unusual act for a Muscovite ruler—to travel with the embassy.

Headed by Lefort, the party of about 250 men set out in March 1697. The sovereign journeyed incognito under the name of Peter Mikhailov. His identity, however, remained no secret to the rulers and officials of the countries he visited or to the crowds which frequently gathered around him. The tsar engaged in a number of important talks on diplomatic and other state matters. But, above all, he tried to learn as much as possible from the West. He seemed most concerned with navigation, but he also tried to absorb other technical skills and crafts, together with the ways and manners and, in fact, the entire life of Europe as he saw it. As the so-called Grand Embassy progressed across the continent and as Peter Mikhailov also took trips of his own, most notably to the British Isles, he obtained some first-hand knowledge of the Baltic provinces of Sweden, Prussia, and certain other German states, and of Holland, England, and the Hapsburg Empire. From Vienna the tsar intended to go to Italy, but instead he rushed back to Moscow at news of a rebellion of the streltsy. Altogether Peter the Great spent eighteen months abroad in 1697–98.

[6] Who had served as his regent.—Ed.

At that time over 750 foreigners, especially Dutchmen, were recruited to serve in Russia. Again in 1702 and at other times, the tsar invited Europeans of every nationality—except Jews, whom he considered parasitic—to come to his realm, promising to subsidize passage, provide advantageous employment, and assure religious tolerance and separate law courts.

The streltsy had already caused trouble to Peter and suffered punishment on the eve of the tsar's journey to the West—in fact delaying the journey. Although the new conspiracy—that was aimed at deposing Peter and putting Sophia [7] in power had been effectively dealt with before the sovereign's return, the tsar acted with exceptional violence and severity. After investigation and torture more than a thousand streltsy were executed, and their mangled bodies were exposed to the public as a salutary lesson. Sophia was forced to become a nun, and the same fate befell Peter's wife, Eudoxia, who had sympathized with the rebels.

If the gruesome death of the streltsy symbolized the destruction of the old order, many signs indicated the coming of the new. After he returned from the West, the tsar began to demand that beards be cut and foreign dress be worn by courtiers, officials, and the military. With the beginning of the new century, the sovereign changed the Russian calendar: henceforth years were to be counted from the birth of Christ, not the creation of the world, and they were to commence on the first of January, not the first of September. More important, Peter the Great rapidly proceeded to reorganize his army according to the Western pattern.

The Grand Embassy failed to further Peter the Great's designs against Turkey. But, although European powers proved unresponsive to the proposal of a major war with the Ottomans, other political opportunities emerged. Before long Peter joined the military alliance against Sweden organized by Augustus II, ruler of Saxony and Poland. . . .

In modern European history the Great Northern War was one of the important wars and Poltava one of the decisive battles. The Russian victory over Sweden and the resulting Treaty of Nystadt meant that Russia became firmly established on the Baltic, acquiring its essential "window into Europe," and that in fact it replaced Sweden as the dominant power in the north of the continent. Moreover, Russia not only humiliated Sweden but also won a preponderant position vis-à-vis its ancient rival Poland, became directly involved in German affairs—a relationship which included marital alliances arranged by the tsar for his and his half-brother Ivan V's daughters—and generally stepped forth as a major European power. . . .

In regard to internal affairs during the reign of Peter the Great, we find that scholars have taken two extreme and opposite approaches. On the one hand, the tsar's reforming of Russia has been presented as a series, or rather a jumble, of disconnected *ad hoc* measures necessitated by the exigencies of the moment, especially by the pressure of the Great Northern

[7] Peter's older half-sister.—ED.

War. Contrariwise, the same activity has been depicted as the execution of a comprehensive, radically new, and well-integrated program. In a number of ways, the first view seems closer to the facts. As Kliuchevsky pointed out, only a single year in Peter the Great's whole reign, 1724, passed entirely without war, while no more than another thirteen peaceful months could be added for the entire period. . . .

Yet a balanced judgment has to allow something to the opposite point of view as well. Although Peter the Great was preoccupied during most of his reign with the Great Northern War and although he had to sacrifice much else to its successful prosecution, his reforming of Russia was by no means limited to hectic measures to bolster the war effort. In fact, he wanted to Westernize and modernize all of the Russian government, society, life, and culture, and even if his efforts fell far short of this stupendous goal, failed to dovetail, and left huge gaps, the basic pattern emerges, nevertheless, with sufficient clarity. Countries of the West served as the emperor's model. We shall see, however, when we turn to specific legislation, that Peter did not merely copy from the West, but tried to adapt Western institutions to Russian needs and possibilities. The very number and variety of European states and societies offered the Russian ruler a rich initial choice. It should be added that with time Peter the Great became more interested in general issues and broader patterns. Also, while the reformer was no theoretician, he had the makings of a visionary. With characteristic grandeur and optimism he saw ahead the image of a modern, powerful, prosperous, and educated country, and it was to the realization of that image that he dedicated his life. Both the needs of the moment and longer-range aims must therefore be considered in evaluating Peter the Great's reforms. Other fundamental questions to be asked about them include their relationship to the Russian past, their borrowing from the West —and, concurrently, their modification of Western models—their impact on Russia, and their durability.

Peter the Great hit Muscovy with a tremendous impact. To many of his contemporaries he appeared as either a virtually superhuman hero or the Antichrist. It was the person of the emperor that drove Russia forward in war and reform and inspired the greatest effort and utmost devotion. It was also against Peter the Great that the streltsy, the Bashkirs, the inhabitants of Astrakhan, and the motley followers of Bulavin staged their rebellions, while uncounted others, Old Believers and Orthodox, fled to the borderlands and into the forests to escape his reach.[8] Rumor spread

[8] We have already noted the revolt of the *streltsy*. In Astrakhan an uprising took place in 1705–1707 against Western influence and was headed by a renegade member of the *streltsy* and a fanatic monk. Bulavin led a revolt of the Don Cossacks in 1707 over the same issue and again with religious overtones. The Bashkirs were Turkish subjects of Peter in the lower Volga area who rebelled against heightened Russian interference at about the same time. All these revolts were eventually put down. The Orthodox party and the Old Believers were conservative factions that were opposed to Peter's Westernization and often involved in revolt.—ED.

and legends grew that the reformer was not a son of Tsar Alexis, but a foreigner who substituted himself for the true tsar during the latter's journey abroad, that he was an imposter, a usurper, indeed the Antichrist. Peter himself contributed much to this polarization of opinion. He too saw things in black and white, hating old Muscovy and believing himself to be the creator of a new Russia. Intolerance, violence, and compulsion became the distinguishing traits of the new regime, and St. Petersburg—built in the extreme northwestern corner of the country, in almost inaccessible swamps at a cost in lives far exceeding that of Poltava—became its fitting symbol. The emperor's very size, strength, energy, and temperament intensified his popular image. . . .

. . . Scholarly investigations of the last hundred years, together with large-scale publication of materials on the reformer's reign, undertaken by a number of men from Golikov to Bogoslovsky, have established beyond question many close connections between Peter the Great and the Muscovite past. Entire major aspects of the reformer's reign, for example, foreign policy and social relations and legislation, testified to a remarkable continuity with the preceding period. Even the reformer's desire to curb and control ecclesiastical landholding had excellent Muscovite precedents. The central issue itself, the process of Westernization, had begun long before the reformer and had gathered momentum rapidly in the seventeenth century. In the words of a modern scholar, Peter the Great simply marked Russia's transition from an unconscious to a conscious following of her historical path.

Although in the perspective of Russian history Peter the Great appears human rather than superhuman, the reformer is still of enormous importance. Quite possibly Russia was destined to be Westernized, but Peter the Great cannot be denied the role of the chief executor of this fate. At the very least the emperor's reign brought a tremendous speeding up of the irreversible process of Westernization, and it established state policy and control, where formerly individual choice and chance prevailed.

Suggestions for Further Reading

THE HISTORIOGRAPHY of Peter the Great divides along the line separating Russian national scholars from Westerners. As we observed in the head-note to the Riasanovsky selection, this separation is a product not only of the Soviet revolution but of the earlier Pan-Slav movement with its deep suspicions of Western influence. Of this viewpoint of Russian nationalist historians, the best example is Vasily O. Kluchevsky, whose *A History of Russia*, tr. C. J. Hogarth, 5 vols. (New York: Russell and Russell, 1960), originally published in Russia between 1911 and 1931, is among the monuments of modern Russian historical writing. The section of Kluchevsky's history dealing with Peter has been separately published: *Peter the Great*, tr. Liliana Archibald (London: Macmillan, 1961). To some extent the views of Kluchevsky are seconded by M. T. Florinsky, *Russia: A History and an Interpretation*, 2 vols. (New York: Macmillan, 1953), which many admirers consider contains the best general account of Peter the Great. See also his *Russia: A Short History* (New York: Macmillan, 1965). For the Soviet views see the essay by C. E. Black, "The Reforms of Peter the Great" in *Rewriting Russian History, Soviet Interpretations of Russia's Past*, ed. Cyril E. Black, 2nd rev. ed. (New York: Random House, 1962).

In the Western tradition, probably the best full-scale biography of Peter is Ian Grey, *Peter the Great, Emperor of All Russia* (Philadelphia: Lippincott, 1960), while the two best brief accounts are B. H. Sumner, *Peter the Great and the Emergence of Russia,* "Teach Yourself History Library" (London: English Universities Press, 1950), and L. Jay Oliva, *Russia in the Era of Peter the Great* (Englewood Cliffs, N.J.: Prentice-Hall, 1969). Students may prefer the exciting popular biography by Harold Lamb, *The City and the Tsar: Peter the Great and the Move to the West, 1648–1762* (New York: Doubleday, 1948). There are three excellent recent biographies of Peter: Matthew S. Anderson, *Peter the Great* (London: Thames and Hudson, 1978), is a brief, solid, up-to-date survey; Alex DeJonge, *Fire and Water: A Life of Peter the Great* (New York: Coward, McCann and Geoghegan, 1980), is also a substantial book but more readable; and Robert K. Massie, *Peter the Great, His Life and World* (New York: Knopf, 1980), is a huge, nine-hundred-page work, the most important aspect of which is its detailed description of the setting, the world of Peter the Great. For the interpretive problems of Peter, see *Peter the Great, Reformer or Revolutionary*, ed. Marc Raeff, rev. ed. (Boston: Heath, 1972) as well as Nicholas V. Riasanovsky, *The Image of Peter the Great in Russian History and Thought* (Oxford and New York: Oxford University Press, 1985).

For the role and setting of such figures as Lomonosov and Shcherbatov, see Hans Rogger, *National Consciousness in Eighteenth-Century Russia* (Cambridge, Mass.: Harvard University Press, 1960), and Marc Raeff, *Origins of the Russian Intelligentsia, the Eighteenth-Century Nobility* (New York: Harcourt, Brace and World, 1966).

Of brief general accounts of Russian history for the background to Peter the Great, the best is Nicholas V. Riasanovsky, *A History of Russia*, 2nd ed. (New York: Oxford University Press, 1969), excerpted in this chapter. But students should also see the fine narrative history, George Vernadsky, *A History of Russia*, 6th rev. ed. (New Haven, Conn.: Yale University Press, 1971), and the exciting and readable James H. Billington, *The Icon and the Axe, An Interpretive History of Russian Culture* (New York: Knopf, 1966). For the role of Russia in Europe, see J. B. Wolf, *The Emergence of the Great Powers, 1685–1715*, cited for the preceding chapter.

The Bettmann Archive

Jean-Jacques Rousseau and the Spirit of Revolution

1712	born in Geneva
1742	moved to Paris
1750	*Discourse on the Sciences and the Arts* wins Dijon prize
1761	wrote *The New Héloïse*
1762	wrote *The Social Contract* and *Émile*
1762–1767	exile in Switzerland and England
1778	died

There was never a more unlikely harbinger of revolution than Jean-Jacques Rousseau nor, for that matter, a more unlikely subject for an enduring literary cult. Yet by the time of his death in 1778, his books were already famous, and scarcely more than a decade later, he was being celebrated as the godfather of the French Revolution.

Rousseau had practically no education. He was born in Geneva in 1712 and orphaned at an early age. Following his parents' deaths, friends and relatives took him in and apprenticed him to a number of crafts, including engraving and watchmaking. Succeeding at none of these, he gave them up for a wandering life that took him to Italy. After a time he returned to Switzerland, where, in Neuchâtel, he passed himself off as a composer and music teacher. In 1742 he departed for Paris with a harebrained scheme for a new system of musical notation he had invented—though he could not read a note of music!

Rousseau's musical notation system came to nothing, but while in Paris he was befriended by Denis Diderot, who allowed him to write some articles on music and political economy for the *Encyclopédie* that he was compiling. In 1749 Diderot encouraged Rousseau to submit an essay to a contest sponsored by the Academy of Dijon on the subject of whether the revival of the sciences and arts had been beneficial or detrimental to morals. Following Diderot's advice, Rousseau took the negative side. His essay won the prize, and Rousseau became an instant literary celebrity.

Despite the limitations of his background, Rousseau had a quick and retentive mind; a breathless, intense, personal style; and a passion for ideas. The Dijon prize essay, his *Discourse on the Sciences and Arts*, was the first of a series of discourses, treatises, articles, and books—each of which was a sensation in one way or another—that made Rousseau the most widely read author of his time, not excepting even the great Voltaire. In 1755 he published a revised and expanded version of his prize-winning essay, *A Discourse on the Origin and Foundations of Inequality*. Then, in the next five years, he wrote *Julie, or the New Héloïse*, a sentimental novel so popular that, as a result of it, Rousseau succeeded the Englishman Samuel Richardson as the leading advocate for the cult of sensibility; a moral-political tract entitled *The Social Contract*; and, finally another novel, *Émile*, which was actually a treatise on education. The ideas that emerged from these writings were so important, the literary style so compelling, and the author himself so controversial that Rousseau's works gained almost universal popularity.

The framework of Rousseau's ideas began to take shape in the prize-winning essay of 1749, in which he argued that civilization, rather than having advanced human morality, had instead corrupted the inherent goodness of human nature. In his revision of the discourse, he expanded this argument, claiming that civilized society had introduced artificial distinctions of wealth and position that further corrupted the sublime equality and moral decency of the state of nature. *The Social Contract* opens with these famous words, "Man was born free, and he is everywhere in chains," and goes on to insist that, by the social contract through which primitive people surrendered their individual rights to the collective society, they did not surrender their claim to practical equality and individual liberty. *Émile* begins with another famous sentence, "Everything is good as it leaves the hands of the Creator; everything degenerates in the hands of man." This novel demonstrates, through the account of its hero's education, how by proper instruction people could regain the happy state now denied them by civilized society and in the process become free and responsible citizens. Rousseau called one of the sections of *Émile* "The Profession of Faith of the Savoyard Vicar," and he put into the mouth of his character a devastating attack upon both Protestantism and Catholicism for their part in the debasement of natural man.

Largely as a result of this attack, Rousseau was condemned by both the Catholic Sorbonne in Paris and the Calvinist Consistory in Geneva, and warrants for his arrest were issued in both cities. Public authorities were already suspicious of Rousseau because of his other radical ideas, for unlike most of his contemporaries, he insisted on publishing his works and proclaiming his ideas under his own name. But the publication of *Émile* was the last straw. Rousseau was forced to flee from one refuge to another across Europe, even stopping briefly in England in 1766, where he was the guest of the historian and philosopher David Hume.

By this time, Rousseau's health had begun to fail, and he suffered from a number of ailments. His actual ailments, real enough, began to blend with others that existed only in his troubled mind. He shunned society and fled from his legion of admirers—in one of his residences, he even had a trap door to the cellar into which he would dart at the approach of a stranger. He quarreled with most of his friends and benefactors, including Hume and Diderot, and accused them of plotting against him. His last years were devoted to attempts to justify his life, his work, and his ideas. The *Confessions* were part of this effort, and, though the book was not published until after his death, he would read from the manuscript in any salon where he could find an audience. Rousseau died in 1778, convinced that he was a failure.

It was Voltaire's opinion that Rousseau was quite mad. This judgment, however, was neither charitable nor entirely correct. Rousseau was certainly a spectacular eccentric, but it was not his eccentricity that bothered critics like Voltaire. Most of them were among the leaders of the broad philosophical and literary movement that dominated the eighteenth century—the Enlightenment. This period is often called the Age of Reason, and with considerable justice, for its leading motif was a belief in reason. The figures of the Enlightenment tended to believe that the capacity for reason belonged not to the great mass of the people but to an intellectual elite. They tended not only to accept monarchy but to extol as the best form of government a monarchy committed to reason, the so-called enlightened despotism. They tended to be hostile to religiosity and contemptuous of organized religion, but they were also optimistic about the future of humanity and had a sublime confidence in the inevitability of progress. Despite the fact that Rousseau shared many of the ideas of the Enlightenment, he did not really belong to it. He was as suspicious of reason as his friends were of religion, and he was as profoundly, if erratically, religious as they were skeptical. Rousseau was an uncompromising democrat and egalitarian, but, at the same time, he was bitterly pessimistic about the future of humanity. His friends and enemies alike simply did not understand him. They rejected his often-proclaimed sincerity as hypocrisy and were convinced that his intense personalism was only self-serving. Voltaire maliciously observed to d'Alembert that "Jean-Jacques would be delighted to be hanged, provided his name was mentioned."[1] Even Hume, in the end, found little to praise in Rousseau except his eloquence, and he doubted gravely that eloquence alone could support the extravagance of Rousseau's ideas.

[1] Quoted in Lester G. Crocker, *Jean-Jacques Rousseau, The Prophetic Voice (1758–1778)* (New York: Macmillan, 1973), p. 244.

Yet those very ideas, so alien to the Enlightenment, were the wave of the future. A modern scholar has called them "the most radical and comprehensive social criticism ever formulated up to his time, a criticism whose impact on modern society was and remains incalculably great."[2] Rousseau's criticism of society was to be the bridge between the Age of Reason and the Age of Revolution. In *Émile* he wrote, "We are approaching a state of crisis and a century of revolutions." The philosopher Ernst Cassirer, in a famous essay on Rousseau, observed that although "Rousseau, the outcast and the eccentric, shied away from the turmoil of the market place and the noise of battle . . . the truly revolutionary impetus emanated from him, not from the men who represented and dominated the public state of mind of contemporary France." [3]

[2] J. Christopher Herold, "The Solitary Wanderer," *Horizon,* 5, no. 3 (1964), 95.

[3] Ernst Cassirer, *The Question of Jean-Jacques Rousseau,* ed. and trans. Peter Gay, (New York: Columbia University Press, 1954), p. 69.

The Social Contract

JEAN-JACQUES ROUSSEAU

The revolutionary impetus of Rousseau's ideas emanated, more than from any of his other works, from the little treatise he wrote in 1762 called The Social Contract. *Considered by one modern authority to be the "capstone" of Rousseau's system of thought,* The Social Contract *was to be the most enduring, the most controversial, and the most influential of his works. It was also to become the manifesto of the French Revolution. Despite its faulty history and naive anthropological constructs, it clearly proclaimed such ideas as popular sovereignty, the general will, the inevitable corruption of princely power, and, of course, the idea of the primal contract among people that is the only possible basis of human society and government—the contract that, at least by inference, the existing governments of Europe had violated.*

We turn now to sample this famous work.

MAN WAS BORN free, and he is everywhere in chains. Those who think themselves the masters of others are indeed greater slaves than they. How did this transformation come about? I do not know. How can it be made legitimate? That question I believe I can answer.

If I were to consider only force and the effects of force, I should say: "So long as a people is constrained to obey, and obeys, it does well; but as soon as it can shake off the yoke, and shakes it off, it does better; for since it regains its freedom by the same right as that which removed it, a people is either justified in taking back its freedom, or there is no justifying those who took it away." But the social order is a sacred right which serves as a basis for all other rights. And as it is not a natural right, it must be one founded on covenants. The problem is to determine what those covenants are. . . .

I assume that men reach a point where the obstacles to their preservation in a state of nature prove greater than the strength that each man has to preserve himself in that state. Beyond this point, the primitive condition cannot endure, for then the human race will perish if it does not change its mode of existence.

Since men cannot create new forces, but merely combine and control those which already exist, the only way in which they can preserve themselves is by uniting their separate powers in a combination strong enough to overcome any resistance, uniting them so that their powers are directed by a single motive and act in concert.

Such a sum of forces can be produced only by the union of separate men, but as each man's own strength and liberty are the chief instruments of his preservation, how can he merge his with others' without putting himself in peril and neglecting the care he owes to himself? This difficulty, which brings me back to my present subject, may be expressed in these words:

"How to find a form of association which will defend the person and goods of each member with the collective force of all, and under which each individual, while uniting himself with the others, obeys no one but himself, and remains as free as before." This is the fundamental problem to which the social contract holds the solution.

The articles of this contract are so precisely determined by the nature of the act, that the slightest modification must render them null and void; they are such that, though perhaps never formally stated, they are everywhere the same, everywhere tacitly admitted and recognized; and if ever the social pact is violated, every man regains his original rights and, recovering his natural freedom, loses that social freedom for which he exchanged it.

These articles of association, rightly understood, are reducible to a single one, namely the total alienation by each associate of himself and all his rights to the whole community. Thus, in the first place, as every individual gives himself absolutely, the conditions are the same for all, and precisely because they are the same for all, it is in no one's interest to make the conditions onerous for others.

Secondly, since the alienation is unconditional, the union is as perfect as it could be, and no individual associate has any longer any rights to claim; for if rights were left to individuals, in the absence of any higher authority to judge between them and the public, each individual, being his own judge in some causes, would soon demand to be his own judge in all; and in this way the state of nature would be kept in being, and the association inevitably become either tyrannical or void.

Finally, since each man gives himself to all, he gives himself to no one; and since there is no associate over whom he does not gain the same rights as others gain over him, each man recovers the equivalent of everything he loses, and in the bargain he acquires more power to preserve what he has.

If, then, we eliminate from the social pact everything that is not essential to it, we find it comes down to this: "Each one of us puts into the community his person and all his powers under the supreme direction of the general will; and as a body, we incorporate every member as an indivisible part of the whole."

Immediately, in place of the individual person of each contracting party, this act of association creates an artificial and collective body composed of as many members as there are voters in the assembly, and by this same act that body acquires its unity, its common *ego*, its life and its will. The public person thus formed by the union of all other persons was once called the *city*, and is now known as the *republic* or the *body politic.* In its passive role it is called the *state*, when it plays an active role it is the *sovereign*; and when it is compared to others of its own kind, it is a *power*. Those who are associated in it take collectively the name of *a people*, and call themselves individually *citizens*, in so far as they share in the sovereign power, and *subjects*, in so far as they put themselves under the laws of the state. . . .

As soon as the multitude is united thus in a single body, no one can injure any one of the members without attacking the whole, still less injure the whole without each member feeling it. Duty and self-interest thus equally oblige the two contracting parties to give each other mutual aid; and the same men should seek to bring together in this dual relationship, all the advantages that flow from it.

Now, as the sovereign is formed entirely of the individuals who compose it, it has not, nor could it have, any interest contrary to theirs; and so the sovereign has no need to give guarantees to the subjects, because it is impossible for a body to wish to hurt all of its members, and, as we shall see, it cannot hurt any particular member. The sovereign by the mere fact that it is, is always all that it ought to be. . . .

Hence, in order that the social pact shall not be an empty formula, it is tacitly implied in that commitment—which alone can give force to all others—that whoever refuses to obey the general will shall be constrained to do so by the whole body, which means nothing other than that he shall be forced to be free; for this is the condition which, by giving each citizen to the nation, secures him against all personal dependence, it is the condition which shapes both the design and the working of the political machine, and which alone bestows justice on civil contracts—without it, such contracts would be absurd, tyrannical and liable to the grossest abuse. . . .

Suppose we draw up a balance sheet, so that the losses and gains may be readily compared. What man loses by the social contract is his natural liberty and the absolute right to anything that tempts him and that he can take; what he gains by the social contract is civil ilberty and the legal right of property in what he possesses. . . .

If the state, or the nation, is nothing other than a legal person the life of which consists in the union of its members and if the most important of its cares is its own preservation, it must have a universal and compelling power to move and dispose of each part in whatever manner is beneficial to the whole. Just as nature gives each man an absolute power over all his own limbs, the social pact gives the body politic an absolute power over all its members; and it is this same power which, directed by the general will, bears, as I have said, the name of sovereignty.

However, we have to consider beside the public person those private persons who compose it, and whose life and liberty is naturally independent of it. Here we have to distinguish clearly the respective rights of the citizens and of the sovereign, and distinguish those duties which the citizens have as subjects from the natural rights which they ought to enjoy as men.

We have agreed that each man alienates by the social pact only that part of his power, his goods and his liberty which is the concern of the community; but it must also be admitted that the sovereign alone is judge of what is of such concern.

Whatever services the citizen can render the state, he owes whenever the sovereign demands them; but the sovereign, on its side, may not impose on the subjects any burden which is not necessary to the community. . . .

The world has seen a thousand splendid nations that could not have accepted good laws, and even those that might have accepted them could have done so only for short periods of their long history. Nations, like men, are teachable only in their youth; with age they become incorrigible. Once customs are established and prejudices rooted, reform is a dangerous and fruitless enterprise; a people cannot bear to see its evils touched, even if only to be eradicated; it is like a stupid pusillanimous invalid who trembles at the sight of a physician.

I am not denying that just as certain afflictions unhinge men's minds and banish their memory of the past, so there are certain violent epochs and revolutions in states which have the same effect on peoples that psychological shocks may have on individuals; only instead of forgetting the past, they look back on it in horror, and then the state, after being consumed by civil war, is born again, so to speak, from its own ashes, and leaps from the arms of death to regain the vigour of youth. Such was the experience of Sparta at the time of Lycurgus, of Rome after the Tarquins, and, in the modern world, of Holland and Switzerland after the expulsion of the tyrants.

But such events are unusual; they are exceptional cases to be explained by the special constitution of the states concerned. It could not even happen twice to the same people; because although a people can make itself free while it is still uncivilized, it cannot do so when its civil energies are worn out. Disturbances may well destroy a civil society without a revolution being able to restore it, so that as soon as the chains are broken, the state falls apart and exists no longer; then what is needed is a master, not a liberator. Free peoples, remember this maxim: liberty can be gained, but never *regained*. . . .

We have seen that the legislative power belongs, and can only belong, to the people. On the other hand, it is easy to see . . . that executive power cannot belong to the generality of the people as legislative or sovereign, since executive power is exercised only in particular acts which are outside the province of law and therefore outside the province of the sovereign which can act only to make laws.

The public force thus needs its own agent to call it together and put it into action in accordance with the instructions of the general will, to serve also as a means of communication between the state and the sovereign, and in a sense to do for the public person what is done for the individual by the union of soul and body. This is the reason why the state needs a government, something often unhappily confused with the sovereign, but of which it is really only the minister.

What, then, is the government? An intermediary body established between the subjects and the sovereign for their mutual communication, a body charged with the execution of the laws and the maintenance of freedom, both civil and political. . . .

Just as the particular will acts unceasingly against the general will, so does the government continually exert itself against the sovereign. And the more this exertion increases, the more the constitution becomes corrupt, and, as in this case there is no distinct corporate will to resist the will of the prince and so to balance it, sooner or later it is inevitable that the prince will oppress the sovereign and break the social treaty. This is the inherent and inescapable defect which, from the birth of the political body, tends relentlessly to destroy it, just as old age and death destroy the body of man. . . .

From these explanations, it follows . . . that the act which institutes the government is not a contract but a law, and that the holders of the executive power are not the people's masters but its officers; and that the people can appoint them and dismiss them as it pleases; and that there is no question of their contracting, but of obeying; and that in discharging the functions which the state imposes on them, they are only doing their duty as citizens, without having any sort of right to argue terms.

Thus when it happens that the people institutes a hereditary government, whether monarchical in one family, or aristocratic in a class of citizens, it does not enter into any undertaking; hereditary government is simply a provisional form that it gives to the administration until such time as it pleases to arrange it differently.

It is true that such changes are always dangerous, and that one should never touch an established government unless it has become incompatible with the public welfare; but such circumspection is a precept of politics and not a rule of law; and the state is no more bound to leave civil authority to its magistrates than military authority to its generals. . . .

In the end, when the state, on the brink of ruin, can maintain itself only in an empty and illusory form, when the social bond is broken in every heart, when the meanest interest impudently flaunts the sacred name of the public good, then the general will is silenced: everyone, animated by secret motives, ceases to speak as a citizen any more than as if the state had never existed; and the people enacts in the guise of laws iniquitous decrees which have private interests as their only end.

Does it follow from this that the general will is annihilated or corrupted? No, that is always unchanging, incorruptible and pure, but it is subordinated to other wills which prevail over it. . . .

Rousseau and the Tyrannical Majority

J. L. TALMON

Rousseau has always been a figure of controversy. As we have seen, he was almost deified by the early leaders of the French Revolution. Not surprisingly, he was hated by its enemies with equal intensity. The Englishman Edmund Burke called him "the insane Socrates of the National Assembly." This controversy has continued in the enormous mass of recent criticism, theorizing, and speculation about Rousseau and especially about his theories of government and society. One of the most influential modern interpretations of Rousseau is that of the distinguished Israeli historian J. L. Talmon, contained in his The Origins of Totalitarian Democracy. *Like many Jewish scholars, Talmon has been interested in discovering the sources of the totalitarianism that produced the Jewish holocaust of Hitler's Germany. He has found at least one source in what he calls the "totalitarian democracy" that had its origin in the eighteenth century and its first historic demonstration in the French Revolution. He sees Rousseau as its prophet.*

Talmon views Rousseau as a "tormented paranoiac," a shattered personality whose prescriptions for society—despite their noble intentions—are as contradictory as the man himself. Those prescriptions, in Talmon's opinion, add up to the most dangerously paradoxical of all modern political notions—totalitarian democracy, the tyranny of the majority. In defense of Rousseau, Talmon notes that we cannot expect an eighteenth-century man to express twentieth-century ideas and that the absolutist nature of his theories, both of the individual and of society, belongs generally to the intellectual order of the eighteenth century. Nevertheless, he claims, Rousseau was the principal architect of the theoretical structure that, in its justification of the tyranny of the majority and the dehumanization of the individual, ultimately produced, in the twentieth century, the fearful tyranny of the right in Nazi Germany and the equally fearful tyranny of the left in Soviet Russia.

Here is Talmon's analysis.

A MOTHERLESS vagabond starved of warmth and affection, having his dream of intimacy constantly frustrated by human callousness, real or imaginary, Rousseau could never decide what he wanted, to release human nature or to moralize it by breaking it; to be alone or a part of human company. He could never make up his mind whether man was made better or worse, happier or more miserable, by people. Rousseau was one of the most ill-adjusted and egocentric natures who have left a record of their predicament. He was a bundle of contradictions, a recluse and anarchist, yearning to return to nature, given to reverie, in revolt against all social conventions, sentimental and lacrimose, abjectly self-conscious and at odds with his environment, on the one hand; and the admirer of Sparta and Rome, the preacher of discipline and the submergence of the individual in the collective entity, on the other. The secret of this dual personality was that the disciplinarian was the envious dream of the tormented paranoiac. *The Social Contract* was the sublimation of the *Discourse on the Origins of Inequality*. . . . Rousseau, the teacher of romantic spontaneity of feeling, was obsessed with the idea of man's cupidity as the root cause of moral degeneration and social evil. Hence his apotheosis of Spartan ascetic virtue and his condemnation of civilization in so far as civilization is the expression of the urge to conquer, the desire to shine and the release of human vitality, without reference to morality. He had that intense awareness of the reality of human rivalry peculiar to people who have experienced it in their souls. Either out of a sense of guilt or out of weariness, they long to be delivered from the need for external recognition and the challenge of rivalry. . . .

It was of vital importance to Rousseau to save the ideal of liberty, while insisting on discipline. He was very proud and had a keen sense of the heroic. Rousseau's thinking is thus dominated by a highly fruitful but dangerous ambiguity. On the one hand, the individual is said to obey nothing but his own will; on the other, he is urged to conform to some objective criterion. The contradiction is resolved by the claim that this external criterion is his better, higher, or real self, man's inner voice, as Rousseau calls it. Hence, even if constrained to obey the external standard, man cannot complain of being coerced, for in fact he is merely being made to obey his own true self. He is thus still free; indeed freer than before. For freedom is the triumph of the spirit over natural, elemental instinct. It is the acceptance of moral obligation and the disciplining of irrational and selfish urges by reason and duty. The acceptance of the obligations laid down in *The Social Contract* marks the birth of man's personality and his initiation into freedom. Every exercise of the general will constitutes a reaffirmation of man's freedom. . . .

Ultimately the general will is to Rousseau something like a mathematical truth or a Platonic idea. It has an objective existence of its own, whether perceived or not. It has nevertheless to be discovered by the human mind. But having discovered it, the human mind simply cannot honestly refuse to accept it. In this way the general will is at the same time outside us and within us. Man is not invited to express his personal preferences. He is not asked for his approval. He is asked whether the given proposal is or is not in conformity with the general will. "If my particular opinion had carried the day, I should have achieved the opposite of what was my will; and it is in that case that I should not have been free." For freedom is the capacity of ridding oneself of considerations, interests, preferences and prejudices, whether personal or collective, which obscure the objectively true and good, which, if I am true to my true nature, I am bound to will. What applies to the individual applies equally to the people. Man and people have to be brought to choose freedom and if necessary to be forced to be free.

The general will becomes ultimately a question of enlightenment and morality. Although it should be the achievement of the general will to create harmony and unanimity, the whole aim of political life is really to educate and prepare men to will the general will without any sense of constraint. Human egotism must be rooted out, and human nature changed. "Each individual, who is by himself a complete and solitary whole, would have to be transformed into part of a greater whole from which he receives his life and being." Individualism will have to give place to collectivism, egoism to virtue, which is the conformity of the personal to the general will. The Legislator "must, in a word, take away from man his resources and give him instead new ones alien to him, and incapable of being made use of without the help of other men. The more completely these natural resources are annihilated, the greater and the more lasting are those which he acquires, and the more stable and perfect the new institutions, so that if each citizen is nothing and can do nothing without the rest, and the resources acquired by the whole are equal or superior to the aggregate of the resources of all individuals, it may be said that legislation is at the highest possible point of perfection." As in the case of the materialists, it is not the self-expression of the individual, the deployment of his particular faculties and the realization of his own and unique mode of existence, that is the final aim, but the loss of the individual in the collective entity by taking on its colour and principle of existence. The aim is to train men to "bear with docility the yoke of public happiness," in fact to create a new type of man, a purely political creature, without any particular private or social loyalties, any partial interests, as Rousseau would call them.

Rousseau's sovereign is the externalized general will, and, as has been said before, stands for essentially the same as the natural harmonious order. In marrying this concept with the principle of popular sovereignty, and popular self-expression, Rousseau gave rise to totalitarian democracy. The mere introduction of this latter element, coupled with the fire of Rousseau's style, lifted the eighteenth-century postulate from the plane of intellectual speculation into that of a great collective experience. It marked the birth of the modern secular religion, not merely as a system of ideas, but as a passionate faith. Rousseau's synthesis is in itself the formulation of the paradox of freedom in totalitarian democracy in terms which reveal the dilemma in the most striking form, namely, in those of will. There is such a thing as an objective general will, whether willed or not willed by anybody. To become a reality it must be willed by the people. If the people does not will it, it must be made to will it, for the general will is latent in the people's will.

Democratic ideas and rationalist premises are Rousseau's means of resolving the dilemma. According to him the general will would be discerned only if the whole people, and not a part of it or a representative body, was to make the effort. The second condition is that individual men as purely political atoms, and not groups, parties or interests, should be called upon to will. Both conditions are based upon the premise that there is such a thing as a common substance of citizenship, of which all partake, once everyone is able to divest himself of his partial interests and group loyalties. In the same way men as rational beings may arrive at the same conclusions, once they rid themselves of their particular passions and interests and cease to depend on "imaginary" standards which obscure their judgment. Only when all are acting together as an assembled people, does man's nature as citizen come into active existence. It would not, if only a part of the nation were assembled to will the general will. They would express a partial will. Moreover, even the fact that all have willed something does not yet make it the expression of the general will, if the right disposition on the part of those who will it was not there. A will does not become general because it is willed by all, only when it is willed in comformity to the objective will.

Exercise of sovereignty is not conceived here as the interplay of interests, the balancing of views, all equally deserving a hearing, the weighing of various interests. It connotes the endorsement of a truth, self-identification on the part of those who exercise sovereignty with some general interest which is presumed to be the fountain of all identical individual interests. Political parties are not considered as vehicles of the various currents of opinion, but representatives of partial interests, at variance with the general interest, which is regarded as almost tangible. It is of great importance to realize that what is to-day considered as an essential concomitant of democracy, namely, diversity of views and interests, was far from being regarded as essential by the eighteenth-century fathers of democracy. Their original postulates were unity and unanimity. The affirmation of the principle of diversity came later, when the totalitarian implications of the principle of homogeneity had been demonstrated in Jacobin dictatorship.

This expectation of unanimity was only natural in an age which, starting with the idea of the natural order, declared war on all privileges and inequalities. The very eighteenth-century concept of the nation as opposed to estates implied a homogeneous entity. Naïve and inexperienced in the working of democracy, the theorists on the eve of the Revolution were unable to regard the strains and stresses, the conflicts and struggles of a parliamentary democratic régime as ordinary things, which need not frighten anybody with the spectre of immediate ruin and confusion. . . .

Like the Physiocrats [4] Rousseau rejects any attempt to divide sovereignty. He brands it as the trick of a juggler playing with the severed limbs of an organism. For if there is only one will, sovereignty cannot be divided. Only that in place of the Physiocratic absolute monarch Rousseau puts the people. It is the people as a whole that should exercise the sovereign power, and not a representative body. An elected assembly is calculated to develop a vested interest like any other corporation. A people buys itself a master once it hands over sovereignty to a parliamentary representative body.

Now at the very foundation of the principle of direct and indivisible democracy, and the expression of unanimity, there is the implication of dictatorship, as the history of many a referendum has shown. If a constant appeal to the people as a whole, not just to a small representative body, is kept up, and at the same time unanimity is postulated, there is no escape from dictatorship. This was implied in Rousseau's emphasis on the all-important point that the leaders must put only questions of a general nature to the people, and moreover, must know how to put the right question. The question must have so obvious an answer that a different sort of answer would appear plain treason or perversion. If unanimity is what is desired, it must be engineered through intimidation, election tricks, or the organization of the spontaneous popular expression through the activists busying themselves with petitions, public demonstrations, and a violent campaign of denunciation. This was what the Jacobins and the organizers of people's petitions, revolutionary *journées*, and other forms of direct expression of the people's will read into Rousseau.

Rousseau demonstrates clearly the close relation between popular sovereignty taken to the extreme, and totalitarianism. . . . In the predemocratic age Rousseau could not realize that the originally deliberate creation of men could become transformed into a Leviathan, which might

[4] A school of eighteenth-century economic philosophers who held that land and agriculture were the only true sources of a nation's wealth (thus opposing the mercantilists) and that taxation should be assessed only on land values. They also supported royal absolutism.—ED.

crush its own makers. He was unaware that total and highly emotional absorption in the collective political endeavour is calculated to kill all privacy, that the excitement of the assembled crowd may exercise a most tyrannical pressure, and that the extension of the scope of politics to all spheres of human interest and endeavour, without leaving any room for the process of casual and empirical activity, was the shortest way to totalitarianism. Liberty is safer in countries where politics are not considered all-important and where there are numerous levels of non-political private and collective activity, although not so much direct popular democracy, than in countries where politics take everything in their stride, and the people sit in permanent assembly.

The Utopian Rousseau

LESTER G. CROCKER

To some scholars, Talmon's interpretation of Rousseau is as controversial as Rousseau himself. The British historian Alfred Cobban, for example, characterizes Talmon's view simply as an "onslaught" on Rousseau that trims the subject to fit Talmon's own preconceptions.[5] *On the other hand, Lester G. Crocker, in his* Jean-Jacques Rousseau, The Prophetic Voice (1758–1778), *the most recent major general treatment of Rousseau, agrees—although somewhat reluctantly—with Talmon's thesis. Crocker maintains, like Talmon, that Rousseau was a man of his time and that he cannot be held responsible for the uses that the future would make of his ideas. He even defends Rousseau's motives as essentially moral and humanitarian. But he also argues that the utopianism inherent in Rousseau's political theory—for all its brilliance, rationalism, and originality—when applied to human affairs makes freedom the inevitable victim.*

The Social Contract is the capstone of Rousseau's rationalistic pyramid. It is one segment of a single sociopolitical system, carefully worked out in his mind and reflecting the needs of his personality, a system designed

[5] Alfred Cobban, *Rousseau and the Modern State* (London: Allen & Unwin, 1964), pp. 29-31.

to make men virtuous and happy. The theoretical mode of political institutions it contains corresponds to the architectonics of his broader plan, his grand plan, to fashion a man and a society "according to his heart." . . .

. . . The most seminal of eighteenth-century writers, he is also the most debated. It has been said that he was "the revolutionary thinker who first inscribed on the political banners of modern times the opposing slogans both of democratic and totalitarian government." "Liberal" would be a better word than "democratic." . . . [Yet] it is obvious that both words, "liberal" and "totalitarian," are partly anachronistic when applied to Rousseau. He did, however, have a clear idea or model, in his beloved Sparta, of a totalitarian collectivity. In any event, the appropriateness of words cannot affect the appropriateness of recognizing clear tendencies. Eighteenth-century thinkers, living in an archaic social and political structure that was out of tune with the economics and ideologies of a new stage in Western culture, were groping for ways to reorganize society on a rational basis and to solve the unending problem of the relation of the individual to the group. . . .

In the *Discourse on Inequality*, Rousseau had painted a vivid picture of a competitive society as one whose values are perverted by a false notion of "progress" and "good," one in which men have every interest in hating each other and in hurting each other. He saw that Western civilization espouses a Christian ethic of brotherhood, but practices a cut-throat, exploitative way of life.

Rousseau's apparent "primitivism" had a powerful appeal to his contemporaries, as well as to men of later times. Some followed the logic of his *Discourse* to its obvious end, dreaming of an egalitarian, communistic society, or even of an anarchistic social state. But Rousseau himself, as he turned to the constructive part of his work and sought a way out of man's dilemma, rejected primitivism. While he urged a simple way of living and abjured none of his criticisms of society, he realized that the simplistic solutions of "abolition" were pure fantasy. There can be no return to innocence. Evolution is an irreversible process.

For Rousseau, society is the original sin, but it is also the testing place, as earthly life is in the Christian tradition. The direction man must take is not a "return to nature"—neither to the hypothetical, metaphysical nature of "natural man," nor to the empirical laws of nature. We must leave all this behind and forge a new destiny, unknown to nature, one that is truly man's own. . . .

However complex and intricate Rousseau's theorizing may become in *The Social Contract*, it rests on this set of simple assumptions. To him they have all the self-evidence and certitude of Descartes' "clear ideas."

Ever since Pascal, the search for happiness and emotional security has been an increasingly important problem in Western civilization. Rousseau was not concerned with men's basic irrationality or the lack of purpose in human existence. He had no feeling of the absurd, of cosmic alienation. Like some other millenarian theorists, he believed that the human problem could be solved in human terms, by the true society.

The Social Contract opens with a famous first sentence: "Man was born free, and everywhere he is in chains." It would be wrong to take these words as a protest. They are only the statement of a fact, that man in society no longer enjoys the freedom of ""natural man." The prime purpose of Rousseau's inquiry, as he says immediately afterwards, will be to determine what conditions justify this civil status; in other words, what are the foundations of a legitimate political society. Here he breaks with most other thinkers of his time, who, like Montesquieu, were seeking to found the body politic on natural laws, or else on a rational "Natural Law." Following his view that society is not natural to man, he looks elsewhere, to artificial and deliberate conventions. In this, Hobbes' influence was doubtless great. In nature, argues Rousseau, there is only force. In society, men create right, which, though using force, supersedes it. Force under law is quite different from force without law. Right comes into being by the convention of the social compact.

Rousseau's version of the social contract theory is brilliantly original. For him, as for Hobbes,[6] it terminates the state of nature, with its natural freedom and equality. But a legitimtae political society gives men, in their stead, something new and far more precious: political liberty (as Rousseau understands it) and civil equality. The compact is the one unanimous act that obviates the need for further unanimity in voting. It creates the obligation to submit to the will of the majority: legally, since the individual has agreed to its rule; morally, since he is still obeying his true will, which is that the general will shall rule. Rousseau shows in detail what is lost forever on accepting the compact, and the gains which, point by point, are substituted for the losses. Possession, for instance, a usurpation which is limited only by strength, becomes property, a right which is both secured and limited by the community. Further, society is assumed, in Rousseau's theory, to be prior to government. The consequence is revolutionary. The so-called rulers of men have no part in the contract; they are only the instruments and servants of the people, in whom all sovereignty inalienably resides, and they may be dispossessed by the simple will of sovereign citizens.

This summary points to the two great problems of *The Social Contract* that have exercised the minds of countless commentators. The first is the expression of the will of the community, which is to be the determinant of justice and social control. This involves Rousseau's famous notion of

[6] Like many of his ideas, the idea of the social contract was not unique with Rousseau. Indeed, it enjoyed a kind of general currency in the eighteenth century, having originated (in all likelihood) with the English political theorist Thomas Hobbes in the previous century. It was first popularized by John Locke, but Rousseau gave the concept its most familiar form.—ED.

the "general will." The general will is to be ascertained or formulated by the process of majority vote, that is, a process of cancellation, in accordance with what Rousseau considered to be the workings of the mathematical laws of probability. But we must not err, as many commentators do, by confusing the nature of the general will with this positivistic process of its expression. The "general will" is essentially a rationalistic notion and involves the same type of hypothesis as "natural man" or the "state of nature." Rousseau does not deny what we might call "empirical man," man as he is, fighting primarily for his own interest. But beyond this he assumes a rational unity among all men, consisting of what their reason would desire if all individual passions and desires could be stilled. This is the "general will." It is questionable whether in majority rule Rousseau has found a procedure that would realize it, or whether he was really convinced that he had. It is on the general will, and on the participation of each citizen in the voting process, that he bases his theory that political and civil liberty consist not in doing what we as individuals want, but in doing what this hypothetical or metaphysical "general will" wants. . . .

Scholars have puzzled over the seeming contradiction between the individualism and spirit of rebellion in the *Discourse on Inequality* and the ideal of submissiveness and docility to the univocal will of an organic society in *The Social Contract*. Rousseau himself denied any real contradiction in his writings, and in this regard, at least, there is none. Rousseau's individualism, like his exaltation of the individual conscience, applies only to existing societies, which are corrupt, unjust, and exploitative. It is in the true society of which he dreams, where men are socialized, that the new, emergent conscience of the community, the "general will," supersedes individual conscience and individual will.

The second difficult problem, the new relationship of the individual citizen to the State, is the inevitable sequel. Is Rousseau's thought totalitarian or liberal? A remarkable quantity of ink has flowed in the attempt to prove it one or the other. Rousseau of course was not thinking in such terms. He wanted only to secure men's happiness, through a just, legitimate, political society. This could not be done without sacrifice and control. If we are to make a successful transition from a natural state of force to a civil state of right, we must think of men as citizens who have become part of a greater whole, and not as independent, self-centered individuals. The mutuality of the sacrifice, the application of laws to all, the respecting of others as we wish them to respect us, the limitation of the sacrifice by the sovereign people itself—this is the theoretical justification.

In the working out of Rousseau's plan, however, both individual dissent and political groupings are excluded. Not only are there no minority rights; there cannot even be minorities. Rousseau constantly uses the word "liberty," but for him it does not have the same meaning as for us. Liberty, for him, is first of all the independence or sovereignty of the

State. Second, it is the independence of any individual from all others, or from group pressures. It is the prevention of exploitation, either by individuals or by groups. This goal is achieved by the complete dependence of all on the collective self—an impersonal, inflexible force like that of nature in the original state of nature. Third, liberty is law self-given, or consented to—in other words, the sovereignty of the people as expressed in the general will. . . .

When we realize what kind of society Rousseau is dreaming of, we can better understand the function of the political processes outlined in *The Social Contract.* Sovereignty belongs to all the citizens and cannot be alienated or limited. This "democratic" doctrine turns out to be an absolutist doctrine. The sovereign power is in effect unlimited, even if it is (supposedly) held by an all-powerful general will rather than a despot. In fact, the potential tyranny is greater, because it is to take on a different coloration, that of impersonal necessity. Oppression by the State becomes, by definition, impossible; no self can want to hurt itself, Rousseau argues. It thereby tends to become unlimited. Rousseau's expressed intention is to reach beyond overt conformity and to "capture wills." . . .

Democracy and totalitarianism are not exclusive terms. Democracy is rule by the people. Totalitarianism is the attempt to impose a single pattern upon the thought, feelings, and actions of a community. The opposite of totalitarianism is not democracy, but the pluralistic society, in which people are free to differ and to judge the law itself, one in which complete conformity is not the test of good citizenship. Obedience to law is one thing; submergence into a "higher unity," surrender of one's judgment and will are quite different. We are inclined to cry out with the other Rousseau, the *romantic* Rousseau, "I am I, a sacred I. Thus far do I surrender myself, thus far do I *belong*, but no further." The libertarian will not accept Rousseau's "people's democracy." The general will belongs to the realm of myth; in the realm of reality, it can be expressed only by an individual or a group that speaks in its name and exercises the real power. It is difficult not to conclude that this is what Rousseau really intended, with his "Lawmakers" and his "guides," and all the mechanisms of control of thought and behavior.

In the ideal society Rousseau so ardently longed for, men are made to be happy, because in each man a harmony is created between wish and possibility, and a harmony among all men by the elimination of exploitation and aggressive, self-centered competition. It will also be a just society. Justice will never come from individual conscience or Natural Law, which are simply useless. They could never form the kind of *social* man of whom he was thinking. In their place he put the general will, a juridical, not a moral phenomenon, one that concerns the general welfare. . . .

Utopianism leads to rigorism, for all other ways are wrong. History shows utopianism to be conducive to cruelty and fanaticism, since its theories ignore the persistent refractory elements of human nature. Rousseau expressly favors fanaticism. Ultimately, then, unlimited control of individuals is implied, because that is what is required to make them act in a fashion consonant with utopianism. Most often, as in Rousseau, a utopian myth serves to rationalize coercion. To be sure, his political theory in *The Social Contract* is an attempt to transcend experience and is unrelated to action. However, when theory is ruthlessly applied to human affairs, freedom is its victim. . . .

Whether or not we like Rousseau's "new society," we feel his incomparable candor and the courage he drew from absolute conviction. In one sense, his message is one of hope. Neither society nor human nature is beyond the reach of man's will and rational powers; under certain conditions, both can be turned in new directions. Rousseau thought he had pointed out the paths toward a more human existence.

The *Discourse on Inequality* tells us what men may have been, in their remote origins, or what they still are in their fundamental substructure, and what has happened to them because of social experience. *The Social Contract*, a purely theoretical work, indicates a new direction. It tells us how to overcome and transform this "natural man" within us. It tells us what men may become—or rather, what Rousseau thought they must become, if the unique *human* experiment in a *natural* universe is to succeed and to survive.

Was he "a false prophet," as Irving Babbitt once called him? We cannot, at this point in history, say that he was wrong. His criticisms of our kind of society have surely lost none of their validity. And in such matters, only history can pronounce the verdict.

Suggestions for Further Reading

ROUSSEAU WAS ONE of the most popular and influential writers of the eighteenth century. Students are encouraged to read further in his most important work, *The Social Contract*, beyond the brief excerpt in this chapter. They will also find useful an excellent, brief, analytical study guide to this work in Hilail Gildin, *Rousseau's Social Contract, The Design of the Argument* (Chicago and London: University of Chicago Press, 1983). If not as important as *The Social Contract*, his *Confessions* were even more popular. See *The Confessions of Jean-Jacques Rousseau* . . . ed. A. S. B. Glover (New York: Heritage Press, 1955). Students may also find interesting *Jean-Jacques Rousseau, Citizen of Geneva: Selections from the Letters* . . . ed. Charles W. Hendel (New York and London: Oxford University Press, 1937), *The First and Second Discourses*, ed. Roger D. Masters (New York: St. Martin's Press, 1964), *Julie, or, The New Eloise* . . . tr. and abridged by Judith H. McDowell (University Park: Pennsylvania State University Press, 1968), or *The Émile of Jean-Jacques*

Rousseau, tr. and ed. William Boyd (New York: Columbia University Press, 1971).

Both because of his influence and because of his slippery, contradictory character, there is an enormous biographical and critical literature on Rousseau. The standard major work is Lester G. Crocker, *Jean-Jacques Rousseau, Vol. 1, The Quest, 1712–1758, Vol. 2, The Prophetic Voice, 1758–1778* (New York: Macmillan, 1968–1973), the second volume excerpted in this chapter. Students may also be interested in Crocker's *Rousseau's Social Contract: An Interpretive Essay* (Cleveland: Case Western Reserve University Press, 1968), in which he goes even further toward an endorsement of J. L. Talmon's controversial views, which students may also wish to examine in greater detail in *The Rise of Totalitarian Democracy* (Boston: Beacon, 1952). As part of the same controversy, students may be interested in William H. Blanchard, *Rousseau and the Spirit of Revolt, A Psychological Study* (Ann Arbor: University of Michigan Press, 1967), a work of psycho-history which examines the conflicting sentiments of tyrant and rebel in Rousseau. Jakob H. Huizinga, *Rousseau: The Self-Made Saint* (New York: Grossman, 1976), is a brilliantly written debunking biography, and Ernst Cassirer, *The Question of Jean-Jacques Rousseau*, ed. and tr. Peter Gay (New York: Columbia University Press, 1954), is a standard work of interpretation by a great contemporary philosopher. An excellent short biography is George R. Havens, *Jean-Jacques Rousseau* (Boston: Twayne, 1978).

Although something of an anti-Enlightenment figure, Rousseau always figures in works on the Enlightenment. A good, brief, introductory essay is Frederick B. Artz, *The Enlightenment in France* (Kent, Ohio: Kent State University Press, 1968), but the most important modern work is Peter Gay, *The Enlightenment, An Interpretation*, 2 vols. (New York: Knopf, 1966–1969), and it is immensely readable. Norman Hampson, *A Cultural History of the Enlightenment* (New York: Pantheon, 1968), is a work that can bear comparison with Gay. Two of the early classic works on the Enlightenment can still be read with profit: Ernst Cassirer, *The Philosophy of the Enlightenment*, tr. Fritz C. A. Koelln and James P. Pettegrove (Princeton, N.J.: Princeton University Press, 1951 [1932]), because it is still the best analytical work on its subject; and Carl L. Becker, *The Heavenly City of the Eighteenth Century Philosophers* (New Haven, Conn.: Yale University Press, 1932), because of its wisdom and urbanity. For the more recent critique of Becker, see *Carl Becker's Heavenly City Revisited*, ed. Raymond O. Rockwood (Hamden, Conn.: Archon Books, 1968).

Leo Gershoy, *From Despotism to Revolution, 1763–1789*, "Rise of Modern Europe" (New York: Harper, 1944), is still one of the best histories of the time of Rousseau, and Joan McDonald, *Rousseau and the French Revolution, 1762–1791* (London: University of London, Athlone Press, 1965), is an important revisionist work dealing with the often noted impact of Rousseau on the revolution.

The Granger Collection

Napoleon: Child or Betrayer of the Revolution?

1769	born on Corsica
1793	first command, against Toulon
1796–1797	the successful Italian campaign
1799–1804	one of three rulers in the Consulate
1804	proclaimed emperor
1805–1807	victories in Europe
1812–1813	the disastrous Russian campaign and defeat at Leipzig
1814	abdication and exile to Elba
1814–1815	"The Hundred Days," defeated at Waterloo, and second exile, to St. Helena
1821	died on St. Helena

Was Napoleon the child of the French Revolution? Napoleon himself felt that he was. And in one sense at least, the assertion is undeniably true. The Revolution had broken the caste system of the old military order, just as it had broken the social order of the Old Regime generally. In the struggling revolutionary republic, threatened with invasion and armed reprisal from every side, any man who showed the ability and the willingness to serve could advance in the military—even such an apparently unpromising officer as the young Napoleon Bonaparte, with his heavy Italian accent, his mediocre record as a military cadet and a junior officer, and his consuming interest in the politics of his native Corsica, which seemed to preclude any involvement in the great events that had been shaking France since 1789.

But Napoleon was not indifferent to those events. As early as 1791, he had become a member of the Jacobin Club in his garrison town of Valence, in the south of France, and was an outspoken advocate of Jacobin radicalism. His political views, rather than any proven military ability, secured for him his first important commission as commander of artillery at the siege of Toulon against the royalists and the British. Napoleon was successful, and he caught the eye of the military commissioner Augustin Robespierre, who praised the young officer in a letter to his brother Maximilien, then at the zenith of his political career in Paris. Napoleon was appointed commandant of artillery in the army of Italy. But Robespierre and his faction soon fell from power, and

Napoleon, deprived of his command, was arrested. After a brief imprisonment, he departed for Paris to try to rescue his fortunes.

In 1795 the National Convention, its tenure running out, submitted to referendum the so-called Constitution of the Year III,[1] with its accompanying decree that two-thirds of the convention's members must be returned to the new legislative assembly. The royalists, enraged at this attempt to insure continued radical domination of the government, rose in revolt. Someone remembered that the young radical Napoleon was in Paris, and he was given effective command of the defense of the convention. As the rebels marched on 13 Vendémiaire, Year IV (October 5, 1795), Napoleon had already positioned his artillery and coolly ordered it to fire. The famous "whiff of grapeshot" carried the day—though there is no record that Napoleon used the phrase—and friends and enemies alike began to call him "Général Vendémiaire." He was now a force to be reckoned with in the politics of the Revolution.

When the new government was formed, headed by a Directory, Napoleon was its military adviser. Within a year, he was given command of the army of Italy. The Italian campaign was at that time verging on failure, but Napoleon turned it around. He gained the loyalty of his troops—largely by authorizing them to live off the land they conquered in lieu of the pay their republic had failed to provide—and he won battles. Within less than a year, Napoleon was the master of Italy. Far exceeding his authority, he set up a series of Italian republics and forced the Austrians out of Italy entirely. Then Napoleon returned to Paris once more to engineer the Treaty of Campo Formio with the defeated Austrians. Although the Directory was far from pleased, Napoleon was fast becoming a popular hero.

Britain, with its formidable sea power and its wealth and industry, was clearly France's most dangerous enemy, and the Directory had formulated a plan for an invasion of England from across the channel. Napoleon was placed in command of the operation. After a cursory inspection, he rejected the plan, arguing instead for a strike at the British lifeline to India—a campaign in Egypt. Napoleon was able to overcome the Directory but not the British sea power and the squadrons of Lord Nelson. The Egyptian campaign was a disaster. But rather than admit defeat, Napoleon returned to France and proclaimed a victory when in fact there was none. The French people believed him.

In 1799 Napoleon, with Abbé Sieyès, an ambitious member of the Directory, engineered a coup d'état. The coup, which took place on 18–19 Brumaire, Year VIII (November 9–10, 1799), was successful, and the Directory was replaced by a Consulate of three men, one of them

[1] The early leaders of the Revolution had proclaimed a new calendar dating from the overthrow of the Old Regime. Napoleon would later return France to the common usage.

Napoleon. Within a matter of weeks, a new "Constitution of the Year VIII" was proclaimed, making Napoleon First Consul and the government of France a military dictatorship. It is true that the constitution was overwhelmingly approved by plebescite, after the fact. It is true that under its authority Napoleon launched far-reaching reforms, moving the nation in the direction of order and stability. But it is also true that the French nation had succumbed to the myth of Napoleon, a myth that was ultimately founded upon his military invincibility and—at least in Napoleon's mind—upon continued military victories.

In 1802 Europe might well have had peace. Even Britain had agreed to the Treaty of Amiens. For achieving this diplomatic coup, Napoleon was granted lifetime tenure as First Consul, but even this did not satisfy his ambition. Napoleon demanded an empire and he got it: on May 18, 1804, he was proclaimed Emperor of the French. In the years that followed, Napoleon compiled an incredible list of military victories: he defeated the Austrians at Ulm and the Austrians and Russians at Austerlitz in the winter of 1805, the Prussians at Jena and Auerstädt in the fall of 1806, and the Russians alone at Eylau and Friedland in the spring and summer of 1807. By this time, Napoleon had redrawn the map of western Europe, and his own relations sat on half a dozen thrones. His plan was to organize the Continent against the stubborn British; to this end, he signed an agreement with the new Russian emperor, Alexander I, dividing Europe between them.

In 1810 Napoleon, standing at the apex of his power, decided to disregard his agreement with Alexander and invade Russia. It was a disastrous miscalculation, and it proved to be the crucial turning point in Napoleon's career. Out of the almost half a million men who had massed on the banks of the Neman in the summer of 1812, fewer than ten thousand remained after the winter's march back from Moscow. The myth of Napoleon was shattered, and the powers of Europe rose up against him. Not only had he defeated and humiliated them, but he had brought them the Revolution. Even if he had subverted the Revolution in France, he had, nevertheless, exported its principles along with his conquests. To the Old Regime of Europe, this was Napoleon's greatest insult, the ultimate betrayal that they could not forgive. But it was also perhaps Napoleon's most enduring claim to having been one of the makers of the Western tradition, for, whatever his motives, Napoleon introduced the Age of Revolution that persisted on the Continent, in one guise or another, through most of the nineteenth century and that fundamentally changed the nature of European government and society.

Napoleon was forced to abdicate and was exiled to the Mediterranean island of Elba. But even as the victors were gathering to undo his work and the Bourbons were returning to France, Napoleon escaped from Elba. This was the beginning of his Hundred Days. As Napoleon, with an escort of grenadiers, approached Grenoble, he met the first battalion sent to intercept him. His secretary, the Marquis de Las Cases, described the scene:

> The commanding officer refused even to parley. The Emperor without hesitation, advanced alone, and one hundred of his grenadiers marched at some distance from him, with their arms reversed. The sight of Napoleon, his costume, and in particular his grey military great coat, produced a magical effect on the soldiers, and they stood motionless. Napoleon went straight up to a veteran whose arm was covered with *chevrons,* and very unceremoniously seizing him by the whisker, asked him whether he would have the heart to kill his Emperor. The soldier, his eyes moistened with tears immediately thrust the ramrod into his musquet, to show that it was not loaded, and exclaimed, "See, I could not have done thee any harm: all the others are the same." Cries of *Vive l'Empereur!* resounded on every side. Napoleon ordered the battalion to make half a turn to the right, and all marched on to Paris.[2]

With every mile resistance melted, and cries of *Vive l'Empereur!* swelled up from the throngs that lined the roads and from garrison troops and militia. Napoleon had returned and France was his. Even after the catastrophe at Waterloo, an officer lying in the mud with a shattered thigh cried out, "He has ruined us—he has destroyed France and himself—yet I love him still." [3]

But what of the Revolution? The old veteran on the road to Grenoble and the wounded officer on the field of Waterloo wept for their emperor, not for the lost cause of the Revolution. Thousands unquestionably shared their views. But many thousands more were convinced that, despite the terrible cost of Napoleon's search for glory, he had carried the Revolution to its proper, even to its inevitable conclusion. Napoleon himself wrote:

> I purified a revolution, in spite of hostile factions. I combined all the scattered benefits that could be preserved; but I was obliged to protect them with a nervous arm against the attacks of all parties; and in this situation it may be truly said that the public interest, *the State, was myself.*[4]

The wheel had come full circle. Napoleon "the child of the Revolution" echoed the words often ascribed to Louis XIV, "I am the state."

[2] The Count de Las Cases, *Memoirs of the Life, Exile, and Conversations of the Emperor Napoleon,* new ed. (New York: Eckler, 1900), III, 295.

[3] Louis Antoine Fauvelet de Bourrienne, *Memoirs of Napoleon Bonaparte,* ed. R. W. Phipps (New York: Scribners, 1891), IV, 204.

[4] Las Cases, *Memoirs,* III, 255-56.

Napoleon's Memoirs

THE COUNT DE LAS CASES

When, after Waterloo, Napoleon was sent into exile again, this time to the tiny, distant island of St. Helena in the south Atlantic, he was only forty-five years old, apparently in the prime of life. Might he not escape once more, even against all odds? Might he even be called back by one or another of the victorious allies, already beginning to quarrel among themselves? Might not France even summon its emperor again? Napoleon was planning for any eventuality, as carefully and methodically as he might plan a military campaign.

Napoleon had, of course, some limited contact with the Bonapartists in France, but this was restricted by the tight control over the island. He was able to carry on some correspondence, though much of it consisted of complaints to the British government about the conditions of his exile. But mainly Napoleon devoted himself to his memoirs, which he dictated to his secretary, the Marquis de Las Cases. Las Cases carefully transcribed the material, and then Napoleon read and corrected it himself.

Memoirs of the Life, Exile, and Conversations of the Emperor Napoleon *is a vast and complicated work—four volumes in its final published form. In addition to Napoleon's own recollections of events, discourses, and opinions, it contains comments, reflections, and interpolations by Las Cases. It details Napoleon's bitter, petty, continuing controversy with the authorities on the island whose task it was to maintain his captivity. But primarily the book is Napoleon's own apologia, the justification for his policies and his career, directed to his own French people, to the allies, and to the tribunal of history. To Napoleon, the book was his final weapon.*

It is in this work, more than in any other place, that we see the precise terms in which Napoleon considered himself the child, the inheritor, the "purifier" of the Revolution.

"THE FRENCH REVOLUTION was not produced by the jarring interests of two families disputing the possession of the throne; it was a general rising of the mass of the nation against the privileged classes." . . . The principal object of the Revolution was to destroy all privileges; to abolish signorial jurisdictions, justice being an inseparable attribute of sovereign authority; to suppress feudal rights as being a remnant of the old slavery of the people; to subject alike all citizens and all property to the burdens of the state. In short, the Revolution proclaimed equality of rights. A citizen might attain any public employment, according to his talent and the chances of fortune. The kingdom was composed of provinces which had been united to the Crown at various periods: they had no natural limits, and were differently divided, unequal in extent and in population. They possessed many laws of their own, civil as well as criminal: they were more or less privileged, and very unequally taxed, both with respect to the amount and the nature of the contributions, which rendered it necessary to detach them from each other by lines of custom-houses. France was not a state, but a combination of several states, connected together without amalgamation. The whole had been determined by chance and by the events of past ages. The Revolution, guided by the principle of equality, both with respect to the citizens and the different portions of the territory, destroyed all these small nations: there was no longer a Brittany, a Normandy, a Burgundy, a Champagne, a Provence, or a Lorraine; but the whole formed a France. A division of homogeneous territory, prescribed by local circumstances, confounded the limits of all the provinces. They possessed the same judicial and administrative organization, the same civil and criminal laws, and the same system of taxation. The dreams of the upright men of all ages were realized. The opposition which the Court, the Clergy, and the Nobility, raised against the Revolution and the war with foreign powers, produced the law of emigration and the sequestration of emigrant property, which subsequently it was found necessary to sell, in order to provide for the charges of the war. A great portion of the French nobility enrolled themselevs under the banner of the princes of the Bourbon family, and formed an army which marched in conjunction with the Austrian, Prussian, and English forces. Gentlemen who had been brought up in the enjoyment of competency served as private soldiers; numbers were cut off by fatigue and the sword; others perished of want in foreign countries; and the wars of La Vendée and of the Chouans, and the revolutionary tribunals, swept away thousands. Three-fourths of the French nobility were thus destroyed; and all posts, civil, judicial, or military, were filled by citizens who had risen from the common mass of the people. The change produced in persons and property by the events of the Revolution, was not less remarkable than that which was effected by the principles of the Revolution. A new church was created; the dioceses of Vienne, Narbonne, Féjus, Sisteron, Rheims, &c., were superseded by sixty new dioceses, the boundaries of which were circumscribed, in Concordat,[5] by new Bulls applicable to the present state of the French territory. The suppression of religious orders, the sale of convents and of all ecclesiastical property, were sanctioned, and the clergy were pensioned by the State. Everything that was the

[5] The agreement (1801) between Napoleon and Pope Pius VII that restored Catholicism to France, though largely on Napoleon's terms.—Ed.

result of the events which had occurred since the time of Clovis, ceased to exist. All these changes were so advantageous to the people that they were effected with the utmost facility, and, in 1800, there no longer remained any recollection of the old privileges and sovereigns of the provinces, the old parliaments and bailiwicks, or the old dioceses; and to trace back the origin of all that existed, it was sufficient to refer to the new law by which it had been established. One-half of the land had changed its proprietors; the peasantry and the citizens were enriched. The advancement of agriculture and manufactures exceeded the most sanguine hopes. France presented the imposing spectacle of upwards of thirty millions of inhabitants, circumscribed within their natural limits, and composing only a single class of citizens, governed by one law, one rule, and one order. All these changes were conformable with the welfare and rights of the nation, and with the justice and intelligence of the age.

The five members of the Directory were divided. Enemies to the Republic crept into the councils; and thus men, hostile to the rights of the people, became connected with the government. This state of things kept the country in a ferment; and the great interests which the French people had acquired by the Revolution were incessantly compromised. One unanimous voice, issuing from the plains of France and from her cities and her camps, demanded the preservation of all the principles of the Republic, or the establishment of an hereditary system of government, which would place the principles and interests of the Revolution beyond the reach of factions and the influence of foreigners. By the constitution of the year VIII the First Consul of the Republic became Consul for ten years, and the nation afterwards prolonged his magistracy for life: the people subsequently raised him to the throne, which it rendered hereditary in his family. The principles of the sovereignty of the people, of liberty and equality, of the destruction of the feudal system, of the irrevocability of the sale of national domains, and the freedom of religious worship, were now established. The government of France, under the fourth dynasty, was founded on the same principles as the Republic. It was a moderate and constitutional monarchy. There was as much difference between the government of France under the fourth dynasty and the third, as between the latter and the Republic. The fourth dynasty succeeded the Republic, or, more properly speaking, it was merely a modification of it.

No Prince ever ascended a throne with rights more legitimate than those of Napoleon. The crown was not presented to him by a few Bishops and Nobles; but he was raised to the Imperial throne by the unanimous consent of the citizens, three times solemnly confirmed.[6] Pope Pius VII, the head of the Catholic religion, the religion of the majority of the French

[6] A reference to the successive plebiscites that Napoleon used to gain approval of his modifications in the government. The last sanctioned his assumption of the imperial title.—ED.

people, crossed the Alps to anoint the Emperor with his own hands, in the presence of the Bishops of France, the Cardinals of the Romish Church, and the Deputies from all the districts of the Empire.[7] The sovereigns of Europe eagerly acknowledged Napoleon: all beheld with pleasure the modification of the Republic, which placed France on a footing of harmony with the rest of Europe, and which at once confirmed the constitution and the happiness of that great nation. Ambassadors from Austria, Russia, Prussia, Spain, Portugal, Turkey, and America, in fine, from all the powers of Europe, came to congratulate the Emperor. England alone sent no ambassador: she had violated the treaty of Amiens, and had consequently again declared war against France. . . .

The English declaration of war (1803) precipitated the imperial phase of Napoleon's career, during which, in victory after victory, he defeated the great powers of Europe. He hoped to complete his plans for Europe and for himself in the attack upon Russia. Here he reflects upon those plans and upon the Russian war.

. . . "That war should have been the most popular of any in modern times. It was a war of good sense and true interests; a war for the repose and security of all; it was purely pacific and preservative; entirely European and continental. Its success would have established a balance of power and would have introduced new combinations, by which the dangers of the present time would have been succeeded by future tranquillity. In this case, ambition had no share in my views. In raising Poland,[8] which was the key-stone of the whole arch, I would have permitted a King of Prussia, an Archduke of Austria, or any other to occupy the throne. I had no wish to obtain any new acquisition; and I reserved for myself only the glory of doing good, and the blessings of posterity. Yet this undertaking failed, and proved my ruin, though I never acted more disinterestedly, and never better merited success. As if popular opinion had been seized with contagion, in a moment, a general outcry, a general sentiment, arose against me. I was proclaimed the destroyer of kings—I, who had created them! I was denounced as the subverter of the rights of nations—I, who was about to risk all to secure them! And people and kings, those irreconcileable enemies, leagued together and conspired against me! All the acts of my past life were now forgotten. I said, truly, that popular favour

[7] Though the pope was present, Napoleon placed the crown on his own head, as depicted in the famous painting of the occasion by the court painter Jacques-Louis David.—ED.

[8] His creation of an independent Poland was an indignity Russia would not endure. It was over this matter that the Russian campaign actually began.—ED.

would return to me with victory; but victory escaped me, and I was ruined. . . ."

The ruin brought upon him by the Russian war was purely fortuitous, claims Napoleon, and in no way can obscure his true accomplishments.

"I closed the gulf of anarchy and cleared the chaos. I purified the Revolution, dignified Nations and established Kings. I excited every kind of emulation, rewarded every kind of merit, and extended the limits of glory! This is at least something! And on what point can I be assailed on which an historian could not defend me? Can it be for my intentions? But even here I can find absolution. Can it be for my despotism? It may be demonstrated that the Dictatorship was absolutely necessary. Will it be said that I restrained liberty? It can be proved that licentiousness, anarchy, and the greatest irregularities, still haunted the threshold of freedom. Shall I be accused of having been too fond of war? It can be shown that I always received the first attack. Will it be said that I aimed at universal monarchy? It can be proved that this was merely the result of fortuitous circumstances, and that our enemies themselves led me step by step to this determination. Lastly, shall I be blamed for my ambition? This passion I must doubtless be allowed to have possessed, and that in no small degree; but at the same time, my ambition was of the highest and noblest kind that ever, perhaps, existed—that of establishing and of consecrating the empire of reason, and the full exercise and complete enjoyment of all the human faculties! And here the historian will probably feel compelled to regret that such ambition should not have been fulfilled and gratified!" Then after a few moments of silent reflection: "This," said the Emperor, "is my whole history in a few words."

On Politics, Literature, and National Character

MADAME DE STAËL

There were many who, like one hostile critic, regarded Napoleon simply as "the Corsican ogre." But there were other, more thoughtful critics who, though they condemned Napoleon, tried to understand why they did so. One of these was Anne-Louise-Germaine, Madame de Staël (1766–1817). She was the daughter of the Swiss banker Jacques Necker, who, as Minister of Finance to Louis XVI, had tried without much success—and without much imagination—to rescue France from fiscal chaos on the eve of the Revolution. Madame de Staël had grown up in the highest circles of the French aristocracy and the court, marrying the Swedish ambassador to France, Eric Magnus de Staël-Holstein, in 1786. She lived through the Revolution and knew most of its leading figures, as she did Napoleon and the men of the counterrevolution.

But Madame de Staël was more than simply a fashionable aristocrat. She was one of the last great luminaries of the Age of Enlightenment and one of the most important European writers of her time. She was also one of Napoleon's most perceptive and persistent critics. Though Madame de Staël was a passionate champion of liberty and an outspoken French patriot, she was no friend of the Revolution. But then, she observed, neither was Napoleon! He was, in her view, nothing less than its most sinister subverter. Napoleon tried first to moderate her views, then to persuade her of his good intentions, but he failed altogether to understand the basis of her hostility. Finally, he sent her into exile, and from Switzerland, Germany, Russia, and England she continued to observe and to write about the unfolding of the events she had foreseen. We turn now to Madame de Staël, On Politics, Literature, and National Character, *and her account of the rise and fall of Napoleon, so different in every way from his own.*

THE DIRECTORY was not inclined to peace, not because it wished to extend French rule beyond the Rhine and the Alps but because it believed war useful for the propagation of the republican system. Its plan was to surround France with a belt of republics. . . .

General Bonaparte was certainly less serious and less sincere than the

Directory in the love of republican ideas, but he was much more shrewd in estimating a situation. He sensed that peace would become popular in France because passions were subsiding and people were weary of sacrifices; so he signed the Treaty of Campo Formio with Austria.

General Bonaparte distinguished himself as much by his character and mind as by his victories, and the imagination of the French was beginning to attach itself to him strongly. A tone of moderation and nobility prevailed in his style, which contrasted with the revolutionary gruffness of the civil leaders of France. The warrior spoke like a magistrate, while the magistrates expressed themselves with martial violence. . . .

It was with this feeling, at least, that I saw him for the first time in Paris. I could find no words of reply when he came to me to tell me that he had sought my father at Coppet and that he regretted having passed through Switzerland without having seen him. But when I was somewhat recovered from the confusion of admiration, a very strong sense of fear followed. Bonaparte at that time had no power; he was even believed to be somewhat threatened by the jealous suspicions of the Directory. So the fear he inspired was caused only by the extraordinary effect of his person upon nearly all who approached him. I had seen men worthy of respect, and I had seen fierce men: there was nothing in the impression Bonaparte produced upon me that recalled either the former or the latter. I very quickly saw, in the various occasions I had to meet him during his stay in Paris, that his character could not be defined by the words we ordinarily use; he was neither good, nor fierce, nor gentle, nor cruel, like others we know. Such a being, having no equals, could neither feel nor arouse any sympathy: he was more than a human being or less than one. His appearance, his mind, and his speech were foreign in nature—an added advantage for subjugating the French.

Far from being reassured by seeing Bonaparte more often, I was made increasingly apprehensive. I had a vague feeling that no emotions of the heart could influence him. He considers a human being a fact or a thing, not a fellow man. He does not hate nor does he love. For him, there is nothing but himself; all others are ciphers.

Every time I heard him speak I was struck by his superiority: yet it had no resemblance to that of men educated and cultivated by study or by social intercourse, such as may be found in England or France. But his speech showed a feeling for the situation, like the hunter's for his prey. . . .

General Bonaparte, at this same time, the end of 1797, sounded public opinion regarding the Directors; he realized that they were not liked but that republican sentiment made it as yet impossible for a general to take the place of civilian officials. The Directory proposed to him the assault upon England. He went to examine the coasts, and, quickly seeing that this expedition was senseless, returned resolved to attempt the conquest of Egypt.

Bonaparte has always sought to seize the imagination of men and, in this respect, he knows well how one must govern when one is not born to the throne. An invasion of Africa, the war carried to an almost fabulous country like Egypt, must make an impression upon every mind. . . .

But in his climb to power, Napoleon depended not only upon his growing military reputation.

The most potent magic that Bonaparte used to establish his power was the terror the mere name of Jacobinism inspired, though anyone capable of reflection knew perfectly well that this scourge could not reappear in France. People readily pretend to fear defeated parties in order to justify harsh measures. Everyone who wants to promote the establishment of despotism forcefully reminds us of the terrible crimes of demagogy. It is a very simply technique. So Bonaparte paralyzed every form of resistance to his will by the words: *Do you want me to hand you over to the Jacobins?* And France bowed down before him, no man bold enough to reply to him: *We shall be able to fight the Jacobins and you.* In short, even then he was not liked, only preferred. He almost always presented himself in competition with another cause for alarm, in order to make his power acceptable as a lesser evil. . . .

We cannot watch too attentively for the first symptoms of tyranny; when it has grown to a certain point, there is no more time to stop it. One man sweeps along the will of many individuals of whom the majority, taken separately, wish to be free but who nevertheless surrender because people fear each other and do not dare to speak their thoughts freely. . . .

General Bonaparte decreed a constitution in which there were no safeguards. Besides, he took great care to leave in existence the laws announced during the Revolution, in order to select from this detestable arsenal the weapon that suited him. The special commissions, deportations, exiles, the bondage of the press—these steps unfortunately taken in the name of liberty—were very useful to tyranny. To adopt them, he sometimes advanced reasons of state, sometimes the need of the times, sometimes the acts of his opponents, sometimes the need to maintain tranquillity. Such is the artillery of phrases that supports absolute power, for "emergencies" never end, and the more one seeks to repress by illegal measures the more one creates disaffected people who justify new injustices. The establishment of the rule of law is always put off till tomorrow. This is a vicious circle from which one cannot break out, for the public spirit that is awaited in order to permit liberty can come only from liberty itself. . . .

It was particularly advantageous to Bonaparte's power that he had to manage only a mass. All individual existence was annihilated by ten years of disorder, and nothing sways people like military success; it takes great power of reason to combat this tendency instead of profiting from it. No one in France could consider his position secure. Men of all classes, ruined or enriched, banished or rewarded, found themselves one by one equally, so to speak, in the hands of power. Bonaparte, who always moved between two opposed interests, took very good care not to put an end to these anxieties by fixed laws that might let everyone know his rights. To one man he returned his property, while another he stripped of his forever. The First Consul reserved to himself the power of determining, under any pretext, the fate of everything and everyone.

Those Frenchmen who sought to resist the ever-increasing power of the First Consul had to invoke liberty to struggle against him successfully. But at this word the aristocrats and the enemies of the Revolution cried "Jacobinism," thus supporting the tyranny for which they later sought to blame their adversaries. . . .

I sensed more quickly than others—and I pride myself on it—Bonaparte's tyrannical character and intentions. The true friends of liberty are in this respect guided by an instinct that does not deceive them. But my position, at the outset of the Consulate, was made more painful by the fact that respectable society in France thought it saw in Bonaparte the man who had saved them from anarchy or Jacobinism. They therefore vigorously condemned the spirit of opposition I displayed toward him. . . .

Madame de Staël's opposition led to her exile. But even in exile she continued to comment upon Napoleon and upon the rise and finally the decline of his military and political fortunes. In 1813, following the Russian disaster, the allies invaded France, heading for Paris.

From the moment the Allies passed the Rhine and entered France it seemed to me that the prayers of the friends of France must undergo a complete change. I was then in London, and one of the English Cabinet Ministers asked me what I wished for. I ventured to reply that my desire was to see Bonaparte victorious and slain. The English had enough greatness of soul to make it unnecessary for me to conceal this French sentiment from them. Yet I was to learn, in the midst of the transports of joy with which the city of the conquerors reverberated, that Paris was in the power of the Allies. At that moment I felt there was no longer a France: I believed Burke's prediction realized and that where France had existed we should see only an abyss. The Emperor Alexander, the Allies, and the constitutional principles adopted through the wisdom of Louis XVIII banished this gloomy presentiment.

There was, nevertheless, something of grandeur in Napoleon's farewell to his troops and to their eagles, so long victorious. His last campaign had been long and skillful: in short, the fatal magic that bound France's military glory to him was not yet destroyed. Thus the conference at Paris must be blamed for having made his return possible. . . .

Many people like to argue that Bonaparte would still be emperor if he had not attempted the expeditions against Spain or Russia. This opinion pleases the supporters of despotism, who insist that so fine a government could not be overthrown by the very nature of things but only by an accident. I have already said, what observation of France will confirm, that Bonaparte needed war to establish and maintain absolute power. A great nation would not have supported the dull and degrading burden of despotism if military glory had not ceaselessly moved or exalted the public spirit. . . .

I shall never forget the moment when I learned, from one of my friends the morning of March 6, 1815, that Bonaparte had landed on the French coast. I had the misfortune to foresee at once the consequences of that event—as they have since taken place—and I thought the earth was about to open under me. I said, "There will be no liberty if Bonaparte wins and no national independence if he loses." Events, it seems to me, have borne out this sad prediction only too well. . . .

. . . Enlightened men could see in Bonaparte nothing but a despot, but by a rather fatal conjunction of circumstances this despot was presented to the nation as the defender of its rights. All the benefits achieved by the Revolution, which France will never willingly give up, were threatened by the endless rashness of the party that wants to repeat the conquest of Frenchmen, as if they were still Gauls. And that part of the nation that most feared the return of the Old Regime thought they saw in Bonaparte a way to save themselves from it. The most fatal association that could overwhelm the friends of liberty was that a despot should join their ranks—should, so to speak, place himself at their head—and that the enemies of every liberal idea should have a pretext for confusing popular violence with the evils of despotism and thus make tyranny appear to be the result of liberty itself. . . . If it was criminal to recall Bonaparte, it was silly to try to disguise such a man as a constitutional monarch. . . .

Whether Napoleon lives or perishes, whether or not he reappears on the continent of Europe, only one reason moves me to speak of him: the ardent wish that the friends of liberty in France completely separate their cause from his and beware of confusing the principles of the Revolution with those of the Imperial *régime*. I believe I have shown that there is no counter-revolution so fatal to liberty as the one he made.

A Modern Napoleon

GEORGES LEFEBVRE

Napoleon has been the most enduringly fascinating figure in modern history, the subject of literally thousands of books—more than 200,000 by some estimates. Recent opinion has tended to divide along precisely the lines that appeared in Napoleon's own time—as suggested in the first two selections of this chapter—either "for" or "against" him, to borrow from the title of a famous book on the Napoleonic tradition.[9] *The following selection is from* Napoleon, From 18 Brumaire to Tilsit 1799–1807, *by the distinguished French historian Georges Lefebvre, considered by many competent critics to have been the best modern scholar of the Napoleonic age. But Lefebvre was also a great authority on the French Revolution, and so we turn to him for his view on the relationship of Napoleon to the Revolution and his answer to the question of whether Napoleon was its child or its betrayer. It is the opinion of Lefebvre that the Revolution had betrayed itself long before Napoleon became its conscious heir; that only in the most elementary sense of its giving him the opportunity to rise to power could Napoleon be considered its offspring; that—as Madame de Staël argued—Napoleon was always the same, from the beginning to the end of his career, an autocrat; and that he did not purify the Revolution but rather manipulated it.*

THAT THE FRENCH Revolution turned to dictatorship was no accident; it was driven there by inner necessity, and not for the first time either. Nor was it an accident that the Revolution led to the dictatorship of a general. But it so happened that this general was Napoleon Bonaparte, a man whose temperament, even more than his genius, was unable to adapt to peace and moderation. Thus it was an unforeseeable contingency which tilted the scale in favour of "la guerre éternelle."

For a long time the republicans had wanted to strengthen the central authority. One need only look at the constitutions they gave to the vassal states: in Holland, the members of the Directory controlled the treasury; in Switzerland, they appointed government officials; in Rome, they appointed judges as well. In the Helvetic and Roman Republics every department already possessed a "prefect." All this is not to mention the

[9] Pieter Geyl, *Napoleon, For and Against*, Olive Renier, trans. (New Haven: Yale University Press, 1949).

Cisalpine Republic, which was Bonaparte's personal fief. . . . The coup d'état of 18 Fructidor had provided the occasion sought by Sieyès, Talleyrand, and Bonaparte, but they let the opportunity slip. In Year VII, however, they hoped to bring about a new one. Without realizing it, the republicans were giving way to a tendency which, ever since the start of the civil and foreign wars, was pushing the Revolution in the direction of a permanent and all-powerful executive, that is to say toward dictatorship. It was this social revolution that drove the dispossessed nobility far beyond insurrection. Subsidized by enemy gold, it exploited the wartime hardships—that inexhaustible source of discontent —and particularly the monetary and economic crisis, thereby intending to turn the people against the government. The French did not want a return to the Old Regime, but they suffered and they held their leaders responsible for it. At every election the counter-revolution hoped to regain power. It was awareness of this danger that led the Mountain [10] in 1793 to declare the Convention in permanent session until the peace. The Thermidorians had intended to restore elective government, but they immediately returned to Jacobin expediency by passing the Decree of the Two-Thirds. Next, the Directory, overwhelmed by the elections of 1797, re-established the dictatorship on 18 Fructidor. Yet as long as the Constitution of Year III continued to exist, this dictatorship, put to the test each year, required a host of violent measures and could never be brought into working order. So it was still necessary to revive the principle of 1793 and invest it with permanence until such time as peace, settled once and for all, would persuade the counter-revolution to accept the new order. It was in this respect that Napoleon's dictatorship became so much a part of the history of the French Revolution. No matter what he may have said or done, neither he nor his enemies were ever able to break this bond, and this was a fact which the European aristocracy understood perfectly well.

In 1799, as in 1793, the Jacobins wished to establish a democratic dictatorship by relying on the Sans-culottes[11] to push it through the councils. Taking advantage of the crisis preceding the victory at Zurich, they succeeded in forcing the passage of several revolutionary measures: a compulsory loan, the abolition of exemptions from military service, the law of hostages, a repeal of assignments on public revenues which had been granted to bankers and government contractors, withholdings on the rente and on salaries, and finally, requisitions. These measures constituted a direct attack on bourgeois interests and brought that class to action. Thus it was symbolic that assignments on public revenues were restored the very night of 19 Brumaire. The Idéologues who gathered around Madame de Condorcet at Auteuil or in the salon of Madame de

[10] The popular name given to the radical faction in the Convention.—ED.

[11] Another popular name for the urban proletariat, especially of Paris, who tended to support Jacobin radicalism.—ED.

Staël wanted neither a democratic dictatorship nor even a democracy. . . . Madame de Staël expressed their desire: to devise a representative system of government which would assure power to the moneyed and talented "notables." Sieyès, who had become a Director, took his inspiration from the Decree of the Two-Thirds. Together with his friends he wanted to select the membership of the newly constituted bodies which would then expand themselves by co-optation, leaving to the nation only the role of electing candidates. Furthermore, those already in office saw in this plan the chance to keep themselves in power.

The people having been eliminated as an obstacle to the dictatorship of the bourgeoisie, only the army remained. The Directory had already sought its help on 18 Fructidor, Year V, and had managed to keep the upper hand, despite serious incursions. Now, however, the situation was very different in that steadfast republicans, not royalists, were to be driven out. Only a popular general could have carried it through, and Bonaparte's sudden return destined that it should be he. The will of the nation which was invoked to justify 18 Brumaire played no part in the event. The nation rejoiced at the news that Bonaparte was in France because it recognized an able general; but the Republic had conquered without him, and Masséna's victory [12] had bolstered the reputation of the Directory. Consequently, the responsibility for 18 Brumaire lies on that segment of the republican bourgeoisie called the Brumairians, whose leading light was Sieyès. They had no intention of giving in to Bonaparte, and they chose him only as an instrument of their policy. That they propelled him to power without imposing any conditions, without even first delimiting the fundamental character of the new regime, betrays their incredible mediocrity. Bonaparte did not repudiate the notables, for he too was not a democrat, and their collaboration alone enabled him to rule. But on the evening of 19 Brumaire, after they had hurriedly slapped together the structure of the Provisional Consulate, they should not have harboured any more illusions. The army had followed Bonaparte, and him alone. He was complete master. Regardless of what he and his apologists may have said, his rule was from its origins an absolute military dictatorship. It was Bonaparte alone who would decide the questions on which the fate of France and Europe hinged.

What sort of a man was he? His personality evolved in so singular a manner that it defies portrayal. He appeared first as a studious officer full of dreams, garrisoned at Valence and Auxonne. As a youthful general, on the eve of the battle of Castiglione, he could still hold a council of war. But in the final years as Emperor, he was stupefied with his own omnipotence and was infatuated with his own omniscience. And yet distinctive traits appear throughout his entire career: power could do no more than accentuate some and attenuate others.

Short-legged and small in stature, muscular, ruddy, and still gaunt at

[12] At Zurich over the Russians.—Ed.

the age of thirty, he was physically hardy and fit. His sensitivity and steadiness were admirable, his reflexes quick as lightning, and his capacity for work unlimited. He could fall asleep at will. But we also find the reverse: cold humid weather brought on oppression, coughing spells, dysuria; when crossed he unleashed frightful outbursts of temper; overexertion, despite prolonged hot baths, despite extreme sobriety, despite the moderate yet constant use of coffee and tobacco, occasionally produced brief collapses, even tears. His mind was one of the most perfect that has ever been: his unflagging attention tirelessly swept in facts and ideas which his memory registered and classified; his imagination played with them freely, and being in a permanent state of concealed tension, it never wearied of inventing political and strategic motifs which manifested themselves in unexpected flashes of intuition like those experienced by poets and mathematicians. This would happen especially at night during a sudden awakening, and he himself referred to it as "the moral spark" and "the after midnight presence of the spirit." This spiritual fervour shone through his glittering eyes and illuminated the face, still "sulphuric" at his rise, of the "sleek-haired Corsican." This is what made him unsociable, and not, as Hippolyte Taine would have us think, some kind of brutality, the consequence of a slightly tarnished *condottiere* being let loose upon the world in all his savagery. He rendered a fair account of himself when he said, "I consider myself a good man at heart," and indeed he showed generosity, and even kindness to those who were close to him. But between ordinary mortals, who hurried through their tasks in order to abandon themselves to leisure or diversion, and Napoleon Bonaparte, who was the soul of effort and concentration, there could exist no common ground nor true community. Ambition—that irresistible impulse to act and to dominate—sprang from his physical and mental state of being. . . .

Ever since his military school days at Brienne, when he was still a poor and taunted foreigner, timid yet bursting with passion, Napoleon drew strength from pride in himself and contempt for others. Destined to become an officer, his instinct to command without having to discuss could not have been better served. Although he might on occasion have sought information or opinion, he alone was master and judge. Bonaparte's natural propensity for dictatorship suited the normal practice of his profession. In Italy and in Egypt he introduced dictatorship into the government. In France he wanted to put himself forward as a civilian, but the military stamp was indelibly there. He consulted often, but he could never tolerate free opposition. More precisely, when faced with a group of men accustomed to discussion, he would lose his composure. This explains his intense hatred of the Idéologues. The confused and undisciplined, yet formidable masses inspired in him as much fear as contempt. Regardless of costumes and titles, Bonaparte took power as a general, and as such he exercised it. . . .

. . . Having entered into a life of action, he still remained a thinker. This warrior was never happier than in the silence of his own study, surrounded by papers and documents. In time he became more practical, and he would boast that he had repudiated "ideology." Nevertheless, he was still a typical man of the eighteenth century, a rationalist, a philosophe. Far from relying on intuition, he placed his trust in reason, in knowledge, and in methodical effort. . . .

He seemed to be dedicated to a policy of realism in every way, and he was, in fact, a realist in execution down to the slightest detail. . . . And yet he was a realist in execution only. There lived in him an alter-ego which contained certain features of the hero. It seems to have been born during his days at the military academy out of a need to dominate a world in which he felt himself despised. Above all he longed to equal the semi-legendary heroes of Plutarch and Corneille. His greatest ambition was glory. "I live only for posterity," he exclaimed, "death is nothing, but to live defeated and without glory is to die every day." His eyes were fixed on the world's great leaders: Alexander, who conquered the East and dreamed of conquering the world; Caesar, Augustus, Charlemagne—the creators and the restorer of the Roman Empire whose very names were synonymous with the idea of a universal civilization. From these he did not deduce a precise formulation to be used as a rule, a measure, or a condition of political conduct. They were for him examples, which stimulated his imagination and lent an unutterable charm to action. . . . That is why it is idle to seek for limits to Napoleon's policy, or for a final goal at which he would have stopped: there simply was none. . . .

That a mind so capable of grasping reality in certain respects should escape it in others . . . can only be due to Napoleon's origins as much as to his nature. When he first came to France, he considered himself a foreigner. Until the time when he was expelled from Corsica by his compatriots in 1791, his attitude had been one of hostility to the French people. Assuredly he became sufficiently imbued with their culture and spirit to adopt their nationality; otherwise he could never have become their leader. But he lacked the time to identify himself with the French nation and to adopt its national tradition to the point where he would consider its interests as a limitation upon his own actions. Something of the uprooted person remained in him; something of the *déclassé* as well. He was neither entirely a gentleman nor entirely common. He served both the king and the Revolution without attaching himself to either. This was one of the reasons for his success, since he could so easily place himself above parties and announce himself as the restorer of national unity. Yet neither in the Old Regime nor in the new did he find principles which might have served as a norm or a limit. . . .

What about moral limits? In spiritual life he had nothing in common with other men. Even though he knew their passions well and deftly turned them to his own ends, he cared only for those that would reduce men to dependence. He belittled every feeling that elevated men to acts of sacrifice—religious faith, patriotism, love of freedom—because he saw in them obstacles to his own schemes. Not that he was impervious to these sentiments, at least not in his youth, for they readily led to heroic deeds; but fate led him in a different direction and walled him up within himself. In the splendid and terrible isolation of the will to power, measure carries no meaning.

Suggestions for Further Reading

NAPOLEON IS LINKED inescapably with both the French Revolution that created him and with the nineteenth-century age of revolution that he created. Thus, the first category of books to be recommended for Napoleon and his age are those which treat this large topic. The best general work is probably Erich J. Hobsbawm, *The Age of Revolution: Europe 1789–1848* (Cleveland: World, 1962); it is a book of ideas rather than a factual survey, and the author is interested in the continuing social and cultural trends of the revolutionary age, in which he includes the topic of England and its industrial revolution. Of the same sort is Norman Hampson, *The First European Revolution, 1776–1850* (New York: Harcourt, Brace and World, 1969), a brief, attractive survey and analysis which plays down the role of Napoleon in favor of the continuity of the idea of revolution. George Rudé, *Revolutionary Europe, 1783–1815* (New York: Harper & Row, 1966), is a good summary, while somewhat more comprehensive is Franklin L. Ford, *Europe, 1780–1830* (London: Longman, 1970); both are excellent, straightforward accounts.

The outstanding modern work on the French Revolution itself is Georges Lefebvre, *The French Revolution*, 2 vols., Vol. 1, tr. Elizabeth M. Evanson (New York: Columbia University Press, 1962), Vol. 2, tr. John Hall Stewart and James Friguglietti (New York: Columbia University Press, 1964), along with Lefebvre's brilliant analytical work, *The Coming of the French Revolution, 1789*, tr. R. R. Palmer (Princeton, N.J.: Princeton University Press, 1947). R. R. Palmer, *The World of the French Revolution* (New York: Harper & Row, 1969), is a highly interpretive, brief, readable, analytical survey, while M. J. Sydenham, *The French Revolution* (New

York: Putnam, 1965), is a brief, largely political history. Alfred Cobban, *The Social Interpretation of the French Revolution* (Cambridge, England: Cambridge University Press, 1964), is a major critical work, revising much of the sociological theorizing about classes that had marked a generation of revolutionary studies. Cobban argues that the land-owning class eventually triumphed in revolutionary France and that in the course of the French Revolution the shift from title to property as the basis for social status was finally made. Norman Hampson, *A Social History of the French Revolution* (Toronto: Toronto University Press, 1963), is a briefer and more balanced treatment of the same themes.

Georges Lefebvre is the most important authority on Napoleon, as he is on the Revolution. See his *Napoleon*, 2 vols., Vol. 1 *Napoleon from 18 Brumaire to Tilsit, 1799–1807*, tr. H. F. Stockhold, Vol. 2 *Napoleon from Tilsit to Waterloo, 1807–1815*, tr. J. E. Anderson (New York: Columbia University Press, 1969) (the first volume is excerpted in this chapter). J. C. Herold, *The Age of Napoleon* (New York: Harper & Row, 1963), is not only a lush and beautiful book but an interpretive study; Herold is not an admirer of Napoleon and considers him at the best an ungrateful child of the Revolution. On the other hand, Robert B. Holtman, *The Napoleonic Revolution* (Philadelphia: Lippincott, 1967), sees Napoleon as a dramatic and important innovator in a score of fields, thus preserving the best gains of the Revolution. Felix M. Markham, *Napoleon and the Awakening of Europe*, "Teach Yourself History Library" (New York: Macmillan, 1954), and his *Napoleon I, Emperor of the French* (New York: New American Library, 1964) are good short biographies. Several special studies are also recommended. For military history see the good, comprehensive, straightforward account in David G. Chandler, *The Campaigns of Napoleon* (New York: Macmillan, 1966), and the detailed study by Christopher L. Hibbert, *Waterloo: Napoleon's Last Campaign* (New York: New American Library, 1967). A related work is the dramatic and exciting Edith Saunders, *The Hundred Days* (New York: Norton, 1964). Two books by R. F. Delderfield deal with the last years of Napoleon's military career, *The Retreat from Moscow* (New York: Atheneum, 1967) and *Imperial Sunset: The Fall of Napoleon, 1813–14* (Philadelphia: Chilton, 1968). An extremely interesting work on a subtopic of Napoleon is J. Christopher Herold, *Bonaparte in Egypt* (New York: Harper & Row, 1962). Pieter Geyl, *Napoleon, For and Against*, tr. Olive Renier, New Haven, Conn.: Yale University Press, 1949), is a famous book of Napoleonic historiography. Finally, highly recommended is the luminous biography by J. Christopher Herold, *Mistress to an Age: A Life of Madame de Staël* (Indianapolis: Bobbs-Merrill, 1958).

The Granger Collection

Charles Darwin and the Evolutionary Revolution

1809	born
1831–1836	the voyage of the *Beagle*
1859	published *The Origin of Species*
1871	published *The Descent of Man*
1882	died

Charles Darwin (1809–1882), the man whose name is indelibly associated with the revolutionary theory of biological evolution, was the son of a prosperous Shropshire physician. His grandfather Erasmus Darwin had been not only a physician but an amateur scientist of some note and an early advocate of evolutionary theory. From the beginning, Darwin was destined for the family profession. At sixteen he was enrolled in the great medical school of the University of Edinburgh but was a dismal failure. He hated the work and could not stand the sight of blood. Darwin's father was convinced that it was a matter not of disposition but of indifference. "You care for nothing but shooting, dogs and rat-catching," he said, "and you will be a disgrace to yourself and all your family." [1] There was more than a little truth in his father's angry charge: Darwin's only real enthusiasms were for hunting and natural history.

The decision was made to send him to Christ's College, Cambridge, to prepare for a career in the church. His academic record at Cambridge was only slightly less dismal than it had been at Edinburgh, and he scraped through his degree finally with a bare "pass" in 1831. In the years at Cambridge, however, Darwin continued his passion for natural history and collecting. It was not an unusual interest, for science was much the vogue in the early nineteenth century and tied in with the generally

[1] Quoted in J. W. Burrow, "Makers of Modern Thought: Charles Darwin," *Horizon*, 8, no. 4 (Autumn 1966), 42.

accepted notions of natural theology, that is, the conviction that the phenomena of nature were the specific evidences of God's wonderfully reasonable order of creation. The intellectual world in which Charles Darwin grew up was smug, orderly, and comfortable.

While at Cambridge, Darwin met two great teachers, the biologist John Stevens Henslow and the geologist Adam Sedgwick. Both men took the young naturalist with them on collecting trips, and Henslow, in particular, made him a kind of protégé. He invited Darwin to the famous Friday evening discussions at his home; he gently urged him to take this course or hear that lecture; he recommended books, encouraged his interests, and taught him the value of patient, careful, minute observation. It was Henslow who recommended Darwin for the job that he himself had reluctantly had to turn down, as unpaid naturalist aboard HMS *Beagle,* about to set out in 1831 on a scientific and mapping voyage to the Southern Hemisphere.

Darwin was offered the position, and, barely overcoming the reluctance of his father, he accepted. As a parting gift, Henslow gave him a copy of the recently published first volume of Charles Lyell's *Principles of Geology,* the work that was to revolutionize geology in the same way—and amid the same furor—that Darwin's would revolutionize biology. For Lyell contended, in contradiction to the accepted biblical chronology, that the earth had not been created in a few thousand years by catastrophic change but rather was millions of years old. It is worth noting that Henslow, while he admired Lyell's method, was unalterably opposed to his conclusions, as he would later be to Darwin's. The captain of the *Beagle,* Robert FitzRoy, confided to Darwin that he hoped that his collections and observations would prove, once and for all, the literal truth of God's creation as set forth in the Bible. At this point, Darwin found nothing strange in such a notion. But in the course of the five-year voyage, his work led him not toward that notion but away from it. The voyage of the *Beagle* was the turning point in Darwin's life.

On his return to England, Darwin was elected a Fellow of the Royal Society, worked briefly for the Geographical Society, and came to know Sir Charles Lyell, whose works he had long admired. Then in 1839 he married his cousin Emma Wedgwood and three years later bought "a good, very ugly house with 18 acres" [2] at Down in Kent, where he spent the rest of his life. Amid the "quiet gladness" of his family, in his study and library and at his modest window-ledge laboratory, Darwin worked out the theories that had begun to emerge in the notebooks and jottings he had made during his voyage half-way around the world. In 1856, as he was preparing the abstract for a paper that would present those theories, he received a communication from another scientist, Alfred Russel Wallace, with a sketch of a paper setting out exactly the same views.

[2] Quoted in Walter Karp, *Charles Darwin and the Origin of Species* (New York: Harper & Row, 1968), p. 85.

Despite the fact that Wallace's work was almost entirely theoretical while his own rested upon a mass of detailed scientific observations and data, the modest Darwin was ready to withdraw from the field. But his friend Lyell intervened, brought the two men together, and arranged for their work to appear as a joint paper, "On the Tendency of Species to Form Varieties; and on the Perpetuation of Varieties and Species by Natural Means of Selection." The paper was read before the Linnaean Society in 1858 and published in the journal of the society for the same year. It caused no stir at all.

But this was not the case when, in the following year, Darwin published his *On the Origin of Species by Means of Natural Selection, or the Preservation of Favoured Races in the Struggle for Life*. The book was a sensation: the first printing sold out in a single day. The theory of evolution was at last before the public essentially in its modern form.

To a considerable extent, the theory of evolution was an idea whose time had come. It had been speculated upon since antiquity, and the theory itself, in broad and general terms, had been revived by the freethinkers and rationalists of the late eighteenth century, including Diderot and Buffon in France and Darwin's own grandfather in England. The work of the French zoologist Lamarck, though theoretically faulty, had clearly anticipated Darwin's. Work in parallel fields, such as Lyell's in geology, was available to support a breakthrough in biological theory. Moreover, the rapidly accumulating data of scientific observation—geological stratification, fossils, the enormous variation in plant and animal species—put an increasing strain upon accepted beliefs. Strain reached the breaking point with the publication of *The Origin of Species*.

And yet Darwin was as modest about his contributions as he was about his abilities. At the end of his autobiography (1876) he wrote:

> My success as a man of science, whatever this may have amounted to, has been determined, as far as I can judge, by complex and diversified mental qualities and conditions. Of these the most important have been —the love of science—unbounded patience in long reflecting over my subject—industry in observing and collecting facts—and a fair share of invention as well as of common-sense. With such moderate abilities as I possess, it is truly surprising that thus I should have influenced to a considerable extent the belief of scientific men on some important points.[3]

In one sense, Darwin was correct in this self-effacing assessment. His great contribution was not the originality of the idea of evolution—as he himself readily admitted. Rather, he gave the theory a solid basis in scientific fact and explained how the mechanisms of evolution really worked.

[3] *The Autobiography of Charles Darwin (1809–1882)*, ed. Nora Barlow (New York: Harcourt, Brace, 1958), pp. 144-45.

While Darwin had enthusiastic supporters, such as the great zoologist T. H. Huxley, the botanist Sir Joseph Hooker, and, of course, Sir Charles Lyell, he had equally zealous opponents. These included both his adored teachers Henslow and Sedgwick and a number of other important scientists, led by Sir Richard Owen, the brilliant and unscrupulous curator of paleontology for the British Museum. His enemies, of course, also included a significant number of important members of the clergy and lay advocates of outraged biblical literalism. But whether scientists or clergy, the bitterness of these opponents—often approaching fanaticism—can be largely attributed to two things: Darwin's work had completely upset the whole comfortable system of natural theology and it had made untenable the notion of special creation. It was "the crime" of Darwin to demythologize humans, to set them down like all other beings with "no pedigree or armorial bearings," creatures of nature in nature's order rather than in God's image. (See p. 97.)

The Origin of Species

CHARLES DARWIN

Darwin himself took little part in the controversies that surrounded him. His health was rapidly failing and there was no time to spare from his work. In 1868 his The Variation of Animals and Plants under Domestication *appeared, followed by* The Descent of Man, Selection in Relation to Sex *(1871),* The Expression of the Emotions in Men and Animals *(1872), a host of technical notes and papers, an enormous correspondence, and endless revisions of* The Origin of Species *until his death in 1882.*

Despite the greater notoriety of The Descent of Man*—with all the clamor over humans and apes—his most important book remained* The Origin of Species, *for it contained the basic assertions of his work in their clearest form. He revised the book tirelessly, incorporating changes arising not only from his own further work and reflection but from the criticism of other scientists. The final version of this most prized of his works contains the "Recapitulation and Conclusion" from which the following excerpt is taken.*

I HAVE NOW recapitulated the facts and considerations which have thoroughly convinced me that species have been modified, during a long course of descent. This has been effected chiefly through the natural selection of numerous successive, slight, favourable variations; aided in an important manner by the inherited effects of the use and disuse of parts; and in an unimportant manner, that is in relation to adaptive structures, whether past or present, by the direct action of external conditions, and by variations which seem to us in our ignorance to arise spontaneously. . . .

It can hardly be supposed that a false theory would explain, in so satisfactory a manner as does the theory of natural selection, the several large classes of facts above specified. It has recently been objected that this is an unsafe method of arguing; but it is a method used in judging of the common events of life, and has often been used by the greatest natural philosophers. The undulatory theory of light has thus been arrived at; and the belief in the revolution of the earth on its own axis was until lately supported by hardly any direct evidence. It is no valid objection that science as yet throws no light on the far higher problem of the essence or origin of life. Who can explain what is the essence of attraction of gravity? No one now objects to following out the results consequent on this unknown element of attraction; notwithstanding that Leibnitz formerly accused Newton of introducing "occult qualities and miracles into philosophy."

I see no good reason why the views given in this volume should shock the religious feelings of anyone. It is satisfactory, as showing how transient such impressions are, to remember that the greatest discovery ever made by man, namely the law of the attraction of gravity, was also attacked by Leibnitz, "as subversive of natural, and inferentially of revealed, religion." A celebrated author and divine has written to me that "he has gradually learnt to see that it is just as noble a conception of the Deity to believe that He created a few original forms capable of self-development into other and needful forms, as to believe that He required a fresh act of creation to supply the voids caused by the action of His laws." . . .

Although I am fully convinced of the truth of the views given in this volume under the form of an abstract, I by no means expect to convince experienced naturalists whose minds are stocked with a multitude of facts all viewed, during a long course of years, from a point of view directly opposite to mine. It is so easy to hide our ignorance under such expressions as the "plan of creation," "unity of design," etc., and to think that we give an explanation when we only re-state a fact. Anyone whose disposition leads him to attach more weight to unexplained difficulties than to the explanation of a certain number of facts will certainly reject the theory. A few naturalists, endowed with much flexibility of mind, and who have already begun to doubt the immutability of species, may be influenced by this volume; but I look with confidence to the future,—to young and rising naturalists, who will be able to view both sides of the question with impartiality. Whoever is led to believe that species are mutable will do good service by conscientiously expressing his conviction; for thus only can the load of prejudice by which this subject is overwhelmed be removed. . . . When we no longer look at an organic being as a savage looks at a ship, as something wholly beyond his comprehension; when we regard every production of nature as one which has had a long history; when we contemplate every complex structure and instinct as the summing up of many contrivances, each useful to the possessor, in the same way as any great mechanical invention is the summing up of the labour, the experience, the reason, and even the blunders of numerous workmen; when we thus view each organic being, how far more interesting,—I speak from experience,—does the study of natural history become!

A grand and almost untrodden field of inquiry will be opened, on the causes and laws of variation, on correlation, on the effects of use and disuse, on the direct action of external conditions, and so forth. The study of domestic productions will rise immensely in value. A new variety raised by man will be a more important and interesting subject for study than one more species added to the infinitude of already recorded species. Our classifications will come to be, as far as they can be so made, genealogies; and will then truly give what may be called the plan of creation. The rules for classifying will no doubt become simpler when we have a definite object in view. We possess no pedigrees or armorial bearings; and we have to discover and trace the many diverging lines of descent in our natural genealogies, by characters of any kind which have long been inherited. Rudimentary organs will speak infallibly with respect to the nature of long-lost structures. Species and groups of species which are called aberrant, and which may fancifully be called living fossils, will aid us in forming a picture of the ancient forms of life. Embryology will often reveal to us the structure, in some degree obscured, of the prototypes of each great class.

When we can feel assured that all the individuals of the same species, and all the closely allied species of most genera, have within a not very remote period descended from one parent, and have migrated from some one birth-place; and when we better know the many means of migration, then, by the light which geology now throws, and will continue to throw, on former changes of climate and of the level of the land, we shall surely be enabled to trace in an admirable manner the former migrations of the inhabitants of the whole world. Even at present, by comparing the differences between the inhabitants of the sea on the opposite sides of a continent, and the nature of the various inhabitants on that continent in relation to their apparent means of immigration, some light can be thrown on ancient geography.

The noble science of Geology loses glory from the extreme imperfection of the record. The crust of the earth with its embedded remains must not be looked at as a well-filled museum, but as a poor collection made at hazard and at rare intervals. The accumulation of each great fossiliferous formation will be recognised as having depended on an unusual concurrence of favourable circumstances, and the blank intervals between the successive stages as having been of vast duration. But we shall be able to gauge with some security the duration of these intervals by a comparison of the preceding and succeeding organic forms. We must be cautious in attempting to correlate as strictly contemporaneous two formations, which do not include many identical species, by the general succession of the forms of life. As species are produced and exterminated by slowly acting and still existing causes, and not by miraculous acts of creation; and as the most important of all causes of organic change is one which is almost independent of altered and perhaps suddenly altered physical conditions, namely, the mutual relation of organism to organism,—the improvement of one organism entailing the improvement or the extermination of others; it follows that the amount of organic change in the fossils of consecutive formations probably serves as a fair measure of the relative, though not actual lapse of time. A number of species, however, keeping in a body might remain for a long period unchanged, whilst within the same period, several of these species, by migrating into new countries and coming into competition with foreign associates, might become modified; so that we must not overrate the accuracy of organic change as a measure of time. . . .

Authors of the highest eminence seem to be fully satisfied with the view that each species has been independently created. To my mind it accords better with what we know of the laws impressed on matter by the Creator, that the production and extinction of the past and present inhabitants of the world should have been due to secondary causes, like those determining the birth and death of the individual. When I view all beings not as special creations, but as the lineal descendants of some few beings which lived long before the first bed of the Cambrian system was deposited, they seem to me to become ennobled. Judging from the past, we may safely infer that not one living species will transmit its unaltered likeness to a distant futurity. And of the species now living very few will transmit progeny of any kind to a far distant futurity; for the manner in which all organic beings are grouped; shows that the greater number of species in each genus, and all the species in many genera, have left no descendants, but have become utterly extinct. We can so far take a prophetic glance into futurity as to foretell that it will be the common and widely spread species, belonging to the larger and dominant groups within each class, which will ultimately prevail and procreate new and dominant species. As all the living forms of life are the lineal descendants of those which lived long before the Cambrian epoch, we may feel certain that the ordinary succession by generation has never once been broken, and that no cataclysm has desolated the whole world. Hence we may look with some confidence to a secure future of great length. And as natural selection works solely by and for the good of each being, all corporeal and mental endowments will tend to progress towards perfection.

It is interesting to contemplate a tangled bank, clothed with many plants of many kinds, with birds singing on the bushes, with various insects flitting about, and with worms crawling through the damp earth, and to reflect that these elaborately constructed forms, so different from each other, and dependent upon each other in so complex a manner, have all been produced by laws acting around us. These laws, taken in the largest sense, being Growth with Reproduction; Inheritance which is almost implied by reproduction; Variability from the indirect and direct action of the conditions of life, and from use and disuse: a Ratio of Increase so high as to lead to a Struggle for Life, and as a consequence to Natural Selection, entailing Divergence of Character and the Extinction of less-improved forms. Thus, from the war of nature, from famine and death, the most exalted object which we are capable of conceiving, namely, the production of the higher animals, directly follows. There is grandeur in this view of life, with its several powers, having been originally breathed by the Creator into a few forms or into one; and that, whilst this planet has gone cycling on according to the fixed law of gravity, from so simple a beginning endless forms most beautiful and most wonderful have been, and are being evolved.

Darwin and the Beagle

ALAN MOOREHEAD

From the rumination of a sick and weary old man contemplating the meaning of his life's work, we turn now to the engaging picture of the vigorous young Darwin in the midst of his preparation for that work, serving as naturalist aboard the Beagle. *The basis of any account of that epochal voyage is, of course, Darwin's own voluminous notebooks, letters, and records. They have been used by Alan Moorehead for his crackling narrative* Darwin and the Beagle, *from which the following selection is excerpted.*

ONE OF THE fascinating things about Charles Darwin is that he really does seem to have been one of those men whose careers quite unexpectedly and fortuitously are decided for them by a single stroke of fortune. For twenty-two years nothing much happens, no exceptional abilities are revealed; then suddenly a chance is offered, things can go either this way or that, but luck steps in, or rather a chain of lucky events, and away he soars into the blue never to return. It all looks so inevitable, so predestined; yet the fact is that in 1831 no one in England, certainly not Darwin himself, had the slightest inkling of the extraordinary future that lay ahead of him, and it is next to impossible to recognize in the brooding, ailing figure of the later years this blithe young extrovert on the brink of his greatest adventure—the voyage of the *Beagle*.

Events moved so quickly that he could hardly take in what was happening. On 5 September 1831 he was summoned to London to meet Robert FitzRoy, captain of HMS *Beagle*, a ship which the Admiralty was sending off on a long voyage round the world, and the suggestion was that Darwin should be offered the post of naturalist on the voyage. It was an astonishing idea. He was only twenty-three years old, he had never met Captain FitzRoy, and a week ago he had never even heard of the *Beagle*. His youth, his inexperience, even his background, seemed all against him; yet against all these odds he and FitzRoy got on famously and the offer was made.

The *Beagle*, FitzRoy explained, was a small ship, but a good one. He knew her well; he had taken over the command of her previous voyage to South America, and had brought her back to England. Now she was being entirely refitted at Plymouth and she had a splendid crew, many of whom had sailed in her before and had volunteered for this new voyage. They had two missions: first they were to continue the charting of the South American coast, and secondly they were to get a more accurate fixing of longitude by carrying a chain of chronological reckonings round the world. The ship would set off in a matter of weeks; they would be away more than two years, perhaps even three or four, but Darwin would be free to leave the ship and return home whenever he chose to do so. He would have ample opportunities for getting ashore, and in the course of the voyage they would be doing many exciting things, exploring unknown rivers and mountains, calling at coral islands in the tropics and sailing far down towards the frozen south. Oh, it was all wonderful. "There is indeed a tide in the affairs of men," Darwin wrote to his sister Susan, "and I have experienced it." . . .

After frustrating delays, the Beagle *sailed, not "in a matter of weeks" but at the end of December 1831—bound across the Bay of Biscay for the Madeiras and the Atlantic. Darwin was wretchedly seasick until they made a first landfall at the Cape Verde Islands. Things began to improve —though Darwin never became a good sailor—as the ship slanted across the Atlantic to the coast of South America. In the spring of 1832, Darwin experienced, for the first time, the richness and variety of tropical forests (and saw the horrors of slavery). As they coasted south toward the tip of the continent, he not only continued his collecting of living specimens but discovered great prehistoric fossil remains along the escarpment of the desolate Patagonian coast.*

What then had exterminated so many species? "Certainly no fact in the long history of the world is so startling as the wide and repeated extermination of its inhabitants." He ruled out the possibility that changes in climate might have caused this exterminaion, and after considering many theories came to the conclusion that the isthmus of Panama might once have been submerged. He was right. For seventy million years there was no isthmus of Panama, South America was an island, and these great animals evolved in isolation. When the isthmus arose and North America was joined to South America the fate of these curious and largely helpless beasts was sealed.

When Darwin took his specimens back on board the *Beagle* Wickham[4] was disgusted at the "bedevilment" of his clean decks and railed against "the damned stuff." FitzRoy later on recalled "our smiles at the apparent rubbish he frequently brought on board." But to Darwin this was no light matter, and it must have been about this time that he first began to argue with FitzRoy about the authenticity of the story of the Flood. How had such enormous creatures got aboard the Ark? FitzRoy had an answer. Not *all* the animals had managed to get aboard the Ark, he explained; for some divine reason these had been left outside and drowned. But, Darwin protested, *were* they drowned? There was much evidence—the seashells, for example—to prove that the coast here had risen above the sea, and that these animals had roamed across the Pampas in much the same way as the guanacos did at the present time. The land had *not* risen, FitzRoy contended; it was the sea that had risen and the bones of these drowned animals were an additional proof of the Flood.

At this early stage of the voyage Darwin was not prepared to put his arguments too forcibly; he was puzzled, he needed more evidence, more time for thought. He was even willing to be persuaded that these new and disturbing ideas that were stirring in his mind were wrong. Certainly he had no wish to deny the truth of the Bible: "No one can stand in these solitudes [the great forests] unmoved," he had written, "and not feel there is more in man than the mere breath of his body." It was just a matter of interpreting its words in the light of modern science. . . .

After a perilous passage "around the Horn" and a difficult session of mapping and charting, the Beagle *began to beat northward along the coast of Chile, with the majestic Andes in sight.*

. . . By now (the spring of 1833), [Darwin] knows the ropes, the last remnants of his hesitancy and inexperience drop away and he becomes a very useful member of the expedition. The idea of his entering the church grew fainter and fainter, and natural history possessed him entirely. "There is nothing like geology," he wrote to Catherine[5]; "The pleasure of the first day's partridge shooting or the first day's hunting cannot be compared to finding a fine group of fossil bones, which tell their story of former times with almost a living tongue . . . I collect every living creature which I have time to catch and preserve." In his journals which he kept up faithfully day by day one can see his confidence steadily in-

[4] The first mate.—ED.
[5] Another sister of Darwin.—ED.

creasing; his ideas form patterns and speculations begin to harden into theories. . . .

But it is the geology of the mountains that engrosses him, and he makes two discoveries that rivet his attention: at 12,000 feet he comes on a bed of fossil seashells, and then somewhat lower down a small forest of snow-white petrified pine trees with marine rock deposits round them. Now at last the "marvellous story" was beginning to unfold. These trees had once stood on the shores of the Atlantic, now 700 miles away; they had been sunk beneath the sea, then raised 7000 feet. Clearly all this part of the South American peninsula was once submerged beneath the sea, and in quite recent geological times had been elevated again. As the Andes were pushed upwards they became at first a series of wooded islands and then a continuous chain of mountains whose cold climate killed off the vegetation as they rose. This movement had been accompanied by earthquakes and volcanic eruptions which acted like safety valves. . . .

By the time the Beagle *reached the Galapagos Islands, Darwin's convictions were becoming more fixed. The great natural laboratory of these fascinating islands, astride the equator off the western coast of South America, was to provide the clinching certainty for his emerging theories.*

Apart from their practical uses there was nothing much to recommend the Galapagos; they were not lush and beautiful islands like the Tahiti group, they were (and still are) far off the usual maritime routes, circled by capricious currents, and nobody lived in them then except for a handful of political prisoners who had been stranded there by the Ecuador government. The fame of the islands was founded upon one thing; they were infinitely strange, unlike any other islands in the world. No one who went there ever forgot them. For the *Beagle* this was just another port of call in a very long voyage, but for Darwin it was much more than that, for it was here, in the most unexpected way—just as a man might have a sudden inspiration while he is travelling in a car or a train—that he began to form a coherent view of the evolution of life on this planet. To put it into his own words: "Here, both in space and time, we seem to be brought somewhat near to that great fact—that mystery of mysteries—the first appearance of new beings on this earth."

But the *Beagle* could not linger, much as Darwin longed to. "It is the fate of most voyagers, no sooner to discover what is [of] most interest in any locality, than they are hurried from it." Back on board he began to sort out his specimens, and was soon struck by an important fact: the majority of them were unique species which were to be found in these islands and nowhere else, and this applied to the plants as well as to the reptiles, birds, fish, shells and insects. It was true that they resembled other species in South America, but at the same time they were very different. "It was most striking," Darwin wrote later, "to be surrounded by new birds, new reptiles, new shells, new insects, new plants, and yet by innumerable trifling details of structure, and even by the tones of voice and plumage of the birds, to have the temperate plains of . . . Patagonia, or the hot dry deserts of northern Chile, vividly brought before my eyes."

He made another discovery: the species differed from island to island, even though many of the islands were only fifty or sixty miles apart. His attention was first drawn to this by comparing the mocking-thrushes shot on various islands, but then Mr. Lawson, an Englishman who was acting as vice-governor of the archipelago, remarked that he could tell by one look at a tortoise which island it came from. Thus the tortoises of Albemarle Island had a different sort of shell from those on Chatham, and both differed again from those on James.

With the little finches these effects were still more marked. The finches were dull to look at, and made dreary unmusical sounds; all had short tails, built nests with roofs, and laid white eggs spotted with pink, four to a clutch. Their plumage varied within limits: it ranged from lava black to green, according to their habitat. (It was not only the finches that were so dully feathered; with the exception of a yellow-breasted wren and a scarlet-tufted flycatcher none of the birds had the usual gaudy colouring of the tropics.) But it was the number of different species of finch, and the variety of their beaks, that so amazed Darwin. On one island they had developed strong thick beaks for cracking nuts and seeds, on another the beak was smaller to enable the bird to catch insects, on another again the beak was adjusted to feeding on fruits and flowers. There was even a bird that had learned how to use a cactus spine to probe grubs out of holes.

Clearly the birds had found different foods available on different islands, and through successive generations had adjusted themselves accordingly. The fact that they differed so much among themselves as compared with other birds suggested that they had got to the Galapagos islands first; for a period, possibly quite a long one, they were probably without competitors for food and territory, and this had allowed them to evolve in directions which would otherwise have been closed to them. For instance, finches do not normally evolve into woodpecker-like types because there are already efficient woodpeckers at work, and had a small mainland woodpecker already been established in the Galapagos it is most unlikely that the woodpecker finch would ever have evolved. Similarly the finch which ate nuts, the finch which ate insects, and the finch which fed on fruit and flowers, had been left in peace to evolve their best method of approach. Isolation had encouraged the origin of new species.

Somewhere here a great principle was involved. Naturally Darwin did not grasp the full implications of it all at once; for instance, he makes little mention of the finches in the first published edition of his Journal, yet the subject of their diversity and modification later became one of the great arguments in his theory of natural selection. But by this time he must have realised that he was on the edge of a remarkable and disturbing discovery. Until this point he had never openly objected to the current belief in the creation of unchangeable species, though he may well have had secret doubts. But now here on the Galapagos, faced with the existence of different forms of mocking-birds, tortoises and finches on different islands, different forms of the same species, he was forced to question the most fundamental contemporary theories. Indeed, it was more than that; if the ideas that were now buzzing round in his head were proved correct then all the accepted theories of the origin of life on this earth would have to be revised, and the Book of Genesis itself—the story of Adam and Eve and the Flood—would be exposed as nothing more than a superstitious myth. It might take years of research and investigation to prove anything, but in theory at least all the pieces of the jig-saw seemed to be coming together.

Darwin and Darwinism Today

STEPHEN JAY GOULD

The pieces of the jigsaw did indeed come together, as we have seen, to make Darwin the father of modern evolutionary theory. It is the judgment of Sir Julian Huxley and H. B. D. Kettlewell that he "changed the whole framework of human thought, substituting a dynamic and progressive vision of existence for the traditional view" and that "in the process he made important discoveries in geology, botany, paleontology, genetics, reproduction, behaviour, and general natural history; virtually created the new sciences of ecology and ethnology, laid the foundations for a scientific taxonomy; and prepared the way for a rational anthropology."[6]

Despite such claims by his champions, Darwin and the theory of evolution have continued to have their critics—largely of the same stripe and promoting the same arguments as those who first opposed Darwin in the mid-nineteenth century. In the famous Scopes trial of 1925, the

[6] Julian Huxley and H. B. D. Kettlewell, *Charles Darwin and His World* (New York: Viking, 1965), pp. 127–28. Also see pp. 147–48, for a reference to Darwin and the controversy.

controversy gained international publicity. A Tennessee high-school teacher, John T. Scopes, was on trial for teaching evolutionary theory in violation of a state law prohibiting the teaching of any doctrine denying the divine creation of human beings taught in the Bible. The issues of science versus religious fundamentalism were argued respectively by Clarence Darrow and William Jennings Bryan. The technical verdict went to Bryan and to the state, but the popular victory went to Darrow. For a generation or more Darwinism gained wider acceptance than it had ever enjoyed, but the opponents did not go away. In the decade of the 1980s, the issues of this long debate have once more surfaced.

In the following excerpt, those issues are reviewed. The excerpt is from the essay "Evolution as Fact and Theory," by Stephen Jay Gould, reprinted from his book Hen's Teeth and Horse's Toes *(1983). Gould is a Harvard scientist and scientific popularizer, the author of the monthly column "This View of Life" in* Natural History, *and himself an important contributor to evolutionary theory. The essay is only one of many such that he has written and is a blistering attack on the dogma of "scientific creationism" and an eloquent defense of Darwin and the theory of evolution.*

KIRTLEY MATHER, who died [in 1982] at age ninety, was a pillar of both science and Christian religion in America and one of my dearest friends. The difference of a half-century in our ages evaporated before our common interests. The most curious thing we shared was a battle we each fought at the same age. For Kirtley had gone to Tennessee with Clarence Darrow to testify for evolution at the Scopes trial of 1925. When I think that we are enmeshed again in the same struggle for one of the best documented, most compelling and exciting concepts in all of science, I don't know whether to laugh or cry.

According to idealized principles of scientific discourse, the arousal of dormant issues should reflect fresh data that give renewed life to abandoned notions. Those outside the current debate may therefore be excused for suspecting that creationists have come up with something new, or that evolutionists have generated some serious internal trouble. But nothing has changed; the creationists have presented not a single new fact or argument. Darrow and Bryan were at least more entertaining than we lesser antagonists today. The rise of creationism is politics, pure and simple; it represents one issue (and by no means the major concern) of the resurgent evangelical right. Arguments that seemed kooky just a decade ago have reentered the mainstream.

The basic attack of modern creationists falls apart on two general counts before we even reach the supposed factual details of their assault against evolution. First, they play upon a vernacular misunderstanding of the word "theory" to convey the false impression that we evolutionists are covering up the rotten core of our edifice. Second, they misuse a popular philosophy of science to argue that they are behaving scientifically in attacking evolution. Yet the same philosophy demonstrates that their own belief is not science, and that "scientific creationism" is a meaningless and self-contradictory phrase, an example of what Orwell called "newspeak.". . .

Well, evolution *is* a theory. It is also a fact. And facts and theories are different things, not rungs in a hierarchy of increasing certainty. Facts are the world's data. Theories are structures of ideas that explain and interpret facts. Facts do not go away while scientists debate rival theories for explaining them. Einstein's theory of gravitation replaced Newton's, but apples did not suspend themselves in mid-air pending the outcome. And human beings evolved from apelike ancestors whether they did so by Darwin's proposed mechanism or by some other, yet to be discovered.

Moreover, "fact" does not mean "absolute certainty." The final proofs of logic and mathematics flow deductively from stated premises and achieve certainty only because they are *not* about the empirical world. Evolutionists make no claim for perpetual truth, though creationists often do (and then attack us for a style of argument that they themselves favor). In science, "fact" can only mean "confirmed to such a degree that it would be perverse to withhold provisional assent." I suppose that apples might start to rise tomorrow, but the possibility does not merit equal time in physics classrooms.

Evolutionists have been clear about this distinction between fact and theory from the very beginning, if only because we have always acknowledged how far we are from completely understanding the mechanisms (theory) by which evolution (fact) occurred. Darwin continually emphasized the difference between his two great and separate accomplishments: establishing the fact of evolution, and proposing a theory—natural selection—to explain the mechanism of evolution. He wrote in *The Descent of Man:* "I had two distinct objects in view; firstly, to show that species had not been separately created, and secondly, that natural selection had been the chief agent of change . . . Hence if I have erred in . . . having exaggerated its [natural selection's] power . . . I have at least, as I hope, done good service in aiding to overthrow the dogma of separate creations."

Thus Darwin acknowledged the provisional nature of natural selection while affirming the fact of evolution. The fruitful theoretical debate that Darwin initiated has never ceased. From the 1940s through the 1960s, Darwin's own theory of natural selection did achieve a temporary hegemony that it never enjoyed in his lifetime. But renewed debate characterizes our decade, and, while no biologist questions the importance of natural selection, many now doubt its ubiquity. In particular, many evolutionists argue that substantial amounts of genetic change may not be subject to natural selection and may spread through populations at random. Others are challenging Darwin's linking of natural selection with gradual, imperceptible change through all intermediary degrees; they are arguing that most evolutionary events may occur far more rapidly than Darwin envisioned. . . .

Creationists pervert and caricature this debate by conveniently neglecting the common conviction that underlies it, and by falsely suggesting that we now doubt the very phenomenon we are struggling to understand.

Secondly, creationists claim that "the dogma of separate creations," as Darwin characterized it a century ago, is a scientific theory meriting equal time with evolution in high school biology curricula. . . .

"Scientific creationism" is a self-contradictory, nonsense phrase precisely because it cannot be falsified. I can envision observations and experiments that would disprove any evolutionary theory I know, but I cannot imagine what potential data could lead creationists to abandon their beliefs. Unbeatable systems are dogma, not science. Lest I seem harsh or rhetorical, I quote creationism's leading intellectual, Duane Gish, Ph.D., from his . . . (1978) book, *Evolution? The Fossils Say No!* "By creation we mean the bringing into being by a supernatural Creator of the basic kinds of plants and animals by the process of sudden, or fiat, creation. We do not know how the Creator created, what processes He used, *for He used processes which are not now operating anywhere in the natural universe* [Gish's italics]. This is why we refer to creation as special creation. We cannot discover by scientific ingestigations anything about the creative process used by the Creator." Pray tell, Dr. Gish, in the light of your last sentence, what then is "scientific creationism?

Our confidence that evolution occurred centers upon three general arguments. First, we have abundant, direct observational evidence of evolution in action, from both field and laboratory. This evidence ranges from countless experiments on change in nearly everything about fruit flies subjected to artificial selection in the laboratory to the famous populations of British moths that became black when industrial soot darkened the trees upon which the moths rest. (Moths gain protection from sharp-sighted bird predators by blending into the background.) Creationists do not deny these observations; how could they? Creationists have tightened their act. They now argue that God only created "basic kinds," and allowed for limited evolutionary meandering within them. Thus toy poodles and Great Danes come from the dog kind and moths can change color, but nature cannot convert a dog to a cat or a monkey to a man.

The second and third arguments for evolution—the case for major changes—do not involve direct observation of evolution in action. They rest upon inference, but are no less secure for that reason. Major evolutionary change requires too much time for direct observation on the scale of recorded human history. All historical sciences rest upon inference, and evolution is no different from geology, cosmology, or human history in this respect. In principle, we cannot observe processes that operated in the past. We must infer them from results that still surround us: living and fossil organisms for evolution, documents and artifacts for human history, strata and topography for geology.

The second argument—that the imperfection of nature reveals evolution—strikes many people as ironic, for they feel that evolution should be most elegantly displayed in the nearly perfect adaptation expressed by some organisms—the camber of a gull's wing, or butterflies that cannot be seen in ground litter because they mimic leaves so precisely. But perfection could be imposed by a wise creator or evolved by natural selection. Perfection covers the tracks of past history. And past history—the evidence of descent—is the mark of evolution.

Evolution lies exposed in the *imperfections* that record a history of descent. Why should a rat run, a bat fly, a porpoise swim, and I type this essay with structures built of the same bones unless we all inherited them from a common ancestor? An engineer, starting from scratch, could design better limbs in each case. Why should all the large native mammals of Australia be marsupials, unless they descended from a common ancestor isolated on this island continent? Marsupials are not "better," or ideally suited for Australia; many have been wiped out by placental mammals imported by man from other continents. This principle of imperfection extends to all historical sciences. When we recognize the etymology of September, October, November, and December (seventh, eighth, ninth, and tenth), we know that the year once started in March, or that two additional months must have been added to an original calendar of ten months.

The third argument is more direct: transitions are often found in the fossil record. Preserved transitions are not common—and should not be, according to our understanding of evolution . . . —but they are not entirely wanting, as creationists often claim. The lower jaw of reptiles contains several bones, that of mammals only one. The non-mammalian jawbones are reduced, step by step, in mammalian ancestors until they become tiny nubbins located at the back of the jaw. The "hammer" and "anvil" bones of the mammalian ear are descendants of these nubbins. How could such a transition be accomplished? the creationists ask. Surely a bone is either entirely in the jaw or in the ear. Yet paleontologists have discovered two transitional lineages of therapsids (the so-called mammal-like reptiles) with a double jaw joint—one composed of the old quadrate and articular bones (soon to become the hammer and anvil), the other of the squamosal and dentary bones (as in modern mammals). . . .

Faced with these facts of evolution and the philosophical bankruptcy of their own position, creationists rely upon distortion and innuendo to buttress their rhetorical claim. If I sound sharp or bitter, indeed I am—for I have become a major target of these practices.

I am both angry at and amused by the creationists; but mostly I am deeply sad. Sad for many reasons. Sad because so many people who respond to creationist appeals are troubled for the right reason, but venting their anger at the wrong target. It is true that scientists have often been dogmatic and elitist. It is true that we have often allowed the white-coated, advertising image to represent us—"Scientists say that Brand X cures bunions ten times faster than . . ." We have not fought it adequately because we derive benefits from appearing as a new priesthood. It is also true that faceless and bureaucratic state power intrudes more and more into our lives and removes choices that should belong to individuals and communities. I can understand that school curricula, imposed from above and without local input, might be seen as one more insult on all these grounds. But the culprit is not, and cannot be, evolution or any other fact of the natural world. Identify and fight your legitimate enemies by all means, but we are not among them.

I am sad because the practical result of this brouhaha will not be expanded coverage to include creationism (that would also make me sad), but the reduction or excision of evolution from high school curricula. Evolution is one of the half dozen "great ideas" developed by science. It speaks to the profound issues of genealogy that fascinate all of us—the "roots" phenomenon writ large. Where did we come from? Where did life arise? How did it develop? How are organisms related? It forces us to think, ponder, and wonder. Shall we deprive millions of this knowledge and once again teach biology as a set of dull and unconnected facts, without the thread that weaves diverse material into a supple unity?

But most of all I am saddened by a trend I am just beginning to discern among my colleagues. I sense that some now wish to mute the healthy debate about theory that has brought new life to evolutionary biology. It provides grist for creationist mills, they say, even if only by distortion. Perhaps we should lie low and rally round the flag of strict Darwinism, at least for the moment—a kind of old-time religion on our part.

But we should borrow another metaphor and recognize that we too have to tread a straight and narrow path, surrounded by roads to perdition. For if we ever begin to suppress our search to understand nature, to quench our own intellectual excitement in a misguided effort to present a united front where it does not and should not exist, then we are truly lost.

Suggestions for Further Reading

AS THE EXCERPTED PASSAGE from *The Origin of Species* demonstrates, Darwin's own works are both readable and comprehensible to nonscientists. Students are encouraged to read further in them. *The Origin of Species* is available in several editions, including *The Origin of Species, A Variorum Text*, ed. Morse Peckham (Philadelphia: University of Pennsylvania Press, 1959), logging the thousands of changes Darwin made throughout many editions of this work. There are also good modern editions of *The Descent of Man, The Expression of the Emotions in Man and Animals, The Variation of Animals and Plants under Domestication*, and *The Different Forms of Flowers on Plants of the Same Species. Charles Darwin's Diary of the Voyage of H.M.S. "Beagle"*, ed. from the manuscript by Nora Barlow (Cambridge, England: Cambridge University Press, 1933), is the best edition of this work. His scientific papers are now available in *The Collected Papers of Charles Darwin*, ed. Paul H. Barrett, 2 vols. (Chicago: University of Chicago Press, 1977). His autobiography is available in two editions, one by his son, the other by his granddaughter: *Charles Darwin's Autobiography, with his Notes and Letters Depicting the Growth of The Origin of Species*, ed. Francis Darwin (New York: Schuman, 1950), and *Charles Darwin. Autobiography* . . . , ed. Nora Barlow (New York: Harcourt, Brace and World, 1958). His son also prepared *The Life and Letters of Charles Darwin* . . . ed. Francis Darwin, 2 vols. (New York: Appleton, 1899). An important collection of the correspondence is *Darwin and Henslow: The Growth of an Idea: Letters 1831–1860*, ed. Nora Barlow (Berkeley: University of California Press, 1967). Students, however, may prefer *The Darwin Reader*, ed. Marston Bates and Philip S. Humphrey (New York: Scribners, 1956), or *Darwin for Today, The Essence of His Works*, ed. Stanley E. Hyman (New York: Viking, 1963). For the storm of controversy caused by Darwin, students should see two excellent books: Peter J. Vorzimmer, *Charles Darwin: The Years of Controversy: The Origin of Species and Its Critics, 1859–1882* (Philadelphia: Temple University Press, 1970), and *Darwin and His Critics: The Reception of Darwin's Theory of Evolution by the Scientific Community*, ed. David L. Hull (Cambridge, Mass.: Harvard University Press, 1973).

G. R. deBeer, *Charles Darwin: Evolution by Natural Selection* (New York: Doubleday, 1963), is probably the best brief introduction to Darwin and his work, but also recommended are Walter Karp, *Charles Darwin and The Origin of Species* (New York: Harper & Row, 1968), and Julian Huxley and H. B. D. Kettlewell, *Charles Darwin and His World* (New York: Viking, 1965); Michael Ruse, *The Darwinian Revolution: Science Red in Tooth and Claw* (Chicago: University of Chicago Press, 1979); and Neal C. Gilespie, *Charles Darwin and the Problem of Creation* (Chicago: University of Chicago Press, 1975). Alan Moorehead, *Darwin and the Beagle* (New York: Harper & Row, 1969), excerpted in this chapter, is an exciting account. Equally exciting on another subject is William Irvine, *Apes, Angels, and Victorians: The Story of Darwin, Huxley, and Evolution* (New York: McGraw-Hill, 1955). There are two important books setting Darwin and his ideas in their own time. John C. Greene, *The Death of Adam: Evolution and Its Impact on Western Thought* (Ames: Iowa State University Press, 1959), and Loren Eiseley, *Darwin's Century: Evolution and the Men Who Discovered It* (New York: Doubleday, 1958). There are two related works, another by Eiseley, *Darwin and the Mysterious Mr. X, New Light on the Evolutionists* (New York: Dutton, 1979), a series of papers and essays centering on an obscure nineteenth-century naturalist named Edward Blyth whose theories anticipated those of Darwin; and Arnold C. Brackman, *A Delicate Arrangement: The Strange Case of Charles Darwin and Alfred Russel Wallace* (New York: Times Books, 1980). Two more good books dealing largely with the impact of Darwinism are Gertrude Himmelfarb, *Darwin and the Darwinian Revolution* (New York: Doubleday, 1959), and Paul B. Sears, *Charles Darwin: The Naturalist as a Cultural Force* (New York: Scribner's, 1950). Students will also enjoy Jacques Barzun, *Darwin, Marx, Wagner: Critique of a Heritage*, rev. 2nd ed. (New York: Doubleday, 1958), a brilliant work in which Barzun considers these three men as the revolutionary influences in the making of the modern world.

Among the books marking the Darwin centenary of 1982 and since are Peter Brent, *Charles Darwin, "A Man of Enlarged Curiosity"* (New York: Harper & Row, 1981), a carefully researched major biography; Ronald W. Clark, *The Survival of Charles Darwin, A Biography of a Man and an Idea* (New York: Random House, 1984), dealing as much with Darwinism as with Darwin; an interesting (if somewhat demanding) book on Darwinism and its impact largely on modern literature, Margot Norris, *Beasts of the Modern Imagination, Darwin, Nietzsche, Kafka, Ernst, and Lawrence* (Baltimore and London: The Johns Hopkins University Press, 1985); and the best of several symposium programs, *Charles Darwin: a Commemoration 1882–1982*, for the Linnean Society of London, ed. R. J. Berry (London, New York, et al.: Academic Press, 1982).

The Granger Collection

Bismarck: The Iron Chancellor

1815 born
1862 became minister-president of Prussia
1864 victory in Schleswig-Holstein War
1866 Prussian victory in Austro-Prussian War
1870 Prussian victory in Franco-Prussian War
1871 proclamation of the German empire
1882 formation of Triple Alliance with Austria and Italy
1887 the "Reinsurance Treaty" with Russia
1890 resigned as chancellor
1898 died

The history of Continental Europe—indeed, of much of the world—in the second half of the nineteenth century was overshadowed by the Empire of Germany. And Germany was overshadowed by the massive, brooding figure of Otto Eduard Leopold von Bismarck, Minister-President of Prussia and Chancellor of the Empire for almost thirty years, the mastermind and creator of modern Germany. The question of the nature of Bismarck's policies is a crucial one—whether he sought German hegemony of Europe to secure the peace (as he claimed) or to satisfy the motives of power, whether he was a great statesman or simply one more German tyrant. For how we answer this question will tend to determine how we look at the history of the world in our own fateful century following hard upon Bismarck's death in 1898. It is almost impossible, in the backwash of two world wars that undeniably stemmed from German aggression, not to regard the question as rhetorical and consequently to condemn both Bismarck the person and Bismarck the statesman. And yet, in the years immediately following World War II, many "good Germans" both in Germany and abroad looked back to the age of Bismarck as a kind of golden age when Germany could have prestige without dishonor, greatness without cruelty, and empire without genocide. The historian Friedrich Meinecke, though he knew very well to what disaster Prussian militarism had led, could still recall how "free and proud" "we Germans often felt in the mightily flourishing

Empire of 1871." [1] And Hajo Holborn, himself an exile from German tyranny, could still argue that Bismarck's empire was founded not only upon naked force but upon German philosophic idealism and the traditions of German Protestantism.

The beginning of the German Empire, regardless of how we view its end, is to be found in Germany's legitimate search for national security. Prussia, the major state among the scattering of German principalities, was nevertheless the smallest and weakest of the so-called great powers that had finally defeated Napoleon. But in the years following the Napoleonic wars, Prince Metternich (1773–1859), architect of France's containment and of the Concert of Europe, kept Prussia subordinated to his own Austria. When the Metternichian Concert began to become unstrung by revolts and revolutions and, after mid-century, to be replaced by the direct competition of the great powers, the Prussian King William I, with some reservation, in 1862 appointed Otto von Bismarck Minister-President of the Kingdom of Prussia.

Bismarck by this time was an experienced diplomat and politician. He had learned to hate the arrogance of Austria as the Prussian envoy to the Federal Diet in 1851. He had been ambassador to Russia from 1859 to 1862 and had gained considerable respect for that great Eastern bear. In 1862 he had been briefly ambassador to Napoleon III of France for whom he had only contempt. But Bismarck reserved his choicest contempt for the notions of popular government and for the abortive Frankfort Parliament of 1849 that had tried in vain to bring the blessings of revolutionary liberalism to Germany. He judged liberalism to be as weak as the "weak men" of Frankfort who advocated it. Indeed, the whole idea of personal liberty—at the heart of the liberal creed—seemed to him not only unattainable but selfish to the point of indecency. People live for the state, for duty, service, order—not for themselves. Bismarck was a conservative through and through, and an autocrat. Shortly after his appointment as chief minister, appearing before the Budget Commission of the Prussian Diet, he delivered his most famous speech. He spoke of the prestige that Prussia enjoyed among the other German states, a prestige that flowed from its power and resolve, not from its liberalism. He spoke of Prussia's need to collect its forces and look to its "natural" frontiers. And he ended, "Not by speeches and majorities will the great questions of the day be decided—that was the mistake of 1848 and 1849—but by iron and blood." [2]

What Bismarck sought in this famous speech was a dramatic increase

[1] Quoted in W. N. Medlicott, *Bismarck and Modern Germany* (London: English Universities Press, 1965), p. 183.

[2] Quoted in Louis L. Snyder, *The Blood and Iron Chancellor, A Documentary-Biography of Otto von Bismarck* (New York: Van Nostrand, 1967), p. 127.

in the military budget. The Diet refused to authorize the necessary taxes. Bismarck levied them anyway, collected them, and used them to enlarge and reorganize the already substantial Prussian army and to supply it with the most modern equipment. Liberals in the Diet charged that the government was acting unconstitutionally; neither Bismarck nor the Prussian people seemed to mind. Prussia, indeed all of Germany, was prospering. The Industrial Revolution was in full swing. The modern world was opening up, and the great majority of Prussians shared Bismarck's views. Order, discipline, and military power seemed more likely to guarantee their future in that brave new world than outworn parliamentarianism.

Bismarck's first opportunity to employ his new army came quickly, in the Schleswig-Holstein dispute of 1863. These two north German provinces were claimed by Denmark and about to be annexed. The German Federal Diet, as sensitive on this question as Bismarck himself, clamored for war. But Bismarck was not a German nationalist, he was a Prussian. And he wanted no part of a war in which Prussian arms would contribute to the prestige of the hated federation. He wanted a Prussian victory for Prussia. To that end, he joined with Austria in 1864 in a war against Denmark, which was quickly defeated. Prussia took Schleswig, and Austria, Holstein.

But the Austrians were not welcome in Holstein, and frictions developed. Bismarck encouraged them. Austria complained to the Federal Diet. Bismarck denied its jurisdiction, accused Austria of aggression, and occupied Holstein. The Diet supported Austria, and in 1866 Austria and most of the rest of the federated states declared war on Prussia. Again Bismarck and the Prussian army were ready. The war lasted just seven weeks and was an unqualified Prussian victory. Then Bismarck simply declared the federal union dissolved, annexed the majority of its northern member states, and organized them into a North German Confederacy, clearly subordinate to Prussia. The North German Confederation was also clearly a half-way house to a Prussian empire.

The powers of Europe were stunned and unsettled by these developments in Germany—none more so than France, justly alarmed at the growth of Prussian power on its border and disillusioned with the failures of Napoleon III. There was almost universal talk of a Franco-Prussian war in the offing. Bismarck hoped that Napoleon III would attempt it on the chance of rescuing his policies at home by military success abroad. For Bismarck was convinced that no such French victory would ensue. And he was also convinced that a Franco-Prussian war would force the remaining south German states, already linked to him by defensive alliances, to unify with Prussia.

In the summer of 1870, on a trivial diplomatic pretext cleverly escalated by Bismarck, Napoleon III did declare war on Prussia. His own folly had robbed him of allies, and Bismarck contrived to make the war seem a wanton French aggression. In any event, it was again a short war and again a decisive Prussian victory. Bismarck caused the issues of the war to be settled and the new German Empire to be proclaimed in the famed Hall of Mirrors of the Palace at Versailles—a dramatic gesture never to be forgotten by the French.

The other German states, except Austria—as Bismarck anticipated—had joined Prussia in the war. They now capitulated to their powerful ally, the North German Confederation was dissolved, and the King of Prussia was transformed into the Emperor of Germany—ruler of what had become overnight the mightiest state in Europe.

France was humiliated, saddled with an enormous indemnity, and forced to give up the rich industrialized border provinces of Alsace and Lorraine. Bismarck's task now became the prevention of a French war of vengeance; it continued to be the preoccupation of his foreign policy. He spread an increasingly complex web of alliances, understandings, secret treaties, and secret protocols of published agreements across Europe—meanwhile proclaiming that he sought only peace. For example, in 1878 he offered his services in the crisis precipitated by a Russian attack on the rotting Turkish Empire that threatened to upset the balance of Western interests in the "Eastern question." At the resulting Congress of Berlin, Bismarck expansively posed, in his phrase, as "the honest broker." Alone among the great powers, Germany refused to make any territorial demands upon Turkey, which nevertheless was effectively partitioned by the agreements reached. Bismarck wanted only peace—and the continued isolation of France.

In the following year he formed a military pact with Austria, which Italy was permitted to join in 1882. Thus was formed the Triple Alliance, the basic alliance of the so-called Central Powers that would carry into World War I. Austria and Italy were thus safely removed from a possible French alliance. England, long averse to continental alliances, was moreover in sharp conflict with France over colonial issues. Only Russia remained a possibility, and a remote one at that, for there seemed no common ground between backward, autocratic Russia and the French Third Republic. But to be careful, Bismarck approached the Russians. Indeed, he had cultivated them since his days as ambassador to St. Petersburg. He had supported Russia in a Polish insurrection in 1863 and prevented Austrian interference. Russia had been induced to remain neutral in the Franco-Prussian war. But Bismarck was blamed by some Pan-Slav extremists for his part in the Congress of Berlin and the consequent thwarting of Russian victory over the Turks. And now, to approach Russia with any kind of proposal in the face of his alliance with Austria, Russia's great foe in the Balkans, took all Bismarck's nerve and skill. He proposed a secret League of the Three Emperors—

of Germany, Russia, and Austria—directed precisely to the preservation of both Austrian and Russian interests in the Balkans and Turkey. But though the parties agreed, the agreement was never implemented; in 1881 Czar Alexander II was assassinated by a terrorist bomb. But Bismarck persevered and in 1887 finally signed with Russia the famous Reinsurance Treaty, a further "insurance" against a possible Franco-Russian alliance. In 1888 Bismarck stood at the zenith of his career; he appeared to be the master of Europe.

The Speech for the Military Bill of February 6, 1888

OTTO VON BISMARCK

At the very moment that he seemed to hold Europe in his hand, Bismarck paradoxically appealed to the Reichstag twice within two months for extraordinary increases in German armaments—on December 9, 1887, and on January 31, 1888. It was in connection with these proposals that he spoke before the Reichstag on February 6, 1888. It was a speech second in fame only to the "Blood and Iron" speech at the beginning of his career. In one respect, it is its superior. For it is —to quote one of Bismarck's most perceptive modern critics— among his "most important and comprehensive" expositions of his foreign policy, "a majestic survey of German policy in the past, present, and future" that "makes this speech a historical document of great value." [3] *We excerpt it below.*

WHEN I SAY that we must constantly endeavor to be equal to all contingencies, I mean by that to claim that we must make greater exertions than other powers in order to attain the same result, because of our geographical position. We are situated in the middle of Europe. We have at least three fronts of attack. France has only its eastern frontier, Russia only its western frontier, on which it can be attacked. We are, moreover, in consequence of the whole development of the world's history, in consequence of our geographical position, and perhaps in consequence of the slighter degree of internal cohesion which the German nation as compared with others has thus far possessed, more exposed than any other people to the risk of a coalition. God has placed us in a situation in which we are prevented by our neighbors from sinking into any sort of indolence or stagnation. He has set at our side the most warlike and the most restless of nations, the French; and he has permitted warlike inclinations, which in former centuries existed in no such degree, to grow strong in Russia. Thus we get a certain amount of spurring on both sides, and are forced into exertions which otherwise perhaps we should not make. The pikes in the European carp pond prevent us from becoming carps, by letting us feel their prickles on both our flanks; they constrain us to exertions which

[3] Joseph Vincent Fuller, *Bismarck's Diplomacy at Its Zenith* (New York: Fertig, 1967), p. 310.

perhaps we should not voluntarily make; they constrain us Germans also to a harmony among ourselves that is repugnant to our inmost nature: but for them, our tendency would rather be to separate. But the Franco-Russian press in which we are caught, forces us to hold together, and by its pressure it will greatly increase our capacity for cohesion, so that we shall reach in the end that state of inseparableness which characterizes nearly all other nations, and which we still lack. But we must adapt ourselves to this decree of Providence by making ourselves so strong that the pikes can do no more than enliven us. . . .

The bill gives us an increase in troops trained to arms—a possible increase: if we do not need it, we need not call for it; we can leave it at home. But if we have this increase at our disposal, and if we have the weapons for it, . . . then this new law constitutes a reinforcement of the guarantees of peace, a reinforcement of the league of peace, that is precisely as strong as if a fourth great power with an army of 700,000 men—and this was formerly the greatest strength that existed—had joined the alliance. This powerful reinforcement will also, I believe, have a quieting effect upon our own countrymen, and lessen in some degree the nervousness of our public opinion, our stock-market, and our press. I hope it will act upon them as a sedative when they clearly comprehend that from the moment at which this law is signed and published the men are there. The armament, too, may be said to be ready, in the shape of what is absolutely necessary: but we must procure a better, for if we form an army of triarians of the best human material that we have,—of the men above thirty, the husbands and fathers,—we must have for them the best weapons there are. We must not send them into the fight with an outfit that we do not regard as good enough for our young troops of the line. The solid men, the heads of families, these stalwart figures that we can still remember from the time that they held the bridge of Versailles,—these men must have the best rifles on their shoulders, the completest armament, and the amplest clothing to protect them from wind and weather. We ought not to economize there.

But I hope it will tranquilize our fellow citizens, if they are really thinking of the contingency (which I do not expect to occur) of our being attacked simultaneously on two sides,—of course, as I have pointed out in reviewing the events of the last forty years, there is always the possibility of any sort of coalition,—I hope it will tranquilize them to remember that if this happens, we can have a million good soldiers to defend each of our frontiers. At the same time we can keep in the rear reserves of half a million and more, of a million even, and we can push these forward as they are needed. I have been told, "That will only result in the others going still higher." But they cannot. They have long ago reached their limits. . . . In numbers they have gone as high as we, but in quality they cannot compete with us. Bravery, of course, is equal among all civilized nations; the Russian and the Frenchman fight as bravely as the German:

but our men, our 700,000 new men, have seen service; they are soldiers who have served their time, and who have not yet forgotten their training. Besides—and this is a point in which no people in the world can compete with us—we have the material for officers and under-officers to command this enormous army. It is here that competition is excluded, because it involves a peculiarly broad extension of popular culture, such as exists in Germany and in no other country. . . .

There is a further advantage that will result from the adoption of this law: the very strength at which we are aiming necessarily makes us peaceful. That sounds paradoxical, but it is true. With the powerful machine which we are making of the German army no aggression will be attempted. If I saw fit—assuming a different situation to exist from that which in my conviction does exist—to come before you here today and say to you, "We are seriously menaced by France and Russia; the prospect is that we shall be attacked: such at least is my conviction, as a diplomatist, on the basis of the military information that we have received; it is to our advantage to defend ourselves by anticipating the attack, and to strike at once; an offensive war is a better one for us to wage, and I accordingly ask the Imperial Diet for a credit of a milliard or half a milliard, in order to undertake today the war against our two neighbors,"—well gentlemen, I do not know whether you would have such confidence in me as to grant such a request. I hope not. But if you did, it would not be enough for me.

If we in Germany desire to wage a war with the full effect of our national power, it must be a war with which all who help to wage it, and all who make sacrifices for it—with which, in a word, all the nation—must be in sympathy. It must be a people's war; it must be a war that is carried on with the same enthusiasm as that of 1870, when we were wickedly attacked. I remember still the joyful shouts that rang in our ears at the Cologne station; it was the same thing from Berlin to Cologne; it was the same thing here in Berlin. The waves of popular approval bore us into the war, whether we liked it or not. So it must be, if a national force like ours is to be brought fully into operation. It will be very difficult, however, to make it clear to the provinces, to the federal states and to their people, that a war is inevitable, that it must come. It will be asked: "Are you so sure of it? Who knows?" If we finally come to the point of making the attack, all the weight of the imponderables, which weigh much more than the material weights, will be on the side of our antagonist whom we have attacked. "Holy Russia" will be filled with indignation at the attack. France will glisten with weapons to the Pyrenees. The same thing will happen everywhere. A war into which we are not borne by the will of the people—such a war will of course be carried on, if in the last instance the established authorities consider and have declared it to be necessary. It will be carried on with energy and perhaps victoriously, as soon as the men come under fire and have seen blood; but there will not be back of it, from the start, the same dash and heat as in a war in which we are attacked. . . .

I do not believe—to sum up—that any disturbance of the peace is an immediate prosepct; and I ask you to deal with the law that lies before you, independently of any such idea or apprehension, simply as a means for making the great force which God has lodged in the German nation completely available in the event of our needing it. If we do not need it, we shall not call for it. We seek to avoid the chance of our needing it. This effort on our part is still, in some degree, impeded by threatening newspaper articles from foreign countries; and I wish to address to foreign countries especially the admonition to discontinue these threats. They lead to nothing. The threat which we receive, not from the foreign government, but in the press, is really a piece of incredible stupidity, if you think what it means—that by a certain combination of words, by a certain threatening shape given to printer's ink, a great and proud power like the German Empire is assumed to be capable of intimidation. This should be discontinued; and then it would be made easier for us to assume a more conciliatory and obliging attitude toward our two neighbors.

Every country is responsible in the long run, somehow and at some time, for the windows broken by its press; the bill is presented some day or other, in the ill-humor of the other country. We can easily be influenced by love and good will,—too easily perhaps,—but most assuredly not by threats. We Germans fear God, but nothing else in the world; and it is the fear of God that makes us love and cherish peace. But whoever, despite this, breaks it, will find that the warlike patriotism that in 1813, when Prussia was weak, small, and exhausted by plunder, brought her whole population under her banners, has today become the common heritage of the whole German nation; and whoever attacks the German nation will find it united in arms, and in every soldier's heart the firm faith "God will be with us."

Bismarck and the Failure of Realpolitik

JOSEPH VINCENT FULLER

The same critic, Joseph Vincent Fuller, who declared the speech for the military bill of 1888 one of the "most important and comprehensive" expositions of Bismarck's foreign policy sees it at the same time not as the ringing defiance it seems to be but a desperate admission that Bismarck and his foreign policy had failed. This, he argues, explains the paradox of Bismarck's appeal for increased military expenditures in the face of apparent diplomatic victory: the victory had already slipped away.

This is the thesis of Fuller's book, Bismarck's Diplomacy at Its Zenith. *The book dates from the early 1920s and is surely in part a result of the author's experience as an attaché to the American delegation at the Paris Peace Conference of 1919, where so much of the tangle of European diplomacy was laid bare, along with the treachery and cynicism of the master diplomats who had done so much to bring about World War I—Bismarck above all. But whatever its inception, the book remains the classic condemnation of Bismarck as the great exponent of* Realpolitik, *the "practical" politics of ruthless opportunism and military power. Fuller believes that the failure of Bismarck's policies was predictable, even inevitable.*

He focuses special attention upon the 1888 speech as the key revelation of Bismarck's failure. Following is his analysis.

THE SPEECH OF February 6, 1888, is probably the most notable in Bismarck's career. Although he was so ill that only recourse to stimulants enabled him to speak at all, and he was obliged to deliver most of his address while seated, he spoke with a power and appeal which brought him a popular triumph unsurpassed in even his brilliant experience. His majestic survey of German policy in the past, present, and future makes this speech a historical document of great value. Next to the *Gedanken und Erinnerungen,*[4] it is the most important and comprehensive exposition of the Chancellor's views on foreign policy which he has handed down. The aspects of it chiefly considered here will be those bearing upon the events of the two or three preceding years.

Bismarck was careful to begin by saying that he undertook his exposi-

[4] "Thoughts and Recollections," the title Bismarck gave to his memoirs, published after his forced retirement in 1890.—ED.

tion less for the sake of convincing the Reichstag of the need for the proposed law than for that of convincing Europe that its passage implied no threat to peace. The events of the recent past were represented as having reached, on the whole, a satisfactory outcome. The interpretation of them was, naturally, calculated to give the impression of German policy which Bismarck wished to produce upon the world—regardless of the deep-lying facts of the case. . . . Yet the Chancellor must justify a proposal to augment her military forces by 700,000 men—the equivalent of a fourth ally.

"I do not anticipate any immediate disturbance of the peace," ran his argument, "and I ask that you treat the proposed law independently of such considerations and anxieties." But he had stipulated beforehand: "The fact that I hold these for the moment unfounded is far from leading me to the conclusion that we need no increase in our armed forces—quite the contrary." And why? Because, after all is said and done, the war on two fronts looms in the future; and Germany must neglect no preparations to face it. His words were impressive and yet reassuring: "I hope our fellow citizens will take comfort in the thought that, if we should be attacked from two sides at once—which I do not anticipate, though the events of the past forty years show that all sorts of coalitions are still possible—we could have a million good soldiers for the defence of each of our frontiers. And we can raise, besides, a half-million, or even a million, reservists in the interior to send forward where needed." This picture of power and security should suffice to convince his hearers of the wisdom of voting as they were asked to do.

But Germany and the world at large must have no idea that this great force would ever be turned to the uses of aggression. The possibility that Germany should have any ends of expansion to achieve was not even considered. But Bismarck did feel called upon to dispel the suspicion that she might sometime undertake a "preventive war." Upon the fantastic assumption that her Chancellor should ever conceive such a project, he ventured to hope that the Diet would withhold its support; and he expressed confidence that the nation would not rise to the occasion. All this was merely persiflage. Had Bismarck desired a "preventive war," he would have found German public opinion the least of his obstacles. On the several occasions when he had appeared to be preparing for a new war, national sentiment outran him if anything; it was the failure of his ostensible occasions to develop properly that averted the explosions.

Such empty considerations brought the speaker round to his dramatic peroration. He had painted a picture of Germany, strong in her own might and in the consciousness of following ever the path of honor—a Germany misunderstood and maligned, standing between jealous neighbors who constituted always a potential threat to peace. Firm in her own peaceful intentions, she would arm to meet that threat in the most dangerous shape it could take. So Bismarck came to the rhetorical flourish which will ring forever in the hearts of his countrymen: "We Germans fear God, but nothing else in the world!"

Leaving rhetoric and misrepresentation aside, what was the situation of Germany as pictured by Bismarck in the great speech of 1888? Certainly it was far different from the situation of three years before, when the German Empire had stood at the centre of a system of alliances and understandings embracing the whole continent of Europe. The year 1888 found that system crumbling to ruin, the friendship with France destroyed and the alliance with Russia undermined. In 1885 Germany was fearlessly challenging England's supremacy in distant colonial fields: in 1888 she was preoccupied with the defence of her own frontiers and dependent upon England's help for preserving the remains of her structure of alliances. In 1885 Germany's diplomacy brilliantly sufficed for the attainment of her most ambitious ends: three years later she was straining every nerve to keep up a military establishment that would enable her to remain mistress of her own destiny. Bismarck's sounding phrases are a confession of the breakdown of his policy. The problem of assuring Germany's future had got so far beyond the resources of his diplomacy that he had nothing left to recommend but reliance on her own brute force. Another formidable military bill hardly a year after the preceding one—such was the culmination of Bismarck's diplomacy in the eventful year 1887. And such was the international situation which Bismarck left as heritage to his successors; for it had changed but little when they took it over two years later.

The only dependable diplomatic resource he left to them was the Austrian alliance, which they correctly appraised as the most solid element in his international system. . . . From the day of its conclusion, the Austrian alliance had been the cornerstone of Bismarck's system; and he had taken care to promote Austrian interests as far as the limits of caution allowed. His successors overstepped those limits in the end; but it is questionable if Bismarck himself could have kept within them indefinitely. His mask of duplicity had slipped so far aside in 1887 that Russia could never again have any real confidence in his professions as "honest broker." The League of the Three Emperors as a complement to the Austrian alliance had definitely ceased to exist.

Its other complement, the Triple Alliance, remained; but Bismarck had never set great store by the friendship of Italy. He rated Italy's material value to his system hardly above that of the Balkan satellites of Austria, and he realized fully the unreliability of her engagements. . . . Bismarck had, it is true, made extensive commitments on Germany's behalf in renewing the alliance, but he never meant to go out of his way to fulfil them. He had made them during a crisis, when there had appeared an especial need for assuring himself of Italy's rôle with regard to both France and the Eastern Question. In the latter connection, he had skilfully contrived to make Italy and England influence each other. He had drawn England into his system by way of an understanding with Italy, and at the same time induced her to share Germany's burden of satisfying Italy's claims of support for her own interests. Masterly as had been the accomplishment of February, 1887, however, it was a *tour de force* of momentary, rather than permanent, significance.

By his dealings with England, Bismarck appeared to have secured a new addition to his international system, making up for the defection of France and the weakening of the Russian connection. But it was a compensation far from satisfactory in his own mind. His lack of confidence in the straightforwardness and continuity of English foreign policy prevented his ever regarding England's friendship as a permanent asset. He had made no serious effort to attach England directly to Germany by any formal bond. He was fully conscious of the fact that, in dealing with her at all, he was only taking advantage of a temporarily favorable situation for temporary ends. His utilization of England was, in reality, inconsistent with even the slight remnant of his old political system, which he had no idea of altering fundamentally. Germany's own relations with Russia, which Bismarck still valued highly, despite the ill services he had rendered her, would necessarily suffer through Germany's intimacy with England.[5] Moreover, the agreement between England and Germany's two allies, brought about in 1887, had practically fulfilled its purpose when Russia abandoned her designs on Bulgaria. Deprived of its immediate object, the bonds of the agreement must slacken, following Bismarck's own theory that England's support could be counted upon only where English interests were pressingly involved.

Pursuing the consequences of the settlement of 1888 still further, they could entail only an increasing alienation of England from the Central Empires. She had nothing to gain through the replacement of Russian influence in the Balkan Peninsula by the Austrian penetration which followed the opening of the railways to Salonica and Constantinople. She was still less gratified by the diversion of Russia's expansive forces into the Far East which accompanied the development of the Trans-Siberian line. And both these tendencies would necessarily have at least the moral approval of even Bismarck's Germany. The weakening of England's connection with Bismarck's international system, therefore, began with the moment the connection was established. It was essentially self-destructive. Its disappearance would inevitably undermine Italy's position in the Triple Alliance. Italy's connection with England was of more importance to her than that with the Central Empires: once England had broken away from them, the Triple Alliance was practically dissolved. So the new Triple Alliance and the Austro-Italian entente with England were legacies of doubtful value at the best.

[5] Because of the hostility lingering between Russia and England from the Crimean War.—ED.

The most perplexing of Bismarck's diplomatic legacies was the Reinsurance Treaty with Russia. His heirs cannot be greatly blamed for renouncing their title to it. His most bitter criticisms of their policy arose from this action; yet it is doubtful if even in his hands this bond of alliance would ever have proved more than a rope of sand. His regard for the Russian connection was beyond question sincere, but it was a regard which embraced only Germany's interest in maintaining it. He was perpetually cut off from a proper appreciation of Russia's interest by his overweening solicitude for the greatness of Austria. He wished to retain the friendship of Russia as a check upon Austria; yet he could not employ it indefinitely as a mask behind which to contrive the balking of all Russia's designs running counter to Austria's. Perhaps he was not consciously striving to injure Russia; but, supposing he believed himself to be acting for her own good, he could not expect her always to accept his definition of her reasonable and salutary expectations. . . . The consequence could only be the acceleration of Russia's drift toward France. The renewal of the Reinsurance Treaty in 1890 could have checked that tendency only if it had been accompanied by a radical change in German policy, such as Bismarck had shown no signs of bringing about. The results of his conduct were inevitable, whether they took shape immediately in the binding and loosing of formal diplomatic ties or not. The diverting of Russia into the Far East, accompanied by a refusal of the means to develop her projects, brought on the Franco-Russian alliance. That alliance gave Russia a partner in the West to reach her a hand for the return to Europe when those projects were undone by a military defeat in the East.

France's action in these developments was no more dependent upon formal agreements than was Russia's. The Reinsurance Treaty alone could not keep Russia away from France: a treaty with Russia was not necessary to assure France's cooperation against Germany. It was less necessary than ever, after the events of 1887. Whatever progress Bismarck had previously made toward a reconciliation with France had been annulled by his conduct in that critical year. The blame for the revival of enmity between France and Germany rests even more clearly on his shoulders than does that for the estrangement between Germany and Russia. . . . The crises of 1887 demonstrated very clearly to France a positive malevolence against which she would do well to provide. Looked at from the western side, then, the Franco-Russian alliance appears again as the fruit of Bismarck's diplomacy. It would have taken more than his mere continuance in office, more than a simple renewal of the Reinsurance Treaty, to prevent this eventual alliance of hatred and suspicion.

Many tributes have been paid to Bismarck's personality, to his impressive renown, to his unequalled grasp of affairs and sureness of touch, as the essential elements in his policy, impossible to transmit to any successor. Such explanations of the failure of his successors needlessly obscure the shortcomings of the policy they inherited. Of the critical period in which Bismarck's diplomacy put its final touches on Germany's destiny, Robertson has written: "The years 1887 and 1888 were . . . the severest touchstones of a German statesman's statecraft. Bismarck's performance was, when we appreciate the complex difficulties, a consummate one. The master proved his mastery." The eulogy bears almost an ironic interpretation when examined in the light of the situation in which Bismarck's statecraft had placed his country. His performance, "consummate" in duplicity and brutality, left the main problem of the period regulated by a one-sided settlement which only entailed new difficulties. It left Germany between two potential foes about to join hands across her frontiers. It left her with but one dependable alliance amid a set of unstable combinations. It left her frankly dependent upon a vast military establishment as the main reliance for her future. Could the "master" himself have found a safe way out of this situation? If Bismarck's successors were to fall below his level in resourcefulness, the outlook was dark indeed! . . .

Without calling Bismarck's early, fundamental achievements into question—which is beyond the scope of this study—it is not possible to indicate what better courses could have been followed. It is at least clear, however, that his diplomacy contained no priceless and unique key to imperial Germany's future, irrecoverable once wantonly thrown away. Rather, it may be maintained that Bismarck's diplomacy, at the zenith of his power, contained all the causes of his Empire's downfall.

Bismarck the Statesman

A. J. P. TAYLOR

As Joseph Vincent Fuller views Bismarck and the events of 1887–1888 from the perspective of the years following World War I, A. J. P. Taylor, the brilliant Oxford diplomatic historian, represents the view of Bismarck and these culminating years of his diplomacy from the perspective of the years following World War II and the cold war of the mid-1950s. Fuller sees Bismarck anticipating a two-front war and preparing for it. Taylor sees that threat as an empty one used by Bismarck to his own ends. Fuller views the Bismarck alliance system as "crumbling to ruin." Taylor views it as alive and well. Fuller sees Bismarck as dependent on England's help to preserve what remained of his structure of alliances. Taylor sees Bismarck using Britain's "Mediterranean agreement" to his own advantage. Fuller charges Bismarck with brutal duplicity and, in the end, with the destruction of the very security he sought to promote. In contrast, Taylor sees the chancellor's policies still as effective as ever at the end of the 1880s and his only goal "to maintain the peace of Europe." The only thing that Bismarck rued, in Taylor's view, was the eminent end of his own mastery of Germany, not by any means the collapse of his diplomacy.

The following selection is from A. J. P. Taylor's stylish biography Bismarck, The Man and the Statesman.

[BISMARCK] KEPT CONTROL of Europe by the most elaborate diplomatic devices—dancing among eggs, one observer called it, juggling with five balls at once, said William I. Yet the basic principle of his diplomacy was clear and simple: maintenance of Austria-Hungry as a Great Power, but no support for her ambitions in the Balkans. . . .

. . . Bismarck had followed this policy steadily since 1879; only its execution became more elaborate and difficult. His most immediate problem was the Triple Alliance. It had been made in 1882 for five years and was due for renewal in May 1887. Originally it had served to bring Austria-Hungary and Italy under German control. Now a flamboyant renewal would seem to capture Germany for an Austro-Hungarian drive against Russia and an Italian drive against France. Bismarck hesitated; and his hesitation pushed England forward. Great Britain had refused to back either Austria-Hungary or Italy so long as Gladstone was in power—hence in part the original Triple Alliance. Now, with Salisbury at the foreign office, British policy returned, more or less, to the line of 1878.

In February 1887 Salisbury made a secret agreement with Italy to support the *status quo* in the Mediterranean, an agreement which Austria-Hungary soon joined. This first "Mediterranean agreement," as it came to be called, was a mere declaration of policy, not a binding alliance. But it was firm enough to lessen the dangers of the Triple Alliance for Bismarck. Henceforth, if Austria-Hungary or Italy appealed for his assistance, he could reply that they should invoke British aid first. He made no further difficulties in renewing the Triple Alliance. Indeed, by a separate treaty, he gave Italy more binding promises against France than before. Since he was now confident that French policy was peaceful, these promises involved little risk. As always, Bismarck made them so as not to have to carry them out.

Russia was a more difficult affair. The Russians had never liked the League of the Three Emperors and the friendship with Austria-Hungary that this implied. They wanted a straight promise of German neutrality, which would leave them free to attack Austria-Hungary or at any rate to threaten such an attack if she interfered with them in the Balkans. Bismarck had refused to give this promise in 1876 and during the crisis before the congress of Berlin. It was still more out of the question now that he was bound by the Austro-German alliance. Always frank when it suited him, he showed the text of this alliance to the Russian ambassador. But he offered mutual neutrality of a limited kind. Germany would remain neutral unless Russia attacked Austria-Hungary; Russia, to make things equal, would remain neutral unless Germany attacked France. This was the basis of the Reinsurance treaty, which Bismarck concluded with Russia on 18 June 1887. In theory Germany was still exposed to the risk of war on two fronts. . . . But war on two fronts was not the pressing danger in 1887. The danger which Bismarck feared was of a Balkan war between Russia and Austria-Hungry; and the Reinsurance treaty did something to lessen it. A secret protocol promised Germany's diplomatic aid to Russia in Bulgaria and at the Straits. Bismarck could not prevent Russia's going to war; but the temptation for her to do so was less if the tsar believed that he could get his way by diplomacy.

The Reinsurance treaty was Bismarck's last great stroke. It has often been described as dishonest and immoral. Dishonest against whom? Whom did it deceive? Bismarck had told the Austrians from the beginning that he would not support them in the Balkans; he had always told the British that, in his view, the *status quo* implied the closing of the Straits even against their fleet; and he had always told the Russians that he would not allow Austria-Hungary to be destroyed. The Reinsurance treaty did no more than repeat these statements. When two Powers or groups of Powers are contending, it always seems immoral to them that another Power should try to remain friendly with both sides. . . . Germany was in the middle of Europe. She had to keep in with both sides, unless indeed she took the lead one way or the other and became after a great war (if she won it) the dominating Power in Europe. This had perhaps appealed to Bismarck in his young revolutionary days at Frankfurt. Now he was elderly, resigned, without ambitions for the future—except to keep things as they were. His only object was to maintain the peace of Europe. Those who admire this call it operating the Balance of Power; those who do not, condemn it as dishonest jugglery.

This is not to say that Bismarck's diplomacy alone preserved peace. Like all successful diplomacy it contained a double bluff. He made the Austrians believe that he would not support them; he made the Russians fear that he would. . . . He managed to put over the bluff by the force of his personality. . . . All he claimed was that it made Alexander III feel more secure and therefore made it easier for him to resist his bellicose advisers. This is the most that diplomacy can ever do. It cannot prevent war; it can merely make peace more attractive.

So events worked out now. Most Russians were weary of the Near East and were only anxious to leave it alone if it would leave them alone. In the summer of 1887 the Bulgarians elected a new prince in defiance of Russia; and she did nothing. It was the sign that there would be no war in the Balkans. But men took some time to read it. The Russians were angry at their humiliation in Bulgaria, even though they would do nothing to remedy it; and on the other side the Austrians wanted to launch a preventive war against Russia in Galicia. Bismarck repeated his diplomacy of the spring in more elaborate form. He conjured up for the Austrians a tighter, more extensive "Mediterranean agreement" with Great Britain and Italy; and he explained frankly to Salisbury the principles of his policy. "We shall avoid a Russian war so long as that is compatible with our interest and security . . . but German policy will always be obliged to enter the struggle if the independence of Austria-Hungary is menaced by a Russian aggression." On the other hand, he brushed the Austrians off with a sharp rebuke when they tried to lure the German generals into staff-talks preparatory to a Russian war; and he did his best to keep on good terms with the Russians, even coming out of his retirement at Friedrichsruh to meet Alexander III at Berlin in November. The interview was not very successful. Aleaxnder III was sulky and resentful, using friendly phrases only to the French ambassador; and Bismarck talked to his intimates of a war against Russia for the resurrection of Poland—only to add that Russo-German friendship would be restored by a new partition of Poland afterwards.

This was a desperate remedy, and not much more than thinking aloud. His actual remedies were desperate enough. On 3 February 1888 he published the text of the Austro-German treaty without waiting for permission from Vienna. This is often described as a gesture against Russia. On the contrary it was a stroke against Austria-Hungary. The Russians had already learnt the terms of the alliance from Bismarck the previous year. Publishing them stressed the defensive nature of the treaty; it was a warning that German strength would not be used, as Bismarck put it, "for Hungarian or Catholic ambitions in the Balkans." He made one concession. He suppressed the final clause which limited the alliance to five years (though with automatic renewal), and thus unwillingly admitted its permanence. Three days later, on 6 February, he introduced a new army-law in the Reichstag, raising the age-limit of the reserve from 32 to 39 years, and spoke on foreign policy for the last time. Germany, he insisted, would defend her interests; she would not follow a policy of power or of prestige. Though she did not fear Russia, she would not be dragged by Austria-Hungary into a policy of Balkan adventure. Implicitly he repudiated the value of all alliances, and declared that Germany must rely on her own strength. "The pike in the European carp-pond prevent us from becoming carp." His last sentence rounded off a career that had begun with "blood and iron": "We Germans fear God and nothing else in the world." It was a strange peroration for a lifetime of apprehensions, where God had often seemed to be the only thing that Bismarck did not fear.

Less than a month later, on 3 March, he appeared at the tribune to announce the death of William I. Tears choked his voice. He wept not only for a beloved master whom he had always claimed to serve though rarely obeyed. He wept still more for the end of his own mastery in Germany.

Suggestions for Further Reading

BISMARCK PROVOKED STRONG REACTIONS, both in his own lifetime and in the critical works on the man and his policies since that time. And those works, even the best of them, tend to divide along the lines represented by the selections from Fuller and Taylor presented in this chapter. The stronger tradition is that hostile to Bismarck, and its classic formulation in modern scholarship is Joseph Vincent Fuller, *Bismarck's Diplomacy at Its Zenith* (New York: H. Fertig, 1967 [1922]), excerpted for this chapter. Fuller's views are shared even by the greatest German authority on Bismarck, whose massive three-volume biography has been scaled down in a one-volume English abridgement: Erich Eyck, *Bismarck and the German Empire* (New York: Macmillan, 1950). This is also the case with the work of Werner Richter, *Bismarck*, tr. Brian Battershaw (New York: Putnam, 1964), a revisionist book directed against the revival of the old patriotic German myth of Bismarck. Gordon A. Craig, *From Bismarck to Adenauer: Aspects of German Statecraft* (Baltimore: Johns Hopkins University Press, 1958), is in the best tradition of historical revision and attempts to present a somewhat more balanced—and favorable—view of Bismarck in this attractive, well-written, and reflective book. Another extremely interesting work—while not on Bismarck himself—tends to exculpate him from many of the charges leveled against him. It is the last work of the great German historian Friedrich Meinecke, *The German Catastrophe: Reflections and Recollections*, tr. Sidney B. Fay (Boston: Beacon, 1964, originally appearing in German in 1946 and an attempt to appraise the events of World War II in historical perspective. The most moderate and even-handed account of Bismarck is probably William N. Medlicott, *Bismarck and Modern Germany*, "Teach Yourself History Library" (London: English Universities Press, 1965), along with Eyck's book the two best brief biographies of him. Louis L. Snyder, *The Blood and Iron Chancellor, A Documentary-Biography of Otto von Bismarck* (Princeton, N.J.: Van Nostrand, 1967), is useful in providing a wide sampling of readings on Bismarck from both sources and secondary works. See also *Otto von Bismarck: A Historical Assessment*, ed. Theodore S. Hamerow, rev. ed. (New York: Harper & Row, 1973). A recent biography, Edward Crankshaw, *Bismarck* (New York: Viking, 1981), is useful for background, stressing the earlier formation of Bismarck's policies.

Bismarck's imperial diplomacy is one of the key subjects of modern European diplomatic history and is therefore treated in any general work on that broad and prolific topic. One of the standard works is William L. Langer, *European Alliances and Alignments, 1871–1890*, 2nd rev. ed. (New York: Knopf, 1950). While somewhat harsher and more anti-German in tone, the brilliant and stylish A. J. P. Taylor, *The Struggle for Mastery in Europe, 1848–1914* (Oxford, England: Clarendon Press, 1954), is the best work since Langer. Of the same sort is the massive, authoritative work of E. Malcolm Carroll, *Germany and the Great Powers, 1866–1914* (New York: Archon Books, 1966 [1938]), and the newer and equally authoritative Gordon A. Craig, *Germany 1866–1945* (New York: Oxford University Press, 1978). Of the broader and more general surveys, Norman Rich, *The Age of Nationalism and Reform, 1850–1890* (New York: Norton, 1970), is a good synthesis, as is the more far-ranging classic Carlton J. H. Hayes, *A Generation of Materialism, 1871–1900*, "Rise of Modern Europe" series (New York: Harper, 1941). Barbara Tuchman, *The Proud Tower, A Portrait of the World Before the War, 1890–1914* (New York: Macmillan, 1962), is a well-regarded, readable popular history. Among a host of more recent reappraisals, the best is probably Norman Stone, *Europe Transformed, 1878–1919* (Cambridge: Harvard University Press, 1984). Two final works on German history are also recommended: Hajo Holborn, *A History of Modern Germany*, vol. 3, 1840–1945 (New York: Knopf, 1969), broad-gauge and reflective and likely to become a standard work on German history; and A. J. P. Taylor, *The Course of German History: A Survey of the Development of Germany Since 1815* (New York: Coward-McCann, 1946), a highly personal interpretive sketch, full of harsh, decisive judgments and interesting to compare with the reflections of Friedrich Meinecke.

Two books can be recommended dealing with the social and economic history of the late nineteenth century. Theodore S. Hamerow, *The Birth of a New Europe: State and Society in the Nineteenth Century* (Chapel Hill: University of North Carolina Press, 1983) is a massive and definitive work on the impact of the industrial revolution on the nature of European society. Arno J. Mayer, *The Persistence of the Old Regime, Europe to the Great War* (New York: Pantheon, 1981) develops the thesis that the entrenched aristocracies and their traditional interests dominated the late nineteenth-century world and finally dragged it into war. But, like many thesis books, this one sometimes overstates its case.

The Granger Collection

Cecil Rhodes and the Dream of Empire

1853	born
1870	first came to South Africa
1888	formation of DeBeers Mining Company
1890	Prime Minister of Cape Colony
1894	establishment of Rhodesia
1895	Jameson's Raid
1899–1902	Boer War
1902	died

If the history of Europe in the second half of the nineteenth century was dominated by Bismarck's German Empire, that of the rest of the world was dominated by the imperial England of Queen Victoria. For in that half century the British Empire reached its greatest extent, and England became the model colonial power of the modern world.

The process had begun centuries before, with the expansion of Europe at the end of the Middle Ages, with the age of exploration and the creation of the first great colonial empires of Portugal and Spain. They were followed by the Dutch, the French, and the British. Colonial rivalries became issues between the major European powers in the seventeenth and eighteenth centuries. But with the coming of the Industrial Revolution, the nature of colonialism was dramatically altered, along with nearly everything else in the modern world.

Interest in underdeveloped areas had formerly been largely commercial and mercantile; it now became exploitative. The Western industrial nations needed raw materials for their factories—rubber, petroleum, copra, hemp, jute, cotton, lumber, copper. European populations demanded vast quantities of meat and grain and such products as coffee, tea, and tobacco. At the same time, the underdeveloped countries of the world represented a new market for industrial goods—for many of which the need itself had to be fabricated as well as the goods.

The industrialized nations turned not only to the colonies they already had but to the entire area now popularly called the Third World. They invested enormous amounts of capital, which was to be protected by their military forces. Colonial policy became an extension of national economic policy. When necessary, both political and economic interests manipulated native political naïveté and exploited native labor, usually with the greedy collusion of native political leaders. Colonialism and all its practices were justified as bringing the blessings of civilization to the less fortunate peoples of the world. By most civilized people this was regarded not only as an opportunity but an obligation, to "take up the white man's burden." Part of that burden was, of course, the responsibility of bringing God's word to the remote places and heathen populations now beginning to become known. Throngs of missionaries went out to establish schools, hospitals, and churches. They were often spectacularly successful. But they were sometimes killed, and when this happened, their martyrdom became the provocation for further extension of colonial control. Even the ideas of Darwin were converted into a social gospel and used to justify the supremacy of the Western industrial nations over the poor, the uneducated, the "less favored" and usually nonwhite peoples of the world.

As Great Britain was the leading industrial power of modern Europe, it was also the leading colonial power. But even imperial Britain was not without rivals in the competition for colonies and spheres of colonial influence—in China, the East Indies, and Southeast Asia, in the Middle East, in Persia, in the lands of the rotting Ottoman Empire, and along the borders of British India. But it was in Africa that the most savage scramble for colonies took place. Even Bismarck's Germany belatedly entered the race.

This was the scene upon which Cecil John Rhodes came in 1870. He was only seventeen years old, the son of a poor Hertfordshire parson. He had been diagnosed as suffering from incipient tuberculosis and, for his health, had decided to join his older brother in South Africa. Shortly after Rhodes' arrival there, the great Kimberley diamond strike was made. Rhodes made his first fortune in this enterprise, and multiplied it many times over by his business acumen. He consolidated existing claims, refinanced bankrupt operations, bought others, and opened new ones. By 1887 his holdings were second only to those of the main Kimberley mine, held by a rough-and-ready diamond merchant and financial genius named Barnett "Barney" Barnato. With backing from the Rothschild Bank, Rhodes bought out his larger rival the following year for more than five million pounds. Thus, he secured absolute control of South African diamond production for his De Beers Consolidated Mines Ltd., the name retained from a former company he had taken over. At the same time, he was deeply involved in gold and had formed the powerful Gold Fields of South Africa Company.

At intervals between making fortunes and between bouts of recurring illness, Rhodes had managed to return to England for several periods of residency at Oxford, where he was graduated in 1881. In that same year, he stood successfully for the Cape Parliament, and his political career began. Politics to Rhodes was simply business by other means, and he was equally successful at it. He quickly became a dominant figure in South African public life. But Rhodes was a British imperialist to the bone. And as he looked to the north, he envisioned British dominion from Cape Colony not only across the Zambezi River to the great lakes of central Africa but to the Sudan and eventually Cairo—to "paint the map of Africa red," as he put it.

Immediately to the north of Cape Colony lay a vast land controlled by native chieftains. The most important of them was Lobengula, King of the Matabele. Rhodes negotiated with him, at the same time hoping to persuade either the Cape government or the British to support his negotiation. Neither was prepared. So Rhodes formed another company, the British South Africa Company, secured a charter for it, and carried through his own negotiations. As a result, he gained virtually sovereign control over the area that would become modern Rhodesia.

Rhodes' further plans were blocked by the opposition of the Boers. The word "boer" means farmer, and the Boer language is an old dialect of Dutch. For the Boers had been Dutch colonists, largely farmers and religious refugees, who had settled in South Africa in the seventeenth century. When the English took control of the Cape following the Napoleonic wars, the Boers had made their "great trek," an epic journey almost a thousand miles to the north. There, they settled in two small republics, the Transvaal and the Orange Free State. They continued to farm, to practice their religion, and to live by a stern, archaic moral code. Their chief representative was Paul Kruger, Prime Minister of the Transvaal. Kruger became Rhodes' most implacable enemy. He disliked Rhodes' plans for British imperial expansion—after all, it was precisely because of such a threat the Boers had fled from the Cape. He distrusted Rhodes' proposal for federation with the other South African states, suspecting that it was no more than a ploy—which it was not. And more generally, like most Boers, Kruger did not care for foreigners—"uitlanders"—financiers and mining speculators. Indeed, the Transvaal government did everything to discourage such people, including high duties on goods crossing its frontiers and ruinous rail tariffs. The situation reached crisis proportions in 1895 after the discovery of further gold and diamond deposits in the Transvaal "on the Rand." Kruger still refused to consider joining a South African federation, stepped up economic resistance, and even sought support from the German imperial government.

Since 1890, Rhodes had been Prime Minister of Cape Colony. He now entered into a conspiracy to overthrow the Kruger government in the Transvaal. He organized a raiding party under the command of a friend, Dr. J. S. Jameson. The Jameson Raid was a military fiasco, and Rhodes' complicity in it was revealed. Such behavior by a head of state was intolerable both for the Cape Colony government and the British. Rhodes was stripped of his office and his seat in Parliament and censured by the British House of Commons, whose inquiry into the matter stopped just short of implicating high officials in the British Colonial Office. Rhodes would never totally recover his influence in South Africa, and the Jameson Raid would become a key incident leading to the Boer War. Rhodes himself died in 1902, not yet fifty years old.

Cecil Rhodes was the most obvious example of nineteenth-century British colonialism. He exemplified all its economic rapacity and political ambition, its chauvinism and its paternalism, its racism and bigotry. He also exemplified the untrammeled gospel of wealth. In a time of robber barons on a worldwide scale—Cornelius Vanderbilt, J. P. Morgan, Andrew Carnegie, John D. Rockefeller, Baron Krupp, and Lord Rothschild—Rhodes was the greatest both in resources and in vision. There was nothing, he thought, that could not be bought, no one who could not be bribed. He used his wealth to gain political ends and political power to further his fortune. And he dreamed dreams of empire that others might applaud or condemn but, for their scope and daring, few could match.

Contemporary Recollections

SIDNEY LOW

While Cecil Rhodes was a doer and a talker of imperial proportions, he was no writer or formal speechmaker. Thus his ideas are not readily found in his own writings. He kept no journal, his letters are of the most routine sort, and he did not live long enough to indulge in the fancy of a memoir—which he would probably have disdained anyhow. But his views were far from unknown. He would and did talk with anybody, often to the disadvantage of his image, his reputation, even his business enterprises. The following excerpt is thus not from Rhodes himself but from the recollections of an exceptionally able journalist, Sidney Low, who knew him well, who interviewed him many times, and who can report the man and his views better, in this instance, than the man himself. The following piece was written on the occasion of Rhodes' death in 1902 for the British popular magazine The Nineteenth Century and After.

MY FIRST INTERVIEW with Rhodes dates back nearly ten years. It occurred on the 10th of December 1892. Up to that time the managing director of the Chartered Company had been to me a vague, and not altogether a sympathetic, figure. I had followed South African affairs with some attention, and I was far from enthusiastic over the methods and constitution of Mr. Rhodes's Company. I recognised the importance of keeping open the road from Cape Colony to the north, and was prepared to admit that the countries of the Matabele and the Mashona should be placed within the British sphere of influence, if only to exclude the possibility of foreign interference. But I held that if the work of conquest or annexation were worth doing, it should be done directly, with a full assumption of responsibility, by the Imperial Government itself. The delegation of the duty to a body of private adventurers, aiming primarily at their own profit, seemed to me a doubtful expedient; and the Chartered Company, with its mixture of high politics and Stock Exchange speculation, I regarded with some distrust. What I could gather of the financial arrangements of the concern did not increase my confidence. . . .

I happened, shortly before the date mentioned, to meet a person much interested in the Chartered enterprise, who attempted, not very successfully, to convert me to a more favourable opinion of the project. He urged me to see Rhodes, and arranged a meeting. At the appointed time I presented myself at the Burlington Hotel. My credentials were duly passed by some members of the little court of secretaries and retainers, whom Rhodes always had about him. He was simple enough in his personal habits, but there was something regal in his dependence upon his suite. He required his trusted favourites and henchmen to be constantly at hand, and he could scarcely write a letter without the assistance of one or other member of his private Cabinet. Eventually I found myself at the end of a large room, in front of a large man, standing before a large fire. Size was the first external impression you received of Cecil Rhodes. In whatever company you met him he seemed the biggest man present. Yet, though tall and broadly built, his stature was not really phenomenal; but there was something in the leonine head, and the massive, loose pose, which raised him to heroic proportions. He received me with a cordial smile and an invitation to sit down in one of the two comfortable arm-chairs, which flanked the fireplace. After a question or two to break the ice, he began to talk, and he went on for an hour almost without intermission. Sometimes I put in a word or two to open the points, and switch him from one track to another; but in the main it was a monologue by Rhodes, or perhaps I should say a lecture on the future of South Africa. As he sat up in his crumpled tweed suit, with his left foot twisted round his right ankle, I lay back in my arm-chair and listened, amazed and fascinated, while the rapid sentences poured out of the broad chest in curiously high notes, that occasionally rose almost to a falsetto. Rhodes's voice was peculiar. It was uneven and apparently under no control. Sometimes it would descend abruptly, but as a rule when he was moved it reached the upper part of the register in odd, jerky transitions. But if it had been full of music and resonance it could have had no more effect upon the listener. I never heard Rhodes make a speech in public, and I am told he was no orator. But a talker he was, of more compelling potency than almost anyone it had been my lot to hear. Readiness, quickness, an amazing argumentative plausibility, were his: illustrations and suggestions were touched off with a rough happy humour of phrase and metaphor: he countered difficulties with a Johnsonian ingenuity: and if you sometimes thought you had planted a solid shot into his defences, he turned and overwhelmed you with a sweeping Maxim-fire of generalisation. Yet in all the intellectual accomplishments of conversation and debate he was inferior to many men one has known. Wittier talkers, more brilliant, far better read, infinitely closer and more logical in argument, it would be easy to name. But these men produced no such impression as Rhodes. It was the personality behind the voice that drove home the words—the restless vivid soul, that set the big body fidgeting in nervous movements, the imaginative mysticism, the absorbing egotism of the man with great ideas, and the unconscious dramatic instinct, that appealed to the sympathies of the hearer. One must add a smile of singular and most persuasive charm. It would break over the stern brickdust-coloured face like the sun on a granite hill, and gave to the large features and the great grey eyes a feminine sweetness that was irresistible. . . .

I came away from my first interview with Rhodes rather fascinated than convinced. It was the character more than the mind one admired. Then, and subsequently, it seemed to me that Rhodes's weakness was on the intellectual side. He was not a clear reckoner or a close thinker, but rather —so he himself admitted—a dreamer of dreams, vague, mighty, somewhat impalpable. Nor did it seem to me that he was an originator of ideas, but one who took up the conceptions of others, expanded them, dwelt upon them, advertised them to the world in his grandiloquent fashion, made them his own. Of late years he has been taken as the typical Imperialist. But in 1892 he seemed to me not an Imperialist at all, in the sense in which we then understood the term. He had risen to power at the Cape, it must be remembered, as the opponent of direct Imperial rule, and of all that was known as "Downing Street." His alliance with the Afrikander Bond was based on joint antipathy against the Colonial Office. When he talked of eliminating the Imperial factor he may have used a casual phrase, with no very precise meaning; but in fact that was what he wanted, though of course he did not mean to eliminate the British flag as well. His ideal was South Africa for the Afrikanders *utriusque juris*. Colonists of both races were to be worked together and federated to form an Afrikander nation, just as the Australians have formed an Australian, and the people of the Dominion a Canadian, nation. To some of us in 1892 the notion of bringing about this result by means of the Dutch, whose hostility to England and the English was well known, seemed dangerous. I asked Mr. Rhodes if the end would not be a secession and the conversion of the Federation to an independent Republic. "Are you going to be the Bismarck or the Washington of South Africa?" I said. Rhodes had his full share of vanity, and was delighted at being linked with these great names; but he hesitated, in order to ponder the question, and then replied with much seriousness, "Oh, Bismarck for choice of course." I suggested that his alliance with the Dutch Nationalists might really involve a danger of separation. He denied it emphatically. He said that he had joined Mr. Hofmeyr, in order to bring the Dutch into Cape constitutional politics and to prepare the way for a United South Africa, able to manage its own affairs, which it had a perfect right to do. "You people at home," he said, "don't understand us." But he laughed at the notion of secession, and he declared that neither Hofmeyr nor any other Dutchman would really want to get rid of English supremacy. "We must have the British Navy behind us," he said, "to keep away foreigners. We all know that." . . .

. . . Rhodes sometimes spoke of England and the English with that kind of irritation which many energetic colonists and Americans feel for this comfortable old country, with its innate conservatism, its arrogant belief in itself, its indifference to new ideas, and its absorption in controversies which, to the pushing new man from beyond the seas, seem time-worn and threadbare. Mr. Kipling's line "What do they know of England who only England know?" had not been written at the date of my first meeting with

Rhodes; but the sentiment it conveyed was shared by him to the full. He thought of the British Isles as a few crowded specks of European territory, whose swarming millions should be given room for expansion in the vacant lands of the ampler continents. He was possessed—I had almost said obsessed—by the fear that if we neglected our chances, they would be taken from us by others, and the English people would be throttled for lack of breathing-space. This work seemed to him of such paramount importance that everything else in politics sank into insignificance beside it. He believed sincerely that the service he had rendered the nation by securing Rhodesia as a field for British colonisation could hardly be over-estimated, and he was astonished that the public took the gigantic benefaction so calmly. . . .

. . . The domestic affairs of some forty millions of people seemed to him hardly worth considering when any question of territorial or colonial expansion was in the balance. Lord Salisbury once recommended the use of "large maps" as a corrective to groundless political alarms. Rhodes was fond of large maps too, but they had a different effect upon him. He would gaze upon the great polygon between the Transvaal and the Zambesi which he had coloured red, and expatiate upon the vastness of the country; then he would run his finger northward, and explain how Africa was to be linked up and thrown open by his Cape-to-Cairo telegraph and railway. It was in my first conversation with him that I heard Rhodes mention this project, which was a novel one to me. I hinted some doubts—whether anyone would want to use the through route, whether the native chiefs and slave traders would not interfere with the poles and wires. Rhodes took up the latter point with one of his touches of cynical humour: "The slavers! Why, before my telegraph had been running six months they would be using it to send through their consignment of slaves." Something was said about the Khalifa,[1] and the obvious difficulty of constructing a railway through the Equatorial Provinces, then in the hands of fanatical barbarians. "You ask me," said Rhodes, in words which, I believe, he afterwards repeated in public, "how I am going to get the railway through the Soudan; well, I don't know. But I tell you, when the time comes we shall deal with the Mahdi[2] in one way or another. If you mean to tell me that one man can permanently check an enterprise like this, I say to you it is not possible." This was very characteristic of Rhodes in two ways. He had a profound belief in destiny and in the power of world-movements to fulfil their ends. And he had also a conviction that almost any man could be "dealt with," if you knew the right way to go to work with him. It was based, I suppose, on his own experience, for he had been singularly successful in manip-

[1] The Caliph, spiritual head of Islam, who was also the Ottoman Sultan, was deeply involved in the colonial scramble in Africa in the late nineteenth century.—Ed.

[2] A fanatic Moslem religious and political leader in the Sudan. His followers besieged Khartoum in 1885 and took the city with great bloodshed. Among the casualties was the British General Charles George "Chinese" Gordon. See also p. 148.—Ed.

ulating and moulding men to his own purposes. From the keen-eyed speculators in Kimberley to the suspicious savages in the Matoppo caves, there were few with whom he had failed to come to terms when he desired to make them his instruments or allies. Partly I am sure that this was due to the mere personal influence, the "magnetism," to which I have already referred. But Rhodes was always a believer in the arts of bargain and management. He held that most people have their price, though the currency is not always notes or cheques or shares. By appealing to a person's vanity, his patriotism, his ideals, or his cupidity, you can generally contrive to get him to do what you want. It was part of the piquancy of Rhodes's character that he mingled the practical shrewdness of the diamond mart and the gambling table wtih his prophetic visions and imaginative enthusiasms. . . .

Whatever inconsistency there may have been in his actions, his opinions, so far as I could perceive, did not vary. In fact, he repeated himself a good deal, having a kind of apostolic fervour in expatiating on the broad simple tenets of the Rhodesian religion. His cardinal doctrines I should say were these: First, that insular England was quite insufficient to maintain, or even to protect, itself without the assistance of the Anglo-Saxon peoples beyond the seas of Europe. Secondly, that the first and greatest aim of British statesmanship should be to find new areas of settlement, and new markets for the products that would, in due course, be penalised in the territories and dependencies of all our rivals by discriminating tariffs. Thirdly, that the largest tracts of unoccupied or undeveloped lands remaining on the globe were in Africa, and therefore that the most strenuous efforts should be made to keep open a great part of that continent to British commerce and colonisation. Fourthly, that as the key to the African position lay in the various Anglo-Dutch States and provinces, it was imperative to convert the whole region into a united, self-governing, federation, exempt from meddlesome interference by the home authorities, but loyal to the Empire, and welcoming British enterprise and progress. Fifthly, that the world was made for the service of man, and more particularly of civilised, white, European men, who were most capable of utilising the crude resources of nature for the promotion of wealth and prosperity. And, finally, that the British Constitution was an absurd anachronism, and that it should be remodelled on the lines of the American Union, with federal self-governing Colonies as the constituent States. . . .

. . . He had a reverence such as is more common now among Americans than Englishmen, for enterprise on an extensive scale. Man in his view was clearly an active animal. He was made to do "big" things, and to do them in a modern, scientific, progressive manner. With the obstructionist, who clogged the wheels of the machine, whether from indolence, ignorance, or an exaggerated regard for the past, he had no patience. Some months before the opening of the South African War I was dining with him and a number of his friends, who were mostly interested in one way or other in Rhodesian or Transvaal affairs. The conversation turned on the condition of Johannesburg, the grievances of the Uitlanders, and the possible attitude of Great Britain. "If I were in the position of the British Government," said Rhodes, "I should say to old Kruger, 'Mr. Kruger, you are interfering with business, and you will have to get out of the way.' " The little speech was characteristic; so, by the way, was the pronunciation of the ex-President's name. Rhodes, as I have said, had no mastery of detail. In his thirty years in South Africa he had not learned how Dutch words should be spoken. He called his ancient enemy "old Krooger," like the man in the street.

My most interesting talk with Rhodes occurred in the early days of February 1896, after the shattering collapse of Jameson's failure, when the deeply compromised Cape Premier hastened to England to "face the music." I was anxious to see him. Knowing that he was an early riser, I thought I should have the best chance of catching him disengaged if I went before most other callers were out of bed. So on the second morning after his arrival, at about eight o'clock, I sent in my name at the Burlington Hotel. My access to Rhodes on this occasion, when few but intimate friends were allowed to approach him, was facilitated by the fact that he had been reading some articles of mine on the events of the preceding month. I was no apologist for the Raid, nor have I ever been able to regard Rhodes's participation in the plot against the Transvaal Republic as anything but an unpardonable breach of trust and a monstrous abuse of the exceptional powers and privileges which had been conferred upon him. But if I did not excuse his conduct, I thought it was possible to explain it; and, as it happened, my explanations were very much on the lines of those which he himself would have framed. On this morning—the 6th of February 1896—I was taken up to Rhodes in his bedroom. He had risen, but was not quite dressed, and as he talked he walked feverishly up and down the room, awkwardly completing his toilet. He had been dining out the evening before; the dress clothes he had worn were scattered in disorder about the room; the large, rather bare, hotel apartment seemed strangely cold and friendless in the chilly light of the grim London morning; and the big man, with the thatch of grey-brown hair, who paced up and down in his shirt-sleeves, was a pathetic, almost a desolate figure. He was much changed by these few bitter weeks of suspense and suffering. Through the ruddy bronze of the sea wind and the veldt breezes his cheeks showed grey and livid; he looked old and worn. He asked me to sit down while he finished dressing; and presently he began to talk about the Raid and the conspiracy. I had felt some diffidence in approaching the subject; but he was full of it—too full to keep silence. He was, as I have said, always candid; but on this occasion, considering the circumstances in which he stood and my own comparatively slight acquaintance with him, I was amazed at his freedom. I thought, indeed, that he was saying too much, and more than once I tried to check him and rose to go; but he evidently wanted to talk—I suppose to ease his mind after a sleepless night—and he begged me to remain till he had finished his story. . . .

. . . From his very candid exposition of his own motives and expectations, I derived a strong, and, I think, perfectly correct impression that Rhodes's intervention in the Johannesburg conspiracy was due quite as much to fear of the Uitlanders as to animosity against Mr. Kruger. Rhodes disliked the reactionary Dutch oligarchy at Pretoria; but he also rather despised it, and believed that it was bound to fall before long by its inherent weakness, which he greatly over-estimated. He was, however, possessed by a genuine apprehension that it might be succeeded by a Republican Government which might be anti-Imperialist and perhaps anti-British. He knew that among the leading reformers at Johannesburg there were Americans, many Australians and Cape Afrikanders, some Germans and other foreigners. They objected to the Krugerite *régime,* which dipped into their pockets and shackled their enterprise; but they had no liking for Downing Street and many of them had even a very qualified affection for the Union Jack. Rhodes put it somewhat in this way:

> I knew that in five years there would be 250,000 white settlers on the Rand. In ten years there might be half a million or more. Now, that large European population, with its enormous wealth and industry, would inevitably become the political centre of all South Africa. If we left things alone, the Uitlanders were certain, sooner or later, to turn out Kruger and his lot, to get possession of the Transvaal administration, and to make the Republic a modern, financial, progressive State, which would draw all South Africa after it. But they would have done it entirely by their own efforts. They would owe no gratitude to England, and, indeed, they might feel a grudge against the Home Government for having left them in the lurch so long. They would take very good care to retain their independence and their flag, with perhaps a leaning towards some foreign power, and all the Afrikander world would gradually recognise their leadership. So that, in the end, instead of a British Federal Dominion, you would get a United States of South Africa, with its capital on the Rand, and very likely it would be ruled by a party that would be entirely opposed to the English connection. In fact, you would lose South Africa, and lose it by the efforts of the English-speaking minority in the Transvaal, who are at present anti-British as well as anti-Kruger. I saw that if left to itself this section would become predominant when the Dutch oligarchy was expelled. That was why I went into the movement. I joined with the wealthy men who were ready to give their money to overthrow Kruger, so that we might be able to turn the revolution in the right direction at the right time. You may say, 'Rhodes should have left it alone; it was no business of his.' Yes; and if I had done so, there was the certainty that the revolution would have been attempted—perhaps not just now, but in two years, three years, or five years—all the same; that it would have succeeded; and then the money of the capitalists, the influence of the leading men in Johannesburg, would have been used in favour of this new and more powerful Republican Govern-

ment, which would have drifted away from the Empire and drawn all South Africa—English as well as Dutch—after it.

I had much more talk with Rhodes on the subject, both on this day and subsequently. But the passage I have reproduced, as nearly as possible in his own words, has always seemed to me the gist of Rhodes's whole defence of his action in 1895.

A South African View of Rhodes

STUART CLOETE

The opinions about Rhodes available in South Africa are, of course, as varied as the political extremes of that troubled region. Most white Rhodesians regard him not only as the founder of their country but as the patron of their way of life. Even the descendants of the South African Boers share many of his views, in particular his racial views. Most black South African intellectuals regard him as the fountainhead of their own present discontent. Stuart Cloete is a native-born white South African who, in a string of highly successful novels, has essayed the hard task of espousing a middle course on the many questions faced by South Africa today. He is a moderate in a land increasingly dominated by extremists. In his assessment of Rhodes he is as moderate as in his other writings, recognizing at once the blight that Rhodes and his sort laid upon South Africa but still able to see the person behind the symbol. The following selection is from his Against These Three: A Biography of Paul Kruger, Cecil Rhodes, and Lobengula: Last King of the Matabele.

RHODES WAS A MAN who parodied his own virtues, whose whole life was a paradox of Machiavellian simplicity. An expatriate who devoted his life to the aggrandizement of the country he had left, and all but ruined the Africa he loved. Hero to some. Murderer to others. The godless man whom men worshipped almost as a god. The Colossus with lungs of clay. The great cynic, the great idealist. The financier who was always in debt. The imperialist who shares with Simón Bolívar the liberator the honor of having a great country named after him. The man who chose a mountain for a tomb. The only white man who ever received the Zulu royal salute of "Bayete" from the very people he had destroyed; and who, exposing another facet of his character, left uncompleted the greatest deal of his life to go to the deathbed of a friend. The maker of a million settlers' homes who had none, in the real sense, of his own. The uncrowned king of half a continent. The man, to whom hundreds of women offered themselves in concubinage or as wives, who never touched a woman. The student of history who forgot men were not bloodless pawns. . . .

He was not a man who lived by rote or thought in terms of precedent. His idea was to force on a reluctant Africa a federation resembling the American federation of states. But he went beyond this. He wanted to get America back and said—"Even from an American point of view, just picture what they have lost." At another time he wrote to Stead, "Fancy the charm to young America to share in a scheme to take the government of the world."

This was Rhodes's master plan—the orderly government of the world by a superstate. The limited plan he came near to achieving was the African federation.

The race for Africa was now really on. The preliminary canter was over. The Belgians were in the Congo—led by Stanley, the explorer; the French were in the Congo—led by another explorer, de Branza. Germans were everywhere hunting, prospecting as engineers for gold, as missionaries for souls. The silences of the great rivers were broken by the shots of the hunters and the hymns of the ministers. Soon they were to echo under the crack of the kiboko and the cries of natives being thrashed for failing to produce their quota of rubber. Portugal was claiming more rights. Germany had established her colonies. France was creeping down the Niger. England must make her way up from the Limpopo and join the Cape to Egypt. Is it wonderful, therefore, that the Boers were afraid? That they sought protection, that they wanted an outlet of their own to the sea? That they, who to live, needed farms so large that they could live by the increase of their herds alone, felt themselves hemmed in? Above all they hated and feared England, and England guided by Rhodes was on the march. "I look upon this territory of Bechuanaland as the Suez Canal of the trade of this country," Rhodes said, ". . . the key of its road to the interior. Some honorable members," he went on, "may say this is immorality. The lands they may say belong to the chief, Mankoroane. . . . Now I have not these scruples. I believe the natives are bound gradually to come under the control of Europeans. . . ." Here Rhodes paraphrased Darwin. He knew what he had to do. He felt conquest his duty—not merely to England, but to the world. . . .

Rhodes always looked older than he was, thirty when he was twenty; forty when he was thirty. He is described as thick and heavy—square, with big hands, a double chin, a sensual mouth, and a high falsetto voice. Bismarck, the maker of Germany and competitor for Africa, another big man, had a similar voice.

Rhodes, the so-called solitary—this is part of the fiction that has been built up about him—hated even to have a meal by himself. He loved to surround himself by friends and if friends were not available enemies would do. He had to talk, he had to have an audience. And often, when he had done talking, his enemies became his friends. He hated loafers and, like many childless men, had definite ideas about education. A good education he felt was essential. "Then kick all the props away. If they are worth anything the struggle will make them better men; if they are not, the sooner they go under the better for the world." Here we get the theory of the survival of the fittest introduced into family life. . . . He investigated God factually and gave God his chance—a fifty per cent chance. He decided that Charles Darwin was the best interpreter of God's work, which in terms of fact appeared to be that "dog eats dog": the bigger dog destroying the lesser. It remained merely for man to follow this lead and God's will was done. [See p. 104.]

God's finest product, according to Rhodes, was the Englishman. Here was the one race which had true ideals of justice, peace, and liberty without any suggestion of equality. . . .

Rhodes's attitude to the natives varied with the political wind. At one time he said—this was when he wanted the natives on his side—"I do not believe they are different from ourselves." But he also said on other occasions, "The natives are children." On the native question at least Rhodes and the Boers had no quarrel. It was their one and lowest common denominator. Rhodes said, "I am no negrophilist"—a superfluous assertion, since he threw so much emphasis on pigmentation. All that was Nordic blond was good to him—in which conclusion he agreed perfectly with the thoughts of Nietzsche, whom he had never seen.

He has been described as overbearing and ruthless. And he was. But he was also reasonable and conciliatory, colloquial; and explanatory when it was worth his while. He was for a time—and not a short time either—successful in being all things to all men. Whether he fooled them or fooled himself, or whether he thought circumstance itself would come to his aid, it seems impossible to determine. He did not believe with Kruger that "alles sal regt kom"—that all would come right; but appears to have thought that he could make things come right if he had control.

Rhodes's charm was undeniable. Barnato said, "You can't resist him." Hofmeyr said, "We had a talk and were friends ever afterwards." The Matabele whom he destroyed said, "You have come again and now all things are clear, we are your children." General Gordon said, "Stay and work with me." Then he asked him to come and help "smash the Mahdi." Rhodes's reply was typical. He would not fight the Mahdi, "but deal with him." To "deal" or to "square" were pleasant euphemisms for bribing: a simpler and a cheaper method of settling difficulties than war. Rhodes is even supposed to have said to Parnell, when he said owing to his divorce, the priests were against him, "Can't you square the Pope?" Nothing daunted Rhodes. After getting Barney Barnato into the Kimberley Club, "to make a gentleman of him" and bring him onto his side of the diamond fence, Barney said, "But your crowd will never leave me in. They will turn me out in a year or two."

"Then we'll make you a life governor," was Rhodes's answer.

This final act of amalgamation took place in Doctor Jameson's cottage. Rhodes and Biet were on one side. On the other were Woolf Joel and Barnato. The stakes were for millions and none of the men concerned was yet thirty-six years old. The argument went on till dawn, Rhodes talking, Rhodes exhorting, cajoling, threatening. Rhodes's high voice stringing out long estimates of costs and profits. Rhodes getting up and sitting down. The room was filled with smoke. The men were drinking as they talked. Someone would lean forward to adjust the light of the lamp, turning the wick up or down. "If you have an idea and it's a good idea, if you will only stick to it, you will come out all right," was Rhodes's argument, and the amalgamation of the diamond fields and consolidation of diamond interests was a good idea. And then, as the sky began to pale, Rhodes threw in his final argument: he promised Barney Barnato a seat in Parliament. That finished it. Barney gave in. Life governor of the Kimberley Club and the right to put the magic letters M.P. after his name.

Ambition. Rhodes's was endless. He even wanted the stars, he said. "These stars that you see overhead at night, these vast worlds which we can never reach. I would annex the planets if I could. I often think of that. It makes me sad to see them so clear and so far away." This takes us back to the story of the old Boer who said there were no minerals in the moon because if there were the British would have taken possession of it long ago.

But what chance had men like Lobengula, and the others who were against him, with Rhodes? The man who wanted the stars, whose thoughts were so big that men were less than ants. Perhaps he saw them as ants toiling to make the world red for England. . . . Rhodes's sense was of the future, always the future; the present meant little to him. Today was no more to Rhodes than the rung which he must climb to attain tomorrow.

An example of Rhodes's sense of timing is given by Fitzpatrick when he describes his negotiations for the sale of a parcel of diamonds worth half a million sterling. What he wanted was a cash offer for the whole lot made on behalf of all the buyers present. They could agree among themselves afterwards as to the proportions they would take, and how the payment should be made, but he alone, acting for the de Beers shareholders, would decide whether the offer they made was adequate or not. The diamonds were laid out on sheets of paper exactly fitting a teak trough twelve inches wide. The sheets overlapped each other like the tiles of a roof and the diamonds on each sheet were carefully sorted and graded by the de Beers experts—the work, perhaps, in a parcel of this size, of several months. The diamonds in each little heap were identical.

The first offer made was not enough and Rhodes said so. He said, "I know the value as well as you do," and, turning to Brink, said, "That's not good enough."

A few minutes later, the buyers agreed to a much higher price which Rhodes accepted.

At this time the diamond market "was in a very nervous condition and it was realized that the sale, releasing of a mass of stones, would have a very serious effect upon prices." Everyone knew this, but the buyers each thought that he would be first in the field and resell quickly. All knew the enormous advantage of buying well-classified stones. Rhodes, when he signed the contract, had said, "I can make no contract with you binding you to hold these stones off the market. . . ." "The buyers were all rivals and none believed that everybody would exercise this restraint or comply with Rhodes's wishes . . . After all, business is business," Harris says. However, all agreed with Rhodes and there was a little chaff about his idealistic touch. Everything was now signed. The lawyers were finished and Rhodes said, casually: "All right, you will get the stones tomorrow when payment is made. They will be here in the de Beers office. Brink will take care of them for you. . . . Come along, Brink, put them away . . . and you understand, delivery tomorrow morning against payment.

"For a moment everyone was happy. Then Rhodes strolled across the room to speak to Brink from the head of the long trough where the diamonds lay grouped on their white paper. A wooden bucket was at the other end of the trough, and as Rhodes told Brink to put them away, he raised the head of the teak trough and shot the whole in a cataract into the bucket. He did it with the most natural movement, just as indifferently as one would toss an old newspaper onto the table. He did not say a word to those round him; was seemingly quite unconscious of what he had done and strolled out of the room without showing any sign of what had happened.

"Believe me, the faces of our people were a treat . . . the whole work of sorting was wiped out in one second and for six or eight months the entire output was kept off the market at surely as if it had been locked in the de Beers' safe. Someone said, 'My God, we have not a word in the contract about the grading or classifying. We just bought the output. . . .' Then someone else said, 'How the Christian beat the Jews!' and there was a roar of laughter such as you would only get from a gathering of Jews, who can, after all, enjoy a story at their own expense. And mind you, Rhodes was perfectly right. Our stones were locked up, but when we could sell them we realized a much better price than we could possibly have done at the time. His judgment was completely justified."

Rhodes and the Twentieth Century

JOHN FLINT

Cecil Rhodes has continued to fascinate not only those whose lives are somehow still touched by his imperial dreams but academic scholars as well, who have brought to their studies both a commitment to impartiality and a distance conducive to perspective. One of the best of these is the Canadian historian John Flint, from whose biography of Rhodes the following selection is excerpted. Flint, as one of his reviewers has pointed out,[3] is the first biographer of Rhodes to bring to his task an authentic expert knowledge of black Africa. What is perhaps more important, Flint is an authority on the British Chartered Companies. He sees Rhodes, therefore, not so much as an imperialist who was a businessman, but as a businessman who intended to use imperialism for his own ends. In this view and in the linkage Flint makes between Rhodes' immediate aims and his darker fancies, he contributes significantly to the modern understanding of this colossal and paradoxical figure.

THE STOCK IMAGE of Rhodes was the one he invented for himself, and the one all his biographers have perpetuated even when critical of his actions: Rhodes the archetype of imperialism, the patriot of empire, embodying in his person the vigor of British individualism and will to expand. The image was also the basis of his popularity in Britain during the last years of his life; it was the Rhodes of the music-hall stage and the Rhodes in the minds of bus drivers and cabbies who hailed him on the streets. No other imperial figure of his day could stand in quite the same unqualified way as "the man of empire." . . .

Rhodes posthumously deluded both his admirers and his critics, for in reality he was by no means a typical figure of the late-Victorian imperialist movement. In the true sense he was not an imperialist at all, for his career and policies had been largely concerned with resisting the metropolitan authority of Britain, with limiting the *imperium* in British imperialism. Rhodes used and exploited British imperialism for his own distinct ends and aims, which did not encompass the extension of direct British power and authority in southern Africa. To him the "imperial factor" was remote, meddling, and dangerously color-blind on racial

[3] "The Duty of an Anglo-Saxon," *Times Literary Supplement* (Nov. 19, 1976), p. 1461.

issues. It could be manipulated where necessary, but it must be a symbolic authority, a majesty to warn off foreigners but not to rule him or his people. The British flag, he told a meeting of De Beers shareholders four days after the relief of Kimberley, was "the best commercial asset in the world." Those who were close to the heart of imperial policies, and especially those with wider experiences of British Imperial questions, seemed to sense Rhodes' propensity to manipulate Imperial symbols; and they distrusted him. Imperial statesmen like Salisbury, Chamberlain or Rosebery kept Rhodes at a certain formal distance, even before the Jameson Raid. The really "typical" figures of British late-Victorian imperialism were the proconsular governors and administrators of the newly acquired or older territories, . . .

Such men, whatever their faults, possessed a certain sense of the awesomeness of the British Imperial system and a feeling for justice and impartial rule, however much some of them at times traduced these principles. Rhodes was too much the white South African, too "colonial," to share such sentiments. If anything he must be described as a colonialist, not an imperialist, in that he dedicated himself to the expansion of the white race in southern Africa. Even the pursuit of this goal was upon his own terms: the whites must expand in his way and to his profit and power. In the last Rhodes' ambitions were ambitions for Rhodes. . . .

The image of Rhodes as the archimperialist, held by admirers and critics alike, has indeed helped to obscure some of his most creative achievements. Politically his dreams evaporated and his schemes collapsed. His major practical political goal, the creation of a South African federation (to include Rhodesia) controlled by an Afrikaner-English alliance under the British flag collapsed under the impact of the Jameson Raid fiasco. Today South Africa has realized Kruger's, not Rhodes' ideas, and is an independent republic outside the British Commonwealth. Even his beloved Rhodesia flies its own green and white flag and is a republic. Rhodes' most original and lasting achievements were economic rather than political. The De Beers company was a multinational corporation, with worldwide shareholding, and a world outlook on the marketing of its product. Though not as dominant in gold mining, the Consolidated Gold Fields company likewise became an international conglomerate. In mining Rhodes was a pioneer innovator in the exploitation of new techniques, and he brought the best of American engineers to South Africa to improve and develop the means of mineral extraction. This determination to develop the means of production in Africa was not confined to minerals. His private and official initiatives in practice established prosperous agriculture in the Cape, where the creation of fruit-growing and the wine industry, also with the help of much American expertise, were major achievements. Joseph Chamberlain has often been credited with initiating economic development in British Africa with his concepts of "developing the Imperial estate." But Rhodes, by directly supervising the application of capital and technology, by stressing planning and pilot schemes, expanded production in actual rather than theoretical terms. . . .

. . . His mystic obsession with his "idea," which was never clearly enunciated, seemed to anticipate the stress on the Leader's intuition in later fascism and Nazism. His companies, like the later fascist parties, operated as states within the formal state; the British South Africa Company openly, the others clandestinely. De Beers had its own police and detective force, ostensibly to curb diamond thefts and illicit diamond buying, but it kept dossiers on prominent South Africans who had little or nothing to do with the diamond business. Rhodes bought into the press, in South Africa and England, to control opinion in his favor and to suppress criticism of his own affairs and information about them. He was never scrupulous in the means he employed to secure his ends, and he thought most men easily corruptible. Like Mussolini after him, Rhodes felt himself Roman. He fancied he bore a likeness to the emperor Hadrian, commissioned dozens of busts and statues of himself, and even arranged for his own funeral to be like that of an emperor. Rhodes' views on race, though not particularly anti-Semitic or unusual for his time, also seemed congenial to extreme right-wing thought in the years between the wars. For Rhodes the achievements of the British were the result of an inner dynamism contained in the "British race"; all other peoples, except the Germanic, were in varying degrees inferior. . . .

In South Africa Rhodes' memory has been cherished best among English-speakers, where there still exists a popular tradition of Rhodes as a heroic figure who might have unified southern Africa with a white colonial regime under the Union Jack had it not been for the impetuous Jameson's tragic mistake in 1895. Many such people would still claim to accept in theory Rhodes' dictum of "Equal rights for all civilized men" while demonstrating in successive elections their increasing willingness to vote Nationalist and support *apartheid* in practice.

Suggestions for Further Reading

THE POWERFUL, complex, and enigmatic figure of Cecil Rhodes continues to elude his biographers, and the definitive, critical biography remains to be written. Sarah Gertrude Millin, *Cecil Rhodes* (New York and London:

Harper & Bros., 1933), is, to an extent, the standard work on him, a colorful and exciting account by an experienced novelist and biographer. Both Felix Gross, *Rhodes of Africa* (New York: Praeger, 1956), and John Marlowe, *Cecil Rhodes: The Anatomy of Empire* (London: Elek, 1972), are superficial popular works. Even J. G. Lockhart and C. M. Woodhouse, *Cecil Rhodes: Colossus of Southern Africa* (New York: Macmillan, 1963), though based more fully on documents than any previous study, is timid and indecisive. John Flint, *Cecil Rhodes* (Boston and Toronto: Little, Brown, 1974), excerpted in this chapter, although a very small book, is probably the best general treatment of him. There are, however, several special studies that can be recommended: John S. Galbraith, *Crown and Charter: The Early Years of the British South Africa Company* (Berkeley: University of California Press, 1974), tells the dramatic story of the founding of Rhodesia and of Rhodes at the height of his power, with an interesting focus on the internal affairs of the company and its dealings; the massive Arthur Keppel-Jones, *Rhodes and Rhodesia: The White Conquest of Zimbabwe, 1884–1902* (Kingston: McGill-Queen's University Press, 1983) is up-to-date and authoritative; Brian Roberts, *Cecil Rhodes and the Princess* (London: Hamilton, 1969), is an intriguing account of a bizarre incident in Rhodes' life, as exciting as an espionage thriller; Jeffrey Butler, *The Liberal Party and the Jameson Raid* (Oxford, England: Clarendon Press, 1968), is a fine study of the political ramifications of a famous incident; and probably the best account of this famous incident is the revised edition of Elizabeth Longford, *Jameson's Raid* (London: Weidenfeld-Nicolson, 1982).

Rhodes was, of course, the quintessential figure of British economic imperialism, and the enormous literature of that subject almost invariably deals with him. A book dealing specifically with South African economic imperialism is Robert V. Kubicek, *Economic Imperialism in Theory and Practice: The Case of South African Gold Mining Finance, 1886–1914* (Durham: Duke University Press, 1979). The definitive work on a key aspect of imperialism is W. L. Langer, *The Diplomacy of Imperialism*, 2nd ed. (New York: Knopf, 1968 [1950]). A smaller book but broader in scope is Heinz Gollwitzer, *Europe in the Age of Imperialism, 1880–1914*, tr. Adam and Stanley Baron (New York: Harcourt, Brace and World, 1969). Raymond F. Betts, *The False Dawn: European Imperialism in the Nineteenth Century* (Minneapolis: University of Minnesota Press, 1975), and *The "New Imperialism": Analysis of Late Nineteenth Century Expansion*, ed. H. M. Wright, rev. ed. (Boston: Heath, 1975), both deal with the theories and arguments about imperialism. But probably the best and most definitive book on the subject is Winfried Baumgart, *Imperialism: The Idea and Reality of British and French Colonial Expansion, 1880–1914* (London: Oxford University Press, 1982). Also of interest is a specialized work on a long-neglected subject, Daniel R. Headrick, *The*

Tools of Empire: Technology and European Imperialism in the Nineteenth Century (London: Oxford University Press, 1981).

With respect to British imperialism, the best survey is Ronald Hyam, *Britain's Imperial Century 1815–1914: A Study of Empire and Expansion* (New York: Barnes and Noble, 1976). A briefer and more lively book dealing with some of the same matter is Bernard Porter, *The Lion's Share: A Short History of British Imperialism, 1850–1970* (New York: Longman, 1975). *British Imperialism: Gold, God, and Glory*, ed. Robin W. Winks (New York: Holt, Rinehart and Winston, 1963), deals with some of the controversies about the nature and motives of British imperialism, as does Richard Faber, *The Vision and the Need: Late Victorian Imperialist Aims* (New York: Humanities Press, 1966). L. H. Gann and Peter Duignan, *Burden of Empire, An Appraisal of Western Colonialism in Africa South of the Sahara* (New York: Praeger, 1967), also deals with the nature and motives of imperialism in Africa; it is a respected cautionary book, asserting that the benefits of colonialism may have outweighed its more publicized disadvantages for all concerned. A shorter book of readings, *The Scramble for Africa: Causes and Dimensions of Empire*, ed. Raymond F. Betts, rev. 2nd ed. (Boston: Heath, 1972), deals with some of the same issues. The fundamental revisionist monograph on the causes and motives of African imperialism is Ronald Robinson and John Gallagher, *Africa and the Victorians: The Climax of Imperialism in the Dark Continent* (New York: St. Martin's, 1961), but students may prefer *Imperialism: The Robinson and Gallagher Controversy*, ed. William R. Louis (New York: New Viewpoints, 1976). Recommended finally is R. Hallett, *Africa Since 1875* (Ann Arbor: University of Michigan Press, 1974), with its focus upon Africa rather than Europe.

The Bettmann Archive

Lenin: Anatomy of a Revolutionary

1870 born
1897 exiled to Siberia
1900 fled to Western Europe
1902 *What Is To Be Done?*, Lenin's first book
1905 Revolution of 1905
1917 returned to Petrograd
1918 Russian surrender to Germany at Brest-Litovsk
1924 died

The factual outline of Lenin's biography is well known. He was born Vladimir Ilyich Ulyanov in 1870, the son of a superintendent of public schools for the province of Simbirsk on the Volga and a member of the lesser nobility that provided most of the minor officialdom of Czarist Russia. Vladimir was a bright student. After high school, he went to study law at the regional university of Kazan. His political activities and growing radicalism led to his arrest, and for a year he was under police surveillance. He was soon arrested again, however, and in 1897 was exiled to Siberia. During his exile, he turned away from the tradition of populism, as the native Russian radicalism was called, and became an ardent Marxist. Later, he was to be the principal force in the unlikely task of applying the doctrines of Marx to vast, peasant Russia.

Returning from exile in 1900, Lenin fled Russia for Western Europe. It was at this time that he began writing under the name Lenin. He became active in the underground of radical émigrés and exiles; published a shoestring newspaper, *Iskra (The Spark);* and began to build a group of disciples who would become the inner circle of his revolutionary party. In 1902 he wrote his first major prescription for revolution, a book entitled *What Is To Be Done?* The following year he seized the leadership of the majority of delegates—the Bolsheviks—to the conventions of the tiny, splintered Russian Social-Democratic Workers Party, meeting in London and Brussels. He hurried back to Russia when the Revolution of 1905 broke out. But the Revolution failed, and Lenin returned to his self-imposed exile in the West. When World War I came, he watched anxiously from Geneva as revolution again broke out in Russia under the stress of war.

Lenin was soon approached by the German government. Would he and his radical followers return to Russia under German safe conduct? The Germans, of course, hoped that Lenin would further radicalize the revolution already under way in Russia, paralyze the government, and destroy military resistance. Lenin agreed, and in what is surely one of the most bizarre incidents in modern history, Lenin and his party were put aboard a train, granted extraterritorial rights to pass through Germany and shipped across Germany to the Baltic and to Petrograd. They arrived at the Finland Station in mid-April 1917.

Lenin quickly became involved in the Revolution and soon was its leading figure. By November he had organized his faction and driven the hopeless Provisional Government of Alexander Kerensky out of power. After the fall of Kerensky, Lenin was elected chairman of the new Council of People's Commissars. He was now, in fact, the head of a new state, ready to implement his theoretical ideas by direct political action. "Not a single problem of the class struggle has ever been solved in history except by violence," he told the Third All-Russian Congress of Soviets on January 24, 1918.

Lenin had already made the bold and controversial decision to take Russia out of "the imperialist World War," not to please the Germans—though it did—but to preserve his revolution and to save his country from sure defeat. The war had been useful as a "powerful accelerator to overturn the filthy and bloodstained cart of the Romanov monarchy," [1] but it served no further useful purpose. Lenin accepted the German peace terms at Brest-Litovsk on March 3, 1918. He called it not so much a surrender as a "compromise" with the "bandits of German imperialism," which would enable the imperialists to do whatever they wished while he and his comrades consolidated their revolution.[2]

The treaty of Brest-Litovsk, however, did not signify the end of war for the Russians. Between the collapse of the old Czarist government and a secure new revolutionary government lay years of civil war and invasion by Russia's former allies, outraged at the surrender at Brest-Litovsk and frightened by the apparent success of the Revolution. Lenin later recalled, "Our Red Army did not exist at the beginning of the war. . . . Nevertheless, we conquered in the struggle against the world-mighty Entente" and did so with "the alliance between the peasants and the workers, under the leadership of the proletarian state." [3] They indeed did conquer, and by the early 1920s modern Soviet Russia was a reality. Lenin had worked ruthlessly and tirelessly. In 1918 he had been seriously

[1] V. I. Lenin, *Selected Works* (New York: International Publishers, 1943), VI, 5.
[2] *Ibid.*, X, 75-76.
[3] *Ibid.*, IX, 246.

wounded in an assassination attempt from which he never fully recovered. Then in 1922 he suffered a stroke, followed by another that partially paralyzed him. In 1924 he died.

Lenin was the most famous figure in Russia and one of the most famous in the world. As "The Father of the Revolution," his picture looked benignly down from giant posters over Red Square, and countless photographs of him appeared in the Western Press. But the man behind the picture was almost unknown—in Russia as well as in the West. Lenin was obsessively secretive about himself. In all his vast collected works, in page after page of mind-boggling theories and bitter polemics, there are no more than a handful of brusque personal anecdotes. When his friends inquired too closely into aspects of his personal life, his tastes, his likes and dislikes, he shoved their questions aside as "trivial" and "unimportant." The cause, the work, the Revolution—these were the things that mattered.

It became almost an obsession with those closest to him to penetrate the "secret corner of his life," that "special room completely to himself," as Lenin called it,[4] in order to understand Lenin the man and to know what made and moved Lenin the leader and revolutionary. His friend the historian M. N. Pokrovsky found the key to Lenin "his tremendous political courage." "Among revolutionaries," Pokrovsky wrote, "there has been no lack of brave people unafraid of the rope and the gallows or of Siberia. But these people were afraid of taking upon themselves the burden of great political decisions." Not so Lenin, "no matter how weighty the decisions." [5] The novelist Maxim Gorky asked a friend, "what, in his opinion, was Lenin's outstanding feature. 'Simplicity! He's as simple as the truth,' he answered without hesitation, as though reiterating a long established fact." [6] Lenin was not simple, of course, and Gorky did not find him so. On the other hand, he never did succeed in identifying to his own satisfaction Lenin's "outstanding feature."

At least two others succeeded somewhat better. And they also isolated what they regarded as the causes that moved Lenin to be the person he was. We turn now to the first of these, Leon Trotsky.

[4] Quoted in N. V. Volsky, *Encounters with Lenin* (London: Oxford University Press, 1968), p. 43.

[5] Quoted in Tamara Deutscher, ed., *Not by Politics Alone—the Other Lenin* (London: Allen & Unwin, 1973), p. 71.

[6] Quoted in George Hanna, ed., *About Lenin*, J. Guralsky, trans. (Moscow: Progress Publishers, n.d.), p. 30.

The Young Lenin

LEON TROTSKY

Like Lenin, Trotsky was both a radical revolutionary intellectual and an exile. He opposed Lenin in the split of the Russian Social-Democratic Congress in 1903 and took a middle position between Lenin's Bolsheviks and the Menshevik "minority." Unlike Lenin, Trotsky was one of the heroes of the unsuccessful Revolution of 1905, after which he was imprisoned. In the successful Revolution of 1917, however, he joined forces with Lenin, and his brilliance, audacity, and organizational ability contributed mightily to its success.

In the power struggle following Lenin's death, Trotsky lost out to Stalin and in 1929 was exiled from Russia. Finally, in 1940, he was assassinated in Mexico, allegedly by Stalinist agents. While in exile, as earlier, Trotsky was a prolific writer, and he continued both his struggle against Stalin and his self-justification in his many books and articles. But he often came back to the subject of Lenin and wrote about him extensively, for example, in his My Life *(1930) and his three-volume* History of the Russian Revolution *(1936). In many ways, the most interesting of Trotsky's works on Lenin is* The Young Lenin, *from which the following selection is taken. The book was written in the early 1930s as the first of two volumes on Lenin's life. The second volume was never finished, delayed by other projects and ultimately by Trotsky's death. The work as it stood was translated by the American journalist and publicist Max Eastman, who had translated Trotsky's other works. Then the manuscript was lost, and it did not turn up again until the late 1960s.* The Young Lenin *was at last published in 1972, almost forty years after it was written.*

More interesting than the curious history of the manuscript is the book's insightful treatment of Lenin's early years, very nearly unique among the memoirs and recollections of other Lenin intimates–including the Reminiscences *of Lenin's wife, which reveal almost nothing about him. Especially intriguing is the importance Trotsky attaches to a series of tragic incidents that occurred at the end of Lenin's adolescence. Trosky finds in these tragedies of Lenin the boy the key to understanding Lenin the man—and the revolutionary.*

"HAPPY FAMILIES are all alike," says Tolstoy. "Each unhappy family is unhappy in its own way." The Ulyanov family had lived a happy life for almost twenty-three years, and been like other harmonious and fortunate families. In 1886 the first blow fell, the death of the father. But misfortunes never come singly. Others followed swiftly: the execution of Alexander, the arrest of Anna. And beyond these there were more, and still more, misfortunes to come. Henceforth everybody, both strangers and intimates, began to consider the Ulyanovs an unhappy family. And they had truly become unhappy, though in their own way. . . .

When Ilya Nikolayevich had completed twenty-five years of service, the ministry retained him for but one supplementary year, and not five as was usual with important government officials. . . . In 1884, simultaneously with the new university constitution, new rules were issued for parish schools. Ilya Nikolayevich was opposed to this reform—not out of hostility to the church, of course, for he zealously saw to it that religion was regularly taught in *zemstvo* schools—but out of loyalty to the cause of education. As the winds of reaction grew strong, the Simbirsk superintendent of public schools, by the very fact that he felt concerned for the cause of literacy, willy-nilly found himself opposing the new course. What had formerly been considered his merit had now, it seemed, become a fault. He was compelled to retreat and adapt himself. His whole life's work was under attack. When an occasion presented itself, Ilya Nikolayevich was not averse to pointing out to his older children the disastrous consequences of revolutionary struggle, and how instead of progress it produced reaction. This was the mood of the majority of peaceful educators of the time.

A Simbirsk landowner, Nazaryev, in sending in his regular dispatch to the editor of the liberal journal *Vestnik Yevropy,* wrote to him confidentially about Ulyanov; "He is not in the good graces of the ministry, and is far from doing well." Ilya Nikolayevich took to heart the government's attack upon the elementary schools, although he obeyed the new policy. His former buoyancy had vanished. His last years were poisoned with uncertainty and anxiety. He fell sick suddenly in January 1886, while preparing his annual report. Alexander was in Petersburg, wholly immersed in his zoology term paper. Vladimir, only a year and a half away from high-school graduation, must have been thinking already about the university. Anna was at home for the Christmas holidays. Neither the family nor the physician took Ilya Nikolayevich's illness seriously. He continued to work on his report. His daughter sat reading some papers to him until she noticed that her father was becoming delirious. The next morning, the twelfth, the sick man did not come to the table, but only came to the dining room door, and looked in—"as though he had come to say good-by," remembered Maria Alexandrovna. At five o'clock the mother, in alarm, called Anna and Vladimir. Ilya Nikolayevich lay dying on the sofa which served him for a bed. The children saw their father shudder twice and go still forever. He was not yet fifty-five years old. The physician described the cause of his death—"hypothetically although with overwhelming probability," to quote his own words—as a cerebral hemorrhage. Thus the first heavy blow fell upon the Ulyanov family. . . .

Anna remained in Simbirsk for a time in order to be near her mother. It was at that time that the elder sister and Vladimir grew close to each other. The winter walks together date from that time, and the long conversations in which her brother revealed himself to her as a rebel and nonconformist, the embodiment of protest—so far, however, only in relation to "high-school authorities, high-school studies, and also to religion." During the recent summer vacation, these moods had not yet existed.

The death of the father had suddenly destroyed the lulling flow of life in a family whose well-being had seemed sure to go on indefinitely. How can we avoid assuming that it was this blow that imparted a new critical direction to Vladimir's thoughts? The answers of the church catechism to questions of life and death must have seemed to him wretched and humiliating, confronted with the austere truth of nature. Whether in reality he threw his cross into the garbage, or whether, as is more likely, Krzhizhanovsky's memory converted a metaphorical expression into a physical gesture, one thing is beyond doubt: Vladimir must have broken with religion abruptly, without long hesitation, without attempts at an eclectic reconciliation of truths with lies, with that youthful courage which was here for the first time spreading its wings.

Alexander was staying up nights engrossed in his work when the unexpected news came of his father's death. "For several days he dropped everything," relates a fellow student at the university, "pacing his room from corner to corner as though wounded." But wholly in the spirit of the family, in which strong feelings went hand in hand with discipline, Alexander did not leave the university, and did not hasten to Simbirsk. He pulled himself together and went back to work. After a few weeks his mother received a letter, brief as always: "I have received a gold medal for my zoological study of annelids." Maria Alexandrovna wept with joy for her son and with grief for her husband. . . .

. . . Life was beginning to move again in its new, narrower channel, when a totally unexpected blow, and a double blow at that, descended upon the family: Both son and daughter were involved in a trial for an attempted assassination of the tsar. It was dreadful even to breathe those words!

Anna was arrested on March 1 in her brother's room, which she had entered while a search was in progress. Shrouded in dreadful uncertainty, the girl was locked up in prison in connection with a case in which she had no part. This, then, is what Sasha was busy with! They had grown up side by side, played together in their father's study with sealing wax and magnets, often fallen asleep together to their mother's music, studied together in Petersburg—and yet how little she knew him! The older Sasha grew, the more he withdrew from his sister. Anna remembered bitterly how, when she visited him, Alexander would tear himself from his books with evident regret. He did not share his thoughts with her. Each time he heard of some new vileness of the tsarist authorities his face would darken, and he would withdraw more deeply into himself. "A penetrating observer could have predicted even then his future course. . . ." But Anna was no penetrating observer. During the last year, Alexander had refused to share an apartment with her, explaining to his companions that he did not want to compromise his sister, who showed no desire for public activity. During that winter Anna saw Alexander with some strange objects in his hands. How far she was from the thought of bombs! . . .

A Petersburg relative of the Ulyanovs wrote of the arrest of Alexander and Anna to a former teacher of the children, asking her to prepare the mother cautiously. Narrowing his young brows, Vladimir stood silent a long time over the Petersburg letter. This lightning stroke revealed the figure of Alexander in a new light. "But this is a serious thing," he said. "It may end badly for Sasha." He evidently had no doubt of Anna's innocence. The task of preparing the mother fell to him. But she, sensing tragedy in the first words, demanded the letter, and immediately began to prepare for a journey.

There was still no railroad from Simbirsk; one had to travel by horse and wagon to Syzran. For the sake of economy and for safety on the journey, Vladimir sought a companion for his mother. But the news had already spread through the town. Everyone turned away fearfully. No one would travel with the mother of a terrorist. Vladimir never forgot this lesson. The days that followed were to mean much in the forming of his character and its direction. The youth became austere and silent, and frequently shut himself up in his room when not busy with the younger children left in his charge. So that is what he was, this tireless chemist and dissector of worms, this silent brother so near and yet so unknown! When compelled to speak with Kashkadamova of the catastrophe, he kept repeating: "It means Alexander could not have acted otherwise." The mother came back for a short time to see the children and told them of her efforts and her dream of a life sentence to hard labor for Sasha. "In that case I would go with him," she said. "The older children are big enough and I will take the younger with me." Instead of a chair at a university and scholarly glory, chains and stripes now became the chief object of the mother's hopes. . . . She was admitted to sessions of the court. In his month and a half of confinement, Alexander had grown more manly; even his voice acquired an unfamiliar impressiveness. The youth had become a man. "How well Sasha spoke—so convincingly, so eloquently." But the mother could not sit through the whole speech; that eloquence would break her heart. On the eve of the execution, still hoping, she kept repeating to her son through the double grating: "Have courage!" On May 5, on her way to an interview with her daughter, she learned from a leaflet given out on the street that Sasha was no more. The feelings that the bereaved mother brought to the grating behind which her daughter stood are not recorded. But Maria Alexandrovna did not bend, did not fall, did not betray the secret to her daughter. To Anna's questions about her brother, the mother answered: "Pray for Sasha." Anna did not detect the despair behind her mother's courage. How respectfully the prison authorities, who knew already of the execution of Alexander, admitted this severe woman in black! The daughter did not yet guess that the mourning for her father had become a mourning for her brother.

Simbirsk was fragrant with all the flowers of its orchards when news came from the capital of the hanging of Alexander Ulyanov. The family of a full state counselor, until then respected on every side, became overnight the family of an executed state criminal. Friends and acquaintances, without exception, avoided the house on Moscow Street. Even the aged schoolteacher who had so often dropped in for a game of chess with Ilya Nikolayevich no longer showed his face. Vladimir observed with a keen eye the neighbors around them, their cowardice and disloyalty. It was a precious lesson in political realism.

Anna was set free some days after the execution of her brother. Instead of sending her to Siberia, the authorities agreed to have her restricted, under police surveillance, to the village of Kokushkino, the home of her mother. . . .

What ideas and moods captivated Vladimir in the summer of 1886, on the eve of his last year at high school? In the preceding winter, according to Anna Yelizarova, he had begun "rejecting authority in the period of his first, so to speak, negative formation of personality." But his criticisms, for all their boldness, still had limited scope. They were directed against high-school teachers, and to some extent against religion. "There was nothing definitely political in our conversations." On her return from the capital, Vladimir did not put any questions to his sister about revolutionary organizations, illegal books, or political groupings among the students. Anna adds: "I am convinced that with our relations being what they were at that time, Volodya would not have concealed such interests from me," had he had any. . . . Vladimir remained completely untouched politically and did not show the slightest interest in those economics books that filled Alexander's shelf in their common room. The name of Marx meant nothing to this young man whose interests were almost exclusively in *belles lettres*. Moreover, he gave himself up to literature with passion. For whole days he drank in the novels of Turgenev, page by page, lying on his cot and carried away in his imagination into the realm of "superfluous people" and idealized maidens under the linden trees of aristocratic parks. Having read through to the end, he would begin all over again. His thirst was insatiable. . . .

Some years later, the Social Democrat Lalayants questioned Lenin about the affair of March 1. Lenin answered: "Alexander's participation in a terrorist act was completely unexpected for all of us. Possibly my sister knew something—I knew nothing at all." As a matter of fact, the sister knew nothing either. The testimony of Lalayants fully corroborates Anna's story and coincides with what we know on this subject from Krupskaya's *Recollections*. In explaining this fact, Krupskaya refers to the difference in their ages, which wholly destroys her own account of the closeness of the brothers. But this reference, inadequate to say the least, does not alter the fact itself. Lenin's grief for his brother must have been colored with bitterness at the thought that Alexander had concealed from him what was deepest and most important. And with remorse over his own lack of attentiveness toward his brother and his arrogant assertions of his own independence. His childish worship of Sasha must have returned now with tenfold strength, sharpened by a feeling of guilt and a consciousness of the impossibility of making amends. His former teacher who handed him the fateful letter from Petersburg, says: "Before me sat no longer the carefree cheerful boy but a grown man buried in thought. . . ." Vladimir went through his final high-school experiences with his teeth clenched. There exists a photograph evidently made for the high-school diploma. On the still unformed but strongly concentrated features with the arrogantly pushed-out lower lip, lay the shadow of grief and of a first deep hatred. Two deaths stood at the beginning of the new period of Vladimir's life. The death of his father, convincing in its physiological naturalness, impelled him to a critical attitude toward the church and the religious myth. The execution of his brother awakened bitter hostility toward the hangmen. The future revolutionary had been planted in the personality of the youth and in the social conditions that formed him. But an initial impulse was needed. And this was provided by the unexpected death of his brother. The first political thoughts of Vladimir must inevitably have arisen out of a twofold need: to avenge Sasha and to refute by action Sasha's distrust.

Lenin the Revolutionary

NIKOLAY VALENTINOV

Like Trotsky and so many of Lenin's other early intimates, N. V. Volsky (d. 1964)—who wrote under the name of Nikolay Valentinov—was fascinated by Lenin even though they broke over philosophical disagreements while Lenin was still in exile, long before the Revolution of 1917. But Volsky's recollections of Lenin remained vivid and became the subject of Encounters with Lenin, *the book from which the following excerpt is taken. In a long chapter entitled "My Attempts to Understand Lenin," Volsky described a singular incident when Lenin dropped his "oriental mask" and allowed a handful of friends into "the secret room of his life." What he revealed was not a moving personal tragedy such as Trotsky relates but a passionate intellectual advocacy for a book whose ideas, Volsky was convinced, made Lenin a revolutionary. The book was* What Is to Be Done? *by Nikolai Chernyshevsky (d. 1889). It is not insignificant, as Lenin himself admitted, that he used this title for the first major proclamation of his own revolutionary program, for Chernyshevsky's book was programmatic. The author had been a leading figure in native Russian radicalism and highly regarded by many Russion radicals before the time of Lenin, though hardly known in the West then or later. But what is perhaps more important than the program of Chernyshevsky was Lenin's passion for the book, a clear indication of the debt he owed to its influence. It is also significant that there existed a bridge between the emotional experience that Trotsky saw as Lenin's center and the intellectual experience described by Volsky. Lenin's dead brother Alexander had loved Chernyshevsky's book. Clearly, young Lenin had read at least one of the books on the shelf in their common room.*

DURING MY ATTEMPTS to understand Lenin, I made some "discoveries" which agreeably surprised me (his love of nature or his attitude to Turgenev, for example), but I also made others which simply nonplussed me. I shall now describe one of these.

At the end of January 1904 I ran into Lenin, Vorovsky, and Gusev in a small café near the square of the Plaine de Plainpalais in Geneva. As I arrived later than the others I did not know how the conversation between Vorovsky and Gusev had started. I only heard Vorovsky mention some literary works which had been very successful in their day but had quickly "dated," and now aroused only boredom and indifference. I remember that he included in this category Goethe's *Werther,* some pieces by George Sand, Karamzin's "Poor Liza," and other Russian works, including Mordovtsev's *A Sign of the Times.* I butted in to say that since he had mentioned Mordovtsev, why not Chernyshevsky's *What is to be Done?* too? "One is amazed," I said, "how people could take any interest or pleasure in such a thing. It would be difficult to imagine anything more untalented, crude and, at the same time, pretentious. Most of the pages of this celebrated novel are written in unreadable language. Yet when someone told him that he lacked literary talent, Chernyshevsky answered arrogantly: 'I am no worse than those novelists who are considered great.' "

Up to this moment Lenin had been staring vacantly into space, taking no part in the conversation. But when he heard what I had just said, he sat up with such a start that the chair creaked under him. His face stiffened and he flushed around the cheek-bones—this always happened when he was angry.

"Do you realize what you are saying?" he hurled at me. "How could such a monstrous and absurd idea come into your mind—to describe as crude and untalented a work of Chernyshevsky, the greatest and most talented representative of socialism before Marx! Marx himself called Chernyshevsky a great Russian writer."

"It wasn't *What is to be Done?* that made Marx call him a great writer. Marx probably didn't read the book," I said.

"How do you know that Marx didn't read it? I declare that it is impermissible to call *What is to be Done?* crude and untalented. Hundreds of people became revolutionaries under its influence. Could this have happened if Chernyshevsky had been untalented and crude? My brother, for example, was captivated by him, and so was I. *He completely transformed my outlook.* When did you read *What is to be Done?*? It is no good reading it when one is still a greenhorn. Chernyshevsky's novel is too complex and full of ideas to be understood and appreciated at an early age. I myself started to read it when I was 14. I think this was a completely useless and superficial reading of the book. But, after the execution of my brother, I started to read it properly, as I knew that it had been one of his favourite books. I spent not days but several weeks reading it. Only then did I understand its depth. This novel provides inspiration for a lifetime: untalented books don't have such an influence."

"So," Gusev asked, "it was no accident that in 1902 you called your pamphlet *What is to be Done?*"

"Is this so difficult to guess?," was Lenin's answer.

Of the three of us I attached the least importance to Lenin's words. On the other hand, Vorovsky became very interested. He began to ask Lenin when he had become acquainted with Chernyshevsky's other works besides *What is to be Done?,* and, in general, which writers had had a particularly strong influence on him before he had become familiar with Marxism. Lenin did not usually speak about himself—this in itself distinguished him from most people. However, on this occasion he broke his rule, and answered Vorovsky's question in great detail. The result was a page of autobiography which has never been recorded in print. In 1919 Vorosky, who was chairman of the Gosizdat (State Publishing House) for a short time, wanted to reconstruct and write down what Lenin said on this occasion. . . .

Vorovsky's reconstruction of Lenin's words throws new light on Lenin's intellectual and political development. I have to admit that it was only very much later that I realized this. It might have been thought that Vorovsky's transcript would be published in the USSR, where even the most worthless scraps of paper connected with Lenin are carefully preserved. However, I have not been able to find it anywhere in the Soviet literature available to me. There is no mention of it whatsoever. What can the explanation be? The point is that Vorovsky records Lenin as saying, in his own words, that he had been "transformed" by Chernyshevsky, and that under his impact he had become a revolutionary before his introduction to Marxism. It is thus impossible, unless one gives credence to a wanton misconception, to believe that Lenin was shaped only by Marx and Marxism. By the time he came to Marxism, Lenin, under Chernyshevsky's influence, was already forearmed with certain revolutionary ideas which provided the distinctive features of his specifically "Leninist" political make-up. All this is extremely important and sharply contradicts both the party canons and Lenin's official biographers. It is very probable that this is the reason why Vorovsky's transcript has not been published. . . .

. . . This is the gist of what Lenin said: "During the year that followed my banishment from Kazan, I used to read greedily from early morning till late at night. I think this was the most intensive period of reading in my whole life, not excluding my time in prison in Petersburg and my exile in Siberia. On the assumption that I might soon be permitted to return to the university, I read my university textbooks. I read a great deal of fiction, I became a great admirer of Nekrasov; what is more, my sister and I used to compete to see who could learn the greater number of Nekrasov's poems by heart. However, I read mainly articles which had once been published in the periodicals *Sovremennik* (Contemporary), *Otechestvennye Zapiski* (Fatherland Notes), and *Vesnik Europy* (Herald of Europe). These periodicals included the best and most interesting social and political writings of the previous decades. Chernyshevsky was my favorite author. I read and reread everything he had published in the *Sovremennik*. Chernyshevsky introduced me to philosophical materialism. It was again Chernyshevsky who first gave me an indication of Hegel's role in the development of philosophical thought, and I got the concept of dialectical method from him; this made it much easier for me to master the dialectic of Marx later on. I read Chernyshevsky's magnificent essays on aesthetics, art, and literature from cover to cover, and Belinsky's revolutionary figure became clear to me. I read all Chernyshevsky's articles on the peasant problem and his notes on the translation of Mill's *Political Economy*. Chernyshevsky's attack on bourgeois economics was a good preparation for my later study of Marx. I read with particular interest and profit Chernyshevsky's surveys of life abroad, which were remarkable for their intellectual depth. I read him pencil in hand, and made long excerpts and abstracts of what I was reading. I kept these notes for a long time. Chernyshevsky's encyclopedic knowledge, the brilliance of his revolutionary views, and his ruthless polemical talent captivated me. I even found out his address and wrote a letter to him; I was very pained when I did not receive any answer, and I was greatly distressed when I heard the news of his death in the following year. Chernyshevsky was hampered by the censorship and could not write freely. Many of his views could only be conjectured at; nevertheless, if one reads his articles carefully for a long time, as I did, one acquires the key to the complete decipherment of his political views, even of those which are expressed allegorically or by means of allusions. It is said that there are musicians with perfect pitch: one could say that there are also people with perfect revolutionary flair. Marx and Chernyshevsky were such men. You can't find another Russian revolutionary who understood and condemned the cowardly, base, and perfidious nature of every kind of liberalism with such thoroughness, acumen, and force as Chernyshevsky did. In the magazines I read there may have been a few things on Marxism too—for example, Mikhaylovsky's and Zhukovsky's articles. I can't say with any certainty whether I read them or not. One thing is certain—they did not attract my attention until I read the first volume of Marx's *Capital* and Plekhanov's book, *Our Differences,* although thanks to Chernyshevsky's articles I had begun to take an interest in economic questions, particularly in Russian rural life. This interest was prompted by essays of Vorontsov, Glep Uspensky, Engelhardt, and Skaldin. Only Chernyshevsky had a real, overpowering influence on me before I got to know the works of Marx, Engels, and Plekhanov, and it started with *What is to be Done?* Chernyshevsky not only showed that every right-thinking and really honest man must be a revolutionary, but he also showed—and this is his greatest merit—what a revolutionary must be like, what his principles must be, how he must approach his aim, and what methods he should use to achieve it. This compensates for all his shortcomings which, in fact, were not so much his fault as a consequence of the backwardness of social relations in his day. . . ."

After this conversation with Lenin, on our way back to the hotel, Gusev said laughingly:

"Ilyich could have scratched your eyes out for your disrespectful attitude to Chernyshevsky. Our old man has apparently not forgotten him to this very day. Still, I would never have believed the extent to which Chernyshevsky turned his head when he was a young man."

I found it even more difficult to believe. Lenin's infatuation with Chernyshevsky was quite incomprehensible and bewildering to me. It seemed strange that such a dreary, tedious, and feeble book as *What is to be Done?* could "transform his whole outlook" and provide "inspiration for a lifetime." It had never occurred to me that there was a special and hidden, yet strongly revolutionary, ideological, political, and psychological line running from Chernyshevsky's *What is to be Done?* to Lenin's *What is to be Done?,* and that there was more to it than the identity of titles. I had to admit that I had not understood an apparently very important part of Lenin's way of thinking.

The Lenin of History

ROBERT V. DANIELS

Western scholars of modern Russian history have also been fascinated by Lenin, the person who, more than any other, made the most significant revolution of the modern world. One of the best of these scholars is the American historian Robert V. Daniels, whose book Red October *provides a detailed account of the opening phase of the Revolution of 1917. Daniels' analysis of Lenin is central to his account, and it is an analysis unobscured by either commitment to or disillusionment with one or another revolutionary ideology. Daniels sees the motives of Lenin—the center of the man—in his ruthless drive for personal power and his cynical manipulation of the very dialectic that he mastered and that has been enshrined in Communist methodology since Lenin's time.*

It would be rash to conclude that Daniels' view of Lenin is more "true" than the views of his earlier comrades or of the current crop of Marxian admirers. But it at least has the virtue of a kind of objectivity we cannot expect from those closer either in time or spirit to Lenin.

THE RUSSIAN Social Democratic Workers Party (of Bolsheviks) had never known any leader but Lenin. It was his personal political creation, starting as a devoted little group of twenty-two Russian *émigrés* (counting Lenin, his wife, and his sister) who met in Geneva in 1904. Their aim was to keep alive his side of the controversy that had split the Russian Marxist movement the year before. . . . Lenin had been adroit enough to seize the label "Bolsheviks"—"Majority men"—for his faction, even though he won only one of the numerous votes that turned around the "hard" political philosophy that he represented. . . .

Lenin had worked out his personal version of Marxist revolutionary philosophy between 1897 and 1900 while serving a sentence of Siberian exile for his revolutionary agitation among the St. Petersburg workers. In 1902, soon after he had left Russia for Western Europe, he published his propositions in the celebrated book, *What Is To Be Done?* Like practically everything Lenin ever said or wrote, the book was couched in the form of a polemic—in this case against the "Economists" because they put the economic progress of the workers ahead of political revolution. "The history of all countries," Lenin insisted, "shows that the working class, exclusively by its own effort, is able to develop only trade union consciousness." What would make them revolutionary, then? "Socialist ideology" and "class political consciousness" that could be "brought to the workers *only from without,* that is, from outside of the economic struggle." By whom? By the Social Democratic Party, and more specifically, "a small compact core of the most reliable, experienced and hardened activists . . . , an organization . . . chiefly of people professionally engaged in revolutionary activity."

Unlike the Mensheviks, who kept to the Marxist doctrine that a bourgeois revolution and capitalism had to precede the proletarian revolution, Lenin took the position that the Russian middle class was too cowardly to revolt, and that the proletariat—led by Lenin—should seize power directly and rule with the peasantry as its "allies." But this revolution would never occur of its own accord. Contrary to Marx, and more in keeping with the tradition of Russian revolutionary conspiracy, Lenin insisted that the proletarian revolution had to be accomplished by the deliberate action of a tightly organized conspiratorial party. He did not trust spontaneous mass movements, and at several crucial moments—in 1905 and in July, 1917—opposed the "adventurism" of Bolsheviks who wanted to exploit a popular outburst. In the fall of 1917, when it seemed as though the proletarian revolution might roll to victory almost as spontaneously as the bourgeois revolution of February, Lenin was beside himself. He was desperate then to demand that his party impose itself by force, to prove its own necessity and keep alive for himself the chance of ruling alone. . . .

Between Lenin and the Mensheviks the basic difference was more temperamental than doctrinal. The Mensheviks, like many earlier critics of Russian injustice, were idealists driven by sympathy for the masses but disinclined to conspire and fight; they admired Western democratic socialism and hoped for a peaceful and legal path to social reform once the Russian autocracy was overthrown. They were appalled by Lenin's elastic political morality and the philosophy they termed "dictatorship over the proletariat."

It is impossible to escape the very strong suspicion that Lenin's deepest motive was the drive for personal power, however he might have rationalized it. Like practically every politician Lenin had a philosophy about the welfare of the people—in his case it was the entire world proletariat—but the philosophy also said or implied that power for him and him alone was the only way this goal could be achieved. Lenin had an inordinate dislike of any sort of political cooperation or compromise, not because it might fail, but because it might succeed, and leave him with less than the whole loaf of power. He never worked honestly under or alongside anyone else, but only as the sole and unquestioned leader of his own forces, even if they had to be whittled down to meet his conditions. He was fascinated by armed force, and did not believe that any revolution worthy of the name could come about without it. "Major questions in the life of nations are settled by force," he wrote when he was a spectator to the Revolution of 1905. "The bayonet has really become the main point on the political agenda . . . , insurrection has proved to be imperative and urgent—constitutional illusions and school exercises in parliamentarism become only a screen for the bourgeois betrayal of the revolution. . . . It is therefore the slogan of the dictatorship of the proletariat that the genuinely revolutionary class must advance."

Many attempts, none very successful, have been made to explain Lenin's psychology. His childhood environment and youthful experiences, hardly exceptional for a family of the nineteenth-century Russian intelligentsia, offer only the sketchiest explanations of the demon that soon came to possess him. He was born in 1870 to a family of the lesser nobility—to be sure, the principal seedbed of the Russian revolutionary movement. His father, Ilya Ulyanov, was the Superintendent of Schools in the Volga city of Simbirsk, also the hometown, interestingly enough, of Alexander Kerensky. Lenin had some traumatic experiences—the untimely death of the father he esteemed; the execution of his older brother Alexander for complicity in an attempt on Tsar Alexander III; and his own expulsion from Kazan University because of a student demonstration. But the most abnormal thing about Lenin was his lack of abnormality among the typically eccentric and extremist Russians. He combined his natural brilliance and energy with an utterly un-Russian rigor and self-discipline which gave him an untold advantage in every political confrontation of his career. "Lenin is sheer intellect—he is absorbed, cold, unattractive, impatient at interruption," wrote John Reed's wife when she met the Bolshevik chief just after the Revolution. In another society Lenin would have risen to Grand Vizier or Corporation Counsel. In fact he did start a legal career in St. Petersburg, in 1893, before the encounter with a circle of Marxist agitators including his future wife Nadezhda Krupskaya finally committed him to the Marxist revolutionary movement.

Most people were either repelled or spellbound by Lenin. He was endowed with an extraordinary force of personality, along with an unbelievably vituperative vocabulary, that made most mortals helpless to opposed him within his own camp—they yielded or left. His extremism attracted many revolutionary romantics of independent mind but none of them were at ease in what Trotsky once called the "barrack regime" of the Bolshevik Party. Lenin hated liberalism and softness and the "circle spirit" of impractical discussion. "Nothing was so repugnant to Lenin," Trotsky recalled, "as the slightest suspicion of sentimentality and psychological weakness." Lenin hated the "spontaneity" of social movements without conscious leadership, and he hated the "opportunism" and "tail-end-ism" of people who went along with such movements. His life was consumed with hatred, and hatred of his rivals for the future of Russia almost more than the old regime. He wrote scarcely anything that was not aimed immediately to abuse an opponent, and usually a democratic and socialist opponent at that.

It is something of a puzzle that young Russian revolutionaries like Lenin embraced the philosophy of Marxism. Literally interpreted, Marx's doctrine of the change of society by deep-seated economic forces held out for an underdeveloped country such as Russia only the prospect of capitalism and middle-class rule for generations—the last thing that the radical intelligentsia wanted. Nor did they plump for Marxism for lack of an alternative philosophy, for the Russian revolutionaries since the 1850's had worked out a substantial body of socialist doctrine—"Populism," it was later termed—based on revolution by the peasants under the direction of the intelligentsia. The conspiratorial methods which so attracted the Russian extremists were an integral part of the Populist philosophy, whereas they were quite foreign to Western Marxism. In short, Marxism did not fit either the way the Russian revolutionaries wanted to work or the goals they wanted to work for, yet they flocked to its banner in ever-increasing numbers. They seem to have been attracted to Marxism because it gave them the secure sense of scientific inevitability and more especially because it stressed the role of the people who were obviously becoming the most vigorous, if small, revolutionary force in Russia, the industrial workers in the big cities. . . .

The stark truth about the Bolshevik Revolution is that it succeeded against incredible odds in defiance of any rational calculation that could have been made in the fall of 1917. The shrewdest politicians of every political coloration knew that while the Bolsheviks were an undeniable force in Petrograd and Moscow, they had against them the overwhelming majority of the peasants, the army in the field, and the trained personnel without which no government could function. Everyone from the right-wing military to the Zinoviev-Kamenev Bolsheviks judged a military dictatorship to be the most likely alternative if peaceful evolution failed. They all thought—whether they hoped or feared—that a Bolshevik attempt to seize power would only hasten or assure the rightist alternative.

Lenin's revolution, as Zinoviev and Kamenev pointed out, was a wild gamble, with little chance that Bolsheviks' ill-prepared followers could prevail against all the military force that the government seemed to have, and even less chance that they could keep power even if they managed to seize it temporarily. To Lenin, however, it was a gamble that entailed little risk, because he sensed that in no other way and at no other time would he have any chance at all of coming to power. This is why he demanded so vehemently that the Bolshevik Party seize the moment and hurl all the force it could against the Provisional Government. Certainly the Bolshevik Party had a better overall chance for survival and a future political role if it waited and compromised, as Zinoviev and Kamenev wished. But this would not yield the only kind of political power—exclusive power—that Lenin valued. He was bent on baptizing the revolution in blood, to drive off the fainthearted and compel all who subscribed to the overturn to accept and depend on his own unconditional leadership.

To this extent there is some truth in the contentions, both Soviet and non-Soviet, that Lenin's leadership was decisive. By psychological pressure on his Bolshevik lieutenants and his manipulation of the fear of counterrevolution, he set the stage for the one-party seizure of power.

Suggestions for Further Reading

LENIN'S OWN VOLUMINOUS WRITINGS, although they do not illuminate his life, nevertheless reveal his ideas and policies and the scathing declamatory style of virtually everything he wrote. The standard English-language edition is his *Collected Works*, 44 vols. (Moscow: Progress Publishers, 1960–1970), but most students will prefer either his *Collected Works*, rev. and annotated, 3 vols. published in 5 vols. (New York: International Publishers, 1927–), or the one-volume *Selected Works* (New York: International Publishers, 1971). There is also a separate edition of *The Letters of Lenin*, tr. and ed. Elizabeth Hill and Doris Mudie (London: Chapman and Hall, 1937), and of his important revolutionary pamphlet, *What Is to Be Done? Burning Questions of our Movement*, ed. V. J. Jerome, tr. J. Fineberg and G. Hanna (New York: International Publishers, 1969).

Lenin was endlessly fascinating to his own close associates—magnetic, harsh, demanding, domineering, but fascinating all the same. This, added to the fame of Lenin the man and Lenin the symbol, has brought into print a steady stream of memoirs and recollections of uneven quality and usefulness. Two of these are excerpted in this chapter: Trotsky's *The Young Lenin*, tr. Max Eastman (New York: Doubleday, 1972) and Valentinov's *Encounters with Lenin*, tr. Paul Rosta and Brian Pearce (London and New York: Oxford University Press, 1968). Both works are valuable and interesting, as is another work by Trotsky, *Lenin: Notes for a Biography*, tr. Tamara Deutscher (New York: Putnam, 1971), a new translation of a work first published in 1925. Valentinov, *The Early Years of Lenin*, tr. R. H. W. Theen (Ann Arbor: University of Michigan Press, 1969), is part of the same memoir as his *Encounters with Lenin*, but its hostility destroys much of its usefulness. Angelica Balabanoff, *Impressions of Lenin*, tr. Isotta Cesari (Ann Arbor: University of Michigan Press, 1964), is the memoir of another early socialist colleague of Lenin. N. K. Krupskaia, *Reminiscences of Lenin*, tr. Bernard Isaacs (Moscow: Foreign Language Publishing House, 1959), is the recollections of Lenin's wife, but it is more political polemic than domestic memoir. *About Lenin*, ed. George Hanna, tr. J.

Guralsky (Moscow: Progress Publishers, n.d.), is a series of readings from fellow revolutionaries and colleagues, published for "official" purposes and carefully sanitized of all unorthodoxy. Much more interesting and useful is *Not by Politics Alone—the Other Lenin*, ed. Tamara Deutscher (London: Allen and Unwin, 1973), an excellent collection of readings from Lenin himself and many of his contemporaries, about his views on a broad range of topics and revealing Lenin as casual and informal as he ever was.

The same fascination with Lenin that prompted the many recollections of those who knew him has created a flood of biographies. The best and most definitive is Louis F. Fischer, *The Life of Lenin* (New York: Harper & Row, 1964). Two straightforward, unbiased, workmanlike shorter biographies are Harold Shukman, *Lenin and the Russian Revolution* (New York: Putnam, 1967), and Robert Conquest, *V. I. Lenin* (New York: Viking, 1972). Isaac Deutscher, *Lenin's Childhood* (London and New York: Oxford University Press, 1970), is the separately published first chapter of a proposed definitive biography by a great authority; it can be favorably compared with Trotsky's *The Young Lenin.* Another work on Lenin's youth and the influences that formed him is R. H. W. Theen, *Lenin: Genesis and Development of a Revolutionary* (Philadelphia: Lippincott, 1973). A classic piece of exciting history and biography is Bertram D. Wolfe, *Three Who Made a Revolution, A Biographical History*, 5th. rev. ed. (New York: Stein and Day, 1984), the interconnected story of Lenin, Trotsky, and Stalin. A collection of Wolfe's essays on Lenin—most of them not previously published—can also be recommended, *Lenin and the Twentieth Century, A Bertram D. Wolfe Retrospective*, ed. Lennard D. Gerson (Stanford: Hoover Institution Press, 1984). More interesting and informative than Krupskaya's own memoirs is Robert H. McNeal, *Bride of the Revolution: Krupskaya and Lenin* (Ann Arbor: University of Michigan Press, 1972). A work on the history of the Soviet Union, by the French authority Hélène Carrere d'Encausse, tr. Valence Ionescu, is organized respectively, around the figures of Lenin, for the first volume and Stalin for the second: see *Lenin, Revolution and Power* (London and New York: Longman, 1982).

Robert V. Daniels, *Red October* (New York: Scribner's, 1967), excerpted in this chapter, is an excellent account of the actual outbreak of the Russian Revolution. Another key event is detailed in J. W. Wheeler-Bennett, *Brest-Litovsk, The Forgotten Peace, March 1918* (London: Macmillan, 1956 [1938]), a brilliant, now classic account. Three important works on the theoretical-intellectual background to Lenin and the revolution must also be recommended: Franco Venturi, *Roots of Revolution: A History of the Populist and Socialist Movements in Nineteenth-Century Russia*, tr. Francis Haskell (New York: Knopf, 1960), is the definitive work on its subject; Edmund Wilson, *To the Finland Station: A Study in the Writing and Acting of History*, rev. ed. (New York: Farrar, Straus, 1972 [1940]), is probably the classic work of the great American social and literary critic, a kind of intellectual history of socialist radicalism ending with Lenin and the outbreak of the Russian Revolution; and Alain Besançon, *The Rise of the Gulag: Intellectual Origins of Leninism*, tr. Sarah Matthews (New York: Continuum, 1980), is a piece of brilliant intellectual history on the ideological framework of the Soviet system and its crucial ties with Lenin's theories. Esther Kingston-Mann, *Lenin and the Problem of Marxist Peasant Revolution* (New York: Oxford University Press, 1983) is a specialized essay dealing with a crucial problem faced by Lenin in adapting classical Marxism to peasant Russia. Finally, Robert V. Daniels, *Russia* (Englewood Cliffs, N.J.: Prentice-Hall, 1964), is an excellent brief book, specifically intended as an introduction to Russia in the twentieth century.

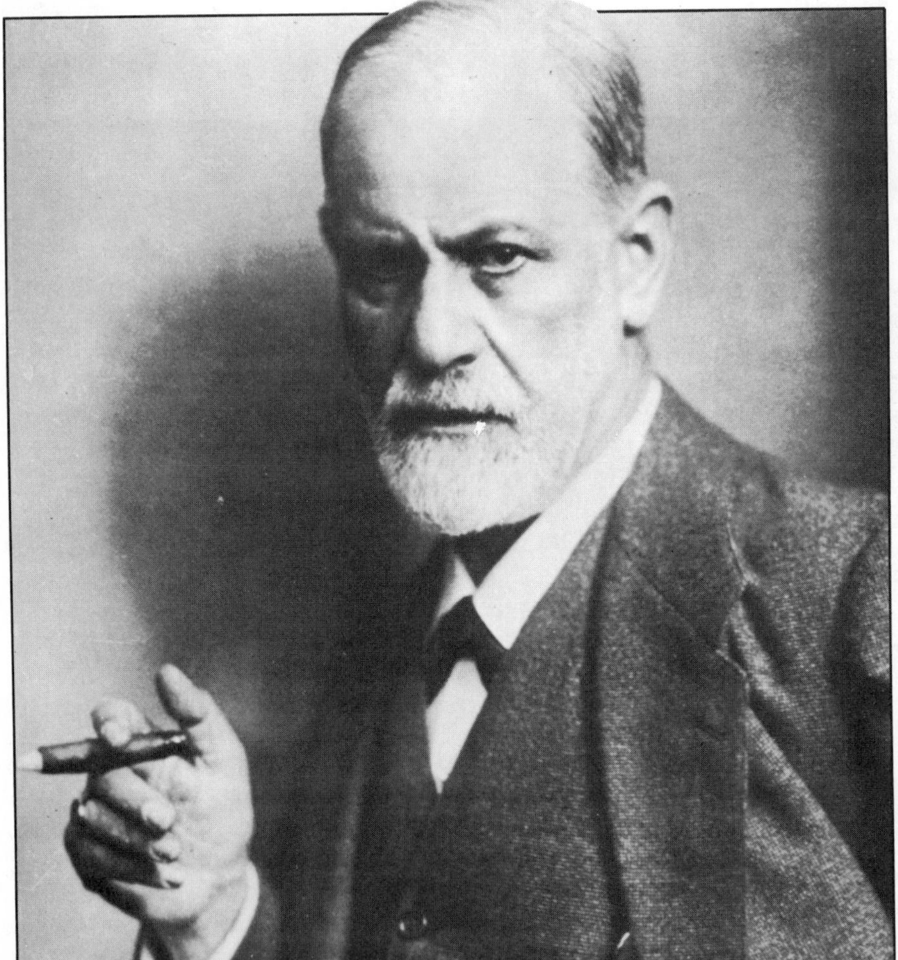

The Granger Collection

Sigmund Freud and the Discovery of the New Self

1856 born
1880 graduated in medicine from the University of Vienna
1897 self-analysis
1900 published *The Interpretation of Dreams*
1923 published *The Ego and the Id*
1938 fled Austria to England
1939 died

The visible, day-to-day events of Sigmund Freud's life are almost totally unrelated to what is important about the man and his work. He lived for almost eighty years in Vienna, where he was trained as a physician, where he practiced, theorized, wrote, and taught. As the favorite child of a well-to-do Jewish merchant family, he was loved and indulged. As an adult, he was happily married, the father of six children, experiencing the joys and sorrows common to ordinary fathers of ordinary families. Yet this man, who was himself staid, conventional, shy, and even "Victorian" about matters of sex, almost single-handedly created the modern "sexual revolution." Though he expected obedience and respect from his own children, he fathered the modern fashion of rebellion against parental authority. His training as a medical scientist taught him to look for clinically verifiable truths, yet he opened up the chaotic, individualistic mirror-world of wish-fulfillment fantasy. And while himself the most gentle and kindly of people, he nevertheless taught others to bring out into the open and express their most terrible hatreds, their most primal aggressions, their most destructive fears. In short, Sigmund Freud caused a revolution in the way people think about themselves and others so profound that it may, in and of itself, set the twentieth century apart from every earlier age in human history.

Freud graduated from the University of Vienna medical school in 1880 and the following year was licensed as a physician. His specialty was neurology, and he had already developed an interest in neuropathology. In addition to his hospital practice with severely disturbed patients, he soon began to see private patients suffering from emotional disorders. Eager to discover new methods of treating his patients, he experimented with hypnosis, which he finally abandoned as a tool of therapy when he found a more reliable instrument in what came to be called "free association." He was beginning to sense the importance of sexual problems in mental and emotional disturbances, and he was discovering with increasing frequency that these problems could be traced back to childhood, even infancy.

In the late 1890s, Freud began a systematic, rigorous, exhausting self-analysis. He had nothing to guide him except his confusing experiences with disturbed patients, combined with a growing conviction that he might find within himself a model for the mental-emotional makeup of all human beings, and that by understanding himself he might be able to understand others and treat them. This was a remarkable insight. Freud did indeed find his model and, in the process, he delineated the methodology that is called psychoanalysis.

Dreams and the Inner Self

SIGMUND FREUD

The source of the model and method for Freud's self-analysis was frankly revealed in his later books, but at the time he was struggling through his self-analysis, it was barely hinted at in his papers and correspondence. Then in 1950 there was discovered and shortly published an extensive corpus of letters from Freud to his friend and fellow physician in Berlin, Wilhelm Fliess. The letters, which dated from 1887 through 1902, reveal an intimate and completely candid account, often an almost day-to-day record, of Freud's self-analysis.

In letters written in the latter part of 1897, Freud excitedly reported to Fliess the beginning of his work in interpreting his dreams, which he believed contained "the most valuable conclusions and evidence." Three years later, he published a book on the subject, The Interpretation of Dreams, *and he never ceased to hold that his work on dreams was "the most valuable of all the discoveries it has been my good fortune to make."*[1] *But regardless of how important one may consider Freud's dream theories to be—and they have aroused considerable controversy—it is nevertheless astonishing to note that, in the accounts and interpretations of his dreams that he wrote to Fliess in 1897, Freud has already begun to talk about such eminently Freudian notions as father-figure conflict, the mother as an object of sexual desire, infantile sexuality, sibling rivalry, transference, and the famous Oedipus complex. Even his much later ideas about psycho-atavism are anticipated.*

We turn now to Freud's own account, in The Origins of Psycho-analysis, Letters to Wilhelm Fliess, Drafts and Notes: 1887–1902.

14.8.97.
Aussee.

My dear Wilhelm,

After a spell of good spirits here I am now having a fit of gloom. The chief patient I am busy with is myself. My little hysteria, which was much intensified by work, has yielded one stage further. The rest still sticks, That is the first reason for my mood. This analysis is harder than any

[1] Quoted in the preface to the third English edition of *The Interpretation of Dreams,* 1931.—ED.

other. It is also the thing that paralyses the power of writing down and communicating what so far I have learned. But I believe it has got to be done and is a necessary stage in my work. . . .

Outwardly very little is happening to me, but inside me something very interesting is happening. For the last four days my self-analysis, which I regard as indispensable for clearing up the whole problem, has been making progress in dreams and yielding the most valuable conclusions and evidence. At certain points I have the impression of having come to the end, and so far I have always known where the next night of dreams would continue. To describe it in writing is more difficult than anything else, and besides it is far too extensive. I can only say that in my case my father played no active role, though I certainly projected on to him an analogy from myself; that my "primary originator" [of neurosis] was an ugly, elderly but clever woman who told me a great deal about God and hell, and gave me a high opinion of my own capacities; that later (between the ages of two and two-and-a-half) libido towards *matrem* was aroused; the occasion must have been the journey with her from Leipzig to Vienna, during which we spent a night together and I must have had the opportunity of seeing her *nudam* (you have long since drawn the conclusions from this for your own son, as a remark of yours revealed); and that I welcomed my one-year-younger brother (who died within a few months) with ill wishes and real infantile jealousy, and that his death left the germ of guilt in me. I have long known that my companion in crime between the ages of one and two was a nephew of mine who is a year older than I am and now lives in Manchester; he visited us in Vienna when I was fourteen. We seem occasionally to have treated my niece, who was a year younger, shockingly. My nephew and younger brother determined, not only the neurotic side of all my friendships, but also their depth. My anxiety over travel you have seen yourself in full bloom.

I still have not got to the scenes which lie at the bottom of all this. If they emerge, and I succeed in resolving my hysteria, I shall have to thank the memory of the old woman who provided me at such an early age with the means for living and surviving. . . .

. . . Last night's dream produced the following under the most remarkable disguises:

She was my instructress in sexual matters, and chided me for being clumsy and not being able to do anything (that is always the way with neurotic impotence: anxiety over incapacity at school gets its sexual reinforcement this way). I saw the skull of a small animal which I thought of as a "pig" in the dream, though it was associated in the dream with your wish of two years ago that I might find a skull on the Lido to enlighten me, as Goethe once did. But I did not find it. Thus it was "a little *Schafskopf*."[2] The whole dream was full of the most wounding ref-

[2] Literally "sheep's head"; figuratively "blockhead."—Ed.

erences to my present uselessness as a therapist. Perhaps the origin of my tendency to believe in the incurability of hysteria should be sought here. Also she washed me in reddish water in which she had previously washed herself (not very difficult to interpret; I find nothing of the kind in my chain of memories, and so I take it for a genuine rediscovery); and she encouraged me to steal "Zehners" (ten-Kreuzer pieces) to give to her. A long chain of association connects these first silver Zehners to the heap of paper ten-florin notes which I saw in the dream as Martha's housekeeping money. The dream can be summed up as "bad treatment." Just as the old woman got money from me for her bad treatment of me, so do I now get money for the bad treatment of my patients; a special role in it was played by Q, who conveyed through you a suggestion that I ought not to take money from her as the wife of a colleague (he stipulated that I should).

A severe critic might say that all this was phantasy projected into the past instead of being determined by the past. The *experimenta crucis* would decide the matter against him. The reddish water seems a point of this kind. Where do all patients derive the horrible perverse details which are often as alien to their experience as to their knowledge?

15.10.97.
IX. Bergasse 19.

My dear Wilhelm,

My self-analysis is the most important thing I have in hand, and promises to be of the greatest value to me, when it is finished. When I was in the very midst of it it suddenly broke down for three days, and I had the feeling of inner binding about which my patients complain so much, and I was inconsolable. . . .

My practice, ominously enough, still allows me plenty of free time.

All this is the more valuable from my point of view because I have succeeded in finding a number of real points of reference. I asked my mother whether she remembered my nurse. "Of course," she said, "an elderly woman, very shrewd indeed. She was always taking you to church. When you came home you used to preach, and tell us all about how God conducted His affairs. At the time I was in bed when Anna was being born" (Anna is two-and-a-half years younger) "she turned out to be a thief, and all the shiny Kreuzers and Zehners and toys that had been given you were found among her things. Your brother Philipp went himself to fetch the policeman, and she got ten months." Now see how that confirms the conclusions from my dream interpretation. I have easily been able to explain the one possible mistake. I wrote to you that she got me to steal Zehners and give them to her. The dream really means that she stole herself. For the dream-picture was a memory that I took money from a doctor's mother, *i.e.,* wrongfully. The real meaning is that the old woman stood for me, and that the doctor's mother was my mother. I was so far from being aware that the old woman was a thief that my interpretation went astray. I also asked about the doctor we had in Freiberg, because I had a dream full of animosity about him. In analysing the dream-personage behind whom he was hidden I remembered a Professor von K., my history master, who did not seem to fit in, as I had no particular feelings about him and indeed got on with him quite well. My mother told me that the doctor of my infancy had only one eye, and among all my masters Professor K. was the only one with the same disability!

It might be objected that these coincidences are not conclusive, because I might have heard that the nurse was a thief in later childhood and to all appearances forgotten the fact until it emerged in the dream. I think myself that that must have been the case. But I have another unexceptionable and amusing piece of evidence. If the woman disappeared so suddenly, I said to myself, some impression of the event must have been left inside me. Where was it now? Then a scene occurred to me which for the last twenty-nine years has been turning up from time to time in my conscious memory without my understanding it. I was crying my heart out, because my mother was nowhere to be found. My brother Philipp (who is twenty years older than I) opened a cupboard for me, and when I found that mother was not there either I cried still more, until she came through the door, looking slim and beautiful. What can that mean? Why should my brother open the cupboard for me when he knew that my mother was not inside it and that opening it therefore could not quiet me? Now I suddenly understand. I must have begged him to open the cupboard. When I could not find my mother, I feared she must have vanished, like my nurse not long before. I must have heard that the old woman had been locked, or rather "boxed" up, because my brother Philipp, who is now sixty-three, was fond of such humorous expressions, and still is to the present day. The fact that I turned to him shows that I was well aware of his part in my nurse's disappearance.

Since then I have got much further, but have not yet reached any real resting-place. Communicating the incomplete is so laborious and would take me so far afield that I hope you will excuse me, and content yourself with hearing the parts which are established for certain. If the analysis goes on as I expect, I shall write it all out systematically and lay the results before you. So far I have found nothing completely new, but all the complications to which by now I am used. It is no easy matter. Being entirely honest with oneself is a good exercise. Only one idea of general value has occurred to me. I have found love of the mother and jealousy of the father in my own case too, and now believe it to be a general phenomenon of early childhood, even if it does not always occur so early as in children who have been made hysterics. (Similarly with the "romanticization of origins" in the case of paranoiacs—heroes, founders of religion.) If that is the case, the gripping power of *Oedipus Rex,* in spite of all the rational objections to the inexorable fate that the story presupposes, becomes intelligible, and one can understand why later fate dramas were such failures. Our feelings rise against any arbitrary, individual fate such as shown in the *Ahnfrau,*[3] etc., but the Greek myth seizes on a compulsion which everyone recognizes because he has felt traces of it in himself. Every member of the audience was once a budding Oedipus in phantasy, and this dream-fulfillment played out in reality causes everyone to recoil in horror, with the full measure of repression which separates his infantile from his present state.

The idea has passed through my head that the same thing may lie at the root of *Hamlet*. I am not thinking of Shakespeare's conscious intentions, but supposing rather that he was impelled to write it by a real event because his own unconscious understood that of his hero. How can one explain the hysteric Hamlet's phrase. "So conscience doth make cowards of us all," and his hesitation to avenge his father by killing his uncle, when he himself so casually sends his courtiers to their death and despatches Laertes so quickly? How better than by the torment roused in him by the obscure memory that he himself had meditated the same deed against his father because of passion for his mother—"use every man after his desert, and who should 'scape whipping?" His conscience is his unconscious feeling of guilt. And are not his sexual coldness when talking to Ophelia, his rejection of the instinct to beget children, and finally his transference of the deed from his father to Ophelia, typically hysterical? And does he not finally succeed, in just the same remarkable way as my hysterics do, in bringing down his punishment on himself and suffering the same fate as his father, being poisoned by the same rival?

Theory as Therapy

ANTHONY STORR

Freud's self-analysis, elaborated in his books and papers, his lectures, and his training of pupils, became the paradigm for the method of modern Freudian psychoanalysis. Psychoanalysts do to their patients almost exactly and literally what Freud did to himself. Both the man and the method have been institutionalized into what Anthony Storr calls "a point

[3] The title of a play by Grillparzer.—ED.

of view, a way of thinking, an attitude to life." Dr. Storr is himself a psychotherapist and the author of several books, including one on C. G. Jung, Freud's great dissident disciple. In the article excerpted below, "Freud on the Couch" (1970), which originally appeared in Horizon, *Dr. Storr describes how Freud's experience of self-analysis and his treatment of patients by the principles he derived became the model for psychoanalysts who came after him. "If ever a man was a living example of his own theories," Storr contends, "it was Freud."*

And if something of the autocratic pose,
The paternal strictness be distrusted, still
Clung to his utterance and features,
It was a protective imitation

For one who lived among enemies so long;
If often he was wrong and at times absurd,
To us he is no more a person
Now but a whole climate of opinion.

OF COURSE W. H. Auden is right. Freud, like Marx and Darwin, those other destroyers of nineteenth-century preconceptions with whom his name is so often linked, is no longer merely a person; he is a point of view, a way of thinking, an attitude to life, and above all, a continuing force to be reckoned with, one who can be neither dismissed nor ignored by anyone concerned with the human predicament. His ideas have become so ubiquitous that it is difficult to imagine how men thought before he formulated them.

Before World War I our grandfathers would have considered themselves as being governed chiefly by reason, although subject to deplorable spells of irrationality. Freud reversed the picture, claiming that reason's voice, though persistent, had but a very small influence upon human conduct. Freud also made us regard both virtue and conventional morality with suspicion. In 1900 the man who displayed altruism and self-sacrifice would have been regarded as simply "good," and if he was celibate, would have been congratulated upon his self-control and spirituality. It would not have occurred to the Victorians to suspect that unselfishness might be self-punishment; that kindness might conceal a patronizing superiority; that altruism could be a mask for self-centeredness, or celibacy an ignominious flight from woman.

Darwin shook man's self-esteem by demonstrating his humble origins and his kinship with other animals. Freud shattered it by showing that man's proudest spiritual achievements were rooted in primitive instinct. Not even children were allowed their "innocence," and the cozy, comfortable love of the Victorian family was shown to be based upon violent sensuality.

Freud tore down many façades, leaving us naked and ashamed, but more realistic. Since his revelations, Western man has become incapable of taking any form of human behavior at face value. It is impossible to think of any other individual who has so affected the way we look at our ordinary daily pursuits. . . .

There follows a sketch of Freud, through his early physiological and neurological training and his experimentation with hypnosis under the influence of Josef Breuer and Jean Martin Charcot, which led him to the important discovery of free association in dealing with hysterics.

Freud's passion for investigation into origins soon led to his exploring the childhood of his patients. Breuer's case had convinced him that some neurotic symptoms were concerned with the suppression of painful memories and that the recovery of these memories was accompanied by the disappearance of the symptoms. Pursuing this idea, Freud soon discovered that many of the distasteful incidents that his patients recalled and that seemed to have caused their illnesses were sexual in nature. Both Breuer and Charcot had, in Freud's hearing, dropped hints that the secrets of the marriage bed were connected with neurotic symptoms. But Freud, who was easily shocked and puritanical in temperament, did not take these remarks seriously and dismissed them from his mind. When he came to investigate his own patients, however, he discovered that a great many of their anxieties and painful memories centered around the facts of sexuality. Moreover, he established that the primary cause of neurosis was the sexuality of childhood.

Today this is taken so much for granted that it is difficult to realize the shock and surprise with which Freud's first announcements about infantile sexuality were received. Indeed, it was somewhat naïve of him not to anticipate that people would be shocked, especially in view of his own primness. But Freud the conventional, bourgeois family man and Freud the relentless seeker after truth were two very different people. If neurosis in adult life was, as seemed probable, the result of trauma in early childhood, and if these traumata were chiefly sexual in nature, then it was Freud's duty as a doctor and a scientist to say so, however unpalatable these truths might be. Freud, like many another Jew, had little expectation of being generally popular in any case, and abuse made him all the more obstinate. Instead of modifying his tone, he interpreted the inevitable attacks as further evidence to support the psychoanalytic view that men are intensely reluctant to face the truth about themselves. For by this time Freud's early belief that neurosis was due to traumatic incidents was gradually becoming modified. Although traumata could and did occur, what neurotics repressed was not simply the memory of such incidents but whole aspects of the primitive and instinctive parts of themselves.

Among Freud's early cases of hysteria were a surprisingly large number of patients who reported incidents of seduction by one or the other parent. At first Freud took these stories literally, but later he came to realize that what a patient told him was largely phantasy and wish-fulfillment, not an account of a real incident. This discovery was at first distressing to Freud, because he thought it represented a failure in his technique. However, he persisted with his investigations, and what finally emerged from this was the importance of the patient's inner world of phantasy. Instead of concentrating on actual childhood traumata, important as they may be, it became more and more a part of psychoanalytic technique to investigate the patient's inner world: that world of hopes, daydreams, fears, loves, and hates that originates in infancy, persists into adult life, and is only tenuously related to the hard facts of the real world.

Freud soon discovered that as the lengthy analysis proceeded, he himself became increasingly important in the patient's inner world. He wrote: "In every analytic treatment there arises, without the physician's agency, an intense emotional relationship between the patient and the analyst, which is not to be accounted for by the actual situation. It can be of a positive or of a negative character and can vary between the extremes of a passionate, completely sensual love and the unbridled expression of an embittered defiance and hatred." Around 1892 Freud began to be aware of the importance of this. The delineation of transference is the second important innovation for which every psychotherapist, Freudian or not, must acknowledge a debt to Freud. When Jung first visited Freud in 1907, Freud asked him, "What do you think of transference?" Jung replied: "It is the alpha and omega in treatment." "You have understood," said Freud.

Transference is, of course, a universal phenomenon. When we enter a new situation in life or are confronted by a new person, we project upon him the prejudices of the past and our previous experience of people. Indeed, getting to know a person is largely a matter of withdrawing projections, of dispelling the smoke screen of prejudice and replacing it with the empirical data.

Thus, when a patient comes into an analyst's consulting room, he brings with him all his past anxieties, fears, prejudices, and hopes. If he is habitually dominant, he will tend to be dominant toward the analyst. If he is submissive elsewhere, he will be so in analysis. Freud's discovery was that if these ingrained (and generally unrecognized) attitudes and prejudices can be made conscious, they can be modified.

No psychotherapeutic treatment of any thoroughness can bypass a repeated discussion of the relationship of the patient to the analyst, and of the changes that take place in this relationship as treatment progresses. Once again, we owe the discovery of a powerful therapeutic weapon to

Freud's reluctance to become too personally involved with his patients. I do not think that transference would have been so clearly delineated if Freud had been of a warmer, less controlled temperament. Because he developed a technique in which he said very little, sat behind the patient, and did not obtrude his own personality, he was more of a blank screen than an active doctor would have been. He therefore tended to be more receptive to his patient's projections than a conventional doctor would have been. It is the unknown person upon whom we project our phantasies, and Freud discovered that being an enigma to his patients produced material of psychological interest from them.

The opening of the inner phantasy world of patients led to the exploration and investigation of all kinds of psychological data that had previously been dismissed as meaningless. The delusions of the insane, the irrational fears with which many people are burdened, and the whole realm of dreams were opened to analytical investigation.

Freud himself regarded dreams as the royal road to the unconscious. His book *The Interpretation of Dreams* was first published in 1900. To the end of his life he continued to regard it as his most important contribution to the understanding of the human mind. Ernest Jones reports that Freud's two favorite books were *The Interpretation of Dreams* and *Three Essays on the Theory of Sexuality*. Of these books he said to Jones: "It seems to be my fate to discover only the obvious: that children have sexual feelings, which every nursemaid knows; and that night dreams are just as much a wish fulfillment as daydreams." *The Interpretation of Dreams* is largely concerned with Freud's own dreams. In October, 1897, during an extended period of self-analysis, he wrote a letter to Wilhelm Fliess in which he describes the basic elements of the Oedipus complex: love for the parent of the opposite sex and jealousy of the parent of the same sex. In his preface to the second edition of *The Interpretation of Dreams* Freud writes: "For me, of course, this book has an additional subjective significance, which I did not understand until after its completion. It revealed itself to me as a piece of self-analysis, as my reaction to the death of my father, that is, to the most important event, the most poignant loss, in a man's life."

This is by no means so for every man, and Freud's assumption underlines the point made above: that psychoanalysis in its original form was a father-oriented psychology. Freud, like many other people who become concerned with the treatment of neurotics, had his own share of neurotic symptoms. He suffered from anxiety attacks in which he had a fear of dying, and he was also overanxious about traveling. In addition, he suffered alternations of mood, being sometimes profoundly distressed, depressed, and unable to work, and more rarely, full of excitement and self-confidence. During the time of his engagement he was tortured by doubt about whether his fiancée really loved him. For a long time he could not tolerate any differences between her opinions and his own, and he demanded that she completely identify with him. This may seem odd in a man so outspokenly opposed to current thought, but it is surely endearing and a sign of Freud's basic humanity that in his private life he certainly did demand support, both from his wife and later from his pupils. The world owes a great deal to Freud's basic insecurity.

Like other men of genius, Freud possessed a personality compounded of many opposing strands. Perhaps its oddest and most interesting feature was his invariable inclination to reduce everything to the lowest common factor. Freud's psychology has often been criticized by other people—notably Jung—on the grounds that it leaves little room for human aspiration, or even for human goodness. On analytical investigation even the most self-sacrificing action tends to be interpreted as distorted self-interest. Indeed, Freud seemed to take an almost masochistic delight in reducing the whole of human endeavor to aggressive or sexual drives of a most basic and primitive kind. Psychoanalysis is a discipline that allows little room for altruism, romance, or spirituality. In this connection it is significant that Freud was so fond of Jewish humor, which often depends upon the deflation of pretension and the reduction of sentiment to self-interest.

If ever a man was a living example of his own theories, it was Freud. His creative energy and his great capacity for work were sublimations bought at the expense of inhibiting more primitive drives. The expression of both his sexuality and his aggression was severely inhibited. It is said that the most shattering discovery in his self-analysis was his deeply buried hatred of the father he thought he had admired and respected. Throughout his life Freud was particularly patient, tolerant, and kind. He always denied being a genius on the grounds that geniuses were intolerable in the home, and his family, he said, would confirm that he was unusually easy to live with. This was undoubtedly true, but it is probable that it was at the price of a certain lack of playfulness or vitality of a more ordinary kind. Freud seems to have been a markedly controlled man, controlled to a point where he revealed very little of himself, either to his patients or to his acquaintances. In 1909, when his work was first beginning to reach a wider audience, he was asked to lecture at Clark Univercity, Worcester, Massachusetts. He traveled across the Atlantic with two colleagues, Jung and Sandor Ferenczi; and the three men spent a good deal of their time analyzing one another's dreams. While in New York, Freud apparently confided in Jung to the extent of telling him about some of his personal difficulties. An intimate dream came up for discussion, and Jung asked for further associations. But Freud refused to give them, saying, so Jung reported: "I can't give you any further associations, for if I did I might lose my authority." Jung's retort was, "Analysis is excellent, except for the analyst."

Even those who were closest to him, like Ernest Jones, felt that there were secrets about Freud that they would never know. Jones says of him: "He was beyond doubt someone whose instincts were far more powerful than those of the average man, but whose repressions were even more potent." He also says, "Everything points to a remarkable concealment in Freud's love life." Although aspects of Freud's self-analysis appear in *The Interpretation of Dreams,* there is a great deal about him that we should like to know but that we shall never know. The man who spent his life investigating the secrets of other people more intimately than any man had done before, was very reluctant to reveal his own.

Freud, Freudianism, and History

ERIK H. ERIKSON

In 1938, Freud, like so many other Jews of every class and station, was forced to flee his country by the threat of Hitler. He died in London the following year. But one need not share Hitler's disparaging opinion of psychoanalysis in order to reject it, much less to raise serious questions about it. Both Freud's basic theories and his methods of treatment were controversial in his own lifetime. Three of his six closest early disciples fell away from him, two of them, Adler and Jung, with much public clamor and considerable bitterness.

Others, even some who have remained in the fold, have nevertheless questioned the very normative features of the psychoanalytic approach we have already noted. Erich Fromm, for example, talks about the stifling orthodoxy of the "dogma" and ritual of psychoanalysis, "the couch with the chair behind it, the four or five sessions every week, the analyst's silence, except when he gives an 'interpretation'—all these factors have been transformed from what once were useful means to an end, into a sacred ritual, without which orthodox psychoanalysis is unthinkable."[4]

Others question the applicability of the laborious individual analytic technique to the mass neuroses of an entire society or its restrictive linkage to medicine, while still others have even more serious

[4] Erich Fromm, *Sigmund Freud's Mission: An Analysis of His Personality and Influence* (New York: Harper, 1959), pp. 106–07.

reservations about the broader social and historical effects of the cult of psychoanalysis. Among the latter critics is the German scholar Erik Erikson. Erikson, who has lived and worked largely in the United States since 1933, has been called the greatest living psychoanalyst; he is certainly one of the most influential. In his Life History and the Historical Moment, *he writes that the very fact that the myth of psychoanalysis has passed into the common history of the Western world cannot be avoided, nor can a sense of responsibility for its implications. A specialist in the psychology of young adulthood, Erikson points with some disquiet to the role of psychoanalytic theory in the youth permissiveness and often the violence of our current culture. He suggests that the Freudian "adjustment to reality" may really be a code phrase for submission by the weak to the strong and ruthless. Perhaps in our attempt to remedy sexual repression, we have come to license the unlimited "use" of one being by another, thus linking psychoanalysis to the other dehumanizing mechanisms of a "technocratic age." Furthermore, orthodox psychoanalysis may well confuse the origin of neurosis with its cause, resulting in rejection of individual responsibility for individual behavior.*

The following selection is an excerpt from Life History and the Historical Moment.

AS HISTORY changes and, with it, the role of psychoanalysis in society, new doubts about the validity of the psychoanalytic kind of enlightenment are added to the "natural" resistance against the recognition of unconscious motivation. And it may well be that we psychoanalysts ourselves carry with us some sense of hybris over being successful practitioners and widely read advocates of what in its beginnings was and in many ways still is and must be a very intimate clinical art-and-science. . . .

. . . When Freud founded this radically introspective branch of the Enlightenment, he still could take much of Western civilization and its belief in enlightened progress for granted and was faced with the changing world of technocracy, with world wars and world revolutions, only toward the end of his life. And he may well have foreseen that psychoanalysis would not only continue to be rejected by reactionaries and moralists —*that* he was proud of—but that in some parts of the world it might be widely accepted and, in fact, flauntingly acted out as well as talked out and yet remain covertly resisted in its essence. If informed youth in the second half of this fast-moving century is attempting, by an alternation of revolt and compliance, to manage the memory and the mandate of the revolutionary changes of the first half, the influence of the Freudian enlightenment is part of that burden. And at times youth does seem to claim mastery over the dangerous knowledge of the unconscious by displaying previously forbidden and denied impulses (such as patricidal wishes or bisexual inclinations) with a mixture of passion and mockery, or by challenging the unconscious with precipitate experiences induced by drugs. But if in this stance we detect an attempt to assimilate the insights of psychoanalysis by means of the overt enactment of wishes once described as either repressed or only symbolically expressed, psychoanalytic enlightenment may, indeed, be faced with new Hippocratic tasks which we must attempt to envisage.

At any rate, today the relationship between the generations and between the sexes can no longer be approached with psychoanalytic concepts without considering the role which these concepts have played and will and should play in the cultural and ideological controversies of our time. . . .

Patients . . . are those members of a given society who—for a variety of etiological reasons—are most inactivated by inner conflicts shared by all. And the public, obscurely aware of this, is so eager for prescriptive slogans defining normal and moral conduct that it will dramatically oversimplify what we conceive to be delicately scientific and therapeutic matters. We may then claim that we have been misunderstood, and that all we wanted to do was to heal specific disturbances or to understand circumscribed aspects of human nature. But perhaps we should take a closer look at the wider applications which our therapeutic enlightenment seems to suggest.

A few brief and simple examples taken from recent history must suffice. Take the matter of "adjustment to reality." Certain types of patients were found to be suffering from partial but distinct denials of verifiable fact. Treatment, we say, must help them to make the reasons for that denial conscious and to bring the whole person up to that level of insight and willpower which we attribute to the "intact" part of the personality—that part which, in fact, makes the person treatable. What we really hope for, especially with our more ambitious treatments, is adaptation rather than adjustment, in that the cured patient, while refusing to overadjust, should learn to *adapt to* what is factual and inevitable and yet also strive by a freer participation in actuality to *adapt to himself* (and to those he cares for) what can and should be changed in his environment. It is this active and effective quality of true adaptation which prompted me to suggest, in a lecture on medical ethics, that the Golden Rule in all its classical brevity, when viewed with modern insights, might be seen to direct us to do to another what will further the other's development even as it furthers our own. Mutual activation is the ethical essence of "my" rule; and it implies that true communality permits and demands it. Yet, before we know it, our vocabulary is seen and used to support a general ideal of *adjustedness*—and this often to conditions which we, in fact, do not believe a person *should* be encouraged to tolerate, precisely because they make mutuality and communality impossible and, in fact, enslave the more sensitive and insightful to conditions which strongly favor other, and often more ruthless characters.

Or take the diagnosis of "sexual repression." Our treatment was intended to lift infantile repressions in order to restore to the adult patient the capacity to make conscious choices—that is, to make it possible to tolerate in oneself and to find an interpersonal style for what is deeply needed and truly wanted, and to discard what is neither. At the same time, it was hoped that new forms of child rearing informed by psychoanalysis would help to alleviate rather than to aggravate the human tendency toward repression. Together with the ideal of adjustability, however—and, of course, in line with a general change of mores—psychoanalytic sexology seemed to prescribe "unrepressed" rules of conduct by which that person is considered the "freest" who can engage in an unlimited use of others for the obsessive expression of all the "techniques" suggested by the sex books.

And yet, we would agree that a common characteristic of all ills, sins, and evils, whether they are spelled in small letters and are accessible to therapies of the mind or are capitalized for higher attention, is the use of another as a mere object, whether the other is thus demeaned as an inferior creature, as cheap merchandise, or as a mere mechanical contrivance. Modern technicism, which tends to make a statistic of each person, may be aggravating just such Evil under the disguise of an ethos of efficiency beyond compassion or awareness of guilt.

Finally, let me point to some consequences of the great clinical invention of reconstructing a detailed *pathogenesis*—the very invention to which we owe the knowledge of early stages and thus the life-historical as well as the case-historical point of view. A resulting emphasis on the earliest "causes" of a disturbance has contributed to decisive insights, and this especially as part of a methodological self-appraisal. However, it can also result in a relative neglect of those conflicts specific for the age of acute onset or aggravation of the disturbance in later life stages. In fact, the general preoccupation with first "causes" has led to a widespread habit of righteous and often vindictive complaints (and this at times on the part of individuals from rather overprotective backgrounds) over having been victimized by progenitors and assorted other exploiters. This, as we have seen, can exhaust itself in a habitual rage not conducive to inner freedom and least of all to a recognition of an adult's responsibility for himself and others.

Historically speaking, then, it seems necessary to be aware of the total moral climate in which psychoanalytic insights take their place in a given period. Certainly, such insights cannot count any more on the particular matrix of an enlightened ethics within the "morality" which Freud "took for granted." No wonder, then, that individual psychotherapy in the classical sense is being complemented by a search for new therapeutic conventions such as therapy in groups or other methods of sharing a wider awareness. But where such search turns to more mystical sources of enlightenment rooted in different civilizations, the question is to what extent they may serve as an escape from the Judeo-Christian heritage which we must come to grips with—even as those civilizations must come to terms with their now internalized values—as humanity enters the technocratic age.

Suggestions for Further Reading

FREUD WAS HIMSELF a prolific writer for all his mature life. The definitive collection of his writings is *The Complete Psychological Works of Sigmund Freud*, tr. and ed. James Strachey and Anna Freud, 23 vols. (London: Hogarth Press, 1953). There is a smaller and less erudite collection, *The Basic Writings of Sigmund Freud*, tr. and ed. A. A. Brill (New York: Modern Library, 1938), and an even smaller, but less satisfactory and more fragmentary *A General Selection from the Works of Sigmund Freud*, ed. John Rickman (New York: Doubleday, 1937). There are separate editions of many of his works: *An Autobiographical Study*, tr. James Strachey (London: Institute of Psycho-analysis, 1950); *The Interpretation of Dreams*, tr. A. A. Brill (New York: Modern Library, 1950); *Totem and Taboo*, tr. James Strachey (New York: Norton, 1950); *Beyond the Pleasure Principle*, tr. C. J. M. Hubback (New York: Boni and Liveright, 1924); and *The Ego and the Id*, tr. Joan Riviere, ed. James Strachey, rev. ed. (New York: Norton, 1962). His letters are among his most important literary and scientific writings. We have excerpted for this chapter a selection from the important collection *The Origins of Psychoanalysis, Letters to Wilhelm Fliess, Drafts and Notes (1887–1902)* (New York: Doubleday, 1954). The balance of this correspondence has now been released by the Freud estate and is scheduled to be published within the next few years. Another important collection is *The Freud-Jung Letters . . . .* , tr. Ralph Manheim and R. F. C. Hull, ed. William McGuire (Princeton, N.J.: Princeton University Press, 1974). There is also a broader, more general collection, edited by his son Ernst, *Sigmund Freud, Letters*, tr. Tania Stern and James Stern, selected and ed. Ernst L. Freud (New York: Basic Books, 1960). Another son, Martin Freud, has written a biographical recollection of his father, *Sigmund Freud: Man and Father* (New York: Vanguard, 1958).

The most extensive and detailed biography of Freud is Ernest Jones, *The Life and Works of Sigmund Freud*, 3 vols. (New York: Basic Books, 1953–1957), which is also available in an abridged edition by Lionel Trilling and Steven Marcus (New York: Basic Books, 1961). Jones celebrated Freud in *Sigmund Freud: Four Centenary Addresses* (New York: Basic Books, 1956), especially the fourth address, "The Man and his Achievements." The conclusions of Jones's adulatory biography have now been challenged by a new generation of scholars. One of these is Herbert Marcuse, whose famous book *Eros and Civilization: A Philosophical Inquiry into Freud* (Boston: Beacon, 1969), discusses the philosophic roots of psychoanalytic theory. Another is Erich Fromm, one of the most perceptive and readable of Freud's critics: see especially two of his books, *Sigmund Freud's Mission: An Analysis of his Personality and Influence* (New York: Harper, 1959), and *Greatness and Limitations of Freud's Thought* (New York: Harper & Row, 1980). Still another critical reevaluation is Marthe Robert, *The Psychoanalytic Revolution: Sigmund Freud's Life and Achievement*, tr. Kenneth Morgan (New York: Harcourt, 1966).

On the other side of the critical question is a recent book by Jeffrey B. Abramson, *Liberation and Its Limits: The Moral and Political Thought of Freud* (New York and London: Free Press and Macmillan, 1984), in which the author argues that our contemporary excesses of liberation represent a perversion of Freud's concept of social responsibility into personal, hedonistic anarchy. Aside from such works, however, there are two books that are nonpolemical and straightforward appraisals of Freud: Reuben Fine, *Freud: A Critical Re-evaluation of His Theories* (New York: McKay, 1962), and Ronald W. Clark, *Freud, The Man and the Cause* (New York: Random House, 1980).

There are three excellent books that deal not so much with Freud's interpretation as the matter of Freud in his own time: Gunnar Brandell, *Freud, A Man of His Century*, tr. Iaian White (Atlantic Highlands, N.J.: Humanities Press, 1979); Frank J. Sulloway, *Freud, Biologist of the Mind: Beyond the Psychoanalytic Legend* (New York: Basic Books, 1979), dealing with the biological and scientific world of the late nineteenth century that formed Freud's scientific thought; and Seymour Fisher and Roger P. Greenberg, *The Scientific Credibility of Freud's Theories and Therapy* (New York: Basic Books, 1977).

In the larger framework of the continuing influence of Freud, see the excellent survey by J. A. C. Brown, *Freud and the Post-Freudians* (Baltimore: Penguin, 1961); Erik Erikson, *Life History and the Historical Moment* (New York: Norton, 1975), excerpted for this chapter; Louis Breger, *Freud's Unfinished Journey: Conventional and Critical Perspectives in Psychoanalytical Theory* (London: Routledge and Kegan Paul, 1981); and finally Janet Malcolm, *Psychoanalysis: The Impossible Profession* (New York: Knopf, 1981), a sharp and well-formulated attack on the effectiveness of the entire mechanism.

The Bettmann Archive

Adolf Hitler: Nightmare of Our Century

1889 born in Linz, Austria
1923 Munich beer hall *Putsch*
1933 became chancellor of Germany
1939 German invasion of Poland: beginning of World War II
1945 died by suicide

In the early 1920s, the Bavarian city of Munich was a gathering place for the most militant and dissatisfied groups of German war veterans. They despised the weak government of the postwar Weimar Republic; they hated the allies who had defeated Germany in World War I and now seemed bent upon destroying it in peace; and they were desperate in the face of German economic collapse, unemployment, and runaway inflation. In this kind of setting, with a weak and harassed central government far away and the Bavarian state authorities—already distrustful of the national government and disposed to separatism—unwilling or unable to threaten them, a rash of splinter political parties flourished. These parties fought bitterly for support among the veterans and among the equally dissatisfied and hard-pressed working classes from which the bulk of the veterans came. At one extreme were the Communists; at the other a cluster of right-wing extremist groups, which, though they battled each other for supporters, shared a hatred for the Communists and for the Jews, who were a handy—and hated—minority to seize upon. One of these right-wing parties was the National Socialist German Workers' Party—*Nationalsozialistische Deutsche Arbeiterpartei*—Nazi for short. Since 1921 its leader was Adolf Hitler.

In November 1923, Hitler and his party command conceived a plan for a *Putsch,* an armed uprising to capture the leaders of the Bavarian state and force them to proclaim a revolution against the Weimar Republic. It was to be the beginning of a new Germany. Hitler had gained the cooperation of General Erich von Ludendorff, one of Germany's war heroes and a right-wing, nationalist fanatic himself, and he was confident that Ludendorff's presence would prevent the military's intervening against the coup. He was also sure that he could count on the Bavarian government's growing hostility toward the government in Berlin. On the evening of November 8, the Bavarian authorities announced a rally and meeting to be held in a Munich beer hall. Hitler and his fellow party leaders—supported by a considerable force of private military police and strong-arm hoodlums already known as stormtroopers—broke into the meeting. They hustled the government officials at gunpoint into a side room and forced them to proclaim a German revolution with Hitler as dictator. As soon as the officials were released, however, they repudiated their action. On the following morning, when the rebels attempted to march on the War Ministry building, they were met by the police. A skirmish ensued and sixteen Nazis were killed. Two days later, Hitler was arrested. The "beer hall *Putsch*" had been a total failure.

The apparently ruined politician who was so ignominiously handled by the Munich police in those autumn days of 1923 had been born in nearby Austria, just across the Bavarian border, in the little town of Braunau, in 1889. The details of his early life are sketchy and contradictory. Hitler's own later accounts of his youth differed as the circumstances demanded, and he generally preferred to remain somewhat mysterious.

His father had been an older man, a retired customs official, stern and domineering. His mother was much younger, usually dominated—if not brutalized—by her husband and idolized by her son. Her death in 1907 was a crushing blow to Hitler. Soon after his mother's death, with his mediocre career in high school completed, Hitler went to Vienna, hoping to be admitted to the state school of art. He failed the entrance examination twice and then drifted into the Viennese underworld of poverty and crime, often near starvation, though he occasionally found work as a sign and postcard painter.

Hitler then went to Munich, and there, with the outbreak of World War I, he joined the German army. Despite a relatively undistinguished military record—he rose only to corporal's rank—the war was the high point in Hitler's life. He belonged at last to a substantial, honored organization engaged in a noble and desperately contested cause. In 1918, as the war was ending, Hitler was hospitalized as the result of a gas attack, and, though not seriously injured, he suffered temporary blindness and loss of speech.

After the war, Hitler joined the obscure political party he was later to lead, and he found a new cause in politics—the obvious end for him being the restoration of the German glory that had come to ruin in 1918. By the time of the failure of the "beer hall *Putsch*," Hitler was a known figure in German radical politics. He should have been finished by the fiasco of the *Putsch*, but he was not. In 1923 his career was only just beginning.

Mein Kampf

ADOLF HITLER

At the instance of the Bavarian authorities, Hitler and the other leaders of the Putsch *were tried, not in the federal court, but a provincial Bavarian court and given the minimum sentence of five years—of which Hitler served less than nine months—in nearby Landsberg prison. In prison he was treated more like an exiled head of state than a common criminal, with exemption from work details, extended visiting hours for the streams of political dignitaries that came to see him, and other special privileges. Despite the failure of his uprising, Hitler still commanded several thousand irregular stormtroopers, even though they were scattered throughout Bavaria. And no one knew how many members his party had, nor the exact extent of his influence. It was in Landsberg prison that his secretary, Rudolf Hess, suggested to Hitler the title* der Fuehrer *(the leader). Hitler liked it and adopted it. It was also in prison that he wrote the book "frequently asked of me" by his followers, which he intended to be "useful for the Movement."* [1] *He called it* Mein Kampf (My Struggle).

The title suggests an autobiography, and in part it is an autobiography, though with much falsification of fact. It is also a political polemic against communism and a distorted vision of history, rife with the most savage and hate-filled racism. But most of all, Mein Kampf *is a vision of the future as Hitler intended it to be under the domination of his party —the Movement. In this respect, the book is both a political manifesto and an incredible, step-by-step prescription for what he planned to do. One of the most thoughtful modern scholars of* Mein Kampf, *Werner Maser, has observed that "from 1925 until his suicide in April 1945, Hitler clung faithfully to the ghastly doctrine set out in* Mein Kampf," *and, even more amazingly, despite the notoriety of his doctrine, "he was able to seize power, to consolidate it and to carry the German people with him into the abyss."* [2]

The passage excerpted below is from the first chapter of the second volume of Mein Kampf, *written in 1927 after Hitler's release from prison. In it he recalls "the first great public demonstration" of the Movement in Munich in 1920. This was the eve of Hitler's takeover of the Nazi party, which was already committed to his ideas. These ideas—world*

[1] Adolf Hitler, *Mein Kampf* (New York: Stackpole, 1939), p. 11.

[2] Werner Maser, *Hitler's Mein Kampf, An Analysis,* R. H. Barry, trans. (London: Faber and Faber, 1970), pp. 11-12.

conquest, brutal direct action, glorification of power, Aryan racial supremacy, anti-Semitism, and anticommunism—show up starkly in the selection that follows.

ON FEBRUARY 24, 1920, the first great public demonstration of our young movement took place. In the festsaal of the Munich Hofbräuhaus the twenty-five theses of the new party's program were submitted to a crowd of almost two thousand and every single point was accepted amid jubilant approval.

With this the first guiding principles and directives were issued for a struggle which was to do away with a veritable mass of old traditional conceptions and opinions and with unclear, yes, harmful aims. Into the rotten and cowardly bourgeois world and into the triumphant march of the Marxist wave of conquest a new power phenomenon was entering, which at the eleventh hour would halt the chariot of doom.

It was self-evident that the new movement could hope to achieve the necessary importance and the required strength for this gigantic struggle only if it succeeded from the very first day in arousing in the hearts of its supporters the holy conviction that with it political life was to be given, not to a new *election slogan*, but to a new *philosophy* of fundamental significance. . . .

Since with all parties of a so-called bourgeois orientation in reality the whole political struggle actually consists in nothing but a mad rush for seats in parliament, in which convictions and principles are thrown overboard like sand ballast whenever it seems expedient, their programs are naturally tuned accordingly and—inversely, to be sure—their forces also measured by the same standard. They lack that great magnetic attraction which alone the masses always follow under the compelling impact of towering great ideas, the persuasive force of absolute belief in them, coupled with a fanatical courage to fight for them.

At a time when one side, armed with all the weapons of a philosophy, a thousand times criminal though it may be, sets out to storm an existing order, the other side, now and forever can offer resistance only if it clads itself in the forms of a new faith, in our case a political one, and for a weak-kneed, cowardly defensive substitutes the battle cry of courageous and brutal attack. . . .

In the first volume I have dealt with the word "folkish," in so far as I was forced to establish that this term seems inadequately defined to permit the formation of a solid fighting community. All sorts of people, with a yawning gulf between everything essential in their opinions, are running around today under the blanket term "folkish." Therefore, before I proceed to the tasks and aims of the National Socialist German Workers' Party, I should like to give a clarification of the concept "folkish," as well as its relation to the party movement.

The concept "*folkish*" seems as vaguely defined, open to as many interpretations and as unlimited in practical application as, for instance, the word "religious. . . ." In it, too, there lie various basic realizations. Though of eminent importance, they are, however, so unclearly defined in form that they rise above the value of a more or less acceptable opinion only if they are fitted into the framework of a political party as basic elements. *For the realization of philosophical ideals and of the demands derived from them no more occurs through men's pure feeling or inner will in themselves than the achievement of freedom through the general longing for it. No, only when the ideal urge for independence gets a fighting organization in the form of military instruments of power can the pressing desire of a people be transformed into glorious reality.*

Every philosophy of life, even if it is a thousand times correct and of highest benefit to humanity, will remain without significance for the practical shaping of a people's life, as long as its principles have not become the banner of a fighting movement which for its part in turn will be a party as long as its activity has not found completion in the victory of its ideas and its party dogmas have not become the new state principles of a people's community. . . .

This transformation of a general, philosophical, ideal conception of the highest truth into a definitely delimited, tightly organized political community of faith and struggle, unified in spirit and will, is the most significant achievement, since on its happy solution alone the possibility of the victory of an idea depends. From the army of often millions of men, who as individuals more or less clearly and definitely sense these truths, and in part perhaps comprehend them, *one* man must step forward who with apodictic force will form granite principles from the wavering idea-world of the broad masses and take up the struggle for their sole correctness, until from the shifting waves of a free thought-world there will arise a brazen cliff of solid unity in faith and will.

The general right for such an activity is based on necessity, the personal right on success.

If from the word "folkish" we try to peel out the innermost kernel of meaning, we arrive at the following:

Our present political world view, current in Germany, is based in general on the idea that creative, culture-creating force must indeed be attributed to the state, but that it has nothing to do with racial considerations, but is rather a product of economic necessities, or, at best, the natural result of a political urge for power. This underlying view, if logically developed, leads not only to a mistaken conception of basic racial forces, but also to an underestimation of the individual. For a denial of the difference between the various races with regard to their general culture-creating forces must necessarily extend this greatest of all errors to the judgment of the individual. The assumption of the equality of the races then becomes a basis for a similar way of viewing peoples and finally individual men. And hence international Marxism itself is only the transference, by the Jew, Karl Marx, of a philosophical attitude and conception, which had actually long been in existence, into the form of a definite political creed. Without the subsoil of such generally existing poisoning, the amazing success of this doctrine would never have been possible. Actually Karl Marx was only the *one* among millions who, with the sure eye of the prophet, recognized in the morass of a slowly decomposing world the most essential poisons, extracted them, and, like a wizard, prepared them into a concentrated solution for the swifter annihilation of the independent existence of free nations on this earth. And all this in the service of his race.

His Marxist doctrine is a brief spiritual extract of the philosophy of life that is generally current today. And for this reason alone any struggle of our so-called bourgeois world against it is impossible, absurd in fact, since this bourgeois world is also essentially infected by these poisons, and worships a view of life which in general is distinguished from the Marxists only by degrees and personalities. The bourgeois world is Marxist, but believes in the possibility of the rule of certain groups of men (bourgeoise), while Marxism itself systematically plans to hand the world over to the Jews.

In opposition to this, the folkish philosophy finds the importance of mankind in its basic racial elements. In the state it sees on principle only a means to an end and construes its end as the preservation of the racial existence of man. Thus, it by no means believes in an equality of the races, but along with their difference it recognizes their higher or lesser value and feels itself obligated, through this knowledge, to promote the victory of the better and stronger, and demand the subordination of the inferior and weaker in accordance with the eternal will that dominates this universe. Thus, in principle, it serves the basic aristocratic idea of Nature and believes in the validity of this law down to the last individual. It sees not only the different value of the races, but also the different value of individuals. From the mass it extracts the importance of the individual personality, and thus, in contrast to disorganizing Marxism, it has an organizing effect. It believes in the necessity of an idealization of humanity, in which alone it sees the premise for the existence of humanity. But it cannot grant the right to existence even to an ethical idea if this idea represents a danger for the racial life of the bearers of a higher ethics; for in a bastardized and niggerized world all the concepts of the humanly beautiful and sublime, as well as all ideas of an idealized future of our humanity, would be lost forever.

Human culture and civilization on this continent are inseparably bound up with the presence of the Aryan. If he dies out or declines, the dark veils of an age without culture will again descend on this globe.

The undermining of the existence of human culture by the destruction of its bearer seems in the eyes of a folkish philosophy the most execrable crime. Anyone who dares to lay hands on the highest image of the Lord commits sacrilege against the benevolent creator of this miracle and contributes to the expulsion from paradise.

And so the folkish philosophy of life corresponds to the innermost will of Nature, since it restores that free play of forces which must lead to a continuous mutual higher breeding, until at last the best of humanity, having achieved possession of this earth, will have a free path for activity in domains which will lie partly above it and partly outside it. . . .

. . . Not until the international world view—politically led by organized Marxism—is confronted by a folkish world view, organized and led with equal unity, will success, supposing the fighting energy to be equal on both sides, fall to the side of eternal truth.

A philosophy can only be organizationally comprehended on the basis of a definite formulation of that philosophy, and what dogmas represent for religious faith, party principles are for a political party in the making.

Hence an instrument must be created for the folkish world view which enables it to fight, just as the Marxist party organization creates a free path for internationalism.

This is the goal pursued by the National Socialist German Workers' Party.

That such a party formulation of the folkish concept is the precondition for the victory of the folkish philosophy of life is proved most sharply by a fact which is admitted indirectly at least by the enemies of such a party tie. Those very people who never weary of emphasizing that the folkish philosophy is not the "hereditary estate" of an individual, but that it slumbers or "lives" in the hearts of God knows how many millions, thus demonstrate the fact that the general existence of such ideas was absolutely unable to prevent the victory of the hostile world view, classically represented by a political party. If this were not so, the German people by this time would have been bound to achieve a gigantic victory and not be standing at the edge of an abyss. What gave the international world view success was its representation by a political party organized into storm troops; what caused the defeat of the opposite world view was its lack up to now of a unified body to represent it. Not by unlimited freedom to interpret a general view, but only in the limited and hence integrating form of a political organization can a world view fight and conquer.

Therefore, I saw my own task especially in extracting those nuclear ideas from the extensive and unshaped substance of a general world view and remolding them into more or less dogmatic forms which in their clear delimitation are adapted for holding solidly together those men who swear allegiance to them. In other words: *From the basic ideas of a general folkish world conception the National Socialist German Workers' Party takes over the essential fundamental traits, and from them, with due consideration of practical reality, the times, and the available human material as well as its weaknesses, forms a political creed which, in turn, by the strict organizational integration of large human masses thus made possible, creates the precondition for the victorious struggle of this world view.*

Hitler and His Germany

ERNST NOLTE

Despite the fact, as Maser reminds us, that the German people had Hitler's plan before them in Mein Kampf, *they followed him anyway. Why? The answer may be, to some extent, that they did not take him seriously. There were, after all, other leaders of lunatic rightist movements in Germany in the 1920s, plumping for German nationalism, spouting anti-Semitic and anti-Communist slogans while the Communists shouted back. But to a greater extent, the German people* did *take Hitler seriously. He preached his doctrine of hatred for the Jews and fear of the Communists, of rabid, militant nationalism more effectively, more tirelessly, more virulently than his competitors—and the German people listened. What Hitler said was crude, but it had a powerful appeal. The Nazi party grew stronger every year, until by the elections of 1932 it was the second most powerful party in Germany. Hitler courted the military establishment, the one great indispensable German national institution, as carefully as he had courted old General Ludendorff in the early 1920s. And he cultivated the economic baronage. Germany's desperate plight was worsened by the world depression of the early 1930s, and the captains of industry, always conservative and disposed to right-wing politics, now frightened by the threat of trade unionism and the Communists, sought a financial-political alliance with Hitler.*

In 1933 the aged President Paul von Hindenburg was compelled by the political situation to name Hitler as chancellor. Hitler persuaded Hindenburg to call for new elections in an effort to achieve a Nazi majority in the Reichstag. Then, on February 27, 1933, a spectacular fire gutted the Reichstag building. It was a case of arson—the arsonist, a Dutch radical, was arrested and confessed—but the fire and the sinister rumors that the Nazis spread of Communist plots provided the excuse for an emergency declaration. In this atmosphere of tension, the Nazis polled a working parliamentary majority in the elections. Upon Hindenburg's death the following year, the offices of chancellor and president were merged for Hitler. The Fuehrer was made. Germany was recovering economically, and part of it was the result of Hitler's military spending that created a vast public debt but also jobs and prosperity. Part of it, too, was the beginning of worldwide recovery. But no matter. Hitler claimed the credit. More Germans supported him, and those who did not were intimidated by open terrorism. Jews had already begun to stream out of Germany.

Hitler was now ready to implement his foreign policy. In 1935 the Rhineland was reclaimed by plebiscite and the following year remilitarized. In 1938 Austria was united with Germany; Czechoslovakia was surrendered to Germany; and on September 1, 1939, Poland was invaded. World War II had begun.

That Hitler was a dangerous psychopath is virtually a cliché of modern European historical studies, and every book that deals seriously with Hitler or his age must come to terms with it and venture a diagnosis. A more interesting question than what particular aberration Hitler suffered from is why the German people were willing to follow a madman, in Werner Maser's phrase, "into the abyss." It is a much more difficult question, a more essential one, and one to which the answers are more diverse. German scholars of the postwar era have been especially preoccupied with this question.

In a now famous essay, Three Faces of Fascism: Action Française, Italian Fascism, National Socialism, *the German historian Ernst Nolte gives his analysis. Although he subjects Hitler to penetrating study and finds him "infantile," "monomaniacal," and "mediumistic," Nolte is unwilling to set him down simply as a madman. Rather, he argues that these very aberrant qualities enabled him to exemplify the experience of his more normal fellow citizens. Hitler told the German people in a passionate and oversimplified way what they themselves wanted to hear, and for this reason he came for a brief time "to be lord and master of his troubled era."*

We turn now to Nolte's analysis.

THE DOMINANT trait in Hitler's personality was infantilism. It explains the most prominent as well as the strangest of his characteristics and actions. The frequently awesome consistency of his thoughts and behavior must be seen in conjunction with the stupendous force of his rage, which reduced field marshals to trembling nonentities. If at the age of fifty he built the Danube bridge in Linz down to the last detail exactly as he had designed it at the age of fifteen before the eyes of his astonished boyhood friend, this was not a mark of consistency in a mature man, one who has learned and pondered, criticized and been criticized, but the stubbornness of the child who is aware of nothing except himself and his mental image and to whom time means nothing because childishness has not been broken and forced into the sober give-and-take of the adult world. Hitler's rage was the uncontrollable fury of the child who bangs the chair because the chair refuses to do as it is told; his dreaded harshness, which nonchalantly sent millions of people to their death, was much closer to the rambling imaginings of a boy than to the iron grasp of a man, and is therefore intimately and typically related to his profound aversion to the cruelty of hunting, vivisection, and the consumption of meat generally.

And how close to the sinister is the grotesque! The first thing Hitler did after being released from the Landsberg prison was to buy a Mercedes for twenty-six thousand marks—the car he had been dreaming of while serving his sentence. Until 1933 he insisted on passing every car on the road. In Vienna alone he had heard *Tristan and Isolde* between thirty and forty times, and had time as chancellor to see six performances of *The Merry Widow* in as many months. Nor was this all. According to Otto Dietrich he reread all Karl May's boys' adventure books during 1933 and 1934, and this is perfectly credible since in *Hitler's Table Talk* he bestowed high praise on this author and credited him with no less than opening his eyes to the world. It is in the conversations related in *Hitler's Table Talk* that he treated his listeners to such frequent and vindictive schoolboy reminiscences that it seems as if this man never emerged from his boyhood and completely lacked the experience of time and its broadening, reconciling powers.

The monomaniacal element in Hitler's nature is obviously closely related to his infantilism. It is based largely on his elemental urge toward tangibility, intelligibility, simplicity. In *Mein Kampf* he expressed the maxim that the masses should never be shown more than *one* enemy. He was himself the most loyal exponent of this precept, and not from motives of tactical calculation alone. He never allowed himself to face more than one enemy at a time; on this enemy he concentrated all the hatred of which he was so inordinately capable, and it was this that enabled him during this period to show the other enemies a reassuring and "subjectively" sincere face. During the crisis in Czechoslovakia he even forgot the Jews over Beneš.[3] His enemy was always concrete and personal, never merely the expression but also the cause of an obscure or complex event. The Weimar system was caused by the "November criminals," the predicament of the Germans in Austria by the Hapsburgs, capitalism and bolshevism equally by the Jews.

A good example of the emergence and function of the clearly defined hate figure, which took the place of the causal connection he really had in

[3] Eduard Beneš, the heroic president of Czechoslovakia who resisted Hitler's schemes and the machinations of the other great powers. He escaped to the United States in 1938. Later, in Britain, he was the head of the Czech government in exile. At the end of the war, he returned to become president of Czechoslovakia once more until his death in 1948.—ED.

mind, is to be found in *Mein Kampf*. Here Hitler draws a vivid picture of the miseries of proletarian existence as he came to know it in Vienna—deserted, frustrated, devoid of hope. This description seems to lead inevitably to an obvious conclusion: that these people, if they were not wholly insensible, were bound to be led with compelling logic to the socialist doctrine, to their "lack of patriotism," their hatred of religion, their merciless indictment of the ruling class. It should, however, have also led to a self-critical insight: that the only reason he remained so aloof from the collective emotions of these masses was because he had enjoyed a different upbringing, middle-class and provincial, because despite his poverty he never really worked, and because he was not married. Nothing of the kind! When he was watching spellbound one day as the long column of demonstrating workers wound its way through the streets, his first query was about the "wirepullers." His voracity for reading, his allegedly thorough study of Marxist theories, did not spur him on to cast his gaze beyond the frontier and realize that such demonstrations were taking place in every city in Europe, or to take note of the "rabble-rousing" articles of a certain Mussolini, which he would doubtless have regarded as "spiritual vitriol" like those in the *Arbeiterzeitung*.[4]

What Hitler discovered was the many Jewish names among the leaders of Austrian Marxism, and now the scales fell from his eyes—at last he saw who it was who, beside Hapsburgs, wanted to wipe out the German element in Austria. Now he began to preach his conclusions to his first audiences; now he was no longer speaking, as until recently he had spoken to Kubizek, to hear the sound of his own voice: he wanted to convince. But he did not have much success. The management of the men's hostel looked on him as an insufferable politicizer, and for most of his fellow inmates he was a "reactionary swine." He got beaten up by workers, and in conversations with Jews and Social Democrats he was evidently often the loser, being no match for their diabolical glibness and dialectic. This made the image of the archenemy appear all the more vivid to him, all the more firmly entrenched. Thirty years later the most experienced statesmen took him for a confidence-inspiring statesman after meeting him personally; hard-bitten soldiers found he was a man they could talk to; educated supporters saw in him the people's social leader. Hitler himself, however, made the following observations in the presence of the generals and party leaders around his table: though Dietrich Eckart had considered that from many aspects Streicher[5] was a fool, it was impossible to conquer the masses without such people, . . . though Streicher was criticized for his paper, *Der Stürmer*; in actual fact Streicher idealized the Jew. The Jew was far more ignoble, unruly, and diabolical than Streicher had depicted him.

[4] A labor newspaper.—ED.

[5] Julius Streicher was the publisher of a radical, anti-Semitic newspaper, *Der Stürmer,* and one of Hitler's earliest supporters. He continued to be a functionary of the party, survived the war, and was convicted of war crimes at Nürnberg.—ED.

Hitler rose from the gutter to be the master of Europe. There is no doubt that he learned an enormous amount. In the flexible outer layer of his personality he could be all things to all men: a statesman to the statesmen, a commander to the generals, a charmer to women, a father to the people. But in the hard monomaniacal core of his being he did not change one iota from Vienna to Rastenburg.

Yet if his people had found that he intended after the war to prohibit smoking and make the world of the future vegetarian it is probable that even the SS would have rebelled. There are thousands of monomaniacal and infantile types in every large community, but they seldom play a role other than among their own kind. These two traits do not explain how Hitler was able to rise to power.

August Kubizek tells a strange story which there is little reason to doubt and which sheds as much light on the moment when Hitler decided to enter politics as on the basis and prospects of that decision. After a performance of *Rienzi*[6] in Linz, Kubizek relates, Hitler had taken him up to a nearby hill and talked to him with shining eyes and trembling voice of the mandate he would one day receive from his people to lead them out of servitude to the heights of liberty. It seemed as if another self were speaking from Hitler's lips, as if he himself were looking on at what was happening in numb astonishment. Here the infantile basis is once again unmistakable. The identification with the hero of the dramatic opera bore him aloft, erupted from him like a separate being. There were many subsequent occasions testifying to this very process. When Hitler chatted, his manner of talking was often unbearably flat; when he described something, it was dull; when he theorized, it was stilted; when he started up a hymn of hate, repulsive. But time and again his speeches contained passages of irresistible force and compelling conviction, such as no other speaker of his time was capable of producing. These are always the places where his "faith" finds expression, and it was obviously this faith which induced that emotion among the masses to which even the most hostile observer testified. But at no time do these passages reveal anything new, never do they make the listener reflect or exert his critical faculty: all they ever do is conjure up magically before his eyes that which already existed in him as vague feeling, inarticulate longing. What else did he express but the secret desires of his judges when he declared before the People's Court: "The army we have trained is growing day by day, faster by the hour. It is in these very days that I have the proud hope that the hour will come when these unruly bands become battalions, the battalions regiments, the regiments divisions, when the old cockade is raised from the dust, when the old flags flutter again on high, when at last reconciliation takes place before the eternal Last Judgment, which we are prepared to face."

[6] An opera by Wagner.—Ed.

His behavior at a rally has often been described: how, uncertain at first, he would rely on the trivial, then get the feel of the atmosphere for several minutes, slowly establish contact, score a bull's-eye with the right phrase, gather momentum with the applause, finally burst out with words which seemed positively to erupt through him, and at the end, in the midst of thunderous cheering, shout a vow to heaven or, amid breathless silence, bring forth a solemn Amen. And after the speech he was as wet as if he had taken a steambath and had lost as much weight as if he had been through a week's strict training.

He told every rally what it wanted to hear—yet what he voiced was not the trivial interests and desires of the day but the great universal, obvious hopes: that Germany should once again become what it had been, that the economy should function, that the farmer should get his rights, likewise the townsman, the worker, and the employer, that they should forget their differences and become one in the most important thing of all—their love for Germany. He never embarked on discussion, he permitted no heckling, he never dealt with any of the day-to-day problems of politics. When he knew that a rally was in a critical mood and wanted information instead of *Weltanschauung,*[7] he was capable of calling off his speech at the last moment.

There should be no doubt as to the mediumistic trait in Hitler. He was the medium who communicated to the masses their own, deeply buried spirit. It was because of this, not because of his monomaniacal obsession, that a third of his people loved him long before he became chancellor, long before he was their victorious supreme commander. But mediumistic popular idols are usually simpletons fit for ecstasy rather than fulfillment. In the turmoil of postwar Germany it would have been *impossible* to love Hitler had not monomaniacal obsession driven the man on and infantile wishful thinking carried him beyond the workaday world with its problems and conflicts. Singly, any one of these three characteristics would have made Hitler a freak and a fool; combined, they raised him for a brief time to be lord and master of this troubled era.

A psychological portrait of Hitler such as this must, however, give rise to doubts in more ways than one. Does the portrait not approach that overpolemical and oversimplified talk of the "madman" or the "criminal"? There is no intention of claiming that this represents a clinical diagnosis. It is not even the purpose of this analysis to define and categorize Hitler as an "infantile mediumistic monomaniac." What has been discussed is merely the existence of infantile, mediumistic, and monomaniacal traits. They are not intended to exhaust the nature of the man Hitler, nor do they of themselves belong to the field of the medically abnormal. Rather do they represent individually an indispensable ingredient of the exceptional. There can be few artists without a streak of infantilism, few ideological politicians without a monomaniacal element in their make-up.

7 "World view."—Ed.

It is not so much the potency of each element singly as the combination of all three which gives Hitler his unique face. Whether this combination is pathological in the clinical sense is very doubtful, but there can be no doubt that it excludes historical greatness in the traditional sense.

A second objection is that the psychological description prevents the sociological typification which from the point of view of history is so much more productive. Many attempts have been made to understand Hitler as typical of the angry petit bourgeois. The snag in this interpretation is that it cannot stand without a psychologizing adjective and almost always suggests a goal which is obviously psychological as well as polemical. What this theory tries to express is that Hitler was "actually only a petit bourgeois," in other words, something puny and contemptible. But it is precisely from the psychological standpoint that the petit bourgeois can best be defined as the normal image of the "adult": Hitler was exactly the reverse. What is correct, however, is that, from the sociological standpoint, bourgeois elements may be present in an entirely nonbourgeois psychological form. It remains to be shown how very petit bourgeois was Hitler's immediate reaction to Marxism. However, it was only by means of that "form" which cannot be deduced by sociological methods that his first reaction underwent its momentous transformation.

The third objection is the most serious. The historical phenomenon of National Socialism might be considered overparticularized if it is based solely on the unusual, not to say abnormal, personality of one man. Does not this interpretation in the final analysis even approach that all too transparent apologia which tries to see in Hitler, and only in him, the "*causa efficiens* of the whole sequence of events"? But this is not necessarily logical. It is only from one aspect that the infantile person is more remote from the world than other people; from another aspect he is much closer to it. For he does not dredge up the stuff of his dreams and longings out of nothing; on the contrary, he compresses the world of his more normal fellow men, sometimes by intensifying, sometimes by contrasting. From the complexity of life, monomaniacal natures often wrest an abstruse characteristic, quite frequently a comical aspect, but at times a really essential element. However, the mediumistic trait guarantees that nothing peripheral is compressed, nothing trivial monomaniacally grasped. It is not that a nature of this kind particularizes the historical, but that this nature is itself brought into focus by the historical. Although far from being a true mirror of the times—indeed, it is more of a monstrous distortion—nothing goes into it that is pure invention; and what does go into it arises from certain traits of its own. Hitler sometimes compared himself to a magnet which attracted all that was brave and heroic; it would probably be more accurate to say that certain extreme characteristics of the era attracted this nature like magnets, to become in that personality even more extreme and visible. Hence from now on there will be little mention of Hitler's psyche, but all the more of the conditions, forces, and trends of his environment to which he stood in some relationship. For whether he merely interpreted these conditions or intervened in them, whether he placed himself on the side of these forces or opposed them, whether he let himself be borne along by these trends or fought them: something of this force or this trend never failed to emerge in extreme form. In this sense Hitler's nature may be called a historical substance.

Hitler: A Study in Tyranny

ALAN BULLOCK

Not only German scholars, as we have seen, but other scholars of modern European history have been intrigued with the question of why and how Hitler rose to power. The most widely respected of these is Alan Bullock, whose most important work is Hitler: A Study in Tyranny. *Bullock tends to share Nolte's opinion about Hitler's infantilism—though he does not use the term. Stressing the fact that Hitler was incapable of real growth or change, Bullock finds him at the end of his career the same as at its beginning, unwilling to admit the possibility of his own error and seeing everyone's faults but his own. But even with such serious flaws of character and personality, Bullock, again like Nolte, is unwilling to dismiss Hitler as a madman. He sees him rather as the possessor of gifts amounting to political genius, evil genius admittedly but genius nonetheless. And he sees Hitler as using those gifts to secure a wholly personal tyranny over Germany. On the question of why Germany followed Hitler, Bullock diverges sharply from Nolte and from many other German scholars. He finds the explanation, not in the terrible German experience of defeat in World War I and depression in the postwar era, but more deeply rooted in German history, in German nationalism, militarism, and authoritarianism—of which Hitler's tyranny was the "logical conclusion."*

We pick up Bullock's account of Hitler at its last moment, late in April 1945, in the chancellery bunker in Berlin. While Russian artillery crashes above him, shattering what remains of his capital, he dictates to his secretary, Frau Junge, his will and his political testament. Hitler is on the point of committing suicide.

FACING DEATH and the destruction of the régime he had created, this man who had exacted the sacrifice of millions of lives rather than admit defeat was still recognizably the old Hitler. From first to last there is not a word of regret, nor a suggestion of remorse. The fault is that of others, above all that of the Jews, for even now the old hatred is unappeased. Word for word, Hitler's final address to the German nation could be taken from almost any of his early speeches of the 1920s or from the pages of *Mein Kampf*. Twenty-odd years had changed and taught him nothing. His mind remained as tightly closed as it had been on the day when he wrote: "During these years in Vienna a view of life and a definite outlook on the world took shape in my mind. These became the granite basis of my conduct. Since then I have extended that foundation very little, I have changed nothing in it." . . .

In the course of Sunday, the 29th, arrangements were made to send copies of the Fuehrer's Political Testament out of the bunker, and three men were selected to make their way as best they could to Admiral Doenitz's and Field-Marshal Schoerner's headquarters. One of the men selected was an official of the Propaganda Ministry, and to him Goebbels entrusted his own appendix to Hitler's manifesto. At midnight on 29 April another messenger, Colonel von Below, left carrying with him a postscript which Hitler instructed him to deliver to General Keitel. It was the Supreme Commander's last message to the Armed Forces, and the sting was in the tail:

> The people and the Armed Forces have given their all in this long and hard struggle. The sacrifice has been enormous. But my trust has been misused by many people. Disloyalty and betrayal have undermined resistance throughout the war. It was therefore not granted to me to lead the people to victory. The Army General Staff cannot be compared with the General Staff of the First World War. Its achievements were far behind those of the fighting front.

The war had been begun by the Jews, it had been lost by the generals. In neither case was the responsibility Hitler's and his last word of all was to reaffirm his original purpose:

> The efforts and sacrifice of the German people in this war [he added] have been so great that I cannot believe they have been in vain. The aim must still be to win territory in the east for the German people. . . .

He now began to make systematic preparations for taking his life. He had his Alsatian bitch, Blondi, destroyed, and in the early hours of Monday, 30 April, assembled his staff in the passage in order to say farewell. Walking along the line, he shook each man and woman silently by the hand. Shortly afterwards Bormann sent out a telegram to Doenitz, whose headquarters was at Ploen, between Lübeck and Kiel, instructing him to proceed "at once and mercilessly" against all traitors. . . .

In the course of the early afternoon Erich Kempka, Hitler's chauffeur, was ordered to send two hundred litres of petrol to the Chancellery Garden. It was carried over in jerricans and its delivery supervised by Heinz Linge, Hitler's batman.

Meanwhile, having finished his lunch, Hitler went to fetch his wife from her room, and for the second time they said farewell to Goebbels, Bormann and the others who remained in the bunker. Hitler then returned to the Fuehrer's suite with Eva and closed the door. A few minutes passed while those outside stood waiting in the passage. Then a single shot rang out.

After a brief pause the little group outside opened the door. Hitler was lying on the sofa, which was soaked in blood: he had shot himself through the mouth. On his right-hand side lay Eva Braun, also dead: she had swallowed poison. The time was half past three on the afternoon of Monday, 30 April, 1945, ten days after Hitler's fifty-sixth birthday.

Hitler's instructions for the disposal of their bodies had been explicit, and they were carried out to the letter. Hitler's own body, wrapped in a blanket, was carried out and up to the garden by two S.S. men. The head was concealed, but the black trousers and black shoes which he wore with his uniform jacket hung down beneath the covering. Eva's body was picked up by Bormann, who handed it to Kempka. They made their way up the stairs and out into the open air, accompanied by Goebbels, Guensche and Burgdorf. The doors leading into the garden had been locked and the bodies were laid in a shallow depression of sandy soil close to the porch. Picking up the five cans of petrol, one after another, Guensche, Hitler's S.S. adjutant, poured the contents over the two corpses and set fire to them with a lighted rag.

A sheet of flame leapt up, and the watchers withdrew to the shelter of the porch. A heavy Russian bombardment was in progress and shells continually burst on the Chancellery. Silently they stood to attention, and for the last time gave the Hitler salute; then turned and disappeared into the shelter. . . .

In this age of Unenlightened Despotism Hitler has had more than a few rivals, yet he remains, so far, the most remarkable of those who have used modern techniques to apply the classic formulas of tyranny.

Before the war it was common to hear Hitler described as the pawn of the sinister interests who held real power in Germany, of the Junkers or the Army, of heavy industry or high finance. This view does not survive examination of the evidence. Hitler acknowledged no masters, and by 1938 at least he exercised arbitrary rule over Germany to a degree rarely, if ever, equalled in a modern industrialized State.

At the same time, from the re-militarization of the Rhineland to the invasion of Russia he won a series of successes in diplomacy and war which established an hegemony over the continent of Europe comparable with that of Napoleon at the height of his fame. While these could not have been won without a people and an Army willing to serve him, it was Hitler who provided the indispensable leadership, the flair for grasping opportunities, the boldness in using them. In retrospect his mistakes appear obvious, and it is easy to be complacent about the inevitability of his defeat; but it took the combined efforts of the three most powerful nations in the world to break his hold on Europe.

Luck and the disunity of his opponents will account for much of Hitler's success—as it will of Napoleon's—but not for all. He began with few advantages, a man without a name and without support other than that which he acquired for himself, not even a citizen of the country he aspired to rule. To achieve what he did Hitler needed—and possessed—talents out of the ordinary which in sum amounted to political genius, however evil its fruits.

His abilities have been sufficiently described in the preceding pages: his mastery of the irrational factors in politics, his insight into the weaknesses of his opponents, his gift for simplification, his sense of timing, his willingness to take risks. An opportunist entirely without principle, he showed considerable consistency and an astonishing power of will in pursuing his aims. Cynical and calculating in the exploitation of his histrionic gifts, he retained an unshaken belief in his historic role and in himself as a creature of destiny.

The fact that his career ended in failure, and that his defeat was preeminently due to his own mistakes, does not by itself detract from Hitler's claim to greatness. The flaw lies deeper. For these remarkable powers were combined with an ugly and strident egotism, a moral and intellectual cretinism. The passions which ruled Hitler's mind were ignoble: hatred, resentment, the lust to dominate, and, where he could not dominate, to destroy. His career did not exalt but debased the human condition, and his twelve years' dictatorship was barren of all ideas save one—the further extension of his own power and that of the nation with which he had identified himself. Even power he conceived of in the crudest terms: an endless vista of military roads, S.S. garrisons and concentration camps stretching across Europe and Asia.

The great revolutions of the past, whatever their ultimate fate, have been identified with the release of certain powerful ideas: individual conscience, liberty, equality, national freedom, social justice. National Socialism produced nothing. . . .

The view has often been expressed that Hitler could only have come to power in Germany, and it is true—without falling into the same error of racialism as the Nazis—that there were certain features of German historical development, quite apart from the effects of the Defeat and the Depression, which favored the rise of such a movement.

This is not to accuse the Germans of Original Sin, or to ignore the other sides of German life which were only grossly caricatured by the Nazis.

But Naziism was not some terrible accident which fell upon the German people out of a blue sky. It was rooted in their history, and while it is true that a majority of the German people never voted for Hitler, it is also true that thirteen millions did. Both facts need to be remembered.

From this point of view Hitler's career may be described as a *reductio ad absurdum* of the most powerful political tradition in Germany since the Unification. This is what nationalism, militarism, authoritarianism, the worship of success and force, the exaltation of the State and *Realpolitik* lead to, if they are projected to their logical conclusion.

There are Germans who will reject such a view. They argue that what was wrong with Hitler was that he lacked the necessary skill, that he was a bungler. If only he had listened to the generals—or Schacht—or the career diplomats—if only he had not attacked Russia, and so on. There is some point, they feel, at which he went wrong. They refuse to see that it was the ends themselves, not simply the means, which were wrong: the pursuit of unlimited power, the scorn for justice or any restraint on power; the exaltation of will over reason and conscience; the assertion of an arrogant supremacy, the contempt for others' rights. As at least one German historian, Professor Meinecke, has recognized, the catastrophe to which Hitler led Germany points to the need to re-examine the aims as well as the methods of German policy as far back as Bismarck.

The Germans, however, were not the only people who preferred in the 1930s not to know what was happening and refused to call evil things by their true names. The British and French at Munich; the Italians, Germany's partners in the Pact of Steel; the Poles, who stabbed the Czechs in the back over Teschen; the Russians, who signed the Nazi-Soviet Pact to partition Poland, all thought they could buy Hitler off, or use him to their own selfish advantage. . . .

Hitler, indeed, was a European, no less than a German phenomenon. . . . The conditions and the state of mind which he exploited, the *malaise* of which he was the symptom, were not confined to one country, although they were more strongly marked in Germany than anywhere else. Hitler's idiom was German, but the thoughts and emotions to which he gave expression have a more universal currency.

Hitler recognized this relationship with Europe perfectly clearly. He was in revolt against "the System" not just in Germany but in Europe, against that liberal bourgeois order, symbolized for him in the Vienna which had once rejected him. To destroy this was his mission, the mission in which he never ceased to believe; and in this, the most deeply felt of his purposes, he did not fail. Europe may rise again, but the old Europe of the years between 1789, the year of the French Revolution, and 1939, the year of Hitler's War, has gone for ever—and the last figure in its history is that of Adolf Hitler, the architect of its ruin. "*Si monumentum requiris, circumspice*"—"If you seek his monument, look around."

Suggestions for Further Reading

STUDENTS ARE ENCOURAGED to read further in Hitler's revealing *Mein Kampf*, beyond the brief passage excerpted in this chapter. The understanding of *Mein Kampf* will be greatly enhanced by reading Werner Maser, *Hitler's Mein Kampf, An Analysis*, tr. R. H. Barry (London: Faber, 1970). Maser, an eminent German authority on Hitler, has also edited *Hitler's Letters and Notes*, tr. Arnold Pomerans (New York: Harper & Row, 1974). Also important for insights into Hitler is *Hitler: Secret Conversations, 1941–1944*, tr. N. Cameron and R. H. Stevens (New York: Octagon, 1972 [1953]), conversations with Hitler's intimates that he himself preserved.

The two best biographies of Hitler are the classic Alan Bullock, *Hitler: A Study in Tyranny*, rev. ed. (New York: Harper & Row, 1962), excerpted in this chapter, and Joachim C. Fest, *Hitler*, tr. Richard and Clara Winston (New York: Harcourt Brace Jovanovich, 1974), which adds some material not available to Bullock. This is the case also with Werner Maser, *Hitler: Legend, Myth and Reality*, tr. Peter and Betty Ross (New York: Harper & Row, 1973). John Toland, *Adolf Hitler* (New York: Doubleday, 1976), is a massive, definitive work on Hitler, based on every shred of material available, but students may still prefer the more interpretive and readable works listed above or the brief, up-to-date, and competent survey by William Carr, *Hitler: A Study in Personality and Politics* (New York: St. Martin's, 1979). There are three interesting psychohistorical works: Walter C. Langer, *The Mind of Adolf Hitler: The Secret Wartime Report* (New York: Basic Books, 1972), the fascinating account of how a team of psychiatrists and psychologists built up a strategic psychological profile of Hitler during World War II; Rudolf Binion, *Hitler Among the Germans* (New York: Elsevier, 1976), a psychohistory of Hitler and his Germany; and Robert G. Waite, *The Psychopathic God: Adolf Hitler* (New York: Basic Books, 1977), more decidedly and professionally psychoanalytic than Binion and more up-to-date than Langer. Three special studies are also recommended: Bradley F. Smith, *Adolf Hitler: His Family, Childhood and Youth* (Stanford: Hoover Institute, 1967), and two excellent, detailed accounts of the beer hall *Putsch*, Harold J. Gordon, *Hitler and the Beer Hall Putsch* (Princeton: Princeton University Press, 1972) and John Dornberg, *Munich 1923, The Story of Hitler's First Grab for Power* (New York: Harper & Row, 1982).

In addition to Ernst Nolte's *Three Faces of Fascism*, tr. Leila Vennewitz (New York: Holt, Rinehart and Winston, 1965), students are urged to read

H. R. Kedward, *Fascism in Western Europe, 1900–1945* (London: Blackie, 1969), or F. L. Carsten, *The Rise of Fascism* (Berkeley: University of California Press, 1967). On German fascism, one of the most complete and comprehensive works is K. D. Bracher, *The German Dictatorship: The Origins, Structure, and Effects of National Socialism*, tr. J. Steinberg (New York: Praeger, 1970). Richard F. Hamilton, *Who Voted for Hitler?* (Princeton, N.J.: Princeton University Press, 1982), is a detailed study of the political functioning of German fascism. Probably the best general survey of political, social, and cultural history is Raymond J. Sontag, *A Broken World, 1919–1939* "Rise of Modern Europe" series (New York: Harper & Row, 1971), but the most readable and exciting popular history is William L. Shirer, *The Rise and Fall of the Third Reich, A History of Nazi Germany* (New York: Simon and Schuster, 1960). A. J. P. Taylor, *From Sarajevo to Potsdam* (New York: Harcourt, Brace and World, 1966), is a vigorous, witty, highly personal interpretive history. Hannah Vogt, *The Burden of Guilt, A Short History of Germany, 1914–1945*, tr. Herbert Strauss (New York: Oxford University Press, 1964), is especially interesting in that it was specifically written for the instruction of post–World War II German young people. Sebastian Haffner, *The Meaning of Hitler*, tr. Ewald Osers (New York: Macmillan, 1979), is a best-selling German book, a reassessment (and condemnation) of Hitler against the tendencies to try to rehabilitate or justify him. Of the several books by those close to Hitler, the best, most important, and most interesting is Albert Speer, *Inside the Third Reich*, tr. Richard and Clara Winston (New York: Macmillan, 1970). Finally, three important books on the German army must be recommended: John W. Wheeler-Bennett, *The Nemesis of Power: The German Army in Politics, 1918–1945* (New York: St. Martin's, 1954); Robert J. O'Neill, *The German Army and the Nazi Party, 1933–1939* (London: Cassell, 1968); and Len Deighton, *Blitzkrieg: From the Rise of Hitler to the Fall of Dunkirk* (New York: Knopf, 1980), an exciting, readable account of the employment of Hitler's army.

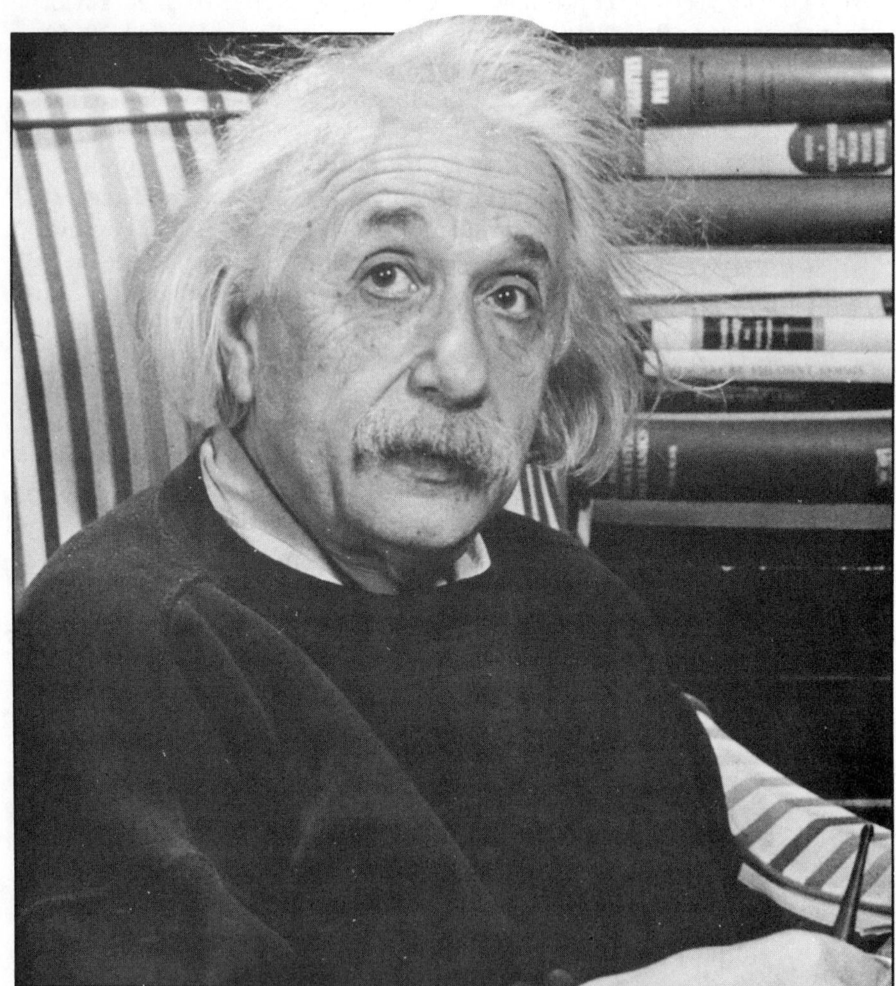

The Granger Collection

Albert Einstein and the Atomic Age: A Question of Responsibility

1879 born
1905 first basic papers published
1916 published fundamental paper on the general theory of relativity
1921 won Nobel Prize in physics
1933 fled from Germany to the United States
1939 Manhattan Project to create the atomic bomb begun
1945 atomic bombs dropped on Hiroshima and Nagasaki
1955 died

By the early 1930s, Albert Einstein was the most famous scientist in the world. Indeed, he had become a kind of symbol for the abstruseness of modern science itself, an expert in a branch of theoretical physics so remote and lofty that—at least according to the popular press—only a dozen other people could even understand his theories, much less explain them.

Long before this time, Einstein had established the fundamental direction of his work. As early as 1905, at the age of twenty-six, he had published very important papers, among them his theory of relativity, his work on statistical mechanics, and the quantum theory of radiation. When these first papers were published, Einstein was working as a patent clerk in Berne since he could not find an academic position, but by 1914 he held a professorship at the University of Berlin and was director of the Institute of Physics in the Kaiser Wilhelm Society for the Development of Sciences and a member of the Royal Prussian Academy of Sciences. In 1916 he published the fundamental paper on the general theory of relativity that established his worldwide fame, and in 1921 he received the Nobel Prize for Physics.

Although Einstein's main interest through the late 1920s was in the development of what came to be called his general field theory, other developments far removed from the abstractions of science had begun to crowd in upon his world. Hitler was on the rise in Germany, and Einstein was a Jew. In 1933 Einstein resigned his academic appointments, severed the associations of a lifetime, and joined the thousands of Jews, humble and famous, who had already begun to flee Hitler's Germany. An honored position was created for him at the Institute for Advanced Study at Princeton University, and there he remained for the rest of his life.

Einstein maintained contact with other brilliant refugee physicists who had fled the tyrannies of Europe, among them his old friend Max Born in England, the Hungarian Leo Szilard in the United States, and dozens of other scholars. These men, through their ties with what remained of the old international community of physicists, began to hear troubling rumors in the mid 1930s of experimental work being done in Europe in the field of atomic energy. Then in 1939 Niels Bohr brought word that Hahn and Strassman of the Kaiser Wilhelm Society in Berlin had actually produced nuclear fission. An atomic bomb was now a practical possibility. The work that Bohr reported and the work that would subsequently be done in Germany, England, and the United States was based, in the last analysis, upon Einstein's theories.

Twenty years before, Einstein had argued in his special theory of relativity that, as an object approached the speed of light, its acceleration would tend to produce not only increased speed but increased mass. He explained the process in the elegantly simple equation $E = mc^2$, in which the potential energy (E) of an object is equal to its mass (m) multiplied by the square of the speed of light (c^2). The enormous product of energy that would result from even the most infinitesimal transformation of mass —with the speed of light computed at 186,000 miles per second—was quite beyond anything but mathematical comprehension and even theoretically possible in terrestrial physics only at the atomic level. Now, working with unstable, heavy elements and apparently quite by accident, German scientists had produced a nuclear chain reaction, the instantaneous transformation of one element into another with exactly the incredible release of energy that Einstein's equation had described. As Leo Szilard would later write, "The dream of the alchemists came true. . . . But while the first successful alchemist was undoubtedly God, I sometimes wonder if the second successful alchemist may not have been the Devil himself." [1]

If German scientists had discovered the secret of atomic fission, it would probably not be long before the German government would have an atomic bomb. This prospect brought Leo Szilard and Eugene Wigner

[1] "Creative Intelligence and Society," in *Collected Works of Leo Szilard . . .* , ed. B. T. Feld and G. W. Szilard (Cambridge, Mass.: M.I.T. Press, 1972), I, 189.

to Einstein. As a result of their discussion, Einstein immediately agreed to take action and eventually signed the now famous letter to President Roosevelt urging government support of research on nuclear chain reactions. Now, with the alarming news from Germany and the push from Einstein, work on the Manhattan Project seriously began, and with it the chain of events leading to the explosions over Hiroshima and Nagasaki in August 1945.

The Complaint of Peace

ALBERT EINSTEIN

Technology is older than science, but through the centuries the two have always been linked together, technology adapting the theoretical findings of science to the practical uses of society. Sad to say, these uses, more often than not, have been military. With "the bomb," society at last had the ultimate weapon, the doomsday machine capable of destroying not only one's enemies but all humanity.

With the bomb there also came the difficult question of the scientists' moral responsibility for the application of their theoretical and experimental work. One of the most troubled by this question was Albert Einstein. In December 1945, within months of the explosions over Japan, Einstein addressed the Nobel Anniversary Dinner in New York, speaking of the parallel between Alfred Nobel and his desire to atone for the invention of "an explosive more powerful than any then known" and the physicists "who participated in producing the most formidable weapon of all time" and who "are harassed by a similar feeling of responsibility, not to say guilt." But, he continued, their choice was as clear as their anguish was real. "We helped create this new weapon in order to prevent the enemies of mankind from achieving it first. . . . The war is won, but the peace is not." [2]

The persistent theme of all Einstein's public statements and the principal concern of the last decade of his life was the creation of a supranational organization to make sure that the bomb would never again be used. Some of Einstein's friends were exasperated with him for his continued refusal to advocate the surrender of the bomb to the United Nations, then in its confident infancy. But Einstein perceived the essential weakness of that organization, later to be so tragically demonstrated: it was not capable of keeping the peace. But his own proposal—the establishment of a world government—was even more unrealistic.

Einstein stated his views in an interview-article with Raymond Swing that originally appeared in the Atlantic Monthly *in November 1945. A slightly revised version of this article, from* Einstein on Peace, *is reprinted below in its entirety. Einstein's statements tended to be brief and simple. But in this piece, it is not his arguments that are striking; rather, it is the*

[2] *Einstein on Peace,* ed. Otto Nathan and Heinz Norden (New York: Schocken Books, 1968), p. 355.

tension between his belief that pure science is essentially unmanageable and his profound sense of the scientist's moral responsibility in the realm of human affairs.

THE RELEASE of atomic energy has not created a new problem. It has merely made more urgent the necessity of solving an existing one. One could say that it has affected us quantitatively, not qualitatively. As long as there are sovereign nations possessing great power, war is inevitable. This does not mean that one can know when war will come but only that one is sure that it will come. This was true even before the atomic bomb was made. What has changed is the destructiveness of war.

I do not believe that the secret of the bomb should be given to the United Nations Organization. I do not believe it should be given to the Soviet Union. Either course would be analogous to a man with capital who, wishing another individual to collaborate with him on an enterprise, starts by giving him half his money. The other man might choose to start a rival enterprise, when what is wanted is his co-operation. The secret of the bomb should be committed to a world government, and the United States should immediately announce its readiness to do so. Such a world government should be established by the United States, the Soviet Union and Great Britain, the only three powers which possess great military strength. The three of them should commit to this world government all of their military resources. The fact that there are only three nations with great military power should make it easier, rather than harder, to establish a world government.

Since the United States and Great Britain have the secret of the atomic bomb and the Soviet Union does not, they should invite the Soviet Union to prepare and present the first draft of a Constitution for the proposed world government. This would help dispel the distrust of the Russians, which they feel because they know the bomb is being kept a secret chiefly to prevent their having it. Obviously, the first draft would not be the final one, but the Russians should be made to feel that the world government will guarantee their security.

It would be wise if this Constitution were to be negotiated by one American, one Briton and one Russian. They would, of course, need advisers, but these advisers should serve only when asked. I believe three men can succeed in preparing a workable Constitution acceptable to all the powers. Were six or seven men, or more, to attempt to do so, they would probably fail. After the three great powers have drafted a Constitution and adopted it, the smaller nations should be invited to join the world government. They should also be free not to join and, though they should feel perfectly secure outside the world government, I am sure they will eventually wish to join. Naturally, they should be entitled to propose changes in the Constitution as drafted by the Big Three. But the Big

Three should go ahead and organize the world government, whether or not the smaller nations decide to join.

Such a world government should have jurisdiction over all military matters, and it need have only one other power. That is the power to interfere in countries where a minority is oppressing the majority and, therefore, is creating the kind of instability that leads to war. For example, conditions such as exist today in Argentina and Spain should be dealt with. There must be an end to the concept of non-intervention, for to abandon non-intervention in certain circumstances is part of keeping the peace.

The establishment of a world government should not be delayed until similar conditions of freedom exist in each of the three great powers. While it is true that in the Soviet Union the minority rules, I do not believe that the internal conditions in that country constitute a threat to world peace. One must bear in mind that the people in Russia had not had a long tradition of political education; changes to improve conditions in Russia had to be effected by a minority for the reason that there was no majority capable of doing so. If I had been born a Russian, I believe I could have adjusted myself to this situation.

It should not be necessary, in establishing a world government with a monopoly of authority over military affairs, to change the internal structure of the three great powers. It would be for the three individuals who draft the Constitution to devise ways for collaboration despite the different structures of their countries.

Do I fear the tyranny of a world government? Of course I do. But I fear still more the coming of another war. Any government is certain to be evil to some extent. But a world government is preferable to the far greater evil of wars, particularly when viewed in the context of the intensified destructiveness of war. If such a world government is not established by a process of agreement among nations, I believe it will come anyway, and in a much more dangerous form; for war or wars can only result in one power being supreme and dominating the rest of the world by its overwhelming military supremacy.

Now that we have the atomic secret, we must not lose it, and that is what we would risk doing if we gave it to the United Nations Organization or to the Soviet Union. But, as soon as possible, we must make it clear that we are not keeping the bomb a secret for the sake of maintaining our power but in the hope of establishing peace through world government, and that we will do our utmost to bring this world government into being.

I appreciate that there are persons who approve of world government as the ultimate objective but favor a gradual approach to its establishment. The trouble with taking little steps, one at a time, in the hope of eventually reaching the ultimate goal, is that while such steps are being taken, we continue to keep the bomb without convincing those who do not have the bomb of our ultimate intentions. That of itself creates fear and suspicion, with the consequence that the relations between rival countries deteriorate to a dangerous extent. That is why people who advocate taking a step at a time may think they are approaching world peace, but they actually are contributing by their slow pace to the possibility of war. We have no time to waste in this way. If war is to be averted, it must be done quickly.

Further, we shall not have the secret of the bomb for very long. I know it is being argued that no other country has money enough to spend on the development of the atomic bomb and that, therefore, we are assured of the secret for a long time. But it is a common mistake in this country to measure things by the amount of money they cost. Other countries which have the raw materials and manpower and wish to apply them to the work of developing atomic power can do so; men and materials and the decision to use them, and not money, are all that is needed.

I do not consider myself the father of the release of atomic energy. My part in it was quite indirect. I did not, in fact, foresee that it would be released in my time. I only believed that it was theoretically possible. It became practical through the accidental discovery of chain reaction, and this was not something I could have predicted. It was discovered by Hahn in Berlin, and he himself at first misinterpreted what he discovered. It was Lise Meitner who provided the correct interpretation and escaped from Germany to place the information in the hands of Niels Bohr.[3]

In my opinion, a great era of atomic science cannot be assured by organizing science in the way large corporations are organized. One can organize the application of a discovery already made, but one cannot organize the discovery itself. Only a free individual can make a discovery. However, there can be a kind of organization wherein the scientist is assured freedom and proper conditions of work. Professors of science in American universities, for instance, should be relieved of some of their teaching so as to have more time for research. Can you imagine an organization of scientists making the discoveries of Charles Darwin?

I do not believe that the vast private corporations of the United States are suitable to the needs of the times. If a visitor should come to this country from another planet, would he not find it strange that, in this country, private corporations are permitted to wield so much power without having to assume commensurate responsibility? I say this to stress my conviction that the American government must retain control of atomic energy, not because socialism is necessarily desirable but because atomic energy was developed by the government; it would be unthinkable

[3] Einstein is in error on a minor point. . . . Lise Meitner did not "escape from Germany to place the information [about atomic fission] in the hands of Niels Bohr." She was already in Sweden at the time.

to turn over this property of the people to any individual or group of individuals. As for socialism, unless it is international to the extent of producing a world government which controls all military power, it might lead to wars even more easily than capitalism because it represents an even greater concentration of power.

To give any estimate as to when atomic energy might be applied for peaceful, constructive purposes is impossible. All that we know now is how to use a fairly large quantity of uranium. The use of small quantities, sufficient, say, to operate a car or an airplane, is thus far impossible, and one cannot predict when it will be accomplished. No doubt, it will be achieved, but no one can say when. Nor can one predict when materials more common than uranium can be used to supply atomic energy. Presumably, such materials would be among the heavier elements of high atomic weight and would be relatively scarce due to their lesser stability. Most of these materials may already have disappeared through radioactive disintegration. So, though the release of atomic energy can be, and no doubt will be, a great boon to mankind, this may not come about for some time.

I myself do not have the gift of explanation which would be needed to persuade large numbers of people of the urgency of the problems that now face the human race. Hence, I should like to commend someone who has this gift of explanation: Emery Reves, whose book *The Anatomy of Peace* is intelligent, clear, brief, and, if I may use the absurd term, dynamic on the topic of war and need for world government.

Since I do not foresee that atomic energy will prove to be a boon within the near future, I have to say that, for the present, it is a menace. Perhaps it is well that it should be. It may intimidate the human race into bringing order to its international affairs, which, without the pressure of fear, undoubtedly would not happen.

Einstein and the Bomb

OTTO NATHAN AND HEINZ NORDEN

Einstein clearly did not consider himself to be the father of the bomb. Indeed, as he stated in the preceding article, he felt his role to be quite indirect. How Einstein came to be involved in the American effort to construct the atomic bomb is a fascinating story, especially in light of the fact that as late as 1939 he did not seem to be very optimistic about practical applications of nuclear fission. But international events finally prompted Einstein to advise President Roosevelt and the American government to undertake the work that became the Manhattan Project and ultimately produced the bomb. The circumstances leading to Einstein's action are described by Otto Nathan, one of Einstein's confidants and the executor of his Last Will, and Heinz Norden in Einstein on Peace, *from which the following selection is excerpted.*

IT WAS ONLY . . . in the early summer of 1939 that Einstein, through Szilard, became involved in the efforts to experiment with the construction of atomic bombs. It would appear that, several years before, Einstein had been very doubtful about the possibility of splitting the atom. At the winter session of the American Association for the Advancement of Science in Pittsburgh in January 1935, reporters asked Einstein whether he thought that scientists would ever be able to transmute matter into energy for practical purposes. In the subsequent newspaper account, which should be considered with caution, Eistein is reported to have replied that he felt almost certain it would not be possible, and to have referred to the vast amount of energy required to release energy from a molecule. "It is," he is reported to have added, "something like shooting birds in the dark in a country where there are only a few birds."

It is possible that Einstein may have learned early in 1939 about the Hahn-Strassmann-Meitner-Frisch work as well as about subsequent publications concerning these developments. It does not appear, however, that he was very optimistic regarding the possibility of a practical application of the new scientific discoveries at an early date. In a statement made in reply to a question submitted to him on the occasion of his sixtieth birthday, March 14, 1939, and published in *The New York Times,* Einstein made the following remarks:

> The results gained thus far concerning the splitting of the atom do not justify the assumption that the atomic energy released in the process could be economically utilized. Yet, there can hardly be a physicist with so little intellectual curiosity that his interest in this important subject could become impaired because of the unfavorable conclusion to be drawn from past experimentation.

Szilard's first contact with Einstein in the matter of nuclear fission took place several months later. When he first considered consulting with Einstein about the new scientific discoveries and their implications, he did not contemplate any approach to the United States Government. Szilard recalls that he and Wigner had by this time become very perturbed by the thought that Germany might obtain large quantities of uranium from the Belgian Congo, the chief source of the material. Germany might thus be greatly helped in her research on atomic energy and ultimately in the production of atomic bombs. Szilard and Wigner felt that the Belgian Government should be advised of these eventualities in order that uranium exports to Germany might be halted if Belgium so desired. Szilard knew that Einstein had for years been on friendly terms with Queen Elizabeth of Belgium. When he and Wigner decided to visit Einstein at Nassau Point, Peconic, Long Island, where Einstein was spending the summer, it was, as Szilard has reported, their intention to suggest to Einstein that he communicate with Queen Elizabeth. It is one of the dramatic aspects of the whole atomic development that this visit, with a relatively modest and probably inconsequential purpose, led to events of completely different and, eventually, momentous import. The visit took place around July 15, 1939.

Szilard recalls that Einstein, when told about the possibility of producing a chain reaction, exclaimed, *"Daran habe ich gar nicht gedacht!"* (That never occurred to me.) Szilard reports that Einstein immediately recognized the implication of Germany's access to uranium in the Congo and declared he would be prepared to assist in informing the Belgian Government accordingly. Several approaches to the problem were discussed by the three scientists. Wigner apparently emphasized not only the desirability of advising the Belgian Government through the Queen or the Belgian Ambassador in Washington of the dangers involved in uranium exports to Germany but also the need for large imports of uranium into the United States. Whether recommendations were made as to how to secure such imports or who might be approached on the matter is not known. Einstein is reported to have favored a suggestion, apparently also offered by Wigner, to submit to the State Department a draft of a projected letter to the Queen of Belgium. The letter would be mailed to the Queen only if no objection were raised by the State Department. There is no information available as to whether, at this original meeting, Einstein, Szilard and Wigner considered advising the American Government of the implications of the new scientific discoveries with a view to engaging its interest in promoting or subsidizing further research in the atomic field.

Even before his visit to Einstein, Szilard had discussed the entire problem with a New York friend in the financial world; he had felt that the financial resources of the physics department of Columbia University would not suffice for the additional research contemplated by Fermi and himself and that outside funds would therefore be necessary. Upon Szilard's return to New York from his visit to Einstein, the finance expert informed him that he had consulted with Dr. Alexander Sachs, a well-known economist connected with the New York banking house of Lehman Brothers and sometimes one of President Roosevelt's unofficial advisers. When it was suggested to Szilard that he communicate with Dr. Sachs, he did so, apparently without delay. It was undoubtedly Sachs who recognized the magnitude and significance of the problem and realized that, to obtain results, the matter should be brought to the attention of the White House. He, therefore, suggested to Szilard that Einstein's letter be addressed to President Roosevelt rather than to the Belgian Queen or the Belgian Ambassador. Sachs offered to see to it that the letter would reach the President personally. Writing to Einstein on July 19, 1939, Szilard stated that, although he had seen Sachs only once in his life and had not been able to form an opinion of him, he nonetheless recommended accepting the course of action outlined by him. Szilard added that this recommendation was also supported by Professor Edward Teller, then guest professor at Columbia University, with whom he had consulted. Szilard further suggested that Einstein's projected letter be entrusted to Sachs since he believed that Sachs was in a position to do as he had promised. Szilard enclosed a draft of the letter. Since Sachs was to play an important role during the ensuing months, and since Einstein's letter to Roosevelt was to release a "chain reaction" which possibly no move by any other individual could have effected at that time, Szilard's casually arranged meeting about an all-important matter with a person completely unknown to him, his subsequent confidence in that person on the basis of a single meeting, and Sachs's perception of Roosevelt's capacity for bold decisions are startling incidents in the drama that was to unfold.

While it is not possible to reconstruct all the developments during the two weeks following Szilard's meeting with Sachs, it is known that, during this period, Szilard once again called on Einstein at his Long Island summer home. Since Wigner was out of town, Szilard was accompanied on his second visit by Edward Teller. At this meeting with Szilard and Teller, if not before by phone or mail, Einstein accepted Sachs's suggestion to bring the matter to the attention of the President and to have a letter to Roosevelt transmitted through Sachs. Einstein dictated to Teller the draft of a letter in German which is preserved in his files. This draft contains some of the main points of the history-making communication to Roosevelt that Einstein was eventually to sign. . . .

Einstein's draft is an indication of how, in possibly less than a week, the initial modest proposition to write a letter to the Belgian Queen had developed into a meaningful and highly suggestive approach to the President of the United States. Whether Einstein's dictated draft was inspired by the draft which Szilard had prepared after his meeting with Sachs and had mailed to Einstein before his second visit cannot be ascertained. On August 2, 1939, Szilard wrote to Einstein that, in his discussions with Sachs about additional recommendations, K. T. Compton, Bernard Baruch and Charles Lindbergh had been suggested for the position of liaison man between the government and the atomic scientists, the position recommended in Einstein's draft and also in his final letter to Roosevelt. Szilard added that Lindbergh was the "favorite" at the time of writing.

On the basis of Einstein's German draft, Szilard prepared, after a further meeting with Sachs, two English versions of a letter to the President, which he forwarded to Einstein in his letter of August 2, 1939. Einstein favored the shorter of the two Szilard drafts. The letter actually sent to Roosevelt and dated August 2, 1939, reads as follows:

Albert Einstein
Old Grove Road
Nassau Point
Peconic, Long Island
August 2, 1939

F. D. Roosevelt
President of the United States
White House
Washington, D.C.

Sir:

Some recent work by E. Fermi and L. Szilard, which has been communicated to me in manuscript, leads me to expect that the element uranium may be turned into a new and important source of energy in the immediate future. Certain aspects of the situation seem to call for watchfulness and, if necessary, quick action on the part of the Administration. I believe, therefore, that it is my duty to bring to your attention the following facts and recommendations.

In the course of the last four months it has been made probable—through the work of Joliot in France as well as Fermi and Szilard in America—that it may become possible to set up nuclear chain reactions in a large mass of uranium, by which vast amounts of power and large quantities of new radium-like elements would be generated. Now it appears almost certain that this could be achieved in the immediate future.

This new phenomenon would also lead to the construction of bombs, and it is conceivable—though much less certain—that extremely powerful bombs of a new type may thus be constructed. A single bomb of this type, carried by boat or exploded in a port, might very well destroy the whole port together with some of the surrounding territory. However, such bombs might very well prove to be too heavy for transportation by air.

The United States has only very poor ores of uranium in moderate quantities. There is some good ore in Canada and the former Czechoslovakia, while the most important source of uranium is the Belgian Congo.

In view of this situation you may think it desirable to have some permanent contact maintained between the Administration and the group of physicists working on chain reactions in America. One possible way of achieving this might be for you to entrust with this task a person who has your confidence and who could perhaps serve in an unofficial capacity. His task might comprise the following:

a) To approach Government Departments, keep them informed of the further developments, and put forward recommendations for Government action, giving particular attention to the problem of securing a supply of uranium ore for the United States.

b) To speed up the experimental work which is at present being carried on within the limits of the budgets of University laboratories, by providing funds, if such funds be required, through his contacts with private persons who are willing to make contributions for this cause, and perhaps also by obtaining the cooperation of industrial laboratories which have the necessary equipment.

I understand that Germany has actually stopped the sale of uranium from the Czechoslovakian mines which she has taken over. That she should have taken such early action might perhaps be understood on the ground that the son of the German Under-Secretary of State, von Weizsäcker, is attached to the Kaiser Wilhelm Institute in Berlin, where some of the American work on uranium is now being repeated.

Yours very truly,

A. Einstein

This letter, addressed by the then greatest living scientist to one of the most important political leaders of the world, bearing on dramatically important scientific and military developments and suggesting crucial moves by the American Government, was actually not submitted to President Roosevelt for over two months, during which period the Germans might have made much progress in the search for a nuclear chain reaction. The available documents in Einstein's files and all other sources of information fail to provide an adequate explanation for the delay in transmitting Einstein's communication. In a letter of September 27, 1939, Szilard conveyed to Einstein his impression that the letter "had already been in Washington for some time." But in another letter, dated October 3, 1939, Szilard reported that he and Wigner had called on Sachs, and Sachs admitted still having Einstein's letter in his possession; Sachs explained that he had gained the impression from several telephone conversations with Roosevelt's secretary that it was advisable to see the President at a later time since he was overburdened with work. In his testimony of November 27, 1945, before the Special Committee on Atomic Energy of the United States Senate, Sachs stated that he had not wanted to accept an appointment with the President as long as the President was involved in revising the existing neutrality legislation. However, the neutrality legislation did not become an acute issue until the war broke out in Europe on September 1, 1939, which was more than four weeks after Einstein had signed the letter.

In his letter to Einstein of October 3, 1939, Szilard remarked that he and Wigner had begun to wonder whether it might not become necessary to entrust another person with the mission Dr. Sachs had volunteered to perform. But Sachs did finally see President Roosevelt on October 11, 1939, and submitted to the President Einstein's letter, a more technical memorandum by Szilard, as well as considerable background material. The Szilard memorandum stated that, if fast neutrons could be used, "it would be easy to construct extremely dangerous bombs . . . with a destructive power far beyond all military conceptions." Sachs also submitted to the President a written statement of his own in which he summarized the main problems involved and listed the steps which he thought should be taken by the United States in the matter of further exploring the problem of nuclear fission.

President Roosevelt acted at once. He appointed an "Advisory Committee on Uranium," which was to report to him as soon as possible; a few days later, he addressed the following letter to Einstein:

The White House
Washington

October 19, 1939

My dear Professor,

I want to thank you for your recent letter and the most interesting and important enclosure.

I found this data of such import that I have convened a board consisting of the head of the Bureau of Standards and a chosen representative of the Army and Navy to thoroughly investigate the possibilities of your suggestion regarding the element of uranium.

I am glad to say that Dr. Sachs will co-operate and work with this committee and I feel this is the most practical and effective method of dealing with the subject.

Very sincerely yours,
Franklin D. Roosevelt

. . . The further history of the many stages in the development of the atomic bomb is recorded in other publications and need not be repeated. What is of interest here are the few instances when Einstein again intervened.

After the first meeting of the Advisory Committee, other scientists were invited to participate in subsequent consultations. Sachs continued to play a very important role as the representative of the President and, as he himself frequently emphasized, as the individual who maintained contact with Einstein: he consulted with Einstein and presented Einstein's opinions and suggestions to the President or the committee orally or in writing, as circumstances would dictate. . . .

Although the Advisory Committee continued to operate, Szilard and

Sachs were perturbed at its relatively slow progress and, in February 1940, they decided once again to secure Einstein's intervention. It took the form of another letter from Einstein, dated March 7, 1940.

In this letter, Einstein reviewed the rapid development of atomic research—Szilard's and Fermi's continuing work, for example, and the likelihood that similar work was going forward in Europe, especially in Germany.

On March 15, 1940, Sachs brought Einstein's second letter to the attention of the President, who, on April 5, 1940, proposed an enlarged meeting of the Advisory Committee on Uranium which would include Einstein and others whom Einstein might suggest. Briggs, the chairman of the committee, invited Einstein to participate in such a meeting. Since Einstein was unable to accept the invitation, he addressed, on April 25, 1940, the following letter to Briggs:

> I thank you for your recent communication concerning a meeting of the Special Advisory Committee appointed by President Roosevelt.
>
> As, to my regret, I shall not be able to attend this meeting, I have discussed with Dr. Wigner and Dr. Sachs particularly the questions arising out of the work of Dr. Fermi and Dr. Szilard. I am convinced as to the wisdom and the urgency of creating the conditions under which that and related work can be carried out with greater speed and on a larger scale than hitherto. I was interested in a suggestion made by Dr. Sachs that the Special Advisory Committee submit names of persons to serve as a board of trustees for a nonprofit organization which, with the approval of the government committee, should secure from governmental or private sources, or both, the necessary funds for carrying out the work. It seems to me that such an organization would provide a framework which could give Dr. Fermi and Dr. Szilard and co-workers the necessary scope. The preparation of the large-scale experiment and the exploration of the various possibilities with regard to practical applications is a task of considerable complexity, and I think that given such a framework and the necessary funds, it could be carried out much faster than through a loose co-operation of university laboratories and government departments.

As far as can be established, Einstein had no further connection either with the work that preceded the atomic bomb project or with the project itself. The Advisory Committee did not continue much longer as such. When, in June 1940, Roosevelt created the National Defense Research Committee, which was to develop into a very significant organization with regard to America's military preparations, he asked that the Advisory Committee be reorganized, again under the chairmanship of Dr. Briggs, as a subcommittee of the newly created National Defense Research Committee. The President specifically assigned to the new committee the responsibility for research on nuclear problems. "This meant," Professor Karl T. Compton, a member of the new committee, remarked, "reviewing and acting upon the recommendations of Dr. Briggs's committee."

Viewed in historical perspective, it would appear that the decision to use Einstein's unique authority in the attempt to obtain the government's direct participation and financial assistance in atomic research may well have been decisive, since his intervention succeeded in securing the attention of President Roosevelt. The Advisory Committee on Uranium was organized by the President as an immediate result of Einstein's intervention and was the germinal body from which the whole huge atomic effort developed. Whether, without Einstein's intervention, similar developments would have taken place around the same period, and whether the atomic bomb would still have been produced around the time it was produced—that is, before the end of the war—are legitimate questions. . . .

. . . We shall never know with any degree of certainty what would have happened if Szilard had not called on Einstein in July 1939, or if Einstein, in turn, had not been immediately willing to lend his authority to supporting a request to the President of the United States that was partly based on scientific assumptions and speculations.

A New Vision Out of the Ashes

BERNARD T. FELD

In this chapter, we have already considered Einstein's own proposal for a world government as the only alternative he saw to nuclear war. And we considered the circumstances leading to Einstein's involvement in the American atom bomb project. Despite Einstein's statement that his role in that project was indirect and passive and his assertion that he did not consider himself "the father of the release of atomic energy," his last years were haunted by the prospect of nuclear war that the "release of atomic energy" had made possible. Those last years were also haunted by a sense of his own culpability—notwithstanding his protests to the contrary. The activities of Einstein in the years following World War II were devoted to his passionate advocacy of peace, a cause he had long advocated but which now became an obsession. These activities are sympathetically described by the MIT physicist and peace activist Bernard T. Feld in the article "Einstein and the Politics of Nuclear Weapons," published as one of the symposium papers in The Centennial Symposium in Jerusalem, one of several such celebrations of the centenary of Einstein's birth in 1979.

IF RELATIVITY CAPTURED the public imagination in the period between the wars, the atomic bomb, which ended World War II, propelled Einstein even more directly into the limelight, but under circumstances that caused him acute moral, as well as personal, embarrassment. To the popular mind, Einstein was, and to a large extent remains, the "father of the atomic bomb." Is there any person so ignorant that he or she does not recognize his famous discovery of the equivalence between mass and energy, $E = mc^2$, which provides the theoretical basis for the release of nuclear energy? Add to this Einstein's audacious intervention with President Franklin D. Roosevelt, to convince him of the military potential of the discovery of nuclear fission, and you have the two ingredients of that aspect of the Einstein legend that he worked most diligently and unsuccessfully, to debunk.

Einstein's role in the successful American effort during World War II to develop a nuclear bomb was indeed peripheral. On this score, he tried hard to put the record straight. Thus, in response to a request from the editor of a Japanese journal demanding to know why Einstein, "as a great scientist who played an important role in producing the atomic bomb, . . . co-operate[d] in [its] production . . . although you were well aware of its tremendous destructive power?" he protested:

> My participation in the production of the atomic bomb consisted of one single act: I signed a letter to President Roosevelt, in which I emphasized the necessity of conducting large-scale experimentation with regard to the feasibility of producing an atom bomb.
>
> I was well aware of the dreadful danger which would threaten mankind were the experiments to prove successful. Yet I felt impelled to take the step because it seemed probable that the Germans might be working on the same problem with every prospect of success. I saw no alternative but to act as I did, *although I have always been a convinced pacifist.*

Yet the myth persisted that through his earlier discovery of the fundamental mass-energy relationship, Einstein somehow bore responsibility for the final outcome. With great patience, he explained:

> Now you seem to believe that I, poor fellow that I am, by discovering and publishing the relationship between mass and energy, made an important contribution to the lamentable situation in which we find ourselves today. You suggest that I should then, in 1905, have foreseen the possible development of atomic bombs. But this was quite impossible since the accomplishment of a "chain reaction" was dependent on the existence of empirical data that could hardly have been anticipated in 1905. But even if such knowledge had been available, it would have been ridiculous to attempt to conceal the particular conclusion resulting from the Special Theory of Relativity. Once the theory existed, the conclusion also existed and could not have remained concealed for any length of time. As for the theory itself, it owes its existence to the efforts to discover the properties of the "luminiferous ether"! There was never even the slightest indication of any potential technological application.

Even now, some forty years later, the importance of Einstein's role in the American development of nuclear weapons before the end of the war against Japan remains a source of legitimate controversy. Some feel it was seminal, that without his intervention the atomic bomb project would never have received the government attention and support that was indispensable to its success. Others believe that the physics was so compelling that once the early (and very inexpensive) demonstrations of the potentiality had taken place—and they would probably have happened even without government support—not even the most obtuse bureaucracy could have resisted the inevitable pressures of the cream of the American physics community. . . .

In any event, Einstein learned of the success of the Manhattan Project as did the rest of the world—by the public announcement on 8 August 1945 that a single bomb using the fission of an isotope of uranium had destroyed the Japanese city of Hiroshima. Einstein is alleged to have responded to this news with the time-honored lament, *"Oy Weh!"* (woe upon us).

There can be no question as to where Einstein would have stood with respect to the dropping of the bombs on Japan. In a letter of 19 March 1955 to Max von Laue, one of the few German physicists with whom he retained a lifelong friendship, he explained:

> My action concerning the atomic bomb and Roosevelt consisted merely in the fact that, because of the danger that Hitler might be the first to have the bomb, I signed a letter to the President which had been drafted by Szilard. Had I known that that fear was not justified, I, no more than Szilard, would have participated in opening this Pandora's box. For my distrust of governments was not limited to Germany.

Unfortunately, I had no share in the warning made against using the bomb against Japan. Credit for this must go to James Franck. If they had only listened to him!

The use of the bomb against Japanese civilians was especially painful to Einstein, because he had formed very strong friendships and a special fondness for the people during his visit to Japan in 1922. Not only was there not a single racist bone in his body, but Einstein never held the Japanese people responsible for the war in the sense that he held the German people responsible. Thus, in an uncharacteristically harsh response to an appeal for a "soft peace" from his old friend and fellow refugee James Franck in December 1945, he wrote:

> I remember too well the campaign of tears staged by the Germans after the First World War to be fooled by its repetition. The Germans slaughtered several millions of civilians according to a well-thought-out plan. If they had murdered you too, some crocodile tears would undoubtedly have been shed. The few decent people who are among them do not change the picture as a whole. I have gauged from several letters received from over there, as well as from the information supplied by some reliable persons, that the Germans do not feel one iota of guilt or sorrow. . . . Dear Franck, do not involve yourself in this dirty mess! They will first misuse your kindness and then they will ridicule you for being a fool. But if I am unable to persuade you to refrain, I, for one, will certainly not get mixed up in this affair. Should the opportunity present itself, I shall publicly oppose the appeal.

Nevertheless, he certainly would have opposed the bomb's use against Germany had it been ready in time, as attested in a letter to a Japanese correspondent written on 23 June 1953:

> I am a *dedicated* [*entschiedener*] but not an *absolute* pacifist; this means that I am opposed to the use of force under any circumstances, except when confronted by an enemy who pursues the destruction of life as an *end in itself*. I have always condemned the use of the atomic bomb against Japan. However, I was completely powerless to prevent the fateful decision for which I am as little responsible as you are for the deeds of the Japanese in Korea and China.
>
> I have never said I would have approved the use of the atomic bomb against the Germans, I did believe that we had to avoid the contingency of Germany under Hitler being in *sole* possession of this weapon. This was the real danger at the time.
>
> I am not only opposed to war against Russia but to all war—with the above reservation. . . .

It is far from surprising, therefore, that with World War II over and the intellectual battle lines forming—between those who would have taken advantage of the American nuclear monopoly to establish the dominance of American military influence over all national and international institutions and those who saw the atomic bomb as an opportunity finally to establish international institutions with the intention *and the power* to provide supranational control over future conflict and war—Einstein again plunged enthusiastically into the arena of public affairs. He firmly supported the fledgling atomic scientists' movement, organized into a Federation of Atomic Scientists, and encouraged its voice, *The Bulletin of the Atomic Scientists*. . . .

In support of the various national and international enterprises of the atomic scientists, Einstein agreed in May 1946 to serve as chairman of an Emergency Committee of Atomic Scientists. Its program was based on an agreed set of principles concerning the dangers of atomic weapons:

> These facts are accepted by all scientists:
>
> 1. Atomic bombs can now be made cheaply and in large number. They will become more destructive.
> 2. There is no military defense against the atomic bomb and none is to be expected.
> 3. Other nations can rediscover our secret processes by themselves.
> 4. Preparedness against atomic war is futile, and if attempted will ruin the structure of our social order.
> 5. If war breaks out, atomic bombs will be used and they will surely destroy our civilization.
> 6. There is no solution to this problem except international control of atomic energy and, ultimately, the elimination of war.
>
> The program of the committee is to see that these truths become known to the public. The democratic determination of this nation's policy on atomic energy must ultimately rest on the understanding of its citizens.

The immediate objective was to raise a fund of $1,000,000 in support of the various educational activities of the atomic scientists aimed at civilian national and international control of future nuclear energy activities. However, although the committee had a certain amount of success in raising money, as time passed it became increasingly clear to Einstein and his fellow committee members that the world was drifting in the wrong direction. In considering the root causes of their failure, Einstein and his colleagues were convinced that the seriousness of the problem demanded more drastic remedies. Their views moved more and more in the direction of "world government" as the only logical solution. . . .

From then on, Einstein became ever more outspoken in his insistence that nothing short of an effective supranational authority able to exercise unquestioned control over international issues of war and peace was needed to save the world from nuclear disaster. He maintained that such an international authority could and should be established promptly through the United Nations, irrespective of whether all the major world powers were ready immediately to join. . . . Although this view was openly and pointedly attacked by Soviet officials, as well as by some Soviet scientists, as playing into the hands of right-wing, anti-Soviet forces, Einstein stood his ground and steadfastly maintained until the end of his life his adherence to the "world government" approach as the only means of saving humankind from the disastrous consequences of the uninhibited national exploitation of inevitable technological progress. . . .

But eternal optimist that he was, Einstein could never give up hope. Thus, in the spring of 1955 he and Bertrand Russell, with typical youthful enthusiasm, launched a project aimed at starting a worldwide movement among scientists to reverse the Cold War trend toward nuclear war. The credo of this movement was the Russell-Einstein Manifesto signed by Einstein on 11 April 1955, exactly one week before his death. The text of this manifesto serves well as a summing up of Einstein's view of the state of the world and of the responsibilities of scientists as world citizens:

> In the tragic situation which confronts humanity, we feel that scientists should assemble in conference to appraise the perils that have arisen as a result of the development of weapons of mass destruction. . . .
>
> We are speaking on this occasion, not as members of this or that nation, continent or creed, but as human beings, members of the species man, whose continued existence is in doubt. The world is full of conflicts; and, overshadowing all minor conflicts, the titanic struggle between Communism and anti-Communism.
>
> Almost everybody who is politically conscious has strong feelings about one or more of these issues; but we want you, if you can, to set aside such feelings and consider yourselves only as members of a biological species which has had a remarkable history, and whose disappearance none of us can desire.
>
> We shall try to say no single word which should appeal to one group rather than to another. All, equally, are in peril, and, if the peril is understood, there is hope that they may collectively avert it. . . .
>
> The general public, and even many men in positions of authority, have not realized what would be involved in a war with nuclear bombs. The general public still thinks in terms of the obliteration of cities. It is understood that the new bombs are more powerful than the old, and that, while one A-bomb could obliterate Hiroshima, one H-bomb could obliterate the largest cities, such as London, New York and Moscow.
>
> No doubt in an H-bomb war great cities would be obliterated. But this is one of the minor disasters that would have to be faced. If everybody in London, New York and Moscow were exterminated, the world might, in the course of a few centuries, recover from the blow. But we now

know, especially since the Bikini test, that nuclear bombs can gradually spread destruction over a very much wider area than had been supposed.

It is stated on very good authority that a bomb can now be manufactured which will be 2,500 times as powerful as that which destroyed Hiroshima.

Such a bomb, if exploded near the ground or under water, sends radioactive particles into the upper air. They sink gradually and reach the surface of the earth in the form of a deadly dust or rain. It was this dust which infected the Japanese fishermen and their catch of fish.

No one knows how widely such lethal radioactive particles might be diffused, but the best authorities are unanimous in saying that a war with H-bombs might quite possibly put an end to the human race. It is feared that if many H-bombs are used there will be universal death—sudden only for a minority, but for the majority a slow torture of disease and disintegration.

Many warnings have been uttered by eminent men of science and by authorities in military strategy. None of them will say that the worst results are certain. What they do say is that these results are possible, and no one can be sure that they will not be realized. We have not yet found that the views of experts depend in any degree upon their politics or prejudices. They depend only, so far as our researches have revealed, upon the extent of the particular expert's knowledge. We have found that the men who know most are the most gloomy.

Here, then, is the problem which we present to you, stark and dreadful and inescapable: Shall we put an end to the human race; or shall mankind renounce war? People will not face this alternative because it is so difficult to abolish war.

The abolition of war will demand distasteful limitations of national sovereignty. But what perhaps impedes understanding of the situation more than anything else is that the term *mankind* feels vague and abstract. People scarcely realize in imagination that the danger is to themselves and their children and their grandchildren, and not only to a dimly apprehended humanity. They can scarcely bring themselves to grasp that they, individually, and those whom they love are in imminent danger of perishing agonizingly. And so they hope that perhaps war may be allowed to continue provided modern weapons are prohibited.

This hope is illusory. Whatever agreements not to use the H-bombs had been reached in time of peace, they would no longer be considered binding in time of war, and both sides would set to work to manufacture H-bombs as soon as war broke out, for, if one side manufactured the bombs and the other did not, the side that manufactured them would inevitably be victorious.

Although an agreement to renounce nuclear weapons as part of a general reduction of armaments would not afford an ultimate solution, it would serve certain important purposes.

First: Any agreement between East and West is to the good in so far as it tends to diminish tension. Second: The abolition of thermonuclear weapons, if each side believed that the other had carried it out sincerely, would lessen the fear of a sudden attack in the style of Pearl Harbor, which at present keeps both sides in a state of nervous apprehension. We should, therefore, welcome such an agreement, though only as a first step.

Most of us are not neutral in feeling, but, as human beings, we have to remember that, if the issues between East and West are to be decided in any manner that can give any possible satisfaction to anybody, whether Communist or anti-Communist, whether Asian or European or American, whether white or black, then these issues must not be decided by war. We should wish this to be understood, both in the East and in the West.

There lies before us, if we choose, continual progress in happiness, knowledge and wisdom. Shall we, instead, choose death, because we cannot forget our quarrels? We appeal, as human beings, to human beings: Remember your humanity and forget the rest. If you can do so, the way lies open to a new paradise; if you cannot, there lies before you the risk of universal death.

Suggestions for Further Reading

EINSTEIN'S OWN STATEMENTS about the atomic bomb and scientific responsibility were as brief and often cryptic as were his public statements on other subjects. His most substantial one is the interview with Raymond Graham Swing reproduced in this chapter ("Einstein on the Atomic Bomb," *Atlantic Monthly*, 176, No. 5 [Nov. 1945], 43–45), but some parallel statements are to be found in his *Out of My Later Years* (New York: Philosophical Library, 1950), especially the section "Science and Life." These, as well as nearly all his other related statements, are reprinted and edited in *Einstein on Peace*, ed. Otto Nathan and Heinz Norden (New York: Simon and Schuster, 1960). Some of his concern comes through in *The Born–Einstein Letters: Correspondence between Albert Einstein and Max and Hedwig Born from 1916–1955*, commentary by Max Born, tr. Irene Born (London: Macmillan, 1971), but this book is much more revealing of Born's anguish. The same sentiment is expressed throughout the world community of nuclear physicists, as Werner Heisenberg, *Physics and Beyond: Encounters and Conversations*, tr. A. J. Pomerans (New York: Harper & Row, 1971) demonstrates, as well as Otto Hahn, *My*

Life . . ., tr. E. Kaiser and E. Wilkins (New York: Herder and Herder, 1970). The same sorts of views are expressed in the United States by J. Robert Oppenheimer in *The Flying Trapeze: Three Crises for Physicists* (London: Oxford University Press, 1964), especially the third crisis dealing with the atomic bomb and the moral responsibility of scientists; and in *The Open Mind* (New York: Simon and Schuster, 1955).

Most of the books about Einstein deal with his scientific and technical work: Lincoln Barnett, *The Universe and Dr. Einstein*, 2nd rev. ed. (New York: W. Sloane, 1957), or Jeremy Bernstein, *Einstein* (New York: Viking, 1973), for example. The best of these scientific biographies is Abraham Pais, *'Subtle is the Lord . . .' The Science and the Life of Albert Einstein* (Oxford and New York: Oxford University Press, 1982). *Some Strangeness in the Proportion: A Centennial Symposium to Celebrate the Achievements of Albert Einstein*, ed. Harry Woolf (Reading, Mass.: Addison-Wesley Publishing Company, Inc., 1980) is also entirely devoted to the evaluation of his work as a scientist and scientific theorist.

The best and most comprehensive book on him, Ronald W. Clark, *Einstein: The Life and Times*, 3rd. ed., (New York: World, 1984), does focus on the political and social implications of his work rather than strictly on the work itself. To a somewhat lesser extent, this is the case with Banesh Hoffman, *Albert Einstein, Creator and Rebel* (New York: Viking, 1972). Antonia Vallentin, *Einstein, A Biography*, tr. M. Budberg (London: Weidenfeld and Nicolson, 1954), is interesting in that it deals more fully than any other book with the intimacies, family relations, and day-to-day affairs of Einstein. This area of his life is also revealed in *Albert Einstein, the Human Side: New Glimpses from His Archives*, ed. Helen Dukas and Banesh Hoffman (Princeton, N.J.: Princeton University Press, 1979).

Lansing Lamont, *Day of Trinity* (New York: Atheneum, 1965), is a fascinating account of the making and employment of the atomic bomb. The implications of that employment are dealt with in several important books: Herbert Feis, *The Atom Bomb and the End of the War in the Pacific*, rev. ed. (Princeton, N.J.: Princeton University Press, 1966), Martin J. Sherwin, *A World Destroyed: The Atomic Bomb and the Grand Alliance* (New York: Knopf, 1975), Gar Alperovitz, *Atomic Diplomacy: Hiroshima and Potsdam; The Use of the Atomic Bomb and the American Confrontation with Soviet Power* (New York: Simon and Schuster, 1965), and in a brilliant and controversial work by a leading defense analyst, Fred Kaplan, *The Wizards of Armageddon* (New York: Simon and Schuster, 1983). Some of these issues and others are conveniently presented in a book of readings, *The Atomic Bomb: The Critical Issues*, ed. Barton J. Bernstein (Boston: Little, Brown, 1975).

UPI/Bettmann Newsphotos

Stalin and the Iron Curtain

1879	born
1913–17	exile in Siberia
1922	Secretary General of the Central Committee of the Communist Party
1934–38	the great purges
1941	German invasion of Russia
1942	Siege of Stalingrad
1943	Conference at Teheran
1945	Conference at Yalta
1945	Conference at Potsdam
1953	died

One of the most momentous results of World War II was the creation of the Soviet bloc, the assembling of most of the states of central and eastern Europe into a community of satellite powers of the Soviet Union. It was a result that had not been envisioned by the leaders of the Western Alliance in the early desperate years of the war, nor was it one that had seemed inevitable in the scheme of things as the war turned surely toward Allied victory. It was instead almost entirely the result of the shrewd military and diplomatic opportunism of the Soviet dictator Joseph Stalin.

Prior to his emergence as one of the leaders of the "Grand Alliance" in World War II—the great friend and faithful ally of Churchill and Roosevelt—Stalin was nearly unknown in the West. To an almost equal extent he was unknown at home, his real character and his personal history hopelessly obscured by the "official" Soviet mythology about him that is only now beginning to be penetrated in Russia and in the West.

Joseph Stalin (1879–1953) came from origins unpromising even for a nineteenth-century Russian revolutionary and almost unimaginable for the greatest dictator of the twentieth, the person who would come to rule more land and people and rule them more absolutely than any other figure in history. He was born Joseph Vissarionovich Dzhugashvili, a Georgian, the son of a washerwoman and a drunken, brutal shoemaker from the tiny village of Gori in what was then a colony of imperial Russia in the Caucasus (he adopted the name *Stalin*, from the Russian word for *steel*, only after he became a revolutionary). He did not speak Russian until he learned it in school and never lost his gutteral Georgian accent. He was short and strongly built, with a mop of straight black hair and dark passionate eyes that stared intently out of a square face pitted with smallpox scars. Stalin looked more like a thug than a thinker, but his appearance was deceiving: Trotsky later made the mistake of underestimating him and paid with his position and influence in the Communist party—and eventually with his life.

Stalin early became a revolutionary, was repeatedly jailed, and at least once was exiled to Siberia for his activities. How much of the account of these activities is fact and how much is Bolshevik legend cannot be determined precisely. In any case, he returned from exile on the eve of the revolution, reached Petrograd on March 25, 1917, and was thus on the scene when the coup of November 1917 occurred. He made himself useful to Lenin and was rewarded with increasingly important jobs in the party: Commissar for Nationalities, Commissar for State Control, and then in 1922 Secretary General of the party's Central Committee, the position he held until his death and which was the real power base for his dictatorship. Unlike Lenin and Trotsky, Stalin was neither an intellectual nor a theoretician. Rather, he was a skilled bureaucrat and a brilliant organizer. Indeed, it is true that he, more than any other person, turned the ideology of the Russian revolution into the organizational reality of the Soviet Union.

Although he had begun to lose the confidence of Lenin in the last months of his life, Stalin became Lenin's successor. He sorted out the jumble of revolutionary ideas and action decisions that Lenin had spawned, setting some aside and implementing others. He shelved for the moment the Marxian goal of world revolution in favor of the more pressing task of socializing the nation. He abandoned Lenin's N.E.P., the New Economic Policy of compromise with peasant capitalists, in favor of socialist agricultural collectivism. Those Kulaks, well-to-do peasant entrepreneurs, who resisted were arrested by the thousands, shot, exiled, and put into the already expanding network of concentration and forced labor camps. An incredible ten million peasants may have perished, but Stalin accomplished agricultural collectivization in Russia and destroyed the pattern of peasant life that had persisted for centuries.

As a corollary to his policy of national agricultural collectivization, Stalin instituted a national policy of industrialization in a series of Five-Year Plans. This process also was accomplished with brutality, intimidation, and total disregard for human life. Whole industrial communities were built from scratch and populated with displaced workers. Public officials and factory managers were blamed for the frequent setbacks and failures and paraded in widely publicized show trials as enemies of the revolution. Yet, despite his methods, Stalin succeeded in converting vast peasant

Russia into an industrialized nation second only to the United States in its volume of production.

Inside the party organization, Stalin proceeded with equal ruthlessness. In the days immediately following Lenin's death, he systematically destroyed his great rival Trotsky. Then, in a series of alliances and betrayals that were Byzantine in their complexity, he displaced all his other rivals. This process culminated in the great purge trials of the mid-1930s. In these highly visible proceedings, he moved against a long list of party functionaries and former associates, cultural and intellectual figures, even marshals and generals of the Red Army. The show trials that featured the noisy denunciation of these leaders were paralleled by a less visible terrorism whose victims numbered into the millions. The result was the creation of a Russian totalitarianism with Stalin as its head.

During this process of consolidating his absolute power in the Soviet Union, Stalin never lost sight of the drift of international affairs. German and Italian fascism were on the march as was Japanese military imperialism. And Stalin had reason to be concerned with events both in the Far East and in Europe. The Axis support for General Franco in the Spanish Civil War of the mid-1930s prompted Stalin to supply arms to the Spanish Republicans including tanks, planes, and military advisers. In the late 1930s, he approached the Western powers with a proposal to form an anti-Hitler pact. In this he failed; Russia was still a diplomatic pariah among the European states. Then, when war appeared inevitable, Stalin entered an alliance with Hitler. He was motivated by the desire to strengthen his own frontier against the west. Under cover of the pact with Hitler, he quickly annexed Lithuania, Estonia, Latvia, and eastern Poland, and extracted territorial concessions from Rumania and Finland. These measures, however, were to no avail. In June 1941, Hitler began his massive invasion of Russia. Stalin, who had earlier appointed himself Chairman of the Council of People's Commissars (i.e., head of state), then assumed supreme military command. He identified himself first with the heroic resistance of the Russian people and the Red Army, then after the defense of Stalingrad had broken the back of the German invasion, he identified himself with the military victories that carried the Red Army into eastern Europe in pursuit of the retreating Wehrmacht. At Teheran in 1943 and at Yalta in 1945, he met to deliberate and negotiate with Prime Minister Churchill and President Roosevelt; later, he met at Potsdam with President Truman and Clement Atlee, as well as Winston Churchill. But whatever he promised or pledged, Stalin never intended to surrender any part of eastern Europe that his forces occupied. At the war's end, the Soviet Union continued to occupy much of these lands, and Stalin moved as quickly as possible to consolidate his control there. The Cold War had begun.

Churchill's Fulton Speech: The Iron Curtain

WINSTON S. CHURCHILL

Winston Churchill, for all his cooperation with Stalin during the war, had never trusted either the man or his motives. At Yalta and Potsdam, Churchill had tried unsuccessfully to insist upon the Soviet Union's making good its commitment to the political freedom of the nations of eastern Europe. With the end of hostilities in Europe—even before the final defeat of Japan—Churchill and his Conservative party were turned out of office in Britain in May 1945. In office or out, Churchill continued to be obsessed with the great themes of the war and the necessity of a lasting peace. Increasingly, he came to see the Soviet threat in eastern Europe as a danger to peace and was almost alone among the leaders of the Western world in taking these views.

He was looking for a forum for his views when, in the spring of 1946, he got an invitation to receive an honorary degree and make a speech at little Westminster College in Fulton, Missouri. He accepted and President Harry Truman, a great friend and admirer of Churchill, agreed to introduce him and sat on the platform as Churchill spoke. It was the perfect occasion: a speech in the heartland of the United States, with the American president in benign attendance, and with international press coverage. Churchill entitled the speech, "The Sinews of Peace," but it is best remembered for another phrase, "the iron curtain;" for its forthright denunciation of Soviet behavior in eastern Europe; and for its call for Britain and especially the United States to keep the peace against the Soviet threat.

THE UNITED STATES stands at this time at the pinnacle of world power. It is a solemn moment for the American Democracy. For with primacy in power is also joined an awe-inspiring accountability to the future. If you look around you, you must feel not only the sense of duty done but also you must feel anxiety lest you fall below the level of achievement. Opportunity is here now, clear and shining for both our countries. To reject it or ignore it or fritter it away will bring upon us all the long reproaches of the after-time. It is necessary that constancy of mind, persistency of purpose, and the grand simplicity of decision shall guide and rule the conduct of the English-speaking peoples in peace as they did in war. We must, and I believe we shall, prove ourselves equal to this severe requirement.

When American military men approach some serious situation they are wont to write at the head of their directive the words "over-all strategic concept." There is wisdom in this, as it leads to clarity of thought. What then is the over-all strategic concept which we should inscribe today? It is nothing less than the safety and welfare, the freedom and progress, of all the homes and families of all the men and women in all the lands. And here I speak particularly of the myriad cottage or apartment homes where the wage-earner strives amid the accidents and difficulties of life to guard his wife and children from privation and bring the family up in the fear of the Lord, or upon ethical conceptions which often play their potent part.

To give security to these countless homes, they must be shielded from the two giant marauders, war and tyranny. . . .

He praises the United Nations as such a shield against war and tyranny and makes a specific proposal that an international armed force be provided for it. But he opposes the sharing of the Atomic Bomb with the UN or with others of the wartime allies—including the Soviet Union. Then he continues.

Now, while still pursuing the method of realising our overall strategic concept, I come to the crux of what I have travelled here to say. Neither the sure prevention of war, nor the continuous rise of world organisation will be gained without what I have called the fraternal association of the English-speaking peoples. This means a special relationship between the British Commonwealth and Empire and the United States. This is no time for generalities, and I will venture to be precise. Fraternal association requires not only the growing friendship and mutual understanding between our two vast but kindred systems of society, but the continuance of the intimate relationship between our military advisers, leading to common study of potential dangers, the similarity of weapons and manuals of instructions, and to the interchange of officers and cadets at technical colleges. It should carry with it the continuance of the present facilities for mutual security by the joint use of all Naval and Air Force bases in the possession of either country all over the world. This would perhaps double the mobility of the American Navy and Air Force. It would greatly expand that of the British Empire Forces and it might well lead, if and as the world calms down, to important financial savings. Already we use together a large number of islands; more may well be entrusted to our joint care in the near future.

The United States has already a Permanent Defence Agreement with the Dominion of Canada, which is so devotedly attached to the British Commonwealth and Empire. This Agreement is more effective than many of those which have often been made under formal alliances. This principle should be extended to all British Commonwealths with full reciprocity. Thus, whatever happens, and thus only, shall we be secure ourselves and able to work for the high and simple causes that are dear to us and bode no ill to any. Eventually there may come—I feel eventually there will come—the principle of common citizenship, but that we may be content to leave to destiny, whose outstretched arm many of us can already clearly see. . . .

But, he continues:

A shadow has fallen upon the scenes so lately lighted by the Allied victory. Nobody knows what Soviet Russia and its Communist international organisation intends to do in the immediate future, or what are the limits, if any, to their expansive and proselytising tendencies. I have a strong admiration and regard for the valiant Russian people and for my wartime comrade, Marshal Stalin. There is deep sympathy and goodwill in Britain—and I doubt not here also—towards the peoples of all the Russias and a resolve to persevere through many differences and rebuffs in establishing lasting friendships. We understand the Russian need to be secure on her western frontiers by the removal of all possibility of German aggression. We welcome Russia to her rightful place among the leading nations of the world. We welcome her flag upon the seas. Above all, we welcome constant, frequent and growing contacts between the Russian people and our own people on both sides of the Atlantic. It is my duty however, for I am sure you would wish me to state the facts as I see them to you, to place before you certain facts about the present position in Europe.

From Stettin in the Baltic to Trieste in the Adriatic, an iron curtain has descended across the Continent. Behind that line lie all the capitals of the ancient states of Central and Eastern Europe. Warsaw, Berlin, Prague, Vienna, Budapest, Belgrade, Bucharest and Sofia, all these famous cities and the populations around them lie in what I must call the Soviet sphere, and all are subject in one form or another, not only to Soviet influence but to a very high and, in many cases, increasing measure of control from Moscow. Athens alone—Greece with its immortal glories—is free to decide its future at an election under British, American and French observation. The Russian-dominated Polish Government has been encouraged to make enormous and wrongful inroads upon Germany, and mass expulsions of millions of Germans on a scale grievous and undreamed-of are now taking place. The Communist parties, which were very small in all these Eastern States of Europe, have been raised to pre-eminence and power far beyond their numbers and are seeking everywhere to obtain totalitarian control. Police governments are prevailing in nearly every case, and so far, except in Czechoslovakia, there is no true democracy.

Turkey and Persia are both profoundly alarmed and disturbed at the claims which are being made upon them and at the pressure being exerted by the Moscow Government. An attempt is being made by the Russians in Berlin to build up a quasi-Communist party in their zone of Occupied Germany by showing special favours to groups of left-wing German leaders. At the end of the fighting last June, the American and British Armies withdrew westwards, in accordance with an earlier agreement, to a depth at some points of 150 miles upon a front of nearly four hundred miles, in order to allow our Russian allies to occupy this vast expanse of territory which the Western Democracies had conquered.

If now the Soviet Government tries, by separate action, to build up a pro-Communist Germany in their areas, this will cause new serious difficulties in the British and American zones, and will give the defeated Germans the power of putting themselves up to auction between the Soviets and the Western Democracies. Whatever conclusions may be drawn from these facts—and facts they are—this is certainly not the Liberated Europe we fought to build up. Nor is it one which contains the essentials of permanent peace. . . .

In front of the iron curtain which lies across Europe are other causes for anxiety. In Italy the Communist Party is seriously hampered by having to support the Communist-trained Marshal Tito's claims to former Italian territory at the head of the Adriatic. Nevertheless the future of Italy hangs in the balance. Again one cannot imagine a regenerated Europe without a strong France. All my public life I have worked for a strong France and I never lost faith in her destiny, even in the darkest hours. I will not lose faith now. However, in a great number of countries, far from the Russian frontiers and throughout the world, Communist fifth columns are established and work in complete unity and absolute obedience to the directions they receive from the Communist centre. Except in the British Commonwealth and in the United States where Communism is in its infancy, the Communist parties or fifth columns constitute a growing challenge and peril to Christian civilisation. These are sombre facts for anyone to have to recite on the morrow of a victory gained by so much splendid comradeship in arms and in the cause of freedom and democracy; but we should be most unwise not to face them squarely while time remains. . . .

I have felt bound to portray the shadow which . . . falls upon the world. I was a high minister at the time of the Versailles Treaty and a close friend of Mr. Lloyd-George, who was the head of the British delegation at Versailles. I did not myself agree with many things that were done, but I have a very strong impression in my mind of that situation, and I find it painful to contrast it with that which prevails now. In those days there were high hopes and unbounded confidence that the wars were over, and that the League of Nations would become all-powerful. I do not see or feel that some confidence or even the same hopes in the haggard world at the present time.

On the other hand I repulse the idea that a new war is inevitable; still more that it is imminent. It is because I am sure that our fortunes are still in our own hands and that we hold the power to save the future, that I feel the duty to speak out now that I have the occasion and the opportunity to do so. I do not believe that Soviet Russia desires war. What they desire is the fruits of war and the indefinite expansion of their power and doctrines. But what we have to consider here to-day while time remains, is the permanent prevention of war and the establishment of conditions of freedom and democracy as rapidly as possible in all countries. Our difficulties and dangers will not be removed by closing our eyes to them. They will not be removed by mere waiting to see what happens; nor will they be removed by a policy of appeasement. What is needed is a settlement, and the longer this is delayed, the more difficult it will be and the greater our dangers will become.

From what I have seen of our Russian friends and Allies during the war, I am convinced that there is nothing they admire so much as strength, and there is nothing for which they have less respect than for weakness, especially military weakness. For that reason the old doctrine of a balance of power is unsound. We cannot afford, if we can help it, to work on narrow margins, offering temptations to a trial of strength. If the Western Democracies stand together in strict adherence to the principles of the United Nations Charter, their influence for furthering those principles will be immense and no one is likely to molest them. If however they become divided or falter in their duty and if these all-important years are allowed to slip away then indeed catastrophe may overwhelm us all. . . .

Stalin's Reply

JOSEPH V. STALIN AND V. M. MOLOTOV

Churchill's words at Westminster College were not lost on the Soviet Union. The speech and the speaker were roundly condemned by every organ of Soviet propaganda. Indeed, ever since, Soviet historians have tended to date the beginning of the Cold War from that speech. So important was it that Stalin himself felt compelled to reply. The occasion was a contrived interview with Pravda, *published on March 13, 1946.*

A FEW DAYS AGO, a *Pravda* correspondent approached Stalin with a request to clarify a series of questions connected with the speech of Mr. Churchill. Comrade Stalin gave clarifications which are set out below in the form of answers to the correspondent's questions:

Q.—How do you assess the last speech of Mr. Churchill which was made in the United States?

A.—I assess it as a dangerous act, calculated to sow the seeds of discord among the Allied governments and hamper their cooperation.

Q.—Can one consider that the speech of Mr. Churchill is damaging to the cause of peace and security?

A.—Undoubtedly, yes. In substance, Mr. Churchill now stands in the position of a firebrand of war. And Mr. Churchill is not alone here. He has friends not only in England but also in the United States of America.

In this respect, one is reminded remarkably of Hitler and his friends. . . .

The German racial theory brought Hitler and his friends to the conclusion that the Germans, as the only fully valuable nation, must rule over other nations. The English racial theory brings Mr. Churchill and his friends to the conclusion that nations speaking the English language, being the only fully valuable nations, should rule over the remaining nations of the world.

In substance, Mr. Churchill and his friends in England and the United States present nations not speaking the English language with something like an ultimatum:

"Recognize our lordship voluntarily and then all will be well. In the contrary case, war is inevitable."

But the nations have shed their blood during five years of cruel war for the sake of liberty and the independence of their countries, and not for the sake of exchanging the lordship of Hitler for the lordship of Churchill.

It is, therefore, highly probable that the nations not speaking English, and which, however, make up an enormous majority of the world's population, will not consent to go into a new slavery. The tragedy of Mr. Churchill lies in the fact that he, as a deep-rooted Tory, cannot understand this simple and obvious truth.

Q.—How do you assess that part of Mr. Churchill's speech in which he attacks the democratic regime of the European countries which are our neighbors, and in which he critizes the good neighborly relations established between these countries and the Soviet Union?

A.—This part of Mr. Churchill's speech is a mixture of the elements of the libel with the elements of rudeness and lack of tact. Mr. Churchill maintains that Warsaw, Berlin, Prague, Vienna, Budapest, Belgrade, Bucharest and Sofia, all these famous cities and the populations of those areas, are within the Soviet sphere and are all subjected to Soviet influence and to the increasing control of Moscow.

Mr. Churchill qualifies this as the "boundless expansionist tendencies of the Soviet Union." It requires no special effort to show that Mr. Churchill rudely and shamelessly libels not only Moscow but also the above mentioned states neighborly to the U.S.S.R.

To begin with, it is quite absurd to speak of the exclusive control of the U.S.S.R. in Vienna and Berlin, where there are Allied Control Councils with representatives of four states, where the U.S.S.R. has only one-fourth of the voice.

It happens sometimes that some people are unable to refrain from libel, but still they should know a limit.

Secondly, one cannot forget the following fact: The Germans carried out an invasion of the U.S.S.R. through Finland, Poland, Romania, Bulgaria, and Hungary. The Germans were able to carry out the invasion through these countries by reason of the fact that these countries had governments inimical to the Soviet Union.

As a result of the German invasion, the Soviet Union irrevocably lost—in battles with the Germans, and also during the German occupation and through the expulsion of Soviet citizens to German slave labor camps—about 7,000,000 people. In other words, the Soviet Union has lost in men several times more than Britain and the United States together.

It may be that some quarters are trying to push into oblivion these sacrifices of the Soviet people which insured the liberation of Europe from the Hitlerite yoke.

But the Soviet Union cannot forget them. One can ask, therefore, what can be surprising in the fact that the Soviet Union, in a desire to insure its security for the future, tries to achieve that these countries should have governments whose relations to the Soviet Union are loyal? How can one, without having lost one's reason, qualify these peaceful aspirations of the Soviet Union as "expansionist tendencies" of our government?

Mr. Churchill further maintains that the Polish government under Russian lordship has been spurred to an unjust and criminal spoliation against Germany. Here every word is a rude and offensive libel.

Contemporary, democratic Poland is led by outstanding men. They have shown in deeds that they know how to defend the interests and worth of their homeland, as their predecessors failed to do.

What reason has Mr. Churchill to maintain that the leaders of contemporary Poland can submit their country to a lordship by representatives of any country whatever? Does Mr. Churchill here libel the Russians because he has intentions of sowing the seeds of discord between Poland and the Soviet Union?

Mr. Churchill is not pleased that Poland should have turned her policy toward friendship and alliance with the U.S.S.R. There was a time when in the mutual relations between Poland and the U.S.S.R. there prevailed an element of conflict and contradiction. This gave a possibility to statesmen of the kind of Mr. Churchill to play on these contradictions, to take Poland in hand under the guise of protection from the Russians, to frighten Russia by specters of war between Poland and herself, and to take for themselves the role of arbiters.

But this time is past. For enmity between Poland and Russia has given place to friendship between them, and Poland, present democratic Poland, does not wish any longer to be a playing-ball in the hands of foreigners. It seems to me that this is just what annoys Mr. Churchill and urges him to rude, tactless outbursts against Poland. After all, it is no laughing matter for him. He is not allowed to play for other people's stakes.

As for Mr. Churchill's attack on the Soviet Union in connection with the extending of the western boundaries of Poland, as compensation for the territories seized by the Germans in the past, there it seems to me that he quite blatantly distorts the facts.

As is known, the western frontiers of Poland were decided upon at the Berlin conference of the three powers, on the basis of Poland's demands.

The Soviet Union repeatedly declared that it considered Poland's demands just and correct. It may well be that Mr. Churchill is not pleased with this decision. But why does Mr. Churchill, not sparing his darts against the Russians in the matter, conceal from his readers the fact that the decision was taken at the Berlin conference unanimously, that not only the Russians voted for this decision but also the English and Americans.

Why did Mr. Churchill have to delude people?

Mr. Churchill further maintains that the Communist parties were very insignificant in all these eastern European countries, but reached exceptional strength, exceeding their numbers by far, and are attempting to establish totalitarian control everywhere; that police-governments prevailed in almost all these countries, even up to now, with the exception of Czechoslovakia, and that there exists in them no real democracy.

As is known, in England at present there is one party which rules the country—the Labor party. The rest of the parties are barred from the government of the country. This is called by Churchill a true democracy.

Meanwhile, Poland, Romania, Yugoslavia, Bulgaria and Hungary are governed by several parties—from four to six parties. And besides, the opposition, if it is loyal, is guaranteed the right to participate in the government. This Churchill calls totalitarian and the government of police.

On what grounds do you expect an answer from Mr. Churchill? Does he not understand the ridiculous situation he is putting himself in by such speeches on the basis of totalitarianism and police rule? Mr. Churchill would have liked Poland to be ruled by Staknovkovski and Anders, Yugoslavia by Mikhailovitch and Pavelitch, Romania by Prince Stirbe and Radescu, Hungary and Austria by some king from the House of Hapsburg, and so on.

Mr. Churchill wants to assure us that these gentlemen from the fascist servants' hall can insure true democracy. Such is the democracy of Mr. Churchill.

Mr. Churchill wanders around the truth when he speaks of the growth of the influence of the Communist parties in eastern Europe. It should, however, be noted that he is not quite accurate. It is not only in eastern Europe, but in almost every country of Europe where fascism has ruled before: Italy, Germany, Hungary, Bulgaria, Romania and Finland, and in countries which have suffered German, Italian or Hungarian occupation—France, Belgium, Holland, Norway, Denmark, Poland, Czechoslovakia, Yugoslavia, Greece, the Soviet Union and so on.

The growth of the influence of Communism cannot be considered accidental. It is a normal function. The influence of the Communists grew because during the hard years of the mastery of fascism in Europe, Communists showed themselves to be reliable, daring and self-sacrificing fighters against fascist regimes, for the liberty of peoples.

Mr. Churchill sometimes recalls in his speeches the common people from small houses, patting them on the shoulder in a lordly manner and pretending to be their friend.

But these people are not so simple-minded as it might appear at first sight. Common people, too, have their opinions and their own politics. And they know how to stand up for themselves.

It is they, millions of these common people, who voted Mr. Churchill and his party out in England, giving their votes to the Labor Party. It is they, millions of these common people, who isolated reactionaries in Europe, collaborators with fascism, and gave preference to Left democratic parties.

It is they, millions of these common people, having tried the Communists in the fire of struggle and resistance to fascism, who decided that the Communists deserve completely the confidence of the people. Thus grew the Communists' influence in Europe. Such is the law of historical development. . . .

The Origins of the Cold War

ADAM B. ULAM

The sides were decisively drawn and the issues laid out in the foregoing statements by Churchill and Stalin. The cold war had begun between the two former war allies, bringing the two superpowers of the twentieth century to face each other across a widening gulf of bitterness and hostility. We turn now to seek the answer to the question of how the cold war became so divisive and deadly an issue.

In the broadest context, the answer lies in the long story of Russia's historic relations with Europe, stretching back to Peter the Great. In the shorter term, it lies in the history of the troubled relations between revolutionary Russia and the West since 1917. In precise terms, it lies in the history of the Soviet Union's role in World War II and in the personal ambition of Joseph Stalin.

These events have, of course, been commented upon, described, and analyzed by many authorities, none more "cogent and convincing"[1] *than Adam B. Ulam in his definitive biography,* Stalin, the Man and his Era, *from which the following excerpt is taken.*

WITH THE RED ARMY'S advance units some fifty miles from Berlin, its Supreme Commander welcomed the President of the United States and the Prime Minister of Great Britain at Yalta, in the Crimea, between February 4 and 11 [1945]. The very day the conference opened Stalin called up the commander of the army group advancing on Berlin, Marshal Zhukov, and ordered him to stop the offensive. Zhukov's army commanders, notably Chuykov of Stalingrad fame, subsequently felt that they had thereby missed a great opportunity to seize Berlin in February. With additional artillery and supplies, they were to argue, they could have easily advanced the remaining fifty miles, and the cost would not have been so great as it was to be in April.

Caution dictated Stalin's decision. Up to then the Russian offensive had rolled at fantastic speed but at prodigious cost in casualties; some Soviet divisions were by now at half their nominal strength. . . . There was no earthly possibility that the Red Army could be beaten now, but a major setback and a retreat while he was negotiating with the Allies were risks he was unwilling to take. The legend of the Red Army's inexhaustible manpower and awesome might was his main card in the game for the distribution of the spoils of war. What if it were realized that the Soviet armies had bled and were almost as exhausted as the Wehrmacht?

As it was, the Yalta conference taxed his diplomatic skill to the utmost. Take Poland. The Anglo-American position on this key issue had stiffened somewhat; Stalin had laid it on too thick with the Supreme Soviet story.[2] Also, the President's attitude toward Stalin was imperceptibly changing. Still determined to do everything in his power to get his trust, Roosevelt could not help feeling a certain resentment that he, a sick and weary man, had had to travel halfway round the world for another conference, while his host, though deferential, had not even seen fit to meet his plane.

[1] In a review in *Commentary*, 56 (April 1974), 66, by Lev Navrozov, who finds the section on Stalin in and after World War II the best part of the book.—ED.

[2] Roosevelt and Churchill had wanted Stalin to withhold recognition of the native Polish Communist faction, the Lublin Committee, as the official government of Poland in favor of the Polish government in exile in London. Stalin, of course, had no such intention and had fabricated the story that the whole matter was out of his hands because the Presidium of the Supreme Soviet had already recognized the Lublin Committee. In fact, the Presidium was little more than a rubber stamp for his policies.—ED.

One side of the territorial aspect of the Polish question had been pretty much settled in Teheran.[3] The President feebly tried to rescue the city of Lvov for Poland. But, as Stalin explained, the frontier between the two countries which he had in mind (i.e., the Molotov-Ribbentrop line) had originally been suggested by Lord Curzon in 1919. Could he be less pro-Russian than Curzon? Also, if he yielded, he would arouse great dissatisfaction and incur political trouble among the Ukrainians. So the official communiqué put the Big Three on record as sanctioning the Soviet demands.

Stalin found the going harder on getting his Polish regime recognized. But he showed himself indefatigable as a negotiator. He kept asking his partners to be fair and to realize that ominous results would ensue if they persisted in their stubbornness on the issue. True, the Lublin government was not a product of elections, but was De Gaulle's, which the Allies had fully recognized? Was the London Polish government? Say what you will, politicians who had been out of their country for four or five years inevitably lost touch with their people. To the query whether British and American observers should not report first as to what was going on in Poland, Stalin retorted that the Poles were a proud nation: they resented foreign interference. Then the President wanted to see the "Lublin Poles." Stalin regretted that his people could not locate the Polish officials to bring them to the Crimea! You could not treat the Poles like the Egyptians (sticking a pin into Churchill); you had here a highly cultured nation with a prewar literacy of 70 per cent. You had to treat them with respect. He sympathized with the troubles Roosevelt and Churchill had with *their* Poles; good people, excellent fighters, great scientists and musicians, but oh how quarrelsome and vain when it came to politics. Wearily, the Western statesmen yielded to this combination of persuasiveness and prevarication. The Soviet protégé, the "Provisional Government of Poland," was to be the nucleus of the future Government of National Unity. Democratic leaders from Poland and abroad would be invited to join it—the process to be supervised in Moscow by a commission composed of Molotov and the British and American ambassadors.

The Polish issue crucially and intimately affected the most important postwar problem: the fate of Germany. Churchill's enthusiasm for moving Poland westward had now abated; a truncated Germany was bound to enhance Russia's domination of the Continent. Stalin was a fervent advocate of Poland's being compensated for her losses in the east by a sizable chunk of Germany up to the Oder–Western Neisse Line—a shift that

[3] This had been the first "summit meeting" of Stalin with Roosevelt and Churchill in November 1943, at Teheran in Iran. It was here that Stalin convinced Roosevelt, if not Churchill, of his willingness to work for a free postwar world. It was here also that Churchill volunteered to accept a larger postwar Poland, at the expense of German territory. Stalin persuaded the other two leaders to defer the question of the Polish government until later meetings, Yalta and Potsdam, as we shall see.—Ed.

would mean, and has meant, the displacement of 6 to 7 million Germans. The principle of Poland's thus being compensated was endorsed by the conference, with the precise details and boundaries to be settled later.

Contrary to what is often believed, Stalin had no clear idea what kind of postwar Germany he wanted. Roosevelt, reflecting America's currently fiercely anti-German mood, still talked of partitioning the country. Churchill, for obvious reasons, was against it. For Stalin, though he felt it diplomatic to agree with the President, the question was academic: Germany was going to be divided into zones of occupation by the Great Powers and (at Churchill's insistence) France, anyway. The Americans were unrealistic to think one could bind the future by agreements and clauses. . . .

It would be wrong to see Stalin—at this in many ways most triumphant moment of his career—as entirely cynical. He had a sense of great historical occasions. The final victory, he knew, would in a sense be anticlimactic; it would bring out the inevitable dissonances and basic contradictions between the partners. For the moment, he enjoyed the glow of camaraderie with two men whose greatness he clearly appreciated, for all his ruthless exploitation of their vulnerabilities, and whose attentions to him he valued. There was also a note of wistfulness, of something which looks suspiciously close to sentimentality in his avowal that he was an old man, in his assertion (for a brief moment he was sincere) that they must work together to spare the world the horrors of another war. Perhaps in his meetings with Roosevelt and Churchill, Stalin felt that he was taking a vacation from his job as a tyrant and his mellowness was not entirely spurious.

The mood could not endure. Within a month of the conference Soviet action contrasted so much with what the Americans took to have been the spirit of Yalta that they were thrown back on the standard explanation: "It was the opinion of the State Department group who were on the President's staff at the conference that Stalin had difficulties with the Politburo when he returned to Moscow for having been too friendly and for having made too many concessions to the two capitalist nations."[4] The Soviet government vetoed most candidates proposed by the Americans and British for the future Polish Government of National Unity as fascists or as otherwise unacceptable to its Polish protégés. In Rumania, King Michael was mercilessly bullied by Vishinsky, whose talents were now applied in the job of Deputy Foreign Minister, and was coerced into appointing a Communist-dominated government. Thereupon President Beneš hastened to designate as head of the Czech government Zdenek Fierlinger, who though nominally a Social Democrat had become during his tenure as ambassador in Moscow a thoroughgoing fellow traveler. The Americans' unhappiness was increased by the undue delays incurred during

[4] Edward R. Stettinius, Jr., *Roosevelt and the Russians* (New York, 1949), p. 309.

the repatriation of American prisoners of war whom the Red Army liberated from German camps as it swept westward. Some of the delays could be attributed to the inevitable red tape and chaotic wartime conditions. But the Soviets refused to let members of the American military mission in Moscow inspect the Soviet facilities where their countrymen were being detained on Polish soil. They were not eager, it was easy to divine, to let stories of what was being done in Poland reach America. The tone of the President's messages to Stalin grew sharp: "The American government has done everything to meet your every wish. . . . Speaking frankly, I cannot understand your unwillingness to allow the American liaison officers to help their countrymen."[5] The amiable Stalin of a few weeks ago had now disappeared: Soviet commanders in Poland were too busy to entertain visiting American officers, and as to the former prisoners of war, they were being better treated in the Soviet rest camps than the Soviet prisoners of war who had been liberated by the Allies in the West.

Stalin's bad humor was mounting. His Polish government was finding it hard going. For all the ordeal of the German occupation and the exhaustion of the people in its wake, most Poles were resisting the Moscow-imposed regime. Stalin had believed that it had been accepted by the Allies and that all it needed was a few democratic trappings. But here the Americans and the British (it was mainly Churchill, he believed) were insisting on its thorough reorganization. Would he have to fight this battle all over again?

He took drastic measures. Sixteen leaders of the Polish underground connected with the London government were contacted and assured of immunity if they came out in the open. They were then invited to a conference with the Soviet military authorities in late March. On their arrival at Marshal Zhukov's headquarters they were seized and taken to Moscow. It was two months before any news of their fate reached the West. . . .

Through his impatience Stalin was risking what all his diplomacy since the inception of the Grand Alliance has been designed to avoid: a clash with the United States, a giant at the height of its industrial and military might, barely bloodied in the war. And to compound his errors, Stalin now made a huge and inexcusable mistake, one which but for a quirk of fate could have had momentous consequences for Russia and for the world.

He was seized by a panic: he had assumed all along that except for some unpleasantness over Poland and for all the transparent intriguing by Churchill, he was leading his allies where he wanted them. But now suddenly it occurred to him that they were fooling *him*. They were about to make a separate arrangement with Germany; the Wehrmacht was going to capitulate in the West and continue fighting the Russians in the

[5] *The Correspondence* . . . , II, 194.

East! He would be robbed of the fruits of victory by the capitalists. For the first time we see in Stalin's handling of foreign affairs an outburst of that paranoid anxiety and irrepressible suspiciousness which had marked his rule over his people.

The occasion was rather trivial. An SS general, Karl Wolff, arrived in Switzerland in March to ascertain possible Allied conditions for a surrender of German forces in northern Italy to Field Marshal Harold Alexander, the Anglo-American commander-in-chief. The British loyally informed Moscow of this secret Nazi proposal and expressed their readiness to have a Soviet representative present when and if the Germans capitulated.

Why should this routine information, the kind to be expected at this stage of the war, throw Stalin into a veritable panic? We now know the probable reason. Some "foreign friend" of the Soviet Union, presumably in the government of Britain or the United States, informed Soviet intelligence that what was discussed in Switzerland was not merely a *local* capitulation by the Germans, but a separate peace in the West.[6] In a sense the information was correct: there had been German soundings of the Allies through various channels about the possibility of a separate peace—though evidently not in this case. The anonymous "well-wisher" of the Soviet Union (who has never been identified) then informed the Soviets that the Allies had rejected the Germans' entreaties. But for Stalin it was the first part of the intelligence report that was important. "That Churchill!" he exclaimed in Zhukov's presence. "He is capable of anything." Orders went out to speed up the opening of the drive on Berlin. At the same time Molotov demanded that the Allied representatives in Switzerland break off their negotiations with the Germans.

This crisis was papered over by the sudden death of President Roosevelt on April 12, 1945.

The new President had to be sized up, so the Supreme Soviet somehow relented and let Molotov go to the United Nations; and on the way to San Francisco he stopped in Washington to see Truman, who dressed him down in a way which was soon to become familiar to various American political figures. He had never been spoken to like that before, exclaimed the "iron bottom." One must assume Molotov meant "spoken to by a foreigner." But in general his report must have been reassuring as were those of anonymous well-wishers who provided the Soviets with information about what the British and Americans were up to. President Truman

[6] This story comes out in Marshal Zhukov's memoirs (pp. 641–42).

was feeling his way in foreign policy; his advisers believed in the possibility of accommodation with Russia.

The Great Fatherland War, as it is styled in the Soviet literature, was nearing its end. Stalin's men got first to Berlin. On April 16 the greatest cannonade in history ushered in the final Soviet drive. . . .

The war with Germany was over, but the arrangement for this ramshackle peace had to be wound up. Just before the demise of the Thousand-Year Reich, there had been a flurry of diplomatic activity which enabled Stalin to undo much of the damage he had done to his cause during his altercation with Roosevelt. As late as April Heinrich Himmler tried to interest the Allies in a separate peace. Churchill rejected these overtures and loyally informed Stalin of them. Again, for a moment, the dictator found a way to the Englishman's heart. "That Churchill is capable of anything," he had exclaimed to Zhukov only a month before, but to the Prime Minister on April 25 went this handsome tribute: "Knowing you, I had full confidence that you would not act differently."[7] Yet Churchill's attempt to exploit this charmed moment to soften the Soviet position on Poland and to reserve some shadow of independence for the unfortunate country met with a harsh refusal: "You, it is clear, do not agree that the Soviet Union has the right to demand for Poland a regime that would be friendly toward the U.S.S.R." Did he, Stalin, interfere with any arrangements the *British* might make in regard to Belgium or Greece?

The Prime Minister, with the famous percentages in Eastern Europe melting into nothingness before his eyes,[8] thought of another stratagem. After the capitulation of Germany the Anglo-American armies should not retreat to their occupation zones, as agreed previously with the Russians, until and unless the latter become more amenable about Eastern Europe. The vision of Russian and Anglo-American soldiers standing eyeball to eyeball and glaring at each other until such time as the Soviets would behave did not meet with approval among the Americans. President Truman, an admirer of Churchill's, perhaps would have gone along with the policy of pressuring the Russians, especially because at San Francisco Molotov was again making trouble about voting procedures and membership in the United Nations. But the American chiefs of staff, whose advice was now decisive, were against any such confrontation with the Soviets. The Americans' attention was on the Pacific war, and contrary to what has sometimes been alleged, military opinion in this country was nearly unanimous on the need of Soviet assistance against Japan. Quite

[7] *The Correspondence of the Chairman of the Council of Ministers of the U.S.S.R. with the Presidents of the United States and Prime Ministers of Great Britain* (Moscow, 1957), I, 339.

[8] Churchill had tried to insist on quotas in the several governments to be set up in eastern Europe—i.e., a balance between factions loyal to the Communists and friendly to the west. It did not work, largely because of Stalin's machinations.—Ed.

apart from professional advice, Churchill's scheme was impractical for psychological and political reasons. Public opinion in both Britain and America was eager for peace and continued friendship with Russia. Few would endanger that friendship for the sake of some Balkan country, or because one person rather than another with an unpronounceable name should become the Prime Minister of Poland. The Soviets were well aware of the facts of life of democratic politics. . . .

With Poland in his pocket, Stalin became all amicability. Oh, there were still problems. At the end of the war against Germany, Lend-Lease had been abruptly stopped. Did someone think Russia could be pressured in this way? "If the Russians were approached on a friendly basis much more could be done, but . . . reprisals in any form would bring about the exactly opposite effect."[9] But he now withdrew the Soviet reservations about the structure of the United Nations. (The Russians still felt obliged to go through their famous act, which never failed to impress the Americans: Molotov would be obdurate and seemingly unyielding; Stalin had to plead with him to accept the American position.) And on the matter which was now uppermost in the Americans' minds, Stalin was very accommodating: on August 8 Russia would be able to enter the war against Japan. . . .

The Potsdam meeting, the last one between the Big Three, which opened in the middle of July was in many ways a replay of Teheran and Yalta. Some of the main actors were different. The new American President, who for all his self-assurance felt some anxiety at meeting his already semi-legendary partners, brought with him the new Secretary of State, his *then* great friend James Byrnes. It is not recorded what impression Stalin formed of either, yet he must have felt relieved at not facing Roosevelt. And it was with mixed emotions that Stalin viewed Churchill's replacement before the end of the conference by Clement Attlee. Chivalry was not one of his strong points, yet as both his daughter Svetlana and Miloyan Djilas astutely recognized, Stalin had a sneaking admiration for Churchill. It was exhilarating to cross swords and best the last real leader of the British Empire, an object of emulation and certain awe by Russia's rulers for over a century. For the British Labour Party, on the other hand, as for socialists everywhere, the Soviets have always had little respect. If Attlee and his Foreign Secretary, Ernest Bevin, ever believed that their alleged ideological propinquity would assure them of warmer relations with the Russians than those enjoyed by the old "imperialist" Churchill, they soon found that the contrary was the case. . . .

But the business meetings of the conference were not unlike those of its predecessors'. Churchill argued, pleaded, occasionally fulminated: Germany should not be required to pay unduly onerous reparations; Poland should not be allowed to help herself to an unduly large part of

[9] Robert E. Sherwood, *Roosevelt and Hopkins* (New York, 1950), p. 897.

Germany; the Russians should cease their scandalous goings-on in Bulgaria and Rumania, where the British and American members of the Allied Control Commissioners were virtual prisoners of the Soviet authorities. Stalin imperturbably parried these arguments: Russia had to be compensated for her vast losses, Poland must get German Pomerania and Silesia; Rumania and Bulgaria had democratic governments that should not be interfered with. The Americans sometimes feebly took the British side; more often they appealed for harmony and compromise. Stalin usually had his way.

The main item of business had been largely settled before: Germany was to be divided into occupation zones. It is obvious that not even Stalin had expected this provisional arrangement to endure for generations, or he would not have insisted that so much German territory go to Poland—which, of course, meant a diminution of any future Communist East Germany. Berlin itself was to be divided, and it is also unlikely that it occurred to him *at the moment* how convenient this arrangement would be for himself and his successors as a means of pressuring the West and by the same token how bothersome it would be to his German Communist protégés. . . .

Throughout the generally unhappy time Churchill was having before and during the first sessions of the conference, one consoling thought stayed with him: the Americans were about to test the atomic bomb. The Prime Minister and the President agreed that they should tell Stalin about the weapon without, needless to say, going into any details. And so after the news of the momentous flash in the New Mexico desert reached Potsdam, Truman went to Stalin and informed him that the United States had a weapon of unusual force. It would have revived Churchill's spirits if Stalin had blanched or asked in a broken voice for details. But Stalin greeted the announcement with aplomb: he was pleased to hear the news and hoped the Americans would use the new weapon against Japan. Marshal Zhukov, who watched the scene, provides some dramatic details. Churchill was closely watching Stalin's expression as Truman gave him the news, and Stalin, according to the worthy Marshal, did not betray his feelings. Only later, in the Soviet quarters, did he turn to Molotov and say smilingly that they were trying to scare him: "Tell Kurchatov[10] to hurry up with the work."[11] Alas, this tale, designed to reveal Stalin's iron nerve, is largely untrue. General Shtemenko gives a more reliable version. Stalin told his chief of staff, General Antonov, about Truman's revelation: "But neither Antonov nor obviously Stalin realized that this was an entirely new type of weapon. In any case, the general staff received no special

[10] Academician Igor Kurchatov, chief scientist of the Soviet atomic project.
[11] George Zhukov, *Recollections and Reflections* (Moscow, 1969), p. 732.

instructions."[12] Soviet nuclear research had begun on a modest scale in 1942, gathered momentum only in January 1945, when espionage reports indicated the Americans were making progress on the weapon. Stalin must have been kept informed but it is unlikely that he realized the full impact of the bomb until after Hiroshima. In any case, Churchill's day was spoiled, though there remained the consoling hope (false, as it was soon to turn out) that the Russians were ignorant of what had been going on in American laboratories and testing grounds.

And, so on September 2, 1945, Stalin shared the emotion of millions of his countrymen: "Glory to our victorious nations." He seemed to share the relief and the fervent wish of millions of human beings everywhere. But in four months the tyrant-teacher had returned. On February 9, 1946, he appeared before his "electors" (elections to the Supreme Soviet were going on) and his listeners (as well as the whole nation) must have realized that this was the pre-June 1941 Stalin who was speaking, that he had never stopped being a tyrant while leading the nation in defeat and victory. The wartime form of address was discarded: no more "Brothers, sisters, my friends, my countrymen." It was again the dry "Comrades." And the same dialectic tone, the same question-and-answer format. Who won the war? No longer the Russian or even the Soviet *nation:* "Our victory means above all that our *social* system has won. . . . Our *political* system has won." And Stalin had built this system. . . .

Nothing on the international or the domestic scene seemed to warrant the dictator's displeasure. Soviet Russia's star shone brightly. Eastern Europe was firmly under Soviet sway. An interesting and promising situation was developing in China. All over the world Communist parties displayed new strength, reflecting the might and glory of the biggest of them. They were linked into a monolithic bloc—more than they had ever been by the formal machinery of the Comintern—by their worship of the greatest Communist. . . .

[12] Sergei Shtemenko, *The General Staff* (Moscow, 1963), p. 359. Soviet generals should read each other's memoirs. Shtemenko's was published only one year before Zhukov's.

Suggestions for Further Reading

THERE IS A SUBSTANTIAL body of writing by Stalin himself available in English, including his *Works*, 13 vols. (Moscow: Foreign Languages Publishing House, 1954–55), ending with his writings and speeches of early 1934. There is a scattering of public speeches and addresses, theoretical or dogmatic statements published in English by the Soviet Foreign Languages Publishing House or by various British and American publishers such as Joseph V. Stalin and V. M. Molotov, *The Soviet Union and World Peace* (New York: New Century Publishers, 1946), which was excerpted for this chapter. They are, for the most part, brief public statements. There are two volumes of selected writings, Joseph Stalin, *Selected Writings* (New York: International Publishers, 1945) and *The Essential Stalin, Major Theoretical Writings, 1905–52*, ed. Bruce Franklin (New York: Doubleday–Anchor, 1972). None of these is revealing of the man or his personal motives and most seem to be the product of Soviet propaganda agencies as much as Stalin's authentic writings. Of somewhat greater value and interest is the official Soviet edition of Stalin's wartime correspondence, *Correspondence Between the Chairman of the Council of Ministers of the U.S.S.R. and the Presidents of the U.S.A. and Prime Ministers of Great Britain during the Great Patriotic War of 1941–1945*, 2 vols (Moscow: Foreign Languages Publishing House, 1957), republished by Capricorn Books, 1965.

There are, however, some glimpses of the real Stalin. Stalin's daughter, Svetlana, defected to the West in the mid-1960s and published a series of private letters, Svetlana Alliluyeva, *Twenty Letters to a Friend*, tr. Priscilla Johnson McMillan (New York: Harper & Row, 1967), that reveal her relations with her father, but are of questionable value. (In the 1980s, Alliluyeva returned to the Soviet Union to live.) Also of questionable value, but great interest, are several works of Stalin's early rival Leon Trotsky, especially his *Stalin: An Appraisal of the Man and his Influence*, ed. and tr. Charles Malamuth (New York: Grosset and Dunlap, 1941), and later editions. Of somewhat greater value are the memoirs of the Yugoslav politician and intellectual Milovan Djilas, *Conversations with Stalin*, tr. M. B. Petrovich (New York: Harcourt, Brace and World, 1962). Among the most interesting and revealing works on Stalin by a contemporary is the speech denouncing him and debunking the "Stalin legend" by Nikita S. Khrushchev, at the Twentieth Congress of the Communist Party, February 24–25, 1956: it is available in two editions, *The Anatomy of Terror . . .* , ed. Nathaniel Weyl (Washington, D.C.: Public Affairs

Press, 1979), and *The Stalin Dictatorship, Khrushchev's 'Secret Speech' and Other Documents*, ed. T. H. Rigby (Sydney: Sydney University Press, 1968). Also of great interest are the accounts and assessments of Stalin by his Western wartime allies. See Winston S. Churchill, *The Second World War*, 6 vols. (Boston: Houghton Mifflin, 1948–53) or its abridgment, *Memoirs of the Second World War*, ed. Denis Kelly (Boston: Houghton Mifflin, 1959); Anthony Eden, *Full Circle* (Boston: Houghton Mifflin, 1960), and *The Reckoning* (Boston: Houghton Mifflin, 1965); and Harry S. Truman, *Memoirs*, 2 vols. (New York: Doubleday, 1956), and *Off the Record: The Private Papers of Harry S. Truman*, ed. Robert H. Ferrell (New York: Harper & Row, 1980). For the other side of the picture, see *Stalin and His Generals: Soviet Military Memoirs of World War II*, ed. Seweryn Bialer (New York: Pegasus, 1969) and *The Memoirs of Marshal Zhukov* (New York: Delacorte Press, 1971).

The many biographies and biographical studies of Stalin represent a wide range of interpretive viewpoints. Probably the best general biography is Adam B. Ulam, *Stalin: The Man and His Era* (New York: Viking Press, 1973), excerpted for this chapter. Two interpretive-biographical collections are also useful: *Stalin*, ed. T. H. Rigby "Great Lives Observed" (Englewood Cliffs, N.J.: Prentice-Hall, 1966) and *Stalinism: Its Impact on Russia and the World*, ed. G. R. Urban (New York: St. Martin's Press, 1982). The latter is a collection of dialogues originally broadcast by Radio Free Europe. Three special studies are also recommended, two of them dealing with the young Stalin: Bertram D. Wolfe, *Three Who Made a Revolution*, 3rd ed. (New York: Stein and Day, 1984), a famous book that deals with the revolution of 1917; and R. C. Tucker, *Stalin as Revolutionary, 1879–1929* (New York: Norton, 1973), an absorbing psychological study emphasizing Stalin's paranoia; and a book dealing with Stalin in World War II, Herbert Feis, *Churchill, Roosevelt, Stalin: The War They Waged and the Peace They Sought* (Princeton: Princeton University Press, 1957). On the broader aspects of Stalinism and Western history, two books may be recommended: Adam B. Ulam, *Expansion and Coexistence: The History of Soviet Foreign Policy, 1917–67* (New York and Washington: Praeger, 1968), and George F. Kennan, *Russia and the West under Lenin and Stalin* (Boston and Toronto: Little, Brown, 1961), the latter by one of the most distinguished American observers and critics of the Soviet Union.

The Granger Collection

Eleanor Roosevelt: "First Lady of the World"

1884 born
1905 married Franklin Delano Roosevelt
1921 Franklin Roosevelt stricken with polio
1928 Franklin Roosevelt elected governor of New York
1933 beginning of Franklin Roosevelt's first term as president
1945 death of Franklin Roosevelt
1946 Eleanor Roosevelt appointed an American delegate to the UN
1962 died

A few days after Franklin Delano Roosevelt's death in the spring of 1945, a newspaper reporter asked Eleanor Roosevelt for a statement. "The story is over," she said quietly.[1] But, of course, it was not over. For Eleanor Roosevelt's story had long since taken on a life and quality of its own. No American president's wife since Dolly Madison had been so visibly involved in her husband's work. Perhaps even more than FDR, Eleanor had become identified with the radical social causes of his New Deal administration and had been praised and vilified along with him.

Yet, there was nothing in her background or early life to suggest that she would play such a role on the nation's stage or come to be widely regarded in her old age as the world's most admired woman. Harry Truman called her "the First Lady of the World."[2] Eleanor was born in 1884 into the aristocracy of New York City and the Hudson Valley, the eldest child of Elliott and Anna Hall Roosevelt. Both her parents died before she was ten, after which she was reared by her stern and demanding maternal grandmother. She was a painfully shy, reticent, awkward little girl, who suffered over her plainness. (Her Aunt Edith, the wife of President

[1] Joseph P. Lash, *Eleanor: The Years Alone* (New York: Norton, 1972), p. 15.
[2] *Ibid.*, p. 219.

Theodore Roosevelt—Eleanor's "Uncle Ted"—dubbed her "the ugly duckling.")

Eleanor was well educated, by tutors at home and at boarding schools in England and France, and prepared to take her place in the comfortable, insular world of money and privilege to which she had been born. In 1905, she married a distant cousin, Franklin Roosevelt. The young couple settled in New York City while Franklin finished law school at Columbia. Upon graduation, he was taken into a prestigious Wall Street law firm, but his real passion was politics.

Franklin was a progressive Democrat—his branch of the family was traditionally Democratic. With the model of Theodore Roosevelt before him, young Franklin confidently anticipated being president himself one day. His political career began in 1910 with his election to the New York Senate. In 1913, he was appointed by President Woodrow Wilson as Assistant Secretary of the Navy, and he served in this job with energy and distinction through World War I. At the 1920 Democratic National Convention, Roosevelt was nominated for vice president, but he and his running mate, James M. Cox, were swept away in the Republican landslide that elected Warren G. Harding and Calvin Coolidge.

Eleanor and Franklin had six children, one of whom died in infancy. Then, in the summer of 1921, tragedy came to the Roosevelt family. Franklin was stricken by polio while at their summer retreat on Campobello Island off the coast of Maine. Almost completely paralyzed and in pain, he began what was to be a slow and only partial recovery. Sara, his devoted but domineering mother, wanted him to surrender to his affliction and return to the family home in Hyde Park, New York, where he could lead a life of leisure as a moneyed invalid. But Eleanor thought otherwise. She urged Franklin to return to politics, and, because he could not attend meetings or cultivate party leaders, she did it for him. Overcoming her lifelong shyness to do so, she in the process developed a lively interest of her own, both in politics and in the capacity of political action to address human problems.

In 1928, Al Smith, the Democratic leader of New York, encouraged Franklin Roosevelt to run for governor at the same time Smith ran for the presidency. Although Smith and the national ticket lost to Herbert Hoover and the Republicans, Roosevelt won the governorship. Despite his physical handicap, he had campaigned with the infectious energy he had displayed before and with enhanced effectiveness—in no small part owing to the shrewd advice of Eleanor. They were becoming political partners. The Great Depression was the preoccupation of New York state politics, as it was across the nation. Largely because of his attention to pocketbook issues, Roosevelt was overwhelmingly reelected governor in 1930. He was already being talked about as a presidential candidate, and he worked to advance his candidacy. After winning the nomination in 1932, he began a vigorous campaign on the program of reform and recovery that he called the "New Deal." He was swept into office for his first term as president.

By this time, Eleanor Roosevelt was experienced, not only as the wife of a public figure, but as a public figure in her own right. Her children were grown, and the years when "I was always just getting over having a baby or about to have one" were behind her.[3] In the early years of her husband's presidency, she became increasingly involved in his administration's liberal social and economic causes that addressed the problems of the Great Depression. But while the first and second Roosevelt terms were dominated by the Depression, the third and what little there was of the fourth term were dominated by World War II. By 1940, as war loomed closer, both Eleanor and Franklin were deeply involved in military preparedness. The president could not even free himself from his commitments to attend the 1940 Democratic National Convention. Eleanor was invited to speak for him and did so. She also accepted the co-directorship of the newly formed Office of Civil Defense. Following the bombing of Pearl Harbor by the Japanese in 1941 and the American declaration of war, Eleanor Roosevelt tirelessly visited hospitals and military bases. In the spring of 1942, she flew to England to check on the war effort and was, among other things, impressed by the total involvement of women. The next year, she flew to United States military bases in the distant South Pacific. Even for such efforts, she was sometimes bitterly criticized—but, equally often, she came off in the polls as the most popular woman in the nation.

As the war neared its victorious end, Eleanor watched with increasing concern the declining health of her husband. The president would not live to see the end of the war he had been so instrumental in winning. He died April 12, 1945—just weeks before the German surrender in Europe—at his retreat in Warm Springs, Georgia.

[3] Quoted in J. William T. Youngs, *Eleanor Roosevelt: A Personal and Public Life* (Boston and Toronto: Little, Brown, 1985), p. 82.—Ed.

Eleanor and the UN: The Next Assignment

ELEANOR ROOSEVELT

Eleanor Roosevelt returned to New York in the spring of 1945 and in the next few months found herself busier than ever with speaking engagements, writing, a syndicated column, a radio show, and seemingly endless correspondence. Then, in December 1945, she was invited by President Truman to be one of the American delegates to the organizational meeting of the UN General Assembly scheduled for London in January 1946. Both Eleanor and Franklin had held the fondest hopes for the United Nations as an instrument for peace and reconciliation after the war. Indeed, Franklin had planned to attend the conference to draft its foundation charter, but he died before it was held. Thus, despite her own misgivings about her ability to serve effectively, Eleanor accepted the president's appointment.

The following is her own account of her work at the UN over the next three years, of her increasing responsibilities and increasing self-assurance. In her view, this was the most important assignment of her life. The excerpt is taken from the third volume of her autobiography, On My Own.

IN DECEMBER OF 1945 I received a message from President Truman. He reminded me that the first or organizing meeting of the United Nations General Assembly would be held in London, starting in January, 1946, and he asked me if I would serve as a member of the United States delegation.

"Oh, no! It would be impossible," was my first reaction. "How could I be a delegate to help organize the United Nations when I have no background or experience in international meetings?"

Miss Thompson,[4] however, urged me not to decline without giving the idea careful thought. I knew in a general way what had been done about organizing the United Nations. After the San Francisco meeting in 1945 when the Charter was written it had been accepted by the various nations, including our own, through their constitutional processes. I knew, too,

[4] Malvina Thompson, "Tommy," Eleanor Roosevelt's longtime secretary and friend.—ED.

that we had a group of people headed by Adlai Stevenson working with representatives of other member nations in London to prepare for the formal organizing meeting. Then, as I thought about the President's offer, I knew that I believed the United Nations to be the one hope for a peaceful world. I knew that my husband had placed great importance on the establishment of this world organization. So I felt a great sense of responsibility.

I talked it over with Tommy and with my son Elliott, and with various other friends, all of whom urged me to accept. At last, I did so in fear and trembling. . . . There was not much time left before the delegates were to leave for London and I had to get ready in a hurry after receiving all kinds of instructions from the Department of State. . . .

Members of the delegation sailed on the *Queen Elizabeth* and the dock was swarming with reporters and news photographers who surrounded the Senators and Congressmen on the delegation to get last-minute statements and pictures. Everything had quieted down, however, when I drove in my own car to the dock and got aboard rather late and managed to find my way to my stateroom.

I was feeling rather lost and quite uncertain about what lay ahead. But as it turned out there was plenty to do even for a confused beginner in such affairs. The first thing I noticed in my stateroom was a pile of blue sheets of paper on the table. These blue sheets turned out to be documents—most of them marked "secret"—that apparently related to the work of delegates. I had no idea where they had come from but assumed they were meant for me so I looked through them. The language was complicated but they obviously contained background information on the work to be taken up by the General Assembly as well as statements of our government's position on various problems.

So, I thought, somebody is putting me to work without delay. I promptly sat down and began reading—or trying to read. It was dull reading and very hard work, I had great difficulty in staying awake, but I knew my duty when I saw it and read them all. By the time I finished I supposed that the Department of State had no more secrets from me, but I would have found it hard to reveal anything because I was seldom really sure of the exact meaning of what was on the blue sheets.

At the time, I feared this was because I couldn't understand plain English when it concerned State Department matters, but I changed my mind on this score because others seemed to have the same difficulty. . . .

But I am getting far ahead of my journey to London. People on the *Queen Elizabeth* were very kind to me, but nevertheless I felt much alone at first. One day, as I was walking down the passageway to my cabin, I encountered Senator Arthur H. Vandenberg, a Republican and before the war a great champion of isolationism. He stopped me.

"Mrs. Roosevelt," he said in his rather deep voice, "we would like to know if you would serve on Committee 3."

I had two immediate and rather contradictory reactions to the question. First, I wondered who "we" might be. Was a Republican Senator deciding who would serve where? And why, since I was a delegate, had I not been consulted about committee assignments? But my next reaction crowded these thoughts out of mind. I suddenly realized that I had no more idea than the man in the moon what Committee 3 might be. So I kept my thoughts to myself and humbly agreed to serve where I was asked to serve.

"But," I added quickly, "will you or someone kindly see that I get as much information as possible on Committee 3?"

The Senator promised and I went on to my cabin. The truth was that at that time I did not know whom to ask for information or guidance. I had no idea where all those blue documents marked "secret" that kept appearing in my cabin came from; for all I knew, they might have originated in outer space instead of in the Department of State. . . .

After our ship docked at Southampton and we were all officially greeted, I drove to London with Senator and Mrs. Tom Connally. . . .

Our offices were on Grosvenor Square about two blocks from the Embassy. When I arrived there my adviser, Durward Sandifer, said that there were one or two members of the delegation's staff who would be available to discuss with me the problems of Committee 3. . . .

As I learned more about my work I realized why I had been put on Committee 3, which dealt with humanitarian, educational and cultural questions. There were many committees dealing with the budgetary, legal, political and other questions, and I could just see the gentlemen of our delegation puzzling over the list and saying:

"Oh, no! We can't put Mrs. Roosevelt on the political committee. What could she do on the budget committee? Does she know anything about legal questions? Ah, here's the safe spot for her—Committee 3. She can't do much harm there!"

Oddly enough, I felt very much the same way about it. On the ship coming over, however, State Department officials had held "briefings" for the delegates. We listened to experts on various subjects explain the problems that would be brought up, give the background on them and then state the general position of the United States on various controversial points. I attended all these sessions and, discovering there also were briefings for newspaper people aboard the ship, I went to all their meetings, too. As a result of these briefings and of my talks with Mr. Sandifer and others, I began to realize that Committee 3 might be much more important than had been expected. And, in time, this proved to be true. . . .

At the early sessions in London, which were largely concerned with technicalities of organization, I got the strong impression that many of the old-timers in the field of diplomacy were very skeptical of the new world organization. They had seen so many failures, they had been through the collapse of the League of Nations, and they seemed to doubt that we would achieve much. The newcomers, the younger people in most cases, were the ones who showed the most enthusiasm and determination; they were, in fact, often almost too anxious to make progress. It was fortunate that such men as Mr. Spaak and Mr. Lie[5] were on hand and skillful enough both to give the veterans new inspiration and to hold the newcomers in check when necessary.

I might point out here that during the entire London session of the Assembly I walked on eggs. I knew that as the only woman on the delegation I was not very welcome. Moreover, if I failed to be a useful member, it would not be considered merely that I as an individual had failed, but that all women had failed, and there would be little chance for others to serve in the near future. . . .

However, it was while working on Committee 3 that I really began to understand the inner workings of the United Nations. It was ironical perhaps that one of the subjects that created the greatest political heat of the London sessions came up in this "unimportant" committee to which I had been assigned.

The issue . . . arose from the fact that there were many displaced war refugees in Germany when the armistice was signed—Ukrainians, Belorussians, Poles, Czechoslovaks, Latvians, Lithuanians, Estonians, and others—a great number of whom were still living there in temporary camps because they did not want to return to live under the Communist rule of their own countries. There also were the pitiful Jewish survivors of the German death camps.

I do not suppose that it had been generally foreseen that this situation would lead to a headline controversy in London, but it did and it flared up in Committee 3. It was raised originally by the Yugoslav representative, Leo Mates, a quick, bright young man whom I came to know well and who became Ambassador to Washington. . . .

The Yugoslav—and, of course, the Soviet Union—position that Mates put forward was that any war refugee who did not wish to return to his country of origin was either a quisling or a traitor to his country. He argued that the refugees in Germany should be forced to return home and to accept whatever punishment might be meted out to them. This position was strongly supported by the Soviet representative, Professor Amazap A. Arutiunian, an Armenian who ably served for a long time in the Russian delegation.

The position of the Western countries, including the United States, was that large numbers of the refugees were neither quislings nor traitors and that they must be guaranteed the right to choose whether or not they would return to their homes. Since the London sessions were largely technical rather than political debates and since Committee 3 was the

[5] Paul Henri Spaak, Belgian foreign minister, and Trygve Lie, the foreign minister of Norway, both key figures in the early years of the UN.—Ed.

scene of one of the early clashes between the Soviet Union and the West, the newspapers found it convenient to make much of the refugee controversy. I felt very strongly on the subject, as did others, and we spent countless hours trying to frame some kind of resolution on which all could agree. We never did, and our chairman, Peter Fraser of New Zealand, had to present a majority report to the General Assembly which was immediately challenged by the USSR.

In the Assembly the minority position was handled, not by the Soviet representative on Committee 3, but by the head of the Soviet Union's delegation, Andrei Vishinsky. . . .

Vishinsky was one of the Russians' great legal minds, a skilled debater, a man with ability to use the weapons of wit and ridicule. And Moscow apparently considered the refugee question of such vital importance that he spoke twice before the Assembly in a determined effort to win over the delegates to the Communist point of view. The British representative on our committee spoke in favor of the majority report. By this time an odd situation had developed. It was apparent that in view of the importance of the issue someone would have to speak for the United States. The question of who this was to be threw our delegation into a veritable dither. There was a hurried and rather uncomfortable consultation among the male members and when the huddle broke up John Foster Dulles approached me rather uncertainly.

"Mrs. Roosevelt," he began, rather lamely, "the United States must speak in the debate. Since you are the one who has carried on for us in this controversy in the committee, do you think you could say a few words to the Assembly? I'm afraid nobody else is really familiar with the subject."

"Why, Mr. Dulles," I replied as meekly as I could manage, "in that case I will do my best."

Actually, I was badly frightened. I trembled at the thought of speaking against the famous Mr. Vishinsky. But when the time came I walked, tense and excited, to the rostrum and did my best. There was a little more than met the eye in this situation. The hour was late and we knew the Russians would delay a vote as long as possible on the theory that some of our allies would get tired and leave. I knew we must, if possible, hold our South American colleagues until the vote was taken because their votes might be decisive. So I talked about Simon Bolivar and his stand for the freedom of the people of Latin America. I talked and I watched the delegates and to my joy the South American representatives stayed with us to the end and, when the vote came, we won.

This vote meant that the Western nations would have to worry about the ultimate fate of the refugees for a long, long time, but the principle of the right of an individual to make his own decisions was a victory well worth while. The argument with Mr. Vishinsky was to be carried on in future meetings of the Assembly and on some occasions he even came to address Committee 3, but we always won out. And finally he gave up carrying the debate and left it to whoever might be the Soviet Union's delegate on Committee 3. . . .

Toward the end of the sessions we worked until late at night. The final night the vote on Committee 3's report was taken so late that I did not get back to the hotel till about one o'clock. I was very tired, and as I walked wearily up the stairs at the hotel I heard two voices behind me. Turning around, I saw Senator Vandenberg and Mr. Dulles. They obviously had something to say to me, but for the life of me I can't recall which one of them said it. Whichever it was, he seemed to be speaking for both.

"Mrs. Roosevelt," he said, "we must tell you that we did all we could to keep you off the United States delegation. We begged the President not to nominate you. But now that you are leaving we feel we must acknowledge that we have worked with you gladly and found you good to work with. And we will be happy to do so again."

I don't think anything could have made the weariness drop from my shoulders as did those words. I shall always be grateful for the encouragement they gave me. . . .

During my years at the UN, it was my work on the Human Rights Commission that I considered my most important task, though as I have explained I was also a delegate to the General Assembly, which at times when the two jobs more or less fused caused some confusion. . . .

As we began our work, the Russian representative designated for the task was Mr. Borisov, but he did not arrive. Instead there appeared a rather young gentleman sent by the Russian Embassy in Washington.

"Mr. Borisov will be here later," he explained. "Meanwhile, I will attend the sessions to listen but I do not have any authorization to cast a vote."

Having learned about Soviet tactics in London, I did not feel any great disappointment because of this development and, after I had been elected chairman of the Commission, I tried to push our work along as rapidly as possible. I might point out here that eventually we decided that our main task was to write an International Bill of Rights. This was to consist of three parts. First, there was to be a Declaration which would be adopted as a resolution of the General Assembly and would name and define all the human rights, not only the traditionally recognized political and civil rights, but also the more recently recognized social, economic and cultural rights. Since the General Assembly is not a world parliament, its resolutions are not legally binding on member states. We therefore decided that the Declaration would be followed by a Covenant (or Covenants) which would take the form of a treaty and would be legally binding on the countries that accepted them. Finally, there was to be a system for the implementation or enforcement of the rights. . . .

Our early debates were lively, but I noted that the young Russian delegate sat quietly by and gave an impression of docility and even timidity.

As the time neared to vote for approval of our preliminary actions Mr. Borisov arrived, and our quiet little man disappeared. Mr. Borisov approached me before the next meeting.

"Mrs. Roosevelt," he said, "I have not been able to attend and I would like to ask you, as chairman, to explain to me the actions on which the Commission has decided informally."

I said I would be delighted and carefully outlined the proposals which had been discussed. When I had finished, everything I had said was translated into Russian for Mr. Borisov. He looked thoughtful for a few moments and then shook his head.

"I am sorry," he said, "but I do not believe I clearly understand your plans. Would you mind explaining to me again?"

I said that of course I would not mind. So I went over the entire proceedings again, explaining as simply as possible what had gone on during Mr. Borisov's absence. Again it was all translated into Russian but again Mr. Borisov shook his head sadly.

"I really don't quite understand," he said. "Would you mind starting again at the beginning?"

After we had gone over it in the same way once more, Mr. Borisov was still frowning thoughtfully. "It is not entirely clear," he announced gravely. "Therefore I will not vote."

So, when we called for a formal vote on presenting our proposals to the Economic and Social Council, the Soviet Union merely recorded its "objections and dissent" to certain agreements and thus did not join in the recommendations of the preparatory Commission. The Council accepted our recommendations and President Truman then nominated me as the United States representative on the Commission, as I stated earlier. Being the first chairman of the Commission in addition to my duties as a delegate to the Assembly kept me on United Nations work during five or six months of the year. . . .

Very early in the meetings of the Commission we discovered that while it would be possible to reach some kind of agreement on the Declaration, we were going to be in for a great deal of controversy with the Russian representatives, particularly Dr. Pavlov,[6] who attempted at every opportunity to write a bit of Communist philosophy into the document. For example, at the end of practically every article the Russians proposed to amend the Declaration to read: "This shall be enforced by the state."

When such an amendment was proposed I, or one of the other Western delegates, would argue against it on the ground that this was an international declaration by the United Nations and that we did not believe it should be imposed by the power of the individual governments. We would then ask for a vote and the amendment would be defeated.

But as soon as the next article was completed the Soviet delegate

[6] Professor A. P. Pavlov, the new Russian delegate in 1948.—Ed.

would again propose the same amendment and we would have to go through the whole business again with the same result—the defeat of the Soviet proposal. This naturally became monotonous but the Russians never gave up trying.

The drafting of the articles continued over many months. During our early work on the Covenants and measures of implementation it became apparent that it was going to be exceedingly difficult to agree on articles that would, if accepted, be legally binding on the various nations. This was difficult enough in regard to civil and political rights that have become fairly well accepted throughout the civilized world, but when it came to economic and social rights at times it seemed to me that agreement would be all but impossible. . . .

Our efforts to write a Charter or International Bill of Human Rights reached a kind of climax at the Paris sessions of the General Assembly in 1948. After our Geneva meeting we made steady progress on the Declaration, despite a good many controversies with the delegates from Communist countries.

Dr. Pavlov was a member of the Commission and he delivered many long propaganda harangues that appeared to be more for the purpose of publicizing the Communist point of view than in the hope of making changes in the Declaration. He was an orator of great power; the words rolled out of his black beard like a river, and stopping him was difficult, indeed. Usually, we had to sit and listen, but on one occasion it seemed to me that the rash accusations he brought up against the United States and Great Britain were proving a real detriment to our work. Dr. Pavlov knew that most of us were getting tired of listening, but toward the end of one week when we were preparing to recess he began speaking again. He seemed likely to go on forever, but I watched him closely until he had to pause for breath. Then I banged the gavel so hard that the other delegates jumped in surprise and, before he could continue, I got in a few words of my own.

"We are here," I said, "to devise ways of safeguarding human rights. We are not here to attack each other's governments and I hope when we return on Monday the delegate of the Soviet Union will remember that!" I banged the gavel again. "Meeting adjourned!"

I can still see Dr. Pavlov staring at me in surprise. But this maneuver may have had some effect, because his orations were brief and to the point for about a week after that.

Eventually we completed a draft of the Universal Declaration of Human Rights that we foolishly felt would be quickly accepted by the General Assembly, which was meeting in Paris in the autumn of 1948.

"I believe," General Marshall, who had become Secretary of State, said before we left for Paris, "that this session of the General Assembly will be remembered as the Human Rights session." . . .

As the session opened I was full of confidence that we could quickly get the Declaration through the formal hearings before Committee 3 and have it approved by the Assembly. My confidence was soon gone. We worked for two months, often until late at night, debating every single word of that draft Declaration over and over again before Committee 3 would approve its transmission to the General Assembly. . . .

In the final vote in Committee 3 on presenting the Declaration to the Assembly, delegates from four Moslem countries abstained, explaining that they believed the article on religious freedom was contrary to the Koran.

This setback came at a critical time near the end of the Paris sessions but, fortunately, we consulted with Sir Zafrulla Khan, the foreign minister of Pakistan, whose delegate on the Commission had abstained, and he courageously rose in the General Assembly to defend the Declaration. Since Pakistan was the largest Moslem nation involved his position was important.

"It is my opinion," he declared, "that our Pakistan delegate has misinterpreted the Koran. I understand the Koran to say: 'He who can believe shall believe; he who cannot believe shall disbelieve; the only unforgivable sin is to be a hypocrite.' I shall vote for acceptance of the Universal Declaration of Human Rights."

In the end there was no vote cast against the Declaration in the General Assembly, but there were some disappointing abstentions. The Soviet Union and its satellite countries abstained, since the Russian delegate contended that the Declaration put emphasis mainly on "eighteenth-century rights" and not enough on economic, social and cultural rights. The delegate from Saudi Arabia, Jamil M. Baroody, abstained, saying that he was quite sure King Ibn Saud would not agree with Sir Zafrulla in interpreting the Koran. South Africa also abstained, I was sad to note; its delegate said that they hoped to give their people basic human rights, but that the Declaration went too far. Two small countries were absent. The Declaration was finally accepted by the General Assembly on December 10, 1948.

The First Lady of the UN

ELIZABETH JANEWAY

In the early 1950s, there was still considerable world opinion that the United Nations might truly become a workable alternative to traditional power politics among nations in the nuclear age. Hence, there was consistent press coverage of its affairs—news stories, editorials, "think pieces." The following passage is from a feature story by Elizabeth Janeway, a popular novelist, critic, and magazine writer. The piece, which appeared in the New York Times Magazine *on October 22, 1950, is also an appreciation of the role Eleanor Roosevelt continued to play in the work of Committee Three, and of the status she had gained by 1950 through her work at the UN.*

OUT AT LAKE SUCCESS, where the General Assembly of the United Nations is meeting, the subject of freedom and human dignity is debated by one of the committees in terms of the long-range obligations of the Governments of the world. This is Committee Three, the Humanitarian, Social and Cultural Committee, which has to deal with that fundamental document known as the Covenant on Human Rights, and to issue to the UN's too-little-known Commission on Human Rights further directives on what the covenant is to include and how it is to be implemented. . . .

The eyes of the visitors move about the circle of faces, pausing at the delegate from the Soviet Union, at the Indian representative in her graceful sari, at the Yugoslav or the Chinese. But in the end they come back and focus on the face they know best, the one that they have most probably come to see, the face of the representative of the United States whose name is Mrs. Franklin D. Roosevelt.

Everyone knows what she looks like: she looks like your favorite aunt. Her clothes and her coiffure both express the truth that it is a great nuisance to be fashionable, and also a nuisance to be at odds with fashion. Her mannerisms are those of a younger and much less important woman. They are endearing because they betray that she is shy and that she is determined to pay as little attention as possible to the distraction of her shyness.

The apologetic little laugh, which occasionally breaks her speeches, is maddening to unsympathetic ears. It is a relic of her past. Once, it can have been her only refuge when confronted with a world which was not as good as she would have liked it to be. The world is still not as good as she would like it to be, but now she has other resources with which to meet it. The laugh is a habit that her mind but not her body has outgrown. Enormously inappropriate to the present, it is a reminder that the only member of the United States delegation who has served at every session of the United Nations was once a sheltered upper-class woman who disliked and dreaded public appearances.

Mrs. Roosevelt is the chairman of the Commission on Human Rights whose work on a draft covenant is to be considered by Committee Three. This is a body appointed by the Economic and Social Council of the U.N. (not to be confused with Unesco, which is a separate but affiliated body with its own delegates). The first duty of the commission was to draw up a Declaration of Human Rights, and this it has done. After some two years of struggling over the principles of contemporary ethics and the minutiae of wording, the Universal Declaration of Human Rights was accepted by the General Assembly in December, 1948. The principles of the declaration have already borne fruit, for both the Indian and Indonesian Constitutions have modeled themselves after it, and it has been referred to in decisions by the Federal courts of the United States.

This, then, is Mrs. Roosevelt's biggest job: to bring down to earth the ideals of the Declaration of Human Rights and contrive, by the lengthy process of discussion and compromise, by bickering and by vote, to get them woven by her committee into an implementation which will be accepted by the United Nations as a whole and by each of the nations singly.

At her job she is untiring. When she first sat as chairman of her commission, she was unfamiliar with parliamentary procedure and was inclined to think common sense an adequate substitute for Robert's "Rules of Order." This was a naive, if good-hearted view. She has since got over it and is quite capable of quoting the procedural rules of the United Nations from memory. . . .

In the daily meetings of the United States delegation Mrs. Roosevelt does not confine her attention to questions before Committee Three. She is au courant with the problems of the Budgetary, Economic, and Political Committees and does not hesitate to comment upon them.

These "briefing" sessions take place before and after meetings, and Mrs. Roosevelt's day will often include a morning session at the United States delegation's offices in New York, continuing in the delegation car on the way to Lake Success, two commission meetings at U.N. headquarters and further discussion in the late afternoon before she goes to a dinner, where she is likely to speak on her work at the United Nations.

Nor are her lunch hours periods of relaxation. The U.N. staff, which used to assemble in awe to watch her pass in the corridor, has got used to seeing her hurry into the delegates' lounge, drop a stuffed briefcase on the most convenient chair and plunge on through toward the cafeteria, where she stands in line to be served, holding her own tray and waiting her turn. Then, if she has time, she will return to the lounge (she has no other office at Lake Success) to meet and talk to a group of students or the members of some organization before the afternoon meeting of the commission. Now that she has added a daily radio program to her schedule, her closest friends are awestruck at the scope of her activities.

This is part and parcel, however, of what she considers a vital part of her job. She is out to cure the country, so far as it is humanly possible for her to do so, of its ignorance about the United Nations and particularly about the great question of human rights. The indefatigable energy which sent her, when she was First Lady, down mines and into hospitals now dispatches her to every speaking engagement she can manage to squeeze in. Convinced, devoted, tireless, endlessly available, she is a symbol of hope for progress throughout the world. . . .

She is alert, too, to the uses of the advisers who sit behind her at meetings. Soviet Foreign Minister Vishinsky once launched into a lengthy speech which included a listing of what he described as American concentration camps. Mrs. Roosevelt noted them down and handed the list to one of her aides who rushed out to phone Washington. By the end of Mr. Vishinsky's oration Mrs. Roosevelt had a report from the Army on the locations mentioned—which had been prisoner-of-war camps, most of them closed.

In her own commission she has used a simple maneuver to cut down the length of speeches. "Have you ever noticed," she will remark with an air of ingenuousness to a long-winded speaker, "about when it is that people begin to remove their headphones? It takes about ten minutes of any speaker's time." Yet her attitude in the chair is one of generous encouragement. "Yes? Yes?" she will say, as if this at last—whatever the subject, whoever the speaker—were bringing her final clarification. "I felt as if she had been waiting all day for me to speak," one delegate said.

The Russians, of course, with their invective, their accusals and their stereotyped denunciations, are a special problem. By the end of the 1949 session of the Commission on Human Rights Mrs. Roosevelt had more or less worked out a basic formula for dealing with them. Whenever she could ignore the rhetoric and charges with which they prolonged the debate she did so, and spoke merely to the point of whatever their actual suggestions for the drafting of the Covenant might be. She had certainly begun her work at the U.N. by attempting to meet the Soviet delegates halfway, but by 1949 she was ready to state publicly that she would never again try to compromise with them.

As for the Soviet Government itself, it had definitely changed its expressed opinion of Mrs. Roosevelt. The Russians began by calling her nothing worse than a "school teacher" (she replied that she was proud to be regarded as a member of the teaching profession), and even two years ago they were willing to appeal to her, in the name of her husband, to cease advocating "imperialism." Such temperance has stopped, however, and Izvestia later referred to her as a "hypocritical servant of capitalism . . . a fly darkening the Soviet sun." In Paris, late in 1948, a Russian delegate was heard to mutter some words in the heat of debate which seemed to characterize Mrs. Roosevelt as a meddling old woman.

An observer was forcefully reminded of Stalin's projected plan for dealing with Lenin's widow, Krupskaya. That unhappy lady was more inclined to Trotsky's view than to Stalin's and for some little time made no bones about saying so. "If that old woman doesn't shut up," Stalin is said to have remarked, "I'll appoint someone else Lenin's widow." There is no doubt he would like to have the power to appoint someone else Franklin D. Roosevelt's widow. . . .

But in the meantime she must speak for the United States in Committee Three and on the Human Rights Commission. This is not always simple. As United States delegate, of course, she must always remember those operative words, "two-thirds of the Senate." A covenant on human rights which is not ratified by the United States Senate will not be a covenant at all, either to America or, practically speaking, to the world at large. No one west of the Iron Curtain can doubt Mrs. Roosevelt's firm adherence to the humanitarian statements of the Declaration of Human Rights. But it is just this adherence to principle which makes her advocate practical compromise.

The United States point of view has thus far excluded from the Covenant of Human Rights economic and social rights, such as the promise of unemployment insurance or material benefits. It has, moreover, restricted very sharply the bringing of petitions for redress against violators of the covenant. Such petitions cannot be presented by distressed individuals, or by organizations representing them, no matter how large a group the organization represents. They can be brought only by national Governments signatory to the covenant.

This puts a wronged human being, whether he be a Czech Democrat, a South African Negro, or a California Japanese subject to the Alien Land Law, in the position of having to discover another national Government willing to bring a case in his behalf against his own Government. To many, such restrictions seem to narrow the covenant to farcical limits; and worse, to invite the bringing of cases as political propaganda. Why does Mrs. Roosevelt support such a position?

Mrs. Roosevelt recognizes both the force and familiarity of this criticism. But she replies on pragmatic grounds. If individual, or even organizational, petitions were permitted, she says, any apparatus for dealing with violations under the covenant would be swamped. "As it is," she points out, "we have letters from people complaining about their rent being raised."

Mrs. Roosevelt goes on to say that she sees this covenant as a first covenant; as a step to be taken so that more can follow. Let us get this covenant ratified—and here the words "two-thirds of the Senate" almost appear in the air over her head—let us take this first step, and then we can go on to work on covenants which can include social and economic rights; to plan for the acceptance first of organizational petitions and then of individual pleas.

Thus she and her critics meet head-on in this ancient philosophic dilemma of ends and means. Mrs. Roosevelt is for means, for the pragmatic approach so typical of American thought. She is for action. Let us do as much as we can, she believes, and, if we cannot do all we want at once, what we do will be better than nothing. Surely we can win the trust of the oppressed millions of the world by honest effort in their behalf, even though our accomplishments at first must be disappointing. . . .

It is because she is an optimist that she is willing to move slowly—she is convinced that the desired end exists ideally, waiting to be achieved. It is because she does actually believe in progress that she can see, in the perspective of her view, this Covenant, and, later, more liberal covenants, as steps toward an ultimate goal.

Eleanor and the UN: A Modern Assessment

JOSEPH P. LASH

With the election of the Republican President Dwight D. Eisenhower in 1952, Eleanor Roosevelt resigned her UN delegate post and even her appointment as United States representative on the Human Rights Commission. Although there were several years left of her term on the commission, she wanted to clear the way for the new president to make his own appointment. President Eisenhower accepted her resignation.

For the ten years that remained of her life, she continued to fight for the UN and for its ideals, for humanitarianism and world peace. She volunteered her services to the American Association for the United Nations, and she accepted invitations to speak and travel everywhere—Japan, India, Israel, Yugoslavia, Russia. In an interview on her seventieth birthday in 1954, she was asked which of her achievements had given her the greatest satisfaction. She replied, "I got the most satisfaction from my work in the UN . . . and I still feel it important to strengthen this organization in every way."[7]

But now, with the perspective of a generation, how are we to interpret the work of Eleanor Roosevelt and the UN in those hopeful years of the late 1940s and early 1950s? For that purpose, we turn to Joseph P. Lash's definitive biography, Eleanor: The Years Alone. *We begin with Eleanor's appointment to the UN by President Truman in December 1945—the point at which we picked up her own narrative of the same events.*

THERE WERE TWO PEOPLE, Truman had told James Byrnes sometime in November, that he had to have on his political team—Henry Wallace, because of his influence with labor, and Mrs. Roosevelt, because of her influence with the Negro voter. He could "take care of Henry" but wanted Byrnes to find an appointment for Mrs. Roosevelt in the field of foreign affairs. "The following week," Byrnes said, "in recommending a list of delegates for the first meeting of the United Nations Assembly in London, I placed Mrs. Roosevelt's name at the top of the list, expressing the belief that because of her husband's deep interest in the success of the UN she might accept. Truman telephoned to her immediately, while I was still in his office, and she did agree to serve." . . .

The delegation was a prestigious one. It consisted of five representatives—Secretary of State James F. Byrnes; Edward R. Stettinius, Jr., who was the U.S. representative on the Security Council; Sen. Tom Connally (D-Texas), chairman of the Senate Foreign Relations Committee; Sen. Arthur H. Vandenberg (R-Michigan), ranking Republican member of the Senate Foreign Relations Committee; and Mrs. Roosevelt. In addition there were five alternates—Rep. Sol Bloom (D-New York), chairman of the House Foreign Affairs Committee; the committee's ranking Republican member, Charles A. Eaton of New Jersey; Frank Walker, former postmaster general and former chairman of the Democratic National Committee; the former chairman of the Republican National Committee, John G. Townsend, Jr., who also was an ex-senator from Delaware. The fifth alternate was John Foster Dulles, chief foreign affairs adviser to Gov. Thomas E. Dewey in the 1944 presidential campaign. . . .

[After a shipboard caucus of the other members of the delegation, Eleanor Roosevelt] was told at the delegation meeting that she had been assigned to Committee III, which—scheduled to deal with humanitarian, social, and cultural matters—was supposed to be a relatively uncontroversial and, therefore, it was thought, safe berth for her. Durward Sandifer

[7] Lash, *Eleanor: The Years Alone*, p. 238.

was her chief adviser. Short, sandy-haired, dryly spoken, he had been an assistant on legal matters in Pasvolsky's office.[8] She quickly came to depend on him. "I went with her to all the sessions," he recalled. "I started carrying her brief case as well as my own—over her protests." She invited him to Claridge's to dinner. She had half a dozen people there, including a cousin. "I rushed home to write a long account of this dinner to Irene [Sandifer]." By the end of the Assembly they were good friends. He should come to lunch at Washington Square once they were back in New York, she urged. He did. "I was so nervous at having lunch with Mrs. Roosevelt," he confided to Tommy afterward, "that I put salt in my coffee." Mrs. Roosevelt overheard him. "You—nervous at having lunch with me? I am the one who should be nervous at having lunch with you. You will never know how frightened I was getting on that boat. I knew what the British thought of Franklin and what they expected of me. You don't know what a help you were to me."

The General Assembly opened. She drove to Westminster with Stettinius—"How your husband planned for this day," he said to her—and in Westminster's Central Hall as the delegations filed in, most of them led by their foreign ministers, and the temporary president mounted to the high podium which was framed from behind by a huge map of the world on a blue and gold background with two great olive branches below it, she felt that FDR's spirit "must be with us." She noted the flowing robes of the Arab representatives and also that there were "very few women on the delegations." She was seated at the end of the U.S. delegation, next to the Soviet group. By mistake she took the seat of V. V. Kuznetzov, who gallantly invited her to join the Soviet delegation and relations between them got off to a good start. . . .

A key issue at this organizational Assembly—and it was a troublesome one—was the election of a secretary-general. Lie of Norway was a candidate, but during the session some members of the U.S. delegation who had favored his election as president of the Assembly had cooled toward him considerably. They were fearful that Norway, sharing a border with Russia, might fall under its domination and influence Lie's policies as secretary-general. Eleanor thought they were wrong both about Norway's vulnerability to Soviet pressure and Lie's staunchness. The United States' first choice for the post was Lester B. Pearson of Canada, but when he proved unacceptable to the Russians, who countered with the candidacy of the foreign minister of Yugoslavia, the United States switched to Lie and persuaded the British to do so as well. . . .

[Meanwhile, Eleanor Roosevelt] was having her own difficulties with the Russians. Contrary to the expectations of the men when they assigned her to Committee III, the hottest East-West issue of the Assembly boiled

[8] Leo Pasvolsky was a State Department official who had been instrumental in drafting the UN charter.—ED.

up in it. "A new type of political refugee is appearing," she noted in her diary after studying a memo on the refugee question, "people who have been against the present governments and if they stay at home or go home will probably be killed." There were approximately one million such refugees in displaced-person camps, most of them from the East. The Communist position was simple, brutally so. They could not see why the refugee question should be a matter of international concern. There were only two categories of refugees in their view: those who wanted to be repatriated and those who did not because they are "quislings, traitors, war criminals or collaborators," and the international community should waste neither sympathy nor resources on this latter group.

She wanted to avoid a collision with the Communists, but drafting a resolution acceptable to them proved impossible. . . .

Debate was endless "and so many words," but finally a vote was reached.

> We defeated the Russians on the three points we disagreed on, they were all fundamental, and I'm afraid while I was brief I was clear in my opposition. Wise Mr. Sandifer of the State Department seemed pleased but whispered "The Russians won't like that."

The Communist amendments would have curbed "propaganda" in the refugee camps and placed the latter under the administrative supervision of officials from the refugees' countries of origin. The item came up again in plenary when Andrei Vishinsky, the head of the Russian delegation, challenged the committee's recommendations and announced he would make a speech on the subject.

> The British had their representative ready to speak but I saw all the heads in our delegation come together because nobody was ready to speak except the woman in Committee 3 whom they had put there, thinking she would be harmless. Finally Mr. Dulles asked me to say a few words and I agreed to do so.

Behind Mr. Dulles's request was a great change in attitude toward Mrs. Roosevelt. New Dealer Benjamin V. Cohen, who was in London as counselor to the State Department, had lunched with Dulles and Vandenberg. While talking with him they also talked to each other, exchanging expressions of amazement at Mrs. Roosevelt's good judgment. They really had not known her before, writing her off as an emotional, rattle-brained woman. "One of the most solid members of the delegation" they now agreed, as Ben Cohen chuckled to himself.

The exchange between Mrs. Roosevelt and Vishinsky, the Soviet Union's wiliest and most formidable debater, provided a moment of high drama. He was the grand inquisitor, the relentless Stalinist prosecutor in the Moscow purge trials, arguing with the twentieth-century embodiment of humanitarianism before a world jury. If democracy had saints, Adlai Stevenson would later say, Eleanor Roosevelt would be among the first canonized. Vishinsky was not happy, Mrs. Roosevelt's aides thought, to find himself ranged against a woman revered for her goodness, who, moreover, bore a name still highly respected in the Soviet Union. His argument was low-keyed. Mankind had paid too much already for tolerance and the right of asylum, he contended. There were limits to liberty. He refused to accept a tolerance "which is known in history by the name of Munich."

She talked over the points she intended to make with Sandifer, but she spoke extemporaneously—"the most important speech ever given by an American delegate without a prepared text," Sandifer later said.

Where Vishinsky sought to exploit the emotional symbolism of Munich, she countered with an equally potent symbol—Spain. Forced repatriation from the refugee camps, Mrs. Roosevelt began, might mean forcing Spanish Republican refugees to return to Spain, "a fascist country." Refugee camps should not be used for political activity, she agreed, but she upheld the right of the refugees to hear good or bad against any UN member. "Are we so weak in the UN that we are going to forbid human beings the right to hear what their friends believe? It is their right to say it and their right to hear it and make their own decision. To say otherwise," she added, would be like saying "I am always right," but "I am not sure my Government or nation will always be right, and we should aim at being so right that the majority will be with us and we can stand having among us those who do not agree."

She recognized that some European countries torn by wars that were both civil and international might take a different view of human rights and human freedom than the United States which, since the Civil War, had no political or religious refugees fleeing its borders, but it was the task of the United Nations "to frame things which will be broader in outlook, which will consider first the rights of man, which will consider what makes man more free: not governments but man!"

The Soviet amendments were again voted down, and afterward she wrote home:

> Yesterday we fought the whole battle over again in the Assembly on refugees which we had fought in Committee & we won again hands down. This time Mr. Vishinsky & I fought it out, evidently they, the Russians, don't let any but delegates speak in the Assembly! The Russians are tenacious fighters but when we finally finished voting at 1 a.m. last night I shook hands & said I admired their fighting qualities & I hoped some day on that kind of question we would be on the same side & they were cordiality itself! Also you will be amused that when Mr. Dulles said good-bye to me this morning he said, "I feel I must tell you that when you were appointed I thought it terrible & now I think your work here

has been fine!" So—against odds, the women inch forward, but I'm rather old to be carrying on this fight! . . .

In Mrs. Roosevelt's clash with Vishinsky over forced repatriation, she had cited the guarantees written into the UN Charter of fundamental human rights. The trampling upon those rights by Nazism and fascism, especially Hitler's persecution of the Jews, was considered by the drafters of the Charter as among the underlying causes of the catastrophe, and a major respect in which the Charter was an advance over the League Covenant was its provision for the establishment of a commission "for the promotion of human rights." It had been the American hope to annex to the Charter a Declaration of Rights, and Durward Sandifer had been assigned to draft such a document. But there was no time before San Francisco to obtain agreement on a Declaration, so its drafting was assigned to the human rights commission as its first order of business.

No delegate in London had more eminently personified the cause of respect for human dignity than Eleanor Roosevelt, and it was not surprising that the Economic and Social Council asked her to serve on the "nuclear" human rights commission whose job it would be to prepare a plan of work and the permanent setup of the Commission. The choice was as widely acclaimed as her appointment as delegate to the London Assembly. Senator Vandenberg, who immediately after FDR's death, had been alarmed by reports that Mrs. Roosevelt might be added to the U.S. delegation to the San Francisco conference, was now enlivening Washington dinner tables with his paeans of praise for Mrs. Roosevelt. "I want to say that I take back everything I ever said about her, and believe me it's been plenty."

"I have cabled Mr. Lie that I would accept," Mrs. Roosevelt informed Secretary Byrnes. "The cable stated that we would meet here in New York City and the meeting would last three weeks and my compensation would be $15 a day and travelling expenses." Would the State Department provide her with an adviser and with secretarial assistance? . . .

The meeting of the "nuclear" commission, as it was called, took place in makeshift quarters in the Hunter College library. The furnishings were of hewn oak, and the delegates sat around tables which had been arranged in the shape of a hollow square in the middle of which sat the interpreters and secretaries. . . .

By the end of the three weeks the group had gotten through its agenda, which included proposals to the Economic and Social Council on the setting up the permanent eighteen-nation Commission on Human Rights and on the drafting and implementation of an international bill of rights. At the very end of its deliberations, the Soviet delegate, a young man from the embassy, was replaced by the permanent representative on the commission, Alexander Borisov, who had just arrived. He asked Mrs. Roosevelt to fill him in and she carefully went over the points that had been accepted, with the concurrence of the Soviet delegate, and asked the interpreter to translate. He did, but Mr. Borisov said he did not understand and asked her to go over the points again. She did so patiently and carefully. Again he claimed he did not understand. She made a third try but still without success, and it finally became clear to her that Mr. Borisov did not want to understand because not only did he refuse to join in the recommendations, but he wanted changed those records showing how his predecessor had voted on those recommendations. This, as chairman, she refused to do. She was "quite annoyed" with Borisov's performance, she confessed a few months later.

> No amount of argument ever changes what your Russian delegate says or how he votes. It is the most exasperating thing in the world, but I have made up my mind that I am going through all the arguments just as though I didn't know at the time it would have no effect. If I have patience enough, in a year from now perhaps the Russians may come with a different attitude.

Borisov's abstention was a portent of things to come, but did not affect the commission's proposals. "I think we have done a helpful piece of work," she summed up. "The real work, of course, remains to be done in the next series of meetings, when the actual writing of an international bill of rights will have to be undertaken. . . .

At her urging, the drafting committee did not spend too much time on the precise wording of the articles. A touchier issue had arisen and was dividing the committee—the binding character of the rights that were to be listed in the Declaration. The small nations in particular wanted something more than a moral manifesto. They wanted states to assume a treaty obligation to grant, protect, and enforce the rights enumerated in the Declaration. Neither the United States nor Russia favored this, but the United States, chiefly as a result of Mrs. Roosevelt's pressure, deferred to the views of the majority. There would be two documents, the committee decided, one a relatively brief declaration of principles that would provide "a common standard of achievement," the other a precise convention that would constitute a treaty binding on the states that ratified it and become a part of their own law. . . .

Public opinion in the United States and the mood in Congress were turning hostile toward additional UN commitments. In part, this was a response to the fact that the end of the war, instead of ushering in an era of peace, order, and friendliness, had brought almost chaotic conditions as well as a perilous confrontation with the Soviet Union. In part, it reflected domestic developments—the postwar swing to the right that culminated in McCarthyism and McCarranism. In part, it was a reaction to Soviet behavior in the United Nations. The readiness of the Soviet Union to exploit the platform and high principles of the United Nations in order to abuse the West and to boycott and paralyze the organs of the United Nations when those principles were invoked against Russia's mundane interests turned congressional sentiment against a legally binding convention, which, it was said, the Russians would disregard, even as they did their own constitution. . . .

Although the department policy group had prepared a U.S. version of what should go into a convention, there was no agreement, as Mrs. Roosevelt prepared in November, 1947, to leave for Geneva, on whether this document should even be circulated to the other members of the Commission as a working paper and basis for discussion. . . .

As chairman, she pushed her Commission relentlessly at Geneva. "I drive hard and when I get home I will be tired! The men on the Commission will be also!" she wrote. Her colleagues called her "a slave driver," the delegate of Panama at one point begging her not to forget the rights of the human beings who are members of the Commission. She was not unresponsive to the beauties and distractions of Geneva. "At last I have seen Mont Blanc!" she exclaimed as the clouds finally rolled away, but they had agreed to work overtime if they took Saturday afternoon off, she reminded them, and kept them in session until seven. Why didn't they shorten the length of their speeches, she suggested, if they objected to the length of the sessions. "No one can ever tell me that women like to talk longer than men!"

A week before Christmas the Declaration was approved by a vote of 13 to 4. Mrs. Roosevelt was not satisfied with the language. It was too professorial, too lawyerlike. "All my advisers are lawyers or I would be lost," she advised a friend, adding, "common sense is valuable now & then I find however!" The Commission approved her resolution asking the drafting committee to prepare a short text, "which will be readily understood by all peoples." On this resolution there was neither abstention nor dissent. . . .

But there was furious debate inside the administration over whether to go ahead with a covenant under which nations would assume a legal obligation to protect the rights enunciated. Officials on the working level in the field of human rights favored a covenant, but would Congress ratify such a treaty? Mrs. Roosevelt came down to Washington after the Geneva meeting to confer with the president and the State Department. Truman's Committee on Civil Rights had just submitted a hard-hitting report that listed ten recommendations to secure minority groups rights in the United States, and southern demagogues, in full cry against those recommendations, were threatening to bolt the Democratic party in 1948. Lovett doubted that the Senate would ratify a covenant that included strong stipulations against discrimination. . . .

The 1948 General Assembly met in Paris at the end of September. It was a moment of tense confrontation with the Communists, who were on the offensive throughout western Europe. Soviet Russia's blockade of

Berlin was being abetted by Communist-instigated strikes, street demonstrations, and violence inside France and Italy. At the heart of the confrontation, in the view of the West, was the issue of human liberty. The Assembly would have before it the draft Declaration. The president and General Marshall thought Mrs. Roosevelt should give a major speech in Paris. . . .

She accepted René Cassin's invitation to come to the Sorbonne and talk on "The Struggle for the Rights of Man."[9] She arrived at the Sorbonne accompanied by General and Mrs. Marshall. The amphitheater, which held 2,500, was packed and many hundreds were unable to gain admittance. The French minister of national defense presided, the French foreign minister was in her audience, and the French Broadcasting System broadcast the entire proceedings. The basic obstacle to peace, she said, sounding her central theme, was the different concept of human rights held by the Soviet Union. It was the battle of the French and American Revolutions all over again. "The issue of human liberty is as decisive now as it was then." Her excellent French and extreme graciousness of manner charmed her audience, as did her ad-libbed departures from her text. . . .

The greatest test of patience was still ahead. The Declaration was on the agenda of the Committee III of the General Assembly. To Mrs. Roosevelt's dismay the Committee insisted on debating the Declaration "exactly as though it was all an entirely new idea and nobody had ever looked at it before." It devoted eighty-five meetings to the subject, "considerably more time than any organ of the General Assembly had spent on any other subject." Again the Soviet bloc delegates sought to delay and postpone, but they met a worthy antagonist in Dr. Malik, chairman of the Committee, who, commented Sandifer, was "the only person I ever knew who succeeded in holding a stopwatch on Pavlov."[10]

The debate was repetitive and tedious. Patiently, she sat through the usual Soviet bloc onslaughts "telling us what dogs we are," happy, she confessed, to escape the "wordy atmosphere" occasionally to do a little Christmas shopping, leaving Sandifer to sit in for her, until finally the Declaration was approved by Committee III and forwarded to the Assembly plenary. . . .

At 3:00 A.M. on December 10 the Assembly adopted the Declaration and she could write "long job finished." The final vote was 48 countries in favor, none against, 2 absent, and 8 abstentions, mostly of Soviet bloc countries. The Assembly delegates, in recognition of Mrs. Roosevelt's leadership, accorded her the rare personal tribute of a standing ovation. . . .

The decision of Mrs. Roosevelt and her advisers to give priority to the Declaration was vindicated. The first United Nations Human Rights prize was awarded to her posthumously.

[9] Rene Cassin was a member of the French delegation.—ED.

[10] Dr. Charles H. Malik, of Lebanon.—ED.

But more than the prize, she would have enjoyed the knowledge that the Declaration was slowly working its way into the ethical conscience of mankind. For as she wrote in 1958:

> Where, after all, do universal human rights begin? In small places, close to home—so close and so small that they cannot be seen on any maps of the world. Yet they *are* the world of the individual persons; the neighborhood he lives in; the school or college he attends; the factory, farm or office where he works. Such are the places where every man, woman and child seeks equal justice, equal opportunity, equal dignity without discrimination. Unless these rights have meaning there, they have little meaning anywhere. Without concerned citizen action to uphold them close to home, we shall look in vain for progress in the larger world.

Suggestions for Further Reading

ELEANOR ROOSEVELT was herself a prolific writer. Her autobiography consists of three volumes, *This Is My Story* (New York: Harper, 1937), *This I Remember* (New York: Harper, 1949), and *On My Own* (New York: Harper, 1958), excerpted for this chapter. She did a monthly column for *Ladies' Home Journal* and later for *McCall's* magazine, excerpts from which were published in *It Seems to Me* (New York: Norton, 1954), frequently reprinted. Another book of the same sort, responses to questions, is *If You Ask Me* (New York and London: Appleton-Century, 1946). In a similar vein is *The White House Press Conferences of Eleanor Roosevelt*, ed. Maurine Beasley (New York and London: Garland, 1983). There are dozens of articles by Eleanor Roosevelt in popular magazines, and there are serious books on a range of issues, such as *It's Up to the Women* (New York: Frederick A. Stokes Co., 1933), *Ladies of Courage* (with Lorena A. Hickok) (New York: Putnam, 1954), *India and the Awakening East* (New York: Harper, 1935), *Tomorrow Is Now* (New York: Harper & Row, 1963), and (with William DeWitt) *UN: Today and Tomorrow* (New York: Harper, 1953).

There are reminiscences of Eleanor Roosevelt by members of her family—*Mother and Daughter: The Letters of Eleanor and Anna Roosevelt*, ed. Bernard Asbell (New York: Coward, McCann and Geoghegan, 1982), one biographical volume by son James, and four biographies by son Elliott. And there are volumes of recollections by her devoted friends such as Lorena A. Hickok, *Eleanor Roosevelt: Reluctant First Lady* (New York: Dodd, Mead, 1962), reprinted 1980, and Archibald MacLeish, *The Eleanor Roosevelt Story* (Boston: Houghton Mifflin, 1965).

There are a number of biographical accounts, from the first full-dress biography by Alfred Steinberg, *Mrs. R: The Life of Eleanor Roosevelt* (New York: Putnam, 1958), a lively and popular book, to the recently published, competent and readable J. William T. Youngs, *Eleanor Roosevelt: A Personal and Public Life* (Boston and Toronto: Little, Brown, 1985). But the best and most definitive biography is in the two substantial volumes of Joseph P. Lash, *Eleanor and Franklin: The Story of Their Relationship, Based on Eleanor Roosevelt's Private Papers* (New York: Norton, 1971), and *Eleanor: The Years Alone* (New York: Norton, 1972), excerpted for this chapter. Lash has also written *A World of Love: Eleanor Roosevelt and Her Friends, 1943–1962* (New York: Doubleday, 1984).

Two books dealing with special topics may also be recommended: *Without Precedent: The Life and Career of Eleanor Roosevelt*, ed. Joan Hoff-Wilson and Marjorie Lightman (Bloomington: Indiana University Press, 1984), a work emphasizing Eleanor's contributions to feminism; and Jason Berger, *A New Deal for the World: Eleanor Roosevelt and American Foreign Policy* (New York: Social Science Monographs, 1981).

The Bettmann Archive, Inc.

Picasso: The Artist of the Century

1881 born
1900 first visited Paris
1906 painted *Les Demoiselles d'Avignon*—the beginning of Cubism
1918 marriage to Olga Khoklova
1937 painted *Guernica*
1958 marriage to Jacqueline Roque
1973 died

Pablo Picasso was born to be an artist, and for most of his long life, he was the quintessential artist of the twentieth century. To the learned critic and the average person alike, his name was synonymous with "modern art" and with all the praise and blame attached to that term. Picasso's father was a Spanish art teacher who fostered the artistic talent of his son. At the age of fifteen, Picasso was accepted at La Lonja, the Barcelona School of Fine Arts, where his father then taught. In the following year, Picasso entered the prestigious Academy of Fine Arts in Madrid, but, after only a few weeks there, the young man grew restless with the barren traditionalism of the academy. He returned to Barcelona where he frequented popular artists' cafés and eagerly entered into the endless talk about the various schools of late nineteenth-century art.

In 1900, when he was just nineteen, Picasso went to Paris, the city that was to be his home for most of the rest of his life. In many ways, his life and his work blended with the life of the city, which was on the verge of becoming the focal point for the early twentieth-century avant-garde—in painting and sculpture, in music and ballet, in literature and philosophy. Picasso was to become a major, formative figure in the avant-garde movement, as well as a popular symbol of it. But that role lay some years in the future.

He settled in a borrowed studio in Montmartre and began to paint. He was deeply influenced by the posters of Toulouse-Lautrec and by the

Collection, The Museum of Modern Art, New York.

paintings of Van Gogh and Cézanne. And he lived in desperate poverty. In later and more prosperous years, he recalled how, when he had eaten the last crust of bread in the house, he would go from one art dealer to another with an armload of paintings, trying without success to sell them, and how the dealers would not even let him stay inside their shops until the rain let up.[1]

Nevertheless, Picasso perserved and began to develop a distinctive style of his own. In the years 1906–1907, he was at work on his first major painting, a huge canvas called *Les Demoiselles d'Avignon*—five nude women, done in the blocky, geometric style of Cézanne. The two figures on the right show the distorted features and disjointed parts originating in Picasso's fascination with African masks and carvings, and all display what would become the characteristics of Cubism. This was the first important movement of modern art to be identified with Picasso. He shared the leadership in the movement with the French painter Georges Braque, who remained his friend for life. (Even so, Picasso's mistress at the time, Fernande Olivier, recalled that the two men shouted at each other over their paintings.) Though the painting *Les Demoiselles*

[1] The incident is reported in a conversation with Picasso by David Douglas Duncan in *The Private World of Pablo Picasso* (New York: The Ridge Press, 1958), p. 86.

d'Avignon was not actually completed for thirty years, it was seen by Picasso's colleagues and was profoundly influential with them.

Picasso's drafts and preliminary drawings were sold at handsome prices. There were now dealers for his paintings, and buyers, and he began to prosper. And he began to be a social lion in Paris salons and studios. Gertrude Stein, the American expatriate writer, numbered herself among his friends and wrote that "his friends in Paris were writers rather than painters, why have painters for friends when he could paint as he could paint. It was obvious that he did not need to have painters in his daily life and this was true all his life."[2] Yet, Stein was only partially right. He was friends with—and his studio was frequented by—such avant-garde poets, playwrights, and critics as Guillaume Apollinaire, Alfred Jarry, Max Jacob, André Salmon, and Maurice Raynal. In addition, Georges Braque often joined his circle, as did André Derain, Fernand Léger, and his fellow Spanish artist Juan Gris.

By the beginning of World War I, Picasso had started to lose interest in Cubism. His friends were drifting off to the war or to voluntary exile out of France. The world was "becoming very strange and not exactly reassuring."[3] He became interested in ballet set and costume design, under the influence of the poet-playwright Jean Cocteau. In 1917, Picasso celebrated his growing affluence by moving to a more fashionable section of Paris. A year later, he married the Russian ballet star Olga Khokhlova. Their apartment-studio was decorated in the most expensive taste of the time, and they rented an Art Nouveau villa for summers at the beach in Brittany. Their son Paulo, born in 1921, even had an English nanny.

In the early 1920s, Picasso indulged in a period of wide-ranging experimentation in his work, including a brief fling at Surrealism. He began to do sculpture—as radically innovative as his paintings had been—as well as book illustrations and collages.

[2] Gertrude Stein, *Picasso* (New York: Dover, 1984), p. 3.

[3] Cited in Lael Wertenbaker, *The World of Picasso* (New York: Time-Life Books, 1967), p. 63.

Picasso Speaks

PABLO PICASSO

By the early 1920s, Picasso was a world famous artist, and, inevitably, he came to be regarded as something of a philosopher-sage. Yet, he had almost no formal learning. Instead, his head was crammed with the ideas and programs and catchphrases of his avant-garde literary friends—some of which made sense, most of which made none. Even in the realm of art, he had no systematic knowledge of art history or aesthetic theory. He was a working artist, a brilliant one, and all his notions about art ultimately derived from his own work. He did write—some fragmentary verse, a long surrealist poem, and later two short plays, all nearly incomprehensible and in no way related to his real work as an artist. They may indeed have been no more than elaborate private jokes. But mainly Picasso talked rather than wrote, and nearly everything we know about his opinions on art comes from statements either noted at the time by his listeners or recalled later. Some of these statements, especially the more comprehensive ones, were solemnly "approved" as authentic by Picasso himself. And then he would later contradict them! Adding to the complication was Picasso's own elfin sense of humor. He was always vastly amused by his own celebrity—especially by his spurious reputation as an intellectual—and he was apt to give an outrageous response to some pompous critic's pronouncement or an equally outrageous answer to some earnest reporter's question that he thought irrelevant. Picasso loved to be enigmatic.

How, then, can we know what opinions he did hold? We can really only speculate. The following excerpt is one of two lengthy statements that Picasso gave. This one, given in 1923, was translated into English and published in the New York magazine The Arts *under the title "Picasso Speaks," the other in 1935 for a French art journal. The former piece, especially, deals with his ideas on art in general and his art in particular. That the sentiments are genuine can be cautiously inferred from two sets of facts: (1) they are consistent with the body of his artistic work and (2) they are sentiments he often expressed.*

In the following statement, Picasso uses the term research *in the broadest and most general way. By it, he seems to mean any sort of reference—historic, occasional, even ideational or symbolic—that might be connected to the inspiration of a work of art. And he rejects such inspiration out of hand. To him, a work of art must be entirely visual and must be inspired only by the artist's choice of form and color, with no reference to the natural world. This leads him to argue that art is not naturalism and never has been, even with the so-called great naturalistic artists of the past like David or Ingres. Nor, he continues, does art have a history or an evolution. It lives in an eternal present. And finally he uses the art of Cubism, with which he had been so closely associated, to illustrate his points.*

I CAN HARDLY UNDERSTAND the importance given to the word *research* in connection with modern painting. In my opinion to search means nothing in painting. To find, is the thing. Nobody is interested in following a man who, with his eyes fixed on the ground, spends his life looking for the pocketbook that fortune should put in his path. The one who finds something no matter what it might be, even if his intention were not to search for it, at least arouses our curiosity, if not our admiration.

Among the several sins that I have been accused of committing, none is more false than the one that I have, as the principal objective in my work, the spirit of research. When I paint my object is to show what I have found and not what I am looking for. In art intentions are not sufficient and, as we say in Spanish: love must be proved by facts and not by reasons. What one does is what counts and not what one had the intention of doing.

We all know that Art is not truth. Art is a lie that makes us realize truth, at least the truth that is given us to understand. The artist must know the manner whereby to convince others of the truthfulness of his lies. If he only shows in his work that he has searched, and researched, for the way to put over lies, he would never accomplish anything.

The idea of research has often made painting go astray, and made the artist lose himself in mental lucubrations. Perhaps this has been the principal fault of modern art. The spirit of research has poisoned those who have not fully understood all the positive and conclusive elements in modern art and has made them attempt to paint the invisible and, therefore, the unpaintable.

They speak of naturalism in opposition to modern painting. I would like to know if anyone has ever seen a natural work of art. Nature and art, being two different things, cannot be the same thing. Through art we express our conception of what nature is not.

Velázquez left us his idea of the people of his epoch. Undoubtedly they were different from what he painted them, but we cannot conceive a Philip IV in any other way than the one Velázquez painted. Rubens also made a portrait of the same king and in Rubens' portrait he seems to be quite another person. We believe in the one painted by Velázquez, for he convinces us by his right of might.

From the painters of the origins, the primitives, whose work is obviously different from nature, down to those artists who, like David, Ingres and even Bouguereau, believed in painting nature as it is, art has always been art and not nature. And from the point of view of art there are no concrete or abstract forms, but only forms which are more or less convincing lies. That those lies are necessary to our mental selves is beyond any doubt, as it is through them that we form our aesthetic point of view of life.

Cubism is no different from any other school of painting. The same principles and the same elements are common to all. The fact that for a long time cubism has not been understood and that even today there are people who cannot see anything in it, means nothing. I do not read English, an English book is a blank book to me. This does not mean that the English language does not exist, and why should I blame anybody else but myself if I cannot understand what I know nothing about?

I also often hear the word evolution. Repeatedly I am asked to explain how my painting evolved. To me there is no past or future in art. If a work of art cannot live always in the present it must not be considered at all. The art of the Greeks, of the Egyptians, of the great painters who lived in other times, is not an art of the past; perhaps it is more alive today than it ever was. Art does not evolve by itself, the ideas of people change and with them their mode of expression. When I hear people speak of the evolution of an artist, it seems to me that they are considering him standing between two mirrors that face each other and reproduce his image an infinite number of times, and that they contemplate the successive images of one mirror as his past, and the images of the other mirror as his future. While his real image is taken as his present. They do not consider that they all are the same images in different planes.

Variation does not mean evolution. If an artist varies his mode of expression this only means that he has changed his manner of thinking, and in changing, it might be for the better or it might be for the worse.

The several manners I have used in my art must not be considered as an evolution, or as steps toward an unknown ideal of painting. All I have ever made was made for the present and with the hope that it will always remain in the present. I have never taken into consideration the spirit of research. When I have found something to express, I have done it without thinking of the past or of the future. I do not believe I have used radically different elements in the different manners I have used in painting. If the subjects I have wanted to express have suggested different ways of expression I have never hesitated to adopt them. I have never made trials nor experiments. Whenever I had something to say, I have said it in the manner in which I have felt it ought to be said. Different motives inevitably require different methods of expression. This does not imply either evolution or progress, but an adaptation of the idea one wants to express and the means to express that idea.

Arts of transition do not exist. In the chronological history of art there are periods which are more positive, more complete than others. This means that there are periods in which there are better artists than in others. If the history of art could be graphically represented, as in a chart used by a nurse to mark the changes of temperature of her patient, the same silhouettes of mountains would be shown, proving that in art there is no ascendant progress, but that it follows certain ups and downs that might occur at any time. The same occurs with the work of an individual artist.

Many think that cubism is an art of transition, an experiment which is to bring ulterior results. Those who think that way have not understood it. Cubism is not either a seed or a foetus, but an art dealing primarily with forms, and when a form is realized it is there to live its own life. A mineral substance, having geometric formation, is not made so for transitory purposes, it is to remain what it is and will always have its own form. But if we are to apply the law of evolution and transformation to art, then we have to admit that all art is transitory. On the contrary, art does not enter into these philosophic absolutisms. If cubism is an art of transition I am sure that the only thing that will come out of it is another form of cubism.

Mathematics, trigonometry, chemistry, psychoanalysis, music and what-not have been related to cubism to give it an easier interpretation. All this has been pure literature, not to say nonsense, which brought bad results, blinding people with theories.

Cubism has kept within the limits and limitations of painting, never pretending to go beyond it. Drawing, design and color are understood and practiced in cubism in the spirit and manner that they are understood and practiced in all other schools. Our subjects might be different, as we have introduced into painting objects and forms that were formerly ignored. We have kept our eyes open to our surroundings, and also our brains.

We give to form and color all their individual significance, as far as we can see it; in our subjects, we keep the joy of discovery, the pleasure of the unexpected; our subject itself must be a source of interest. But of what use is it to say what we do when everybody can see it if he wants to?

Guernica

RUDOLF ARNHEIM

By the early 1930s, Picasso's marriage to the cool and elegant Olga was a shambles, and in 1935 they were divorced. Picasso had already taken up with a series of mistresses, and his work had gone off in several directions. Then, in the summer of 1936, civil war broke out in Spain. A conservative member of the Cortes, *or parliament, was assassinated. A cadre of right-wing army officers took the occasion to revolt against the weak and ineffectual left-wing Popular Front government of the Spanish Second Republic. The revolt spread, and General Francisco Franco seized the leadership. He was particularly successful against the disorganized government loyalist forces—mainly a few isolated military units and the trade unions. By October, Franco had declared himself* Generalissimo, *head of state. Divided and warring Spain immediately became the testing ground for the opposing political ideologies then coming to the fore in Europe. Franco was supported by Nazi Germany and Fascist Italy: the loyalists were supported by the Soviet Union. Perhaps for that reason the Spanish Civil War riveted the attention and aroused the passions of the intellectual-artistic circle to which Picasso belonged. But for Picasso, added to this sort of ideological identification with the issues of the war, was his own deep native love of Spain. He listened to the war news in an agony of apprehension and actively supported the loyalist cause with his reputation and his wealth. He contributed an estimated 400,000 francs from his own pocket and did a series of etchings entitled* The Dream and Lie of Franco *in which he excoriated the Fascist dictator and his brutalities: the revenues from the sale of these etchings went to the loyalists.*

Then, in January 1937, Picasso eagerly accepted a commission from the Spanish Government in Exile to paint a mural for its exhibit at the World's Fair in Paris. On April 26, 1937, while Picasso was still casting about for a theme, German military airplanes attacked the ancient Spanish-Basque town of Guernica; bombers unloaded high-explosive and incendiary bombs, and fighter planes strafed the fleeing civilian population. Guernica had no military garrison and no military value, and the attack was an act of pure and blatant terrorism. Picasso had his theme.

Within ten days, he had made a series of preparatory sketches. He then rented a large building and set up an enormous canvas: it was 25 feet long and 11 feet high. Despite the size of the room, the ceiling was not tall enough to accommodate the canvas. It had to be placed on a slant, and

Picasso worked standing on a ladder and using a special long-handled brush. In a month of furious work, the painting was done. Its rapidly developing stages were cataloged in a fascinating series of photographs taken by his mistress at the time, Dora Maar. Entitled simply Guernica, *it was to be Picasso's most famous work.*

Guernica, *which was displayed inside the entrance to the Spanish Pavilion at the World's Fair, set off a storm of political and artistic controversy that has continued to surround the work. It is obviously a political statement. Picasso, moreover, was quoted as saying that it was intended to express his "abhorrence of the military caste which has sunk Spain in an ocean of pain and death."[4] But he was uncomfortable with the work and the controversy over its meaning. After all, he had often said that a work of art should have no exterior meaning or affiliation with object, nature, occasion, even symbolism. Yet, here was clearly an objective, even naturalistic painting, although its natural objects were fragmented, exploded; it was clearly identified with the horrifying occasion it depicted; and it was equally clearly symbolic. Picasso later tried, somewhat lamely, to rescue some shred of philosophic consistency for his work and to isolate* Guernica *as a special case. In the last days of World War II, he gave an interview to an American military correspondent, Jerome Sickler, in which he said, "My work is not symbolic. Only the Guernica mural is symbolic. But in the case of the mural, that is allegoric. That's the reason I've used the horse, the bull and so on. The mural is for the definite expression of a problem and that is why I used symbolism." In the same interview, he said, "Yes, the bull there represents brutality, the horse the people." Yet, curiously, he refused to identify the bull with Fascism, "darkness and brutality, yes, but not fascism."[5] Picasso's refusal is even more curious because, during World War II, he had become a Communist, and, in the interview with Sickler, he said, "I am a Communist and my painting is Communist painting."[6] Still later, in reaction against ideological analysis of the painting by the critic Juan Larrea, he said, "This bull is a bull and this horse is a horse," and he continued, "The public who look at the picture must see in the horse and bull symbols which they interpret as they understand them. There are some animals. That's all, so far as I'm concerned. It's up to the public to see what it wants to see."[7]*

The controversy over the meaning of Guernica *continues. There are a number of books that attempt to explain it in one framework or another. One of the best is the art historian Rudolf Arnheim's* Picasso's Guernica: The Genesis of a Painting, *from which the following excerpt is taken.*

[4] *Ibid.*, p. 127.

[5] Dore Ashton, ed. *Picasso on Art: A Selection of Views* (New York: Viking Press, 1972), pp. 136–37, 139.

[6] *Ibid.*, p. 140.

[7] Ashton, ed., *Picasso on Art*, p. 155.

Arnheim stresses precisely the symbolism of the painting, not so much as historical-political symbolism as the more generalized symbolism "of suffering and of hope."

The account begins with Picasso's commission to paint the mural.

THE COMMISSION GIVEN PICASSO required him to convey in one image the sense of the drama of his fatherland ravished by the Fascists. A war is a long and complex event, likely to furnish the attentive spectator with innumerable facts, strategic, political, statistical, with photographs of warfare, of destroyed cities, of heroism and death, with descriptions by eyewitnesses evoking precise images. Add to this a Spaniard's knowledge of Spain in general—its history, its landscapes, its portrayal in Spanish literature and painting—plus the immense panorama of personal memories, covering the first nineteen years of an alert young man's life and supplemented by later excursions to his homeland. There was, furthermore, the reservoir of images of every kind accumulated in fifty-six years, gathered from everyday observation, from dreams and fantasy, from readings and pictures, from his own prolific oeuvre. Keep in mind, finally, that Picasso works in a century in which society no longer provides rules, conventions, or even suggestions as to the form such a presentation is expected to take. All the styles ever used to picture a public event were at his disposal: the wall decorations in the tombs of the Egyptian kings and in medieval churches, such as those of Romanesque Catalonia; the etchings on the disasters of the Napoleonic war in Spain by his compatriot Goya; the Hellenistic mosaic of the battle of Alexander the Great; or the historical spectacles by Poussin, Velázquez, Rubens, Delacroix. This terrifying wealth and the freedom to use it or to reject it confronted the artist when he attempted to show the drama of Spain to the eyes of the world.

The bombing of Guernica on April 26, 1937, acted as the catalyst for the creative invention. It came as close as any actual event could come to embodying the nature of the total situation Picasso was called upon to depict. The event did not provide him with the image itself, but with the substance of it. . . .

The "totality" of the event was impressive. This was not just "damage"; it came as close as possible to the total devastation of a complete, peaceful human community. Nor was it merely an attack by the rebellious general; it was the manifestation of Fascist brutality in its universal sense represented by the foreign airplanes and crews. Furthermore, Guernica was not just any small town. There had been earlier air raids on other towns in the Biscay area. In the consciousness of every Spaniard, Guernica represented the very spirit of their ancient pride and freedom. In sum, the murderous incident was pregnant with historical and human meaning. By thus concentrating and externalizing a relevant theme, reality often does preparatory work for the artist.

How does the subject matter of the mural compare with the facts? Obviously, Picasso condensed the event in time and space. No painting can present a sequence of happenings as a film or story can. It is, however, worth noticing that the view is limited to an extremely close environment: the corner of a room plus the lower stories of one or two façades. There is no panorama of the town with the many shells of burned-out, roofless buildings. There is no house of parliament, no church. In other words, this is not a historical chronicle, but a tragedy of human beings envisaged within the close range of the eyes of the peasants terrorized by the disaster. The same approach is apparent in Picasso's use of the figures. In 1937 Guernica had more than 10,000 inhabitants. They could not be crowded into a picture; but what should be noticed is that the mural presents no crowd at all. There are nine figures, each in a different role and clearly distinguished from all the others: four women, one child, a statue of a warrior, a bull, a horse, and a bird. Although all nine are concerned with one and the same event, there is no grouping through duplication of function. Picasso is not a painter of crowds. . . .

The plot is acted by women. The one man, half sculpture, half human, is no more than a fragment, an immobile base. Equally immobile is the bull—a monument rather than an actor—whereas the women scream, push, run, and fall. It is true that at the time of the attack Guernica was largely a town of women and children: many of the men were fighting at the front. But there is more to Picasso's choice. The women make *Guernica* the image of innocent, defenseless humanity victimized. Also, women and children have often been presented by Picasso as the very perfection of mankind. In innumerable paintings and drawings he has celebrated their beauty and grace, their vitality and nobility. An assault on women and children is, in Picasso's view, directed against the very substance of mankind.

Guernica was attacked on a sunny spring afternoon at 4:30. Soon the streets were dark with the smoke of fires; but the bombing did not occur at night, whereas the painting clearly suggests darkness. The black setting, then, which is broken by the figures, flames, and lamps as though by erratic flashes of light, must have been chosen because of its immediate symbolism. Thus, the event is interpreted as being visible—existent—only because of the lamps and the flames. The fire is the companion of brutal destruction, but its flickering reflections are also enlightening because the Fascist attack dramatized the rape of the Spanish people. There are two lamps—a duplication that seems bothersome at first. One of these is pushed violently and forcefully into the center of the scene. It is a modest oil lamp, thrust forward by the woman who leans out of the window; but it is also the apex of the compositional triangle which comprises the warrior, the horse, and the running woman, and which is at the same time a pyramid of light. Placed at so dominant a spot, the small lamp, held by a townswoman—whose head is, however, transfigured into the shape of a dazzlingly white comet—is not merely a means of uncovering the events of the night. It is also a beacon on the top of an almost invisible but nevertheless powerful central column—a potential support—which is all but hidden by the chaos of destruction. Compared with the strength of the oil lamp, the large luminary at the ceiling is almost inert. It is not propelled by anybody, and its effect as a giver of light is not apparent since it is outside the cone of illumination. It is lamp, sun, and eye, but these meanings interfere with rather than support each other. This sun is nothing but a lamp, the pupil of this eye is nothing but a bulb; there is the coldness of an inefficient power, whose somewhat disheveled rays, isolated in the dark and casting shadows as though they were paper cut-outs, do not seem to warm or brighten anything. Here, then, is a symbol of detached "awareness," of a world informed but not engaged. The apparent duplication of the light source actually expresses a significant contrast between the true, small light, whose participation brightens the scene, and the powerful, but blind instrument of a consciousness without conscience.

One further deviation from the historical facts should be mentioned here. The enemy is not present. On the fateful Monday afternoon, says an eyewitness, "Five minutes did not elapse without the sky being black with German airplanes." There is no sky in the painting, and there are no airplanes. The composition is not based on the contrast of two antagonistic parties, as in Picasso's later political works: the robots with their automatic rifles facing Korean women, or the germ-spreading devil on his chariot advancing toward the fighter with the dove of peace on his shield. There is no such dualistic antagonism in *Guernica*, which keeps the mural from being a political statement. It depicts the effects of a brutality that strikes from nowhere; it speaks of suffering and of hope.

I am treating Picasso's objects as symbols—by necessity, because they are expressive shapes in a work of art. All expression communicates the possession of certain properties, and all properties are generic, not particular. It is upon these generic properties that we focus when we treat an object as a work of art. In this sense, then, *Guernica* is like the art of any other period. There is, however, an important difference in the degree to which the pictorial style of a work is made to serve the representation of the subject matter. . . . Neither the broken warrior nor the bull nor the bird is a stranger in the setting of the picture, in the sense in which—to use one more comparison—the female figure of Liberty, waving the flag in Delacroix' *Liberty Leading the People on the Barricades*, is a stranger among the faithfully portrayed contemporaries of the painter. By 1937 the art of painting had made possible a reality level at which deformities of shape and space and incongruities of subject matter portray the world as it *is*. At that level the broken warrior and the frightened women have equal reality status. But in order to establish this level, the painter had not only to remove the appearance of the women and of the setting sufficiently from that of the actual Basque town and its inhabitants, he had also to dematerialize each object and to break up the continuity of physical space. The fragmentary statue could not assume the same status as the horse if the volume of the horse's body were not similarly decomposed into fragments in the cubist manner. In other words, the search for the proper style, which, as the sketches will show, was a principal concern of Picasso's, cannot be considered a matter of whim or taste. Since the reality level required by the meaning of the picture strictly determined the amount and kind of deviation from realism he could introduce, he had to find for his shapes the style that corresponded to the appropriate ratio between the faithful portrayal of a historic episode and the expression of certain ideas. His way of drawing an eye or hand anywhere in the picture determined whether the bull would appear as a domestic animal in a Spanish town, as an apparition, a miracle, an allegory, or as one of a number of figures intended to depict suffering and hope through a war episode.

Portrait of the Artist as an Old Man

ROBERTO OTERO

In the years following World War II, nothing could detract from Picasso's celebrity. He had become the artist of the century. Even his advocacy of Communist causes in the growing chill of the Cold War somehow failed to diminish his image. Perhaps it was the widespread acceptance of Euro-communism among the left-leaning intellectuals of the circle he moved in—Jean-Paul Sartre, Albert Camus, Jean Cocteau, and others. Perhaps it was his own obvious political innocence. He was—and remained—an artist, not a doctrinaire.

And he remained an active, innovative artist. He took up new forms and techniques—for example, pottery and lithography—and returned to sculpture. But the artistic themes remained the same—the figure, the still life, flowers, an occasional political statement, and the bullfight, a Spanish passion he had never outgrown.

From the late 1940s, Picasso preferred to spend his time in the warm and comfortable south of France. There he bought a succession of homes, two of which, the Chateau de Notre Dame de Vie and a large, ugly villa named La Californie, he began to fill with his paintings, his sculpture, his ceramics, and the clutter of objects he loved to live with. He liked to live and work at La Californie especially, in the company of a considerable retinue of retainers, associates, two dogs and a goat, and a new mistress, Jacqueline Roque, who was a third his age and whom he would eventually marry. Occasionally, his two younger children by former mistress Françoise Gilot—a son Claude and a daughter Paloma—would visit. Technical assistants like Jacques Frelaut, the master printmaker, or Picasso's potter, Jules Agar, would come and go, often staying for extended periods. And there was an endless parade of Picasso's friends who might stay for the afternoon, for dinner, or for a week. But few strangers were permitted to intrude. Jaime Sabartès, a boyhood friend who had joined Picasso in his early Paris years, and Jacqueline tried desperately to protect the Maestro's privacy.

But Picasso had an affinity for people he found interesting and could almost never say "no." One such person was a Spanish filmmaker named Roberto Otero who proposed making a documentary film of Picasso. Picasso agreed, and Otero became part of the household, residing mainly at the larger house of Notre Dame de Vie, from 1966 until a few months before Picasso's death in 1972. The film was never made: Picasso did not really want to bother with it, and Otero could not raise the money in any case. But he stayed on, took still photographs, and made notes on the marathon conversations he and others had with Picasso. Eventually, when it was clear that the film would not be made, Otero decided to assemble his photos and notes into a book, aptly titled Forever Picasso. *It is excerpted in the following selection. It makes no pretense of being a formal biography. Rather it is a sort of diary, the dated entries giving impressions of Picasso, of his prejudices and preferences, and his quirks, and revealing him in his old age to be just as enigmatic, quixotic, contradictory, and mercurial as ever.*

The first entry is from late October 1966 when preparation was being made for a major exhibition of Picasso's work in Paris.

ONE MORNING, while the Louvre people are hard at work loading the heavy sculptures into one of the trucks parked in the garden, Jacqueline invites us to La Californie. She wants to add several ceramics to the pieces going to Paris, even though the number of works seems to have reached saturation point. These ceramics are gathering dust somewhere in

Picasso's previous residence. We go in two cars so that the pieces can be sent back to Notre Dame de Vie for cataloguing and wrapping as soon as possible. If we are quick, they can go in one of the trucks, which are almost ready to start for Paris.

The moment we reach La Californie, we go down to the half-basement, where several rooms are joined by a labyrinthine passage. They are low-ceilinged, and most of them are tiny. Despite the spaciousness of the upper floors, Picasso generally worked in one of these rooms. Now they are used for storage. One contains an ancient printing press. Picasso once began to experiment with printing his own graphics, but changed his mind when he realized how many complex technical procedures go into every edition of a print. But he continues to do the first, truly creative part of the edition, which is incising the metal or linoleum plates. During Picasso's years at La Californie, the master printer Jacques Frelaut printed his engravings on this ancient press. Frelaut would come from Paris whenever Picasso needed his help, and during those visits Picasso would drop the four other phases of his artistic life—painting, sculpture, drawing, and ceramics—to supervise the printing of each engraving. . . .

Jacqueline sorts out the key for each room from a huge key-ring. We go into two rooms stacked with boxes and ceramics. Once again we are amazed by her prodigious memory. She can put her hand on every forgotten painting, work of art, or even straight pin in Picasso's terrestrial kingdom. She goes straight to a fish painted in black, white, and red on an earth-colored background. She unwraps another plate, which shows a black-and-white owl. She decides not to take it because she remembers she already has a similar one at Notre Dame de Vie. She gathers up a couple of pitchers and hands them over to us. The last object we must unearth is an impressive bull's head, a bull with human eyes, in which green and jet black are the dominant tones. We now have more than twenty pieces, which we load into the minitruck. The chauffeur drives off slowly, well aware of the fragility and the immeasurable value of his cargo.

We go back into the house. Jacqueline decides to take a survey of some small sculptures which seem to have taken shape magically in the dusky shadows of the big main room. One of them is the famous head of a bull constructed from the handlebars and seat of a bicycle. For safety, I put it in my car trunk, wrapped in a couple of traveling blankets. Back at Notre Dame de Vie, someone unloads the trunk but does not realize that the head of the bull is under the blanket. As a result, I drive around the center of Cannes with the sculpture still in the car. When I discover the "bull" in the trunk, I return to the house, bring out the sculpture, and describe its itinerary.

"You're a fool," Picasso says. "You could have exchanged it for a real bicycle and nobody here would have been the wiser. Do you know how I happened to do this?" he continues, almost without taking a breath. "Well, I was with Sabartès on the way to someone's funeral and I saw this bicycle seat thrown into an empty lot. A little later, in another empty lot, I saw the handlebars. It didn't occur to me all at once what I could do with them, but I realized later that I was turning the matter over in my head. As we left the cemetery I told Sabartès about them, and we stopped to pick up the two parts. Curious, isn't it? I've often felt like leaving this sculpture just anywhere. And it wouldn't surprise me at all if someone found it and said: 'What a nice head of a bull! You know, you could make a bicycle out of it.' "

While I set the sculpture down in a corner of the studio, it crosses my mind that this anecdote sums up Picasso's attitude toward life and art, and even a curious aspect of his complex thought process, better than any other statement. This thought process achieves its most characteristic expression in paradox and in a sense of humor that smacks of both the Spanish *pueblo* and personal intuition. In a way, the game of creating a synthesis out of opposites is encompassed in this singular story, something of an obsession with the contrast between reality and fiction, between life and artistic creation. Of course, this is only one aspect of Picasso among many others. He is not easy to explain, and perhaps that is why so many hundreds of books on his life and work have been written without ever really plumbing the depths of the mystery.

The Louvre packers have finished with the sculptures and are now loading the paintings which were accumulated in the "secret room" early in October. Everyone is busy bringing canvases down to the sculpture room, where the specialists in delicate cargoes are gathering them to take out to the trucks. One of the packers, referring to his long experience in packing paintings, says to Picasso with natural pride:

"Don't worry, Maestro, I was with *La Gioconda* and *Venus* in Tokyo and New York."

Later that evening, Picasso repeats the boast and goes on to say:

"He talked about *La Gioconda* and *Venus* as if they were his girlfriends—how should I put it—as if they were whores. And as if that weren't enough, now he can use the same tone of voice and tell the next painter who has an homage show: "Don't worry, Maestro, I was with Picasso in the Petit and Grand Palais.". . .

Our only duty now is to wrap the ceramics. To save time, Jacqueline decides on a very efficient way to catalogue them. Using an old-fashioned box camera, she photographs each piece in the garden just before it is taken to the sculpture room for wrapping. Then she supervises the meticulous work of the packers, who are busily rolling each ceramic in a protective straw blanket.

When the light begins to fail, we have an aperitif with the people from the Louvre in the sculpture room. Tomorrow the packers will leave with the treasure trove, protected by a tight police escort. As he stretches long strips of adhesive tape across the glass on some of the paintings, one of the packers, who has already amused Picasso with his conversation, remarks seriously:

"Oh well. That's life at the château!"

The phrase becomes a durable household catchphrase for almost any situation.

"Life at the château!" Actually, the phrase is only valid for someone who is on the outside looking in, dazzled by the deceptive exterior of Notre Dame de Vie. For the Master of the Castle, on the other hand, "life at the château" means working like a monster with twelve arms from the moment he wakens until he goes to bed. The only interruptions consist of meals and the time which friends and strangers "miserably" rob from him. Yet, thinking it over, there was a grain of truth in that phrase. Had it not been for Picasso's one and only experience with surgery a while ago—it will be a year exactly on the day the Paris exhibition opens—he would never have known such a long period of idleness. "Life at the château," even if he did not know it himself, is this period in 1966 which is now drawing to a close. The Master of Mougins has already begun intense drawing sessions, and soon he will be painting one or two canvases a day, as in his most productive periods.

The trucks leave at eleven in the morning. Picasso watches them from his bedroom terrace as they fade into the distance. When I go up to join him I ask a question to which I already know the answer.

"Am I going to Paris? Oh, no. Look, what do I have to do in Paris? Besides, I'm horrified at homage shows. Not only now, but ever since Málaga, when I was to be awarded a medal and didn't even show up. I don't know if it embarrasses me or something like that. I just don't know."

He is enormously shy, though the fact is not immediately apparent because of his flippancy about so many things. In fact, he is so shy that he becomes slightly annoyed at having to talk about the show any more and quickly changes the subject:

"And the sculpture of the man with the sheep?" he asks.

Automatically I look down at the place the sculpture normally occupies in the garden.

"What a fool I am," Picasso goes on. "They just took it with them a moment ago. You laugh, but these things happen, just like asking a widow about her freshly buried husband. The worst part is that I'm going to miss the man with the sheep. I'm so used to pissing on it from the first-floor studio."

As if we had never spoken of it before, he describes the value of urine in developing a really handsome patina on bronze. He is so disconcerted by the commotion of the trucks' departure that he forgets he has already described this process to me. His loss of memory seems to me the result of an attack of shyness.

Speech as well as memory. At supper Picasso appears a million miles off, lost in thought and profoundly quiet. Surely he is thinking of the exhibition. When he can no longer bear it or keep it to himself, he says quite suddenly:

"I really don't know why I let it happen. Basically, I'm against exhibitions and homages, as you know. Moreover, it is of no use to anyone. Painting, exhibiting—what's it all about?"

We are all thunderstruck and do not know what to say. After a few moments, which seem endless, someone remarks playfully, as if to cut short Picasso's somber monologue:

"If you like, I'll go to Paris, to the Grand Palais, and slash all your paintings."

"It's not that either. Do you know what I mean? It's not a matter of slashing the paintings or destroying them, but neither did I have to say yes to the exhibition. None of you understand a thing. All this business about homages is ridiculous. What's the use of it all? Who really cares about what I paint?"

He leaves the meal in the same dispirited mood, with the same thing on his mind. I am quite sure he felt very much the same way at his first showing, at Ambroise Vollard's gallery sixty-five years ago. . . .

12 December 1966

I have just returned from Paris, where I have seen the "Hommage à Picasso" exhibition. It is the most comprehensive showing of his work ever mounted. He is less excited than he was the last time I saw him, when the Louvre trucks were leaving, but somewhat more on edge than usual. He goes to the heart of the matter immediately:

"How was it? Tell me. Tell me everything."

Since I know full well that other visitors have already raved to him about this enormous show and that he has also read the critics and their eulogies in the newspapers, I decide to say something totally nonsensical:

"Absolutely hideous."

"Ah, yes? I said it would be. You see, Jacqueline? At last the truth is out about this whole Paris business. I told you this would happen."

A short pause and I go on:

"First of all, the paintings were too close together."

"You see? Do you see how right he is? It looked that way to me from a photo I saw in a magazine."

"Besides, there are a lot of paintings hung upside down."

"What a mess! I knew it would be like that."

The truth is I did see one painting hung upside down, but the joke is going so well it seems a pity to let it drop. He takes the catalogue from the table and looks for the painting in question. Finally I have to find it for him. It is *Guitarre*, a collage done with cloth, string, nails, and paper, and dated 1926.

"You're right."

"Don't worry. It's the only one."

Picasso, who had understood from the first that we were half joking, answers without a second's hesitation:

"You're wrong. There another one."

And he goes through the voluminous catalogue for a long time without finding one. In the end he goes back to *Guitarre* and draws some arrows on either side of the photographic reproduction—also upside down—to indicate "how it must be seen." He turns back to the first page and dedicates the catalogue, as is his custom, and adds a little drawing.

"Take it as a souvenir of the 'most hideous' exhibition of the century."

While handing me the catalogue, he goes on:

"This reminds me of a very nice Uruguayan painter who came to visit us once at La Californie. He was quite nervous, and after looking at my paintings he couldn't think of anything to say but: 'It's awful. Awful.' No one has ever expressed his admiration in such an odd way."

Suddenly he becomes serious and goes back to the previous subject:

"To tell the truth, even if they had turned half the paintings upside down, what difference would it have made? Basically it's all the same, isn't it?" . . .

In the entry of 3 June 1968 they are discussing contemporary literature.

Then, quite unexpectedly, he begins to talk about Françoise Gilot's book.[8] It is a theme he finds repugnant, and he avoids it whenever the book is mentioned. If he is asked about it, he immediately changes the subject. Today, however, he is the one to bring it up, probably because of the photos of Kiki de Montparnasse.[9]

"What I can't understand," he says, "is why they didn't publish that book, Françoise's, with pictures of me in the buff, like Kiki. Though, of course, they would have been a little difficult to come by."

"Don't you know, Pablo, they do wonders with photography? They could have made a photomontage combining your face and some pornographic photos."

"Of course! I don't know why the devil they didn't think of that. People really aren't very imaginative. They would have made a lot more money by now if they *had* done it that way. Have you read the book?"

"Yes."

[8] A revealing account of her life with Picasso, published some four years earlier.—ED.

[9] A notorious libertine Picasso had known years before who was featured in an erotic book they had just been discussing.—ED.

"What did you think of it?"

"Bad. But you don't come out in as unfavorable a light as you think. Just 50 percent is unfavorable."

"Well, I've been told otherwise. And some paragraphs have been read to me. The part that makes me laugh is when she has me pontificating about Michelangelo, Van Gogh, Velázquez, and God knows who! As if I were an art critic! Did I say an art critic? As if I were a professor at the Royal Academy of San Fernando!" . . .

"Besides, as everybody knows, I detest talking seriously about painting. And even more, I detest talking seriously about anything at all. It's the best way for people not to understand each other. Don't you think so?"

As I agree with him, I think that this friend of mine, Picasso, is an incredible character—in short, a real rebel. There is not the slightest doubt that the so-called "intellectual"—whether he is an art critic or an art historian—has always passed the same judgment on Picasso that today's young rebels pass on the academic discourses delivered by the majority of their professors.

"What I can't fathom is why they're forever making me say improbable things. If I were a taciturn, silent type like Miró, for instance, then I could understand why they'd have to invent conversation. But I'm not. I'm forever jabbering. I remember once a critic reading aloud the first sentence of a book he was doing on me. It went like this, more or less: 'Picasso confessed to me not long ago that the shortest distance between two points was a straight line.' Can you imagine? Naturally, I didn't let him read any further, but said; 'Listen here. Are you sure I discovered that?' "

And, after a pause:

"I also thought that if I had been the Greek who invented that law, I would most certainly have stated it differently."

Well, maybe yes, maybe no. But that does not matter, as Picasso himself says about almost anything. What does matter is what he is trying to say when he says what he says. And my experience is that if one knows how to listen to him, one sees that his reasoning is as sharp as that of Cervantes. So I say:

"Pablo, the problem is one of 'communication,' as they say nowadays. One has to have the 'key.' Not only to understand you, but every other human being. Even if it happens to be more complicated in your case than it is with other people."

"Of course, that's it. The problem is the 'key.' . . .

14 February 1969

We are dining in Antibes with Christian and Yvonne Zervos. The publisher of the famous Picasso catalogue has had 295 of the master's recent paintings photographed today, and he is satisfied with his work.

ZERVOS: "There are periods when it is very difficult to do anything with him, as you know, periods when he doesn't want to see anybody. This isn't the first time I've had to spend a long time waiting in Cannes to see him. But years ago it was different, and sometimes he even accompanied me to pick up paintings I needed to photograph—paintings he didn't have at home. I remember once—it must have been in 1934 or 1935—we went to the Bank of France, where he stored a number of canvases in a room rented in the basement. Well, we chose the paintings and set them aside to pick up another day, when they'd be carefully packed. The bank guards closed the door after us and then Picasso said to me, winking his eye like a mischievous schoolboy: 'I have two more rooms. Do you want to see them?' I said I did, of course, and he had another armored room opened for us."

Zervos, well aware of the interest he has kindled in us, pauses while he carefully consumes a delectable sea urchin and savors his white wine. He continues:

"Haven't I ever told you this story? Wait till you see what happens. You'll see. Well, the second room was even bigger than the first, almost as big as this restaurant. To my amazement, there were no paintings in it, but only packages, piled one atop the other to the height, say, of Picasso. Between these piles of packages there was a kind of labyrinthine trench that enabled one to reach the packages piled against the walls. I thought they were drawings, or engravings, or letters—perhaps the Apollinaire archives—in short, something on that order."

Another pause to eat another couple of sea urchins and to drink a few more glasses of wine. The very least one can say about Zervos is that this fastidious notary of Picasso's work is also a genuine master of suspense.

ZERVOS: "Well, as I was saying, Picasso goes up to one of the packages like a mischievous child, tears the paper off one of the corners, and shows me what's inside. And do you know what there was inside? *Bank Notes!* Yes, sir, bank notes, the largest denomination that existed in France then, which was enormous."

The theme and variations on "Picasso and Money" have been wildly fantasized in books and magazines the world over, but I had never read nor imagined a tale like this.

ZERVOS: "As you see, instead of depositing his money in a bank account and earning interest, as any other person in his position would have done, he preferred having it in bundles, wrapped in newspaper. He's always been a bit of a peasant about many things, not only this. He's really no different from the country bumpkin who keeps his savings sewn into his mattress."

A few days later I ask Picasso if what Zervos told us is true. He answers in the affirmative, not giving the matter the slightest importance.

"How awful." I say, exaggerating a bit in the hope of making him talk. "You must have lost a bit here and there, what with inflation and the post-war devaluation."

"You're wrong. Not so. I haven't lost one cent."

And he tells me this marvelous story about Jorge Bomberg:

PICASSO: "I had a friend in Paris during my Rue de la Boëtie days who was Argentinian, the son of bankers or something like that. He had never done a lick of work in his life. In those days, Argentinians were very fashionable in Paris, and people fought to have one or two as permanent guests at their gatherings. The ideal Argentinian could sing tangos and dance like a ballroom professional. Of course, those ideal Argentinians weren't all that easy to come by. My Argentinian could neither sing nor dance, but he had another rare virtue. He was the best Picasso counterfeiter who ever existed." . . .

"And what happened to the paintings?"

"Well, I don't know. Good heavens, you're right! Probably they're in circulation. In museums. Good heavens!"

The thought of this eventuality makes Picasso burst into laughter, but I don't want to lose track of our original conversation.

"What I can't understand is Bomberg's connection to your bank notes."

"Well, one day he wrote me saying I should send my money to Switzerland because it was going to be worthless in France. And I sent it to Switzerland because I trusted him. And that's how I saved it."

It seems we have reached the end of the story with this bank transfer which he owed to the advice of his most dedicated forger. But Picasso goes on: "Of course, I never saw the money again. They invested it there; then the war came along and I forgot about it. Occasionally, a banker comes to see me and says: 'There are no longer so-and-so-many thousand pesetas but so-and-so-many something elses.' Always a little more, according to the bank man. But I haven't seen it since. Actually, I think it would have been better if I had left it as it was, don't you?"

Some guests are announced, and he only has time for one last remark:

"Anyway, it's all the same. What the devil difference is the money to me? My life is my work!"

Suggestions for Further Reading

PICASSO'S OWN CREATIVE WRITINGS, though they have little to do with his artistic works or his career as an artist, are nevertheless available: they include his long poem *Hunk of Skin*, tr. Paul Blackburn (San Francisco: City Lights Books, 1968), and two short plays, *Playscript 25* "desire caught by the tail," tr. Roland Penrose (London: Calder and Boyars, 1970), and *Playscript 32* "the four little girls," tr. Roland Penrose (London: Calder and Boyars, 1970), first published in France, respectively, in 1945 and 1949. More relevant to his career as an artist are the many statements and comments he made about himself and his art. There are several collections of these, including the one excerpted for this chapter, *Picasso on Art: A Selection of Views*, ed. Dore Ashton (New York: Viking Press, 1972). But see also *Picasso says . . .* ed. Hélène Parmelin, tr. Christine Trollope (London: Allen and Unwin, 1969). Another work that features such comments by Picasso is *Picasso*, statements by Pablo Picasso, preface by Alfred H. Barr, Jr., commentaries by Roland Penrose (Basel: Steiner and Co., 1967–68).

The foregoing book is also an expanded catalog of the Picasso 85th Anniversary Exhibition at the Bryeler Gallery in Basel. There are dozens of such collections of his works, but the most comprehensive is the catalog of the 85th Anniversary Exhibition in Paris, called *Hommage à Pablo Picasso* (Paris: Ministère d'Etat, Affaires Culturelles, 1966). One of the best collections is Jean Leymarie, *Picasso: The Artist of the Century* (London: Macmillan, 1972).

Closely related to Picasso's statements are the reminiscences and accounts of him by friends and associates. Many of these are available in a handy book, *A Picasso Anthology: Documents, Criticism, Reminiscences*, ed. Marilyn McCully (Princeton: Princeton University Press, 1982). There are the memoirs of three of his mistresses: Fernande Olivier, *Picasso and His Friends*, tr. Jane Miller (New York: Appleton Century, 1965 [1933]); Françoise Gilot and Carlton Lake, *Life with Picasso* (New York, Toronto, London: McGraw-Hill, 1964); and Geneviève Laporte, *Sunshine at Midnight: Memoirs of Picasso and Cocteau*, tr. and ed. Douglas Cooper (New York: Macmillan, 1973). There are also the reminiscences of Gertrude Stein, *Picasso* (New York: Dover, 1984 [1938]), and the more comprehensive *Gertrude Stein on Picasso*, ed. Edward Burns (New York: Liveright, 1970); and of André Malraux, *Picasso's Mask*, tr. and ed. June and Jacques Guicharnaud (New York: Holt, Rinehart and Winston, 1976).

There are several good biographies of Picasso. The best—virtually the standard work on him—is by his lifelong friend Roland Penrose, *Picasso, His Life and Work*, 3rd. ed. (Berkeley and Los Angeles: University of California Press, 1981). Another excellent comprehensive biography is Patrick O'Brian, *Picasso, A Biography* (New York: Putnam, 1976). A readable life-and-times book is Lael Wertenbaker, *The World of Picasso* (New York: Time-Life Books, 1967). There is also an interesting and gossipy account by Jean-Paul Crespelle, *Picasso and His Women* (New York: Coward-McCann, 1969). Mary Matthews Gedo, *Picasso: Art as Autobiography* (Chicago and London: University of Chicago Press, 1980), attempts to derive an account of Picasso's life strictly from the pictorial evidence of his works. The definitive work on the youth and background of Picasso is Juan-Eduardo Cirlot, *Picasso, Birth of a Genius* (New York and Washington: Praeger, 1972), and revealing of Picasso in his later years are David Douglas Duncan, *The Private World of Pablo Picasso* (New York: The Ridge Press, 1958), and Roberto Otero, *Forever Picasso, An Intimate Look at His Last Years*, tr. Elaine Kerrigan (New York: Abrams, 1974), excerpted for this chapter; both these works are by professional photographers.

A good sampling of the critical evaluation of Picasso is *Picasso in Perspective*, ed. Gert Schiff (Englewood Cliffs, N.J.: Prentice-Hall, 1976). On his most famous work, the most famous book is the controversial Juan Larrea, *Guernica* (New York: Valentin, 1947). But newer and more sophisticated studies are Frank D. Russell, *Picasso's Guernica, The Labyrinth of Narrative and Vision* (Montclair, N.J.: Allenheld and Schram, 1980), an excellent iconographic analysis, and Rudolf Arnheim, *Picasso's Guernica: The Genesis of a Painting* (Berkeley and Los Angeles: University of California Press, 1962), excerpted for this chapter.

ACKNOWLEDGMENTS (continued from p. iv)

flections in Natural History, by Stephen Jay Gould, with the permission of W. W. Norton & Company, Inc. Copyright © 1983 by Stephen Jay Gould.

BISMARCK: From *Bismarck's Diplomacy at Its Zenith* by Joseph Vincent Fuller, Harvard University Press, 1922. Reprinted by permission. From *Bismarck: The Man and the Statesman*, by A. J. P. Taylor. Copyright © 1955 by A. J. P. Taylor. Reprinted by permission of Alfred A. Knopf, Inc.

CECIL RHODES: From *Against These Three: A Biography of Paul Kruger, Cecil Rhodes, and Logenbula, Last King of the Matabele* by Stuart Cloete. Copyright © 1945 by Stuart Cloete. Reprinted by permission of JCA Literary Agency Inc. From *Cecil Rhodes* by John Flint, copyright © 1974 by John Flint. Reprinted by permission of Little, Brown and Company and Hutchinson Publishing Group Ltd.

LENIN: From *The Young Lenin* by Leon Trotsky. Translated by Max Eastman and edited by Maurice Friedburg. Copyright © 1972 by Doubleday & Company, Inc. and reprinted with their permission. From *Encounters With Lenin* by Nikolay Valentinov, translated by Paul Rosta and Brian Pierce. Published by Oxford University Press in 1968 and reprinted with their permission. From *Red October* by Robert V. Daniels. Reprinted by permission of Charles Scribner's Sons. Copyright © 1967 Robert V. Daniels.

SIGMUND FREUD: From Letters 67, 70, and 71 of *The Origins of Psycho-Analysis: Letters to Wilhelm Fliess, Drafts and Notes: 1887–1902* by Sigmund Freud. Edited by Marie Bonaparte, Anna Freud, and Ernst Kris and translated by Eric Mosbacher and James Strachey. Copyright 1954 by Basic Books, Inc., Publishers, New York. Reprinted by permission of Basic Books, Inc. From "Freud on the Couch" by Anthony Storr. *Horizon* (Winter 1970). Copyright © 1970, American Heritage Publishing Company, Inc. Reprinted with permission. From *Life History and the Historical Moment* by Erik H. Erikson. Copyright © 1975 by Rikan Enterprises, Inc. Reprinted with the permission of W. W. Norton & Company, Inc.

ADOLF HITLER: From *Mein Kampf* by Adolf Hitler, translated by Ralph Manheim. Copyright 1943 and © renewed 1971 by Houghton Mifflin Company. Reprinted by permission of the publisher. From *Three Faces of Fascism* by Ernst Nolte. Translated by Leila Vennewitz. Copyright © 1963 by R. Piper & Co. Verlag, Munich. Translation © 1965 by R. Piper & Co. Verlag, Munich. Reprinted by permission of Holt, Rinehart and Winston, Publishers. From *Hitler: A Study in Tyranny* by Alan Bullock, completely revised edition. Copyright © 1962 by Alan Bullock. Reprinted by permission of Harper & Row, Publishers, Inc. and Newnes Books, a Division of The Hamlyn Publishing Group Ltd.

ALBERT EINSTEIN: "Atomic War or Peace" by Albert Einstein as told to Raymond Swing, *Atlantic Monthly*, 176, No. 5 (November 1945). Reprinted in *Einstein on Peace*, edited by Otto Nathan and Heinz Norden, published by Schocken Books. Copyright © 1960 by The Estate of Albert Einstein. This and excerpt from pp. 290–302 of *Einstein on Peace* reprinted by permission of the Hebrew University in Jerusalem, Israel. From *Albert Einstein: Historical and Cultural Perspectives: The Centennial Symposium in Jerusalem*, Gerald Holton and Yehuda Elkana, eds. Copyright © 1982 by Princeton University Press. Excerpt, pp. 371–387 reprinted with permission of Princeton University Press.

STALIN: From *Stalin: The Man and His Era* by Adam B. Ulam, 1973, Viking Penguin. Copyright © 1973 by Adam B. Ulam. Reprinted by permission of The Julian Bach Literary Agency.

ELEANOR ROOSEVELT: From *On My Own* by Eleanor Roosevelt, pp. 39–89, 1958, Harper & Row. Reprinted by permission of the trustee under the will of Eleanor Roosevelt. From "First Lady of the UN" by Elizabeth Janeway, October 22, 1950,

Magazine. Copyright © 1950 by The New York Times Company. Reprinted by permission. From *Eleanor; The Years Alone* by Joseph P. Lash, by permission of W. W. Norton & Company, Inc. Copyright © 1972 by Joseph P. Lash.

PICASSO: From *Picasso on Art: A Selection of Views,* edited by Dore Ashton. Copyright © 1972 by Dore Ashton. Reprinted by permission of Viking Penguin, Inc. From *Picasso's Guernica, the Genesis of a Painting,* by Rudolf Arnheim, © 1962, 1972 The Regents of the University of California, pp. 18–22; reprinted by permission of The Regents of the University of California. From *Forever Picasso, An Intimate Look at His Last Years* by Roberto Otero, trans. Elaine Kerrigan, Harry N. Abrams, Inc. 1974. Reprinted with permission of Harry N. Abrams, Inc.